PREDICTIVE SENTENCING

Predictive Sentencing addresses the role of risk assessment in contemporary sentencing practices. Predictive sentencing has become so deeply ingrained in Western criminal justice decision-making that despite early ethical discussions about selective incapacitation, it currently attracts little critique. Nor has it been subjected to a thorough normative and empirical scrutiny. This is problematic since much current policy and practice concerning risk predictions is inconsistent with mainstream theories of punishment. Moreover, predictive sentencing exacerbates discrimination and disparity in sentencing. Although structured risk assessments may have replaced 'gut feelings', and have now been systematically implemented in Western justice systems, the fundamental issues and questions that surround the use of risk assessment instruments at sentencing remain unresolved. This volume critically evaluates these issues and will be of great interest to scholars of criminal justice and criminology working in the area.

Predictive Sentencing

Normative and Empirical Perspectives

Edited by
Jan W de Keijser
Julian V Roberts
Jesper Ryberg

• HART •
OXFORD • LONDON • NEW YORK • NEW DELHI • SYDNEY

HART PUBLISHING

Bloomsbury Publishing Plc

Kemp House, Chawley Park, Cumnor Hill, Oxford, OX2 9PH, UK

HART PUBLISHING, the Hart/Stag logo, BLOOMSBURY and the Diana logo are trademarks of Bloomsbury Publishing Plc

First published in Great Britain 2019

A catalogue record for this book is available from the British Library.

Library of Congress Cataloging-in-Publication data

Names: Keijser, Jan Willem de, 1968- editor. | Roberts, Julian V., editor. | Ryberg, Jesper, editor.

Title: Predictive sentencing : normative and empirical perspectives / edited by Jan W de Keijser, Julian V Roberts, Jesper Ryberg.

Description: Oxford, UK ; Chicago, Illinois : Hart Publishing, 2019. | Includes bibliographical references and index.

Identifiers: LCCN 2018057412 (print) | LCCN 2018057924 (ebook) | ISBN 9781509921423 (EPub) | ISBN 9781509921416 (hardback)

Subjects: LCSH: Sentences (Criminal procedure) | BISAC: LAW / Criminal Law / General.

Classification: LCC K5121 (ebook) | LCC K5121 .P736 2019 (print) | DDC 345/.0772—dc23

LC record available at https://lccn.loc.gov/2018057412

ISBN: HB: 978-1-50992-141-6
ePDF: 978-1-50992-143-0
ePub: 978-1-50992-142-3

Typeset by Compuscript Ltd, Shannon

ACKNOWLEDGEMENTS

The essays contained in this volume were discussed at an international seminar held at the Faculty of Law, University of Oxford, April 12–15, 2018. The editors thank the following for their financial support: Roskilde University; The Research Support Fund in the Faculty of Law, University of Oxford and the Institute for Criminal Law and Criminology at Leiden University. We are also grateful to Bill Asquith and Linda Staniford from Hart Publishing for their support of the volume.

Jan W. de Keijser
Julian V. Roberts
Jesper Ryberg
Oxford, December 15, 2018

CONTENTS

NOTES ON CONTRIBUTORS

Andrew Ashworth is Vinerian Professor of English Law Emeritus at the University of Oxford, Emeritus Fellow of All Souls College, Oxford and Adjunct Professor of Law at the University of Tasmania.

Jan W de Keijser is Professor of Criminology at the Institute for Criminal Law and Criminology, Leiden University.

Thomas Douglas is Senior Research Fellow in Philosophy at the University of Oxford and a Hugh Price Fellow at Jesus College, Oxford.

Seena Fazel is Professor of Forensic Psychiatry at the University of Oxford.

Richard S Frase is Benjamin N Berger Professor of Criminal Law at the University of Minnesota Law School.

Kelly Hannah-Moffat is Professor of Criminology at the Centre for Criminology and Sociolegal Studies and Vice President of Human Resources & Equity at the University of Toronto.

Rhys Hester is an assistant professor in the Department of Sociology, Anthropology and Criminal Justice at Clemson University.

Zachary Hoskins is Assistant Professor in Philosophy at the University of Nottingham.

Douglas Husak is Distinguished Professor of Philosophy at Rutgers University.

Julian V Roberts is Professor of Criminology at the University of Oxford and fellow of Worcester College, Oxford.

Jesper Ryberg is Professor of Ethics and Philosophy of Law at Roskilde University.

Christopher Slobogin is the Milton Underwood Professor of Law at Vanderbilt University.

Kelly Struthers Montford is a postdoctoral research fellow in punishment, law and social theory at the Centre for Criminology and Sociolegal Studies, University of Toronto.

Michael Tonry is Professor of Law and Public Policy at the University of Minnesota.

Esther FJC van Ginneken is Assistant Professor of Criminology at the Institute for Criminal Law and Criminology, Leiden University.

Sigrid GC van Wingerden is Associate Professor of Criminology at the Institute for Criminal Law and Criminology, Leiden University.

Lucia Zedner is Senior Research Fellow at All Souls College and Professor in the Faculty of Law, University of Oxford. She is also Conjoint Professor in the Faculty of Law, UNSW, Sydney.

1

Introduction

Normative and Empirical Perspectives on Predictive Sentencing

JAN W DE KEIJSER, JULIAN V ROBERTS AND JESPER RYBERG

At sentencing, courts look backwards to punish the offender for the crime, and forwards to prevent further offending. The primary objectives of sentencing therefore fall into one of two categories: retributive and preventive. Retributive sentencing focuses on the seriousness of the offence and the offender's culpability. Establishing the degree of harm and blameworthiness is challenging, but a court is at least dealing with a crime which has occurred. Preventive sentencing is a very different matter. Here the court is required to establish the offender's risk of further offending and then craft a sentence to address this level of risk. The punishment is imposed for what offenders may do, not for what they have already done. Rather than addressing the past, the court must predict the future. Retributive sentencing creates ethical challenges for sentencers; preventive sentencing throws up even more controversies. This volume explores the normative, ethical and empirical challenges arising from predictive, risk-based sentencing.

With the introduction of the concept of selective incapacitation in the 1970s (see Greenberg 1975; Greenwood and Abrahamse 1982), predictive sentencing immediately attracted much academic attention and debate. While the phrase may often be associated with pseudo-science and crystal balls, predictive sentencing has become a vast enterprise, both in terms of the scientific development of risk assessment instruments and its application to criminal justice. All Western jurisdictions currently deploy a multitude of risk assessment instruments to guide aspects of criminal justice decision making. Consequently, it is used for a myriad of decisions, including bail, sentencing and release from imprisonment.

Risk assessment instruments attempt to predict future offending by combining a variety of static and dynamic criminogenic factors (see Mills, Kroner and Morgan 2011; Otto and Douglas 2010). High-risk offenders may be considered eligible for longer prison terms, while low-risk offenders may be considered more eligible for diversionary measures. Risk assessments are also used to identify criminogenic 'needs' that subsequent behavioural interventions may target (according to the 'risk, needs, responsivity' model; see Andrews and Bonta 2010). Structured risk assessment instruments are also promoted because they eliminate or minimise the subjective element in criminal justice decision making; that is, they replace more intuitive decision making (see Latessa and Lovins 2014).

I. Predictive Sentencing: A Widely Used But Controversial Practice

Predictive sentencing can be defined as using risk of future offending to influence the nature and quantum of punishment imposed. Although widely used, the practice remains inherently problematic. Concerns are often expressed about the accuracy of risk assessment instruments. Such instruments ascribe a particular risk level to individual offenders by applying statistical group-based models that combine a variety of risk factors. Risk scales may contain a small or a large number of such factors. Some of those factors are believed to reduce the risk of recidivism, while others are supposed to increase the risk of re-offending. These models inevitably produce errors, most importantly in terms of false positive predictions of dangerousness. Predictive sentencing also raises many fundamental legal and normative questions about its justification and application (see also Tonry 1987).

Predictive sentencing has become so deeply ingrained in Western criminal justice decision making that despite the early discussions about the ethics of selective incapacitation, it currently attracts little critique from practitioners. Nor has the practice been subjected to a comprehensive normative and empirical scrutiny. This is problematic since, as Tonry (2014: 170) noted, 'much current policy and practice concerning risk predictions is flatly inconsistent with mainstream normative theories of punishment'. But the problems of predictive sentencing do not end there. Which characteristics are considered to be risk factors and why are they – or have they become – risk factors? These questions raise concerns about the discriminatory effects of using risk assessments at sentencing. Predictive sentencing appears to exacerbate discrimination and disparity in sentencing (*cf* Monahan and Skeem 2016). As such, Starr (2014) has described it as the scientific rationalisation of discrimination (see also van Eijk 2017). Although structured risk assessments may have replaced sentencers' 'gut feelings' and have now been systematically implemented in Western justice systems, many fundamental issues remain unresolved.

II. Justifying Predictive Sentencing

A. Retributivism

The justifications for predictive sentencing may be sought in the expected future effects of risk-based sentencing or they may be sought in desert. A full retributive justification dictates a deserved punitive response to wrongdoing that is proportional to the harm done and the culpability of the offender. So is there a desert-based justification for predictive sentencing? At first glance, the answer would seem to be no. After all, desert is retrospectively focused on the issues of blameworthiness and harm. Moreover, predictive sentences would quickly be trumped by concerns for proportionality and equality at sentencing (von Hirsch and Kazemian 2009). Predictive sentencing therefore offends desert-based principles. Can someone be censured or blamed for their risk of criminal behaviour in the future, even if re-offending is almost a certainty? Put differently, does future risk affect the offender's current penal desert? Moreover, does variation in assessed risk *ceteris paribus* justify variation in the severity of sentences? Despite such direct and obvious conflicts with desert, conceptualising risk or dangerousness as a reprehensible act or state of mind in itself draws risk assessment into the domain of retributivism.

Another role for retributivism with respect to predictive sentencing may lie in providing a limiting principle (grounded in desert) for constraining preventive interventions based on risk (see, eg, Morris and Miller 1985). However, as a limiting principle, the role for retributivism falls short of providing a general justifying aim (*cf* Hart 1968) for predictive punishment. Within retributivism, then, there are different forms of predictive sentencing. The views range from those who reject risk-based sentencing even for the most dangerous criminals (*cf* Petersen 2014) to others who accept risk within a retributive framework, albeit to a limited extent (eg, Duff 1998; Husak 2011; Morse 1996; Morris and Miller 1985). Obviously, for desert theory, these are difficult issues, but justifying predictive sentencing from a consequentialist point of view is also challenging.

B. Utilitarianism

Utilitarians justify interventions by reference to their net benefit for society. In order to be justified from this perspective, the benefits of predictive sentencing must outweigh the costs. However, it is unclear whether the benefits from taking risk into account do in fact outweigh the (added) harm arising from predictive sentencing. While an instrumentalist approach to predictive sentencing would appear obvious, it does grapple with the predictive validity of the risk assessment instruments as well as with the actual benefits that (predictive) sentencing produces. Moreover, if left unconstrained, an instrumentalist approach to predictive sentencing elicits the classic ethical concerns about justifying draconian or inhumane penal measures as well as justifying punishing those who have yet to commit a criminal offence. But there is more. The individual preventive effects of criminal sentences are not as great as one may expect. Thus, any justification of predictive sentencing is linked to the more general question of whether punishment can be justified on utilitarian grounds. Looking at the available empirical evidence, it is not obvious that that is the case.

For example, the literature shows that incapacitation is a very costly penal strategy, while the preventive effects, mainly as a result of overestimating the residual criminal careers, are modest (*cf* Auerhahn 2002; Blokland and Nieuwbeerta 2007; see also Stolzenberg and D'Alessio (1997) regarding the effectiveness of 'three strikes' sentencing laws). Similarly, individual deterrent sanctions (especially imprisonment) do not seem to achieve their intended effects (*cf* Nagin, Cullen and Jonson 2009; Wermink et al 2018), perhaps not even to the extent that we would expect for a sufficient instrumentalist justification. And finally, considering rehabilitation, the research has shown us that in order to have a chance to achieve rehabilitation, every intervention needs to be tailored to individual risk, criminogenic needs and offender responsivity to the treatment (Andrews and Bonta 2010; Smith, Gendreau and Swartz 2009). But even while such interventions generally produce lower rates of recidivism than custodial sentences, the question remains as to whether these are still sufficient to satisfy the instrumental justification for such interventions.

III. Prediction Issues: Validity and Relevance

Any justification of predictive sentencing must include a discussion of the predictive validity of the risk assessment instruments. How well do specific instruments predict who will re-offend and who will not (eg, Childs et al 2013; Farrington and Tarling 1985; Vincent et al 2008)? Of course, the higher the predictive validity of risk assessment instruments, the better an instrumental justification for predictive sentencing can stand its ground. Incapacitating offenders (most notably through imprisonment), in part or even largely based on such wrongful predictions, inflicts penal suffering and incurs criminal justice costs that cannot be justified. Nevertheless, at the aggregate level, it may still be rational (and cost-effective) to accept a certain proportion of false positives in order to preserve risk assessment in the sentencing equation. The challenge then lies in identifying the 'tipping point': what level of false positive predictions is considered acceptable in order to obtain a degree of collective crime prevention benefits? Morris and Miller (1985) argued that using predictions of dangerousness requires a policy judgement on how to balance the predicted risk and harm with the intrusions on individual liberties that result from intervening because of that prediction. It is disconcerting that neither the end-users nor criminal justice policy makers seem aware of or concerned about the issue. On the other hand, from a principled point of view, it has been pointed out that this can only be a conditional challenge to predictive sentencing (von Hirsch and Kazemian 2009). After all, with the continuous scientific development of these instruments and more validation studies which combine static and dynamic risk factors, the diagnostic value of risk assessments has increased over the past few decades. As such, the problem of false positives may diminish as an objection to predictive sentencing (*cf* Lippke 2008).

What if we were able to predict dangerousness with great accuracy? Could – or should – 'pure preventive detention' as a form of pre-emptive criminal justice strike be permitted (see Morse 2004; and also Morris and Miller 1985)? But there is more to this. Again, from a principled point of view, if dangerousness itself is to be considered a punishable condition or 'act', then the whole issue of false positive predictions becomes trivial. In an individual case, the label 'high risk' as the outcome of a risk assessment instrument is unaffected by this person's actual future behaviour.[1]

IV. The Current Volume

If predictive sentencing conflicts with mainstream rationales for punishment, can it be justified? Moreover, as the practice has been so widely embraced by criminal justice practitioners, how strong is the societal support base for predictive sentencing? What do we currently know about the predictive validity of risk assessment tools and what developments or improvements can we expect from them in the future? Can such developments and improvements alleviate some of the more fundamental concerns that are being addressed? How are risk assessments integrated into sentencing practices in different jurisdictions and how are the immediate concerns related to fairness, human dignity, discrimination and validity dealt with in these practices? Answering these interrelated questions requires the collaboration of diverse disciplines. The contributors to this volume not only explore these questions from their own disciplinary backgrounds, but they also engage with contributions from other disciplines.

This volume aims to add to the existing literature on risk assessment at sentencing by keeping a focus on predictive sentencing and by bringing together and integrating empirical, legal and moral perspectives. The variation in disciplinary backgrounds of the contributors is most directly reflected in this volume by the rough division of chapters into two parts; the first part of the volume contains contributions with a normative and legal outlook on the issues at hand. Some contributors squarely focus on defining a consistent principled justification for the practice, while other contributors take a closer look at considerations external to mainstream moral legal rationales for punishment. This is done by some by reflecting on possibilities and constraints that are derived from concerns for human rights, fairness and dignity. Others compare predictive sentencing to other

[1] Morris and Miller (1985: 18–19) clarify this distinction between a condition (ie, dangerousness) and a result (ie, a future harmful behaviour) by drawing the analogy with unexploded bombs from the Second World War that were found in the post-war period. These unexploded bombs rarely caused death or severe injuries upon removal, but no one would say that because a bomb proved to be a false positive, it was not dangerous.

legal, social and economic practices in order to examine justifications for using risk assessments at sentencing. These include prior record enhancements, indeterminate sentences, the medical practice of quarantine, and exploration of the concept of non-punitive incapacitation.

The second part of the volume contains chapters with a predominantly empirical orientation. The contributors critically discuss the developments in predictive validity and application of risk assessment instruments, discuss the discriminatory effects of risk assessment instruments for offenders and for society, address societal views on predictive sentencing and explain the integration of risk assessments in specific sentencing practices.

The mix of moral, legal and empirical perspectives will invite the reader to weigh both moral theory and practice against one another. The empirical and normative contributions to this volume will first be preceded by an overview of predictive sentencing in Chapter 2, describing the historical development of risk assessment instruments and practices of predictive sentencing within and across various jurisdictions. As such, the overview chapter will set the stage for what follows.

This volume does not explore two issues relevant to predictive sentencing. The first concerns protective factors that diminish the risk of committing future crimes. While most contributions to the current volume focus on positive risk factors (ie, factors that are positively correlated with risk of future offending), does that mean that we are addressing only half the story? We think not. After all, criminal justice interventions aimed at creating or strengthening protective factors carry with them the same fundamental problems as those related to the use of positive risk factors for sentencing purposes. Not only do we need to address the predictive validity and effectiveness of (rehabilitative) efforts aimed at strengthening protective factors, but we also need to address the moral justification for such interventions. The punitive effect of such interventions may only be an unintended side-effect and, as a result, not in need of justification. Taking the punitive bite out of the equation in that manner is a rhetorical trick; something described by Hart as a 'definitional stop' argument (Hart 1968: 5). Second, the question of the relative effectiveness of criminal sanctions is not discussed. Of course, the issues of crime preventive effects, but also of harmful consequences of sanctions (see, for example, Welsh and Rocque 2014) are closely connected to the instrumental justification of predictive sentencing. As the effectiveness debate is relevant for any consequentialist justification of sentences per se, we have decided to keep the focus of the current volume squarely on risk assessment and its role in predictive sentencing.

References

Andrews, DA and Bonta, J (2010) 'Rehabilitating Criminal Justice Policy and Practice' 16 *Psychology, Public Policy, and Law* 39.

Auerhahn, K (2002) 'Selective Incapacitation, Three Strikes, and the Problem of Aging Prison Populations: Using Simulation Modelling to see the Future' 1 *Criminology & Public Policy* 353.

Blokland, AAJ and Nieuwbeerta, P (2007) 'Selectively Incapacitating Frequent Offenders: Costs and Benefits of Various Penal Scenarios' 23 *Journal of Quantitative Criminology* 327.

Childs, KC, Ryals, J, Frick, PJ, Lawing, K, Phillippi, SW, and Deprato, DK (2013) 'Examining the Validity of the Structured Assessment of Violence Risk in Youth (SAVRY) for Predicting Probation Outcomes Among Adjudicated Juvenile Offenders' 31 *Behavioral Sciences and the Law* 256.

Duff, RA (1998) 'Dangerousness and Citizenship' in A Ashworth and M Wasik (eds), *Fundamentals in Sentencing Theory: Essays in Honour of Andrew Von Hirsch* (Oxford, Clarendon Press).

Farrington, DP and Tarling, R (1985) *Prediction in Criminology* (Albany, State University of New York Press).

Greenberg, DF (1975) 'The Incapactitative Effect of Imprisonment: Some Estimates' 541 *Law & Society Review* 1974.

Greenwood, PW and Abrahamse, AF (1982) *Selective Incapacitation* (Santa Monica, RAND).

Hart, HLA (1968) *Punishment and Responsibility* (Oxford, Clarendon Press).

Husak, D (2011) 'Lifting the Cloak: Preventive Detention as Punishment' 48 *San Diego Law Review* 1173.

Latessa, EJ and Lovins, B (2014) 'Risk Assessment, Classification, and Prediction' in GJN Bruinsma and D Weisburd (eds), *Encyclopedia of Criminal Justice* (New York, Springer).

Lippke, RL (2008) 'No Easy Way out: Dangerous Offenders and Preventivce Detention' 27 *Law and Philosophy* 383.

Mills, JF, Kroner, DG and Morgan, RD (2011) *Clinician's Guide to Violence Risk Assessment* (New York, Guilford Press).

Monahan, J and Skeem, JL (2016) 'Risk Assessment in Criminal Sentencing' 12 *Annual Review of Clinical Psychology* 489.

Morris, N and Miller, M (1985) 'Predictions of Dangerousness' 6 *Crime and Justice: An Annual Review of Research* 1.

Morse, SJ (1996) 'Blame and Danger: An Essay on Preventive Detention' 76 *Boston University Law Review* 113.

——. (2004) 'Preventive Confinement of Dangerous Offenders' 32 *Journal of Law, Medicine & Ethics* 56.

Nagin, DS, Cullen, FT and Jonson, CL (2009) 'Imprisonment and Reoffending' 38 *Crime and Justice: An Annual Review of Research* 115.

Otto, RK and Douglas, KS (eds) (2010) *Handbook of Violence Risk Assessment* (New York, Routledge).

Petersen, TS (2014) '(Neuro)prediction, Dangerousness, and Retributivism' 18 *Journal of Ethics* 137.

Smith, P, Gendreau, P and Swartz, K (2009) 'Validating the Principles of Effective Intervention: A Systematic Review of the Contributions of Meta-analysis in the Field of Corrections' 4 *Victims & Offenders* 148.

Solzenberg, L and D'Alessio, SJ (1997) '"Three Strikes and You're out": The Impact of California's New Mandatory Sentencing Law on Serious Crime Rates' 43 *Crime & Delinquency* 457.

Starr, SB (2014) 'Evidence-Based Sentencing and the Scientific Rationalization of Discrimination' 66 *Stanford Law Review* 803.

Tonry, M (1987) 'Prediction and Classification: Criminal Justice Decision Making' 9 *Crime and Justice: A Review of Research* 367.

——. (2014) 'Legal and Ethical Issues in the Prediction of Recidivism' 26 *Federal Sentencing Reporter* 167.

Van Eijk, G (2017) 'Socioeconomic Marginality in Sentencing: The Built-in Bias in Risk Assessment Tools and the Reproduction of Social Inequality' 19 *Punishment & Society* 463.

Vincent, GM, Odgers, CL, McCormick, AV and Corrado, RR (2008) 'The PCL: YV and Recidivism in Male and Female Juveniles: A Follow-up into Young Adulthood' 31 *International Journal of Law and Psychiatry* 287.

Von Hirsch (1986) *Past or Future Crimes: Deservedness and Dangerousness in the Sentencing of Criminals* (Manchester, Manchester University Press).

Von Hirsch, A and Kazemian, L (2009) 'Predictive Sentencing and Selective Incapacitation' in A Von Hirsch, A Ashworth and J Roberts (eds), *Principled Sentencing: Readings on Theory and Policy*, 3rd edn (Oxford, Hart Publishing).

Welsh, BC and Rocque, M (2014) 'When Crime Prevention Harms: A Review of Systematic Reviews' 10 *Journal of Experimental Criminology* 245.

Wermink, HT, Nieuwbeerta, P, Ramakers, AAT, de Keijser, JW and Dirkzwager, JE (2018) 'Short-Term Effects of Imprisonment Length on Recidivism in the Netherlands' 64 *Crime & Delinquency* 1057.

2

The Use of Risk Assessment in Sentencing

ESTHER FJC VAN GINNEKEN

I. A Brief History of Risk Assessment in Sentencing

Over the years, risk, as the likelihood of future criminal behaviour, has played a role in sentencing in different forms and at different stages in the criminal justice process. A general shift can be observed from a welfare-oriented approach to a neoliberal approach, with a declining role for (clinical) experts and a shift of responsibilities from state authorities to the individual (Feeley and Simon 1992; Garland 2001). However, it would be amiss to paint this development with a broad brush only, as there is substantial variation in practice across jurisdictions. This chapter discusses these variations in current and (recent) past practices of risk-based sentencing, and also gives an overview of the main debates around risk assessment. Many of these debates will be examined in more detail in the chapters that follow.

The development of risk assessment instruments over time can be aligned with changes in their function in the criminal justice process. The previous century witnessed the popularity and subsequent decline of the rehabilitative ideal, which was followed by a greater prominence of retributive (deserved punishment) and crime control concerns. Today, risk assessment may be said to serve the primary function of efficient offender management, although there is also still attention for rehabilitative, retributive and incapacitative goals.

A. First Generation: Clinical Judgement and Penal Welfarism

In the heyday of the rehabilitative ideal (roughly the 1950s and 1960s, beginning its descent in the 1970s), it was generally believed that the causes of criminality could be 'diagnosed' and 'treated' using an individual approach (Phelps 2011). Consequently, many offenders received indeterminate sentences that were terminated upon the apparent rehabilitation (and thus low risk) of the individual. This put a great deal of sentencing discretion at the back door with parole boards, as judges would only impose a sentencing range or maximum sentence. These judgments by parole boards about rehabilitation (ie, future dangerousness) were normally informed by clinical assessments of dangerousness, which were not restricted by rules or guidelines about the use of information to reach decisions. Unstructured clinical risk assessments are considered to be the first generation of risk instruments and they have been criticised for their lack of reliability and predictive validity (Hanson and Morton-Bourgon 2009; Monahan 1981).

B. Second Generation: Actuarial Assessment and Selective Incapacitation

In the 1970s and 1980s, dissatisfaction with the rehabilitative potential of prison programmes as well as critiques on indeterminate sentencing contributed to a shift towards determinate sentencing on the basis of retributive and crime control considerations. As part of a large research programme funded by the US National Institute of Justice, a 1982 RAND study claimed that crime could be reduced through selective incapacitation of offenders who are most likely to re-offend (Greenwood and Abrahamse 1982). The study's authors had identified correlates of self-reported offending frequency through a survey of prisoners convicted of robbery and burglary, and advocated the use of an actuarial tool that used these correlates to identify high-rate offenders (for a discussion of methodological and ethical problems, see Auerhahn 1999). The idea of selective incapacitation chimes with the notion that a high proportion of crimes are committed by a small proportion of the most prolific offenders (Wolfgang, Figlio and Sellin 1972). However, even selective incapacitation may incur higher costs than the benefits gained from the crimes it prevents (Blokland and Nieuwbeerta 2007).

A defining characteristic of second-generation risk assessment instruments is that they only include static factors: these factors are fixed and unamenable to intervention (eg, age at first arrest and number of prior convictions). These instruments are actuarial risk assessments in the sense that they calculate risk based on a formula, which may be a regression equation or simple adding of points, and can combine more information than the typical human expert (but see Dressel and Farid 2018). A widely used second-generation instrument is the Static-99 for predicting sexual offending. This instrument consists of 10 items, including age, offence history, victim typology and whether the offender lives with a partner. A total risk score is calculated by adding points for each risk factor, where a total score of 6 or more (range 0–12) is labelled 'high risk'. The initial validation study found a violent recidivism rate of 59 per cent after 15 years for sex offenders who fell in this high-risk category (Hanson and Thornton 1999).

One of the prime criticisms launched at the early actuarial tools was that they had a high false-positive rate, ie, non-recidivists classified as high risk. To some extent, this was remedied by later actuarial tools that used a probabilistic model to estimate the likelihood of future offending. Actuarial risk assessments compare an individual's characteristics to a reference group and calculated risk scores reflect the degree of similarity between an individual and a group: a high-risk offender basically shares many characteristics with past recidivists and a low-risk offender shares many characteristics with past non-recidivists. While this conveys a level of uncertainty, these risk scores still inform decisions that have the same consequences as false positives and false negatives associated with dichotomous categorisation.

In the 1990s, there was growing attention to danger and risk in society more generally (Beck 1992; Giddens 1990), which manifested itself in the criminal justice domain as a preoccupation with risk assessment and management (Feeley and Simon 1992). Yet, the 'promise' of actuarial justice and risk assessment to enhance administrative efficiency (Feeley and Simon 1992, 1994) did perhaps not materialise to the extent envisaged until much more recently (Rothschild-Elyassi, Koehler and Simon in press). The 1990s bore witness to rising crime rates and the introduction of tougher sentences, as well as rapidly growing prison populations. The new generation of risk assessment challenged the dominant focus on punitive responses and incapacitation to some extent by a greater focus on treatment potential.

C. Third and Fourth Generations: Risk-Needs Assessment and Offender Management

The Risk-Needs-Responsivity (RNR) model (Andrews and Bonta 2010) forms the theoretical foundation from which the third and fourth generations of structured professional risk assessments have been developed. Third-generation risk assessment instruments include static and dynamic factors, where dynamic factors (sometimes called 'needs') can change over time or through intervention. This new generation of instruments targets some of the shortcomings of first- and second-generation risk assessments, which were less reliable (particularly professional judgements) and, in the case of second-generation instruments, did not allow for improvements (ie, decreases) in risk because they were based on static factors.

The RNR model outlined the principles for successful interventions in combination with risk assessment. First, the level of treatment should be proportionate to the risk of re-offending (risk principle); this means that offenders with a low risk of re-offending are not unnecessarily targeted for intervention. Second, interventions should target criminogenic needs, or dynamic factors that are correlated with recidivism (needs principle). Here, Andrews and Bonta (2010) distinguished between criminogenic needs (eg, pro-criminal attitudes and substance abuse) and non-criminogenic needs (eg, self-esteem and major mental disorders). Third, interventions should incorporate effective cognitive social learning strategies and tailor them to a person's learning style. Briefly, it could be said that risk refers to *who* should be treated, needs to *what* should be treated and responsivity to *how* to treat. The RNR-based risk assessment instruments are thus used not only to predict risk, but also to assist in reducing it.

Structured professional risk assessments are a combination of clinical judgement and actuarial risk assessment, although they are often carried out by non-clinical professionals (eg, probation officers). They provide guidance on which risk factors to take into consideration and how to score them, but also allow a degree of professional discretion in the assessment and weighing of certain indicators of risk (and even overrides in the final recommendation). These structured professional risk assessments are often also used to keep a record of progression throughout the completion of a sentence. The development of third-generation instruments into fourth-generation instruments is characterised by the combination of risk assessment with offender management and the incorporation of the responsivity principle. Fourth-generation instruments are designed to guide supervision, intervention and release decisions from intake through case closure (Andrews, Bonta and Wormith 2006).

A typical example of a third-generation instrument is the Level of Service Inventory-Revised (LSI-R), which is used on a large scale in Canada and the US, and was developed and tested by Andrews and Bonta (1995). It comprises 54 items across 10 domains: criminal history, education/employment, financial, family/marital, accommodation, leisure/recreation, companions, alcohol/drug problems, emotional/personal and attitudes/orientation. Similar instruments are used in England and Wales (the Offender Assessment System (OASys)) and other European countries (eg, Risk Assessment Scales (RISc) in the Netherlands). The LSI-R was later revised into a fourth-generation instrument, the Level of Service/Case Management Inventory (LS/CMI; Andrews, Bonta and Wormith 2004), which – among other changes – includes additional non-scored sections that provide qualitative information that may be relevant for offender supervision and treatment. Further, it allows the test administrator to designate a subcomponent as 'strength', which could also inform an offender's case plan.

The LSI-R has strong advocates as well as fierce critics. There are numerous studies in support of the utility of the LSI-R in predicting recidivism (Gendreau, Little and Goggin 1996; Vose, Cullen and Smith 2008). Nevertheless, the reliability and validity of lengthy instruments such as the LSI-R have been questioned; only a few of the LSI-R items appear to predict recidivism and there are issues with inter-rater disagreement on ratings of items and risk level (Austin et al 2003; Dowdy, Lacy and Unnithan 2002). Static predictors are more consistently scored and have higher predictive value. This has prompted suggestions to separate risk predictions from needs assessment and case planning (Baird 2009; Caudy, Durso and Taxman 2013; *cf* Labrecque et al 2014).

The developments sketched above cannot simply be characterised as an increase in punitiveness: on the one hand, risk assessments are used to identify high-risk offenders and subject them to greater control and often long-term incarceration; on the other hand, they are also used to identify low-risk offenders and divert them from prison. It is recognised that imposing control and interventions on low-risk offenders may actually have adverse effects. Furthermore, later-generation instruments explicitly regard the offender as capable of change and are used to inform 'treatment' (perhaps not the most fitting term for the dominant cognitive behavioural interventions on offer; see Duguid 2000: 197). It may therefore be more appropriate to speak of a hybrid model of penology (see, for example, Hannah-Moffat 2005; O'Malley 1999), which combines different aims of sentencing including rehabilitation, rather than of a 'new penology' of actuarial justice, as characterised by Feeley and Simon (1992, 1994).

II. Issues around the Use of Risk Assessment in Sentencing

The use of risk assessment in sentencing has been criticised on various grounds, including empirical concerns about validity and normative concerns about fairness. This section will briefly discuss the main debates, many of which will be reviewed in more detail in the following chapters.

A. Normative Concerns

One the most prominent and elaborately discussed criticisms of risk-based sentencing is its violation of the retributive norms of proportionality. Just deserts theory holds that the severity of a punishment should correspond to the seriousness of the offence, which comprises harm and culpability (von Hirsch 1976). Retributive sentencing is thus backwards-looking. Risk assessment brings concerns about the future into calculations of sentence severity, which means that offenders who have committed crimes of equal seriousness may receive differential sentences based on future risk, although, arguably, even within a retributive framework, it is possible to envisage differential sentences for equally serious crimes that are responsive to risk (Ryberg, Chapter 4 in this volume). There is debate among retributivist scholars on whether it is justified to consider prior convictions in sentencing (Bagaric 2001; Lee 2010; von Hirsch 2010). Risk-based sentencing is more compatible with utilitarian approaches to punishment, in particular to advance the aim of crime control through the incapacitation of high-risk offenders or risk reduction by targeted intervention.

A related concern is that the use of risk assessment in sentencing in effect holds offenders responsible for factors that are static (eg, age and gender) or are often outside their direct control (eg, employment). Tonry notes that 'there is something fundamentally unethical or immoral about apportioning punishments or other intrusions on liberty on the basis of ascribed characteristics for which no coherent argument can be made that offenders bear personal responsibility for them'

(2014: 171). To the extent that variable risk factors are a choice, it is still problematic to attach penal consequences to lawful life choices.

So far, however, the use of risk assessment in sentencing decisions has survived legal challenge. The fourth-generation instrument Correctional Offender Management Profiles for Alternative Sanctions (COMPAS) is used across the US to inform sentencing decisions as well as offender management. It assesses risk on the basis of 137 factors and was developed by a commercial organisation, Northpointe, which makes the algorithm proprietary. In *State v Loomis*,[1] Loomis argued that the proprietary nature of COMPAS prevented him from challenging the accuracy and validity of the instrument and that using the instrument in sentencing is an improper form of gendered assessment. The Wisconsin Supreme Court ruled that the court's use of the COMPAS risk score as an element (rather than the sole factor) in determining Loomis's sentence did not violate his due process rights to be sentenced individually and using accurate information, and by taking gender and race into account. A petition to the US Supreme Court to challenge this decision was denied.[2]

B. Predictive Validity and the Meaning of 'Risk'

Another key concern with the use of risk assessment in sentencing is the imperfect predictive validity (see also Fazel, Chapter 11 in this volume). Risk is by definition uncertain: it may or may not materialise into harm. This is reflected in the probability scores that are generated by modern risk assessments, which convey information about the average recidivism rate for a group of offenders who share the same characteristics (included in the instrument) as the individual subjected to the assessment. Yet, often, these raw probability scores are reduced to simplistic categories of low, moderate or high risk in communication to the courts. Predictive validity refers to a risk assessment instrument's ability to correctly assess the likelihood of (serious) re-offending.

Any decision based on a risk score has the potential to make a wrong assumption about actual recidivism: the so-called false positives (ie, a prediction of re-offending when this would not have occurred) and false negatives (ie, a prediction of no re-offending when this will occur). The error rate of risk assessment is substantial; while the most commonly used risk assessment instruments appear fairly accurate at predicting low risk of offending, they have a high rate of false

[1] *State v Loomis* 881 NW2d 749 (Wis 2016).

[2] COMPAS does not use race as an explicit risk factor. The instrument received criticism after journalistic platform ProPublica published an article showing that black defendants were more likely to receive false positive (high-risk) scores than white defendants, while white defendants were more likely to receive false negative (low-risk) scores (Angwin et al 2016). Overall accuracy was the same for white and black defendants. Others have criticised these findings for their limited assessment of fairness, as other criteria showed no racial disparities (Flores, Bechtel and Lowenkamp 2016; Chouldechova 2017).

positives (Fazel et al 2012). The most commonly used measure of predictive accuracy for risk assessment instruments is the area under the Receiver Operating Characteristic (ROC) curve. The area under the curve (AUC) can be interpreted as the probability that a randomly selected recidivist has a higher risk score than a randomly selected non-recidivist. Most risk instruments have an AUC value of between 0.66 and 0.78 (Singh, Grann and Fazel 2011), which means that they have moderate discriminatory power.[3] Even given the AUC value of a particular instrument, the likelihood of false positives and false negatives varies depending on the cut-off score that is used to make decisions about risk: the higher the cut-off score on an instrument for labelling an offender as high-risk, the greater the specificity (ie, positive predictive value), but the lower the sensitivity of detecting true positives. In practice, users of risk assessment instruments are likely to cast a wider net, which classifies a relatively substantial proportion of offenders as high risk, in order to maximise sensitivity and avoid the possibility that any high-risk offenders go undetected; this also means that, inadvertently, a considerable proportion of offenders is inaccurately labelled as high risk (ie, false positives). Of course, this may have consequences at the sentencing stage (see also Hester, Chapter 12 in this volume).

A further consideration is the reliability of the information that is fed into the measure: 'no risk-assessment device can be better than the data from which it is constructed' (Gottfredson and Moriarty 2006: 183). Instruments with low levels of transparency into how scores are calculated can be criticised because the validity cannot be checked or challenged; this is one of the greatest problems with machine learning approaches to risk assessment (see also section IV below and Hannah-Moffat, Chapter 10 in this volume).

Other validity problems are that risk estimates do not include an assessment of the potential effect of specific sentences (or interventions as part of a sentence) on recidivism and that the sample used for developing an instrument may not be representative for the population on which it is used (Starr 2014). Fazel et al conclude that 'risk assessment tools in their current form can only be used to roughly classify individuals at the group level, and not to safely determine criminal prognosis in an individual case' (2012: 5). The use of group data to make predictions about individual cases is not only empirically flawed, but also ethically dubious (Hart, Michie and Cooke 2007; Netter 2007; Starr 2014; *cf* Skeem and Monahan 2011), as it holds individuals responsible for group-based tendencies.

Finally, one should also consider the type of outcome that is predicted and its practical relevance. 'Risk' can have a variety of meanings: it can mean the likelihood of parole violation, re-arrest, a criminal charge, reconviction, re-imprisonment or any specific type or seriousness of re-offending. Instruments that were developed using official statistics (particularly arrests and parole

[3] A systematic review on the reporting of predictive validity in violence risk assessment studies found that AUC results were often misinterpreted (Singh, Desmarais and van Dorn 2013).

violations) partly reflect police and probation practices rather than actual (harmful) behaviour (Harcourt 2007). Regardless, validation studies use a wide variety of outcome measures, so it needs to be questioned to what extent they measure the intended construct. It is also important to understand that someone who falls into a 'high-risk' category does not necessarily pose a great risk of *serious* offending (or causing serious harm); in other words, risk does not equal dangerousness. Many conceive of 'dangerousness' as a function of risk (in terms of likelihood) and harm.[4] The meaning of dangerousness may vary across jurisdictions and is fluid over time, depending partly on public and political concerns about crime at any given time (Pratt 1995). Post-1970, dangerousness has come to be understood as mainly (risk of) violent and sexual offending, which is also reflected in current legislation in England and Wales, discussed in section III.B below. Given the low prevalence rate of serious violent offending, it is inherently difficult to predict its occurrence (but much easier to predict its non-occurrence; see Hester, Chapter 12 in this volume). Many instruments are therefore validated to predict general or any violent offending (including threats or attempts of violence without bodily harm) (Singh, Grann and Fazel 2011; Yang, Wong and Coid 2010). Overall, then, 'high risk' can be easily misinterpreted if decision makers are not given information on error rates and the nature of the outcome that is predicted.

C. Discrimination and Responsibilisation

Some argue in favour of risk assessment for reasons of fair treatment: it can – to some extent – eliminate judicial bias, enhance transparency in sentencing, and prevent unnecessary intervention and the infliction of harm on low-risk offenders. However, there are also concerns that risk-based sentencing results in sentencing disparity and reproduces or even exacerbates social inequality. There are various possible explanatory mechanisms for such an effect. First, risk assessment instruments may have mixed predictive validity for different groups, such as men and women, or individuals with a different ethnic background (Raynor and Lewis 2011; Skeem, Monahan and Lowenkamp 2016; *cf* Skeem and Lowenkamp 2016). Risk and need factors may vary across groups, operate differently and be experienced differently (eg, Hannah-Moffat 2016; van Voorhis et al 2010). Second, the predictive fairness of risk-based sentencing may be compromised because factors that are correlated with recidivism are also correlated with ethnicity and social class (eg, employment status, marital status, education level and substance abuse), which has to be understood in a socio-economic and historical context (Holtfreter, Reisig and Morash 2004; van Eijk 2017). For instance, the correlation between criminal history and race may not only reflect differential participation of ethnic minorities in crime, but also

[4] But see Slobogin (2012), who defines dangerousness as simply the likelihood of re-offending.

differential selection through disproportionately high arrest, prosecution and conviction rates (Harcourt 2007):

> Use of marital status, employment, education, family status, and residential stability as factors in prediction instruments systematically disadvantages minority defendants. The social and economic disadvantages that disproportionately afflict blacks and Hispanics in America are partly the products of historic and ongoing discrimination and bias. (Tonry 2014: 173)

If risk assessment is employed to send high-risk offenders to prison, it is likely to simply reinforce destructive cycles of incarceration and associated social disadvantage (Hannah-Moffat 2016; van Eijk 2017). As a result, the risk assessments will help to sustain the inequalities that are the root causes of many forms of delinquent behaviour, including exclusion from society and economic disadvantage.

Finally, risk assessment may be criticised for depoliticising issues of social justice. Forward-looking, risk-based sentencing diverts attention away from the underlying causes of crime and instead holds individuals fully responsible not only for past crimes, but also for their future risk (known as 'responsibilisation', which transfers the responsibility for solving problems from state authorities to individuals). In other words, one might easily confuse the causes of crime with the causes of individual differences in crime. In risk assessment, the terms 'needs' and 'dynamic risk' are used interchangeably, which devalues the importance of non-criminogenic needs (alterable circumstances which are not directly, empirically linked to recidivism). Valid needs, then, are only those that are potential targets of risk reduction, because they have a statistically proven association with offending. While these needs are often connected to structural constraints (including poverty), they are presented as individual deficits, which are also an individual's responsibility to overcome (Hannah-Moffat 2016; Holtfreter, Reisig and Morash 2004; van Eijk 2017). This bypasses political debate about what should be done about crime – apart from incarcerating high-risk offenders – and to what extent it is a political and societal responsibility to *collectively* reduce risk factors of crime.

III. The Role of Risk Assessment in Sentencing

We can roughly distinguish two functions of risk assessment in sentencing: risk assessment can be used either to limit (judicial) discretion or to inform how discretion in sentencing may be used. Instances of the former function are primarily observed in jurisdictions that make use of sentencing guidelines, which can contain an implicit form of risk assessment in themselves, or alternatively can contain provisions that require judges to make a risk assessment and apply it in a certain way. Risk assessment can also be used to inform judges (as well as parole boards) in more discretionary decisions regarding the type and length of sentences. These various uses of risk assessment are discussed in turn and are illustrated with typical examples.

A. Limiting Discretion: Sentencing Guidelines

Sentencing guidelines have a more or less prescriptive function in sentence calibration, not only in relation to offence seriousness, but also in relation to risk. They can be regarded as a form of risk assessment in themselves as they normally incorporate at least offence history in the recommendation of a sentence (range); in addition, they may also explicitly require or advise the consideration of risk in sentencing decisions. Most guidelines states in the US employ a sentencing grid, which recommends sentencing options based on two criteria: the seriousness of the current offence and an offender's prior record. The length of a prison sentence can vary greatly depending on the number of prior convictions (Frase and Hester 2015). In particular, sentencing grids limit judicial discretion in the sense that prior convictions are uniformly associated with higher recommended sentences; therefore, the presence of this particular risk factor is not subject to much interpretation (see also Roberts and Frase, Chapter 9 in this volume).[5] It has been argued that such sentencing grids function more to standardise judicial practice in line with logics of control and incapacitation than as a form of risk assessment or actuarial justice (Rothschild-Elyassi, Koehler and Simon in press). Matters are more complicated when sentencing guidelines include the recommendation to consider risk assessment in the sentencing decision, primarily in order to divert low-risk offenders from prison.

Risk assessments integrate more information than prior records into a calculation of recidivism risk and judges have the risk scores available in addition to sentencing guidelines. The *2011 Guiding Principles Report* by the National Working Group on the use of offender risk and needs assessment information at sentencing outlines how risk assessments should be used, with the ultimate aim of reducing recidivism in a cost-effective way (Casey, Warren and Elek 2011). Importantly, the guiding principles explicitly separate the punitive aim of sentencing from crime reduction aims and state that risk and needs assessments (RNAs) should only be used for the latter purpose. In other words, the outcomes of RNAs should not be used to make sentences more or less punitive, which is in line with the judgment in *Malenchik v Indiana*,[6] in which the Supreme Court of Indiana found that risk assessment scores should not be interpreted as mitigating or aggravating factors in the determination of the length of a sentence. Rather, the Court recommended that RNAs should be used primarily for deciding whether to suspend (part of)

[5] In *United States v Booker* 543 US 220 (2005), the US Supreme Court ruled that federal mandatory sentencing guidelines were unconstitutional, which consequently made sentencing guidelines advisory.

[6] *Malenchik v Indiana* 928 NE2d 564 (Ind 2010).

a sentence and for assigning programmes, treatment or specific requirements. Therefore, the guiding principles only apply to offenders who are probation-eligible according to state sentencing guidelines. While (additional) probation or treatment requirements may not be *intentionally* punitive, it should be kept in mind that they may certainly be experienced as such (see, for example, Durnescu 2011; van Ginneken and Hayes 2017).

The state of Virginia has gone further than most other states in its use of risk assessment at the sentencing stage, which it introduced to offset the anticipated increase in the occupation of prison beds resulting from truth-in-sentencing legislation and the abolition of parole. The Virginia Criminal Sentencing Commission (2011) developed a Nonviolent Risk Assessment (NVRA) that has been used since 2002 to identify drug and property offenders with the lowest risk of committing further crimes and recommend them for diversion from prison. A few interesting observations can be made about Virginia's experience with risk assessment at sentencing. First, the instrument calculates a score primarily based on offence history and current offence characteristics. The only offender characteristics are age (lower age yields higher risk score) and gender (males receive higher scores). Employment and marital status were included initially, but were excluded from the most recent versions due to difficulties with verification and negligible loss of predictive validity (Ostrom and Kauder 2012). The NVRA is therefore a rather straightforward actuarial instrument. Second, there is substantial discrepancy in relation to the extent to which recommendations from the NVRA are followed by judges. Under half of the eligible offenders who scored 'low risk' actually received an alternative sanction (Garrett, Jakubow and Monahan 2018), including diversion from prison to jail. The same study found that there was substantial variation across the circuit court districts in the imposition of alternative sentences. The majority of judges rated the availability of alternative interventions within their jurisdiction as inadequate (Monahan, Metz and Garrett 2018). Thus, while Virginia achieved its aim of diverting at least 25 per cent of the lowest risk drug and property offenders from prison, there is no consistent application (Garrett, Jakubow and Monahan 2018).

Increasingly, other states also report risk and needs information at the sentencing stage, typically as part of the pre-sentence investigation (PSI) report. Most states that conduct RNA prior to sentencing use state-specific instruments, but the LSI-R, LS/CMI and COMPAS are also used (Elek, Warren and Casey 2015; Vera Institute of Justice 2011). Most of these instruments are much more elaborate than Virginia's NVRA. For example, the Indiana Risk Assessment System requires probation officers to score criminal history; education, employment and financial situation; family and social support; neighbourhood problems; substance abuse; peer associations; and criminal attitudes and behavioural patterns (Elek, Warren and Casey 2015). Overall, the US does not attach binding consequences to specific levels of risk, but sentencing guidelines recommend diversionary sanctions for offenders with low risk scores, while (lengthy) prison sentences are reserved for offenders with high risk scores. Yet, despite clear directions on how judges should interpret and apply risk scores, the research discussed above shows that judges are still likely to use their discretion to deviate from the recommendations on using risk scores.

B. Assessments of Dangerousness and Indeterminate Sentences

The serious consequences of being deemed a 'high-risk offender' are most aptly illustrated with a discussion of the practice of indeterminate sentencing in England and Wales. Sentencing guidelines in England and Wales are developed by the Sentencing Council and must be followed by judges, unless it is not in the interests of justice to do so (section 125(1) of the Coroners and Justice Act 2009). They tend to offer a fairly wide range of penalty options, the choice of which is guided by considerations of culpability, harm, aggravating factors (including relevant previous offences) and mitigating factors. Of particular interest regarding these guidelines is the assessment of dangerousness that judges *must* make for serious specified offences (section 224 of the Criminal Justice Act 2003), which can result in an indeterminate sentence of life imprisonment.

In cases where judges have to make a discretionary assessment of whether to impose a life sentence or extended sentence for certain violent or sexual offences, they do so under the dangerousness provisions outlined in section 229 of the Criminal Justice Act (CJA) 2003. In effect, this appraisal of dangerousness constitutes a risk assessment. A life sentence must be imposed by the court if it is available for the committed offence and 'the court considers that the seriousness of the offence, or of the offence and one or more offences associated with it, is such as to justify the imposition of a sentence of imprisonment for life' (section 225(2)). The judge assesses dangerousness by consideration of the nature and circumstances of the offence, the nature and circumstances of previous offences, any pattern of behaviour including the aforementioned offence(s), and any information about the offender (section 229). This information should normally be included in a pre-sentence report prepared by the National Probation Service (NPS). Such a report also includes an analysis of the likelihood of re-offending and risk of harm.[7] The courts may also consider psychiatric reports and other expert opinion.

England and Wales have – for Western European standards – an exceptionally high proportion of offenders sentenced to indeterminate prison sentences. At the end of 2017, 7,144 prisoners were serving a life sentence, which accounts for

[7] In practice, this involves a combination of actuarial and structured risk assessments (eg, Offender Group Reconviction Scores (OGRS) and Offender Assessment System (OASys)). The NPS also allocates cases based on risk for future management purposes, using the (actuarial) Risk of Serious Recidivism tool (Robinson 2017). See PI 04/2016 'Determining Pre-Sentence Reports'.

11 per cent of their prison population (Ministry of Justice 2018).[8] Life imprisonment is the mandatory sentence for offenders over 21 convicted of murder, a discretionary maximum sentence for offenders over 21 convicted of serious offences such as manslaughter, rape and armed robbery, and an automatic sentence for a second listed offence under conditions outlined in section 122 in the Legal Aid, Sentencing and Punishment of Offenders Act (LASPOA) 2012 (inserted as section 224A into the CJA 2003). At sentencing, the judge also imposes a minimum term that the offender has to serve in prison before they can be considered for parole. At the end of 2017, there were 2,014 prisoners (28 per cent) with a life sentence with an expired tariff (Ministry of Justice 2018). Released life prisoners remain on licence for the remainder of their natural life, which means they can be recalled to prison if this is deemed necessary to protect the public.

C. Imprisonment for Public Protection: A Failed Experiment

The costs of guideline-mandated indeterminate sentences for high-risk offenders are high, which was particularly evident from the brief experiment in England and Wales with another type of indeterminate sentence specifically for 'dangerous offenders': Imprisonment for Public Protection (IPP). The IPP sentence was introduced in section 225 of the CJA 2003 and was abolished in section 123 of the LASPOA 2012. In December 2017, there were still 3,029 prisoners serving an IPP sentence, most of whom (87 per cent) with an expired tariff (Ministry of Justice 2018).

The IPP experiment aptly demonstrates the difficulties with operationalising risk. Initially, there was no minimum offence seriousness threshold for imposing an IPP sentence (apart from commission of a listed offence) and the courts had to make the judgement as to whether an offender was 'dangerous', ie, 'a significant risk to members of the public of serious harm occasioned by the commission by him [sic] of further such offences' (section 229(1) of the CJA 2003). The original legislation contained a presumption of dangerousness, stating that 'the court must assume that there is such a risk' if an offender had committed one of the listed offences. In their risk assessment, the courts were obliged to take into account information about the offence and were allowed to also take into account information about the offender and patterns of behaviour, including the offence. The courts would normally have information from the structured risk assessment OASys at their disposal, but there were no guidelines or case law on how to derive conclusions about dangerousness from these scores (Ashworth and Zedner 2014: 126). Furthermore, the validity of OASys scores was found to be questionable by a report from the Chief Inspector of Prisons and Probation (HMCIP 2008).

[8] Included in this number are 60 prisoners with a whole life order, which means they will not be eligible for parole at any point, with the exception of release on compassionate grounds by the Home Secretary.

As a consequence of the wide net of risk cast by the CJA 2003, offenders were given relatively low commensurate tariffs, but nevertheless faced extended, indeterminate sentences (Jacobson and Hough 2010). The Criminal Justice and Immigration Act 2008 sought to remedy some of the problems with proportionality as well as the expansion of the prison population by removing the presumption of dangerousness and introducing a minimum tariff of two years before an IPP sentence could be imposed. The LASPOA 2012 abolished the IPP sentence altogether and reduced judicial discretion by introducing the automatic life sentence for a second serious violent or sexual offence.

D. Informing Discretion

In jurisdictions with greater judicial discretion at sentencing, the use of risk assessment is less transparent. In civil law countries, judges are not normally bound by guidelines, but instead have to abide by statutory maximum (and sometimes minimum) sentences. As a result, there are no instructions on applying risk scores in a specified manner in sentencing; thus, if and how outcomes from risk assessments should be used for sentencing purposes is left to judicial discretion. Nevertheless, judges often consider risk assessments in some form in their sentencing decisions. While specific preventive policies and measures betray the political preoccupation with risk, we can observe a persistence of rehabilitative ideals among judges and criminal justice professionals (McNeill et al 2009).

Common practice is to convey judgements of risk in the form of pre-sentence (investigation) reports, which are presented in court. Pre-sentence investigation (PSI) reports are widely used and tend to convey information about risk and the criminogenic needs of offenders. In these reports, risk assessments tend to be based on structured and clinical risk assessments, which may incorporate actuarial elements. Research on PSI reports in Belgium, Sweden and Denmark suggests that professional and clinical judgements are most important in determining risk; there is little evidence of the use of actuarial risk assessment at the sentencing stage (Beyens and Scheirs 2010; Persson and Svensson 2012; Wandall 2010). In Canada, on the other hand, structured actuarial risk assessment is a dominant feature of PSIs (Hannah-Moffat and Maurutto 2010).

Even when risk is clearly communicated at the sentencing stage in PSI reports, it is not necessarily interpreted in the same straightforward manner as is the case with sentencing grids and guidelines (ie, sentence enhancements for prior records or diversion from prison in the case of low risk). In the Netherlands, for example, judges appear to respond to risk with a more rehabilitative than incapacitative approach, which may even suggest that criminogenic needs are interpreted as mitigating rather than aggravating factors. A quasi-experimental study (van Wingerden, van Wilsem and Moerings 2014) found that Dutch judges were, contrary to expectations, more likely to sentence offenders identified as 'high risk' by a structured risk-based PSI report to less controlling sentences (ie, a suspended sentence without special conditions) than offenders with the same risk who did not have a PSI report at the time of sentencing. In line with expectations, offenders identified as low risk prior to sentencing were more likely to receive diverting types of sentences (ie, suspended sentence or community sentence) than their counterparts without risk assessment.

E. Beyond Punishment: Preventive Detention and Safety Measures

There are provisions for risk-based sentencing that avoid the engagement with normative issues of punishment through the deployment of what Hart (1968) called a *definitional stop*: if it is not called punishment, it does not have to be justified as such. This is problematic because moral questions and issues cannot be simply 'defined out of existence' (Kleinig 1973: 13). Many continental European jurisdictions have risk-related sanctions or measures that can be imposed at the sentencing stage in addition to or instead of purely offence-related penalties (van der Wolf and Herzog-Evans 2015). The integration of such measures in penal law makes them technically distinct from safety measures created within civil law and they also differ from provisions for safety measures after a sentence has been served, but both of these suffer from some of the same problems discussed below, particularly with respect to the proportionality of suffering inflicted. For example, many US states have the option to detain serious sexual offenders indefinitely under *civil* commitment laws when they have a 'mental abnormality' that predisposes them to sexual violence (*Kansas v Hendricks*).[9] The penal safety measures imposed at sentencing require a *prospective* judgement of risk rather than an assessment of *current* risk to determine safety of release and therefore do not take into account a possible reduction of risk over time.

As these sanctions are not technically punishments – even though they are imposed only when an offence has been committed – they bypass retributive concerns of proportionality; instead, they are intended primarily for public protection. This means that individuals can be deprived of their liberty for much longer than would normally be considered proportionate to the seriousness of the offence. These types of measures should not be confused with those for offenders who are not held criminally responsible for their acts (not discussed in this chapter). De Keijser (2011) has argued elsewhere that the difference between punishment and measure is merely semantic in relation to the infliction of suffering: while punishment involves the intended infliction of suffering, any suffering inflicted by a measure is unintended. Regardless, the deprivation of liberty – unlikely to be the only deprivation resulting from a measure – is inevitably accompanied by pain.

[9] *Kansas v Hendricks* 521 US 346 (1997).

There are many examples of such measures which are preventive in name and punitive in terms of subjective experience (see Ashworth and Zedner (2014) for examples and critiques). The following paragraphs discuss two examples from the Netherlands of penal measures involving liberty deprivation, which provides an interesting case study given that the measures target two very different categories of high-risk offenders: (1) serious violent and sexual offenders; and (2) persistent (low-level) offenders.

The first measure is *terbeschikkingstelling* (TBS, entrustment order). Of particular interest for the purposes of this discussion is the version of TBS which can be imposed in addition to a regular term of imprisonment, meaning that the offender is held (at least partially) criminally responsible.[10] TBS extends a sentence beyond the severity proportionate to the offence, although a TBS order will be served in a TBS institution rather than regular prison; this is not the case in France, for example, where safety detention is executed in prison (van der Wolf and Herzog-Evans 2015). The TBS order incapacitates the offender for its duration, but also entails treatment. The offender may decline treatment, but this would considerably reduce their chances of release. TBS may only be imposed for crimes with a maximum statutory punishment of at least four years, when a psychiatric disorder (to some extent) led to the commission of the offence and when there is a risk of recidivism. Its duration is limited to a maximum of four years for non-violent offenders, although in practice the vast majority of offenders given a TBS order are sentenced for violent offences. For violent offenders, TBS can be extended indefinitely with two-year increments upon review. The decision to impose a TBS order relies primarily on a psychiatric report provided to the court, which is still heavily based on clinical diagnosis and risk assessment. Risk assessments during a TBS order – for example, to determine temporary release – increasingly make use of structured risk assessment tools, such as the Dutch HKT-R and the international HCR20V3.

The second measure is *Inrichting Stelselmatige Daders* (ISD, Institution for Persistent Offenders), which is a determinate custodial measure of a maximum of two years imposed instead of a regular prison sentence. It targets offenders who frequently commit less serious crimes and are seen to be responsible for a disproportionately high number of offences. ISD prisoners are incarcerated on dedicated ISD wings within regular prison facilities. The ISD measure is best understood as a measure to protect society of nuisance rather than danger. Like TBS, ISD imposes a sanction that is more severe than would be justified solely on retributive grounds. It can be imposed at the request of the public prosecutor if a defendant has been convicted at least three times in the preceding five years. The judicial decision is further informed by a pre-sentence report, including risk assessment, provided by the Probation Service. Apart from the public

[10] TBS can also be imposed on offenders not held criminally responsible due to mental illness at the time of the offence.

protection rationale underlying ISD, it is also thought that the duration of the measure is potentially more effective at addressing problems of addiction than repetitive short sentences; there is some evidence that the ISD measure is effective at reducing crime and recidivism (Tollenaar, van der Laan and van der Heijden 2014, 2018).

IV. The Future of Risk Assessment

The use of risk assessment in sentencing is not a new development, but its function and form have changed over the last few decades. While risk assessment is still used at the back door of sentencing to determine safety of release, it is increasingly used at the front door of sentencing. Here, it has two primary (and to some extent, mutually exclusive) functions: (1) to limit judicial discretion by attaching prescribed or advised sentences to offenders' risk; and (2) to inform judicial discretion, mainly in the form of pre-sentence investigation reports containing risk/needs assessments. There is no uniformity in how risk assessment is used and even the consequences attached to it. It can serve to identify low-risk offenders who can be safely diverted from prison, to identify high-risk offenders who should be given indeterminate sentences or safety measures, or to determine the most appropriate type of sentence or conditions. Actuarial assessment has gained some ground, but the remaining influence of professional judgement should not be underestimated. Nevertheless, policies and legislation for dangerous offenders are illustrative of increasing risk aversion and, in effect, limit judicial discretion. This final section reflects on two recent developments that may signal further changes in the shape and methods of risk-based sentencing: (1) the criminalisation of risk; and (2) technological advancements, including machine learning and neurological risk assessment.

While the preceding discussion has focused on risk assessment as part of the sentencing process and in determining release decisions, there is a trend towards an assumption of risk with certain activities. This concerns primarily pre-inchoate or preparatory offences that are thought to indicate risk of further offending that has the potential to cause great harm. Pre-inchoate offences mainly concern activities associated with terrorism (eg, encouragement of terrorism or engaging in any conduct in preparation for acts of terrorism; see the UK's Terrorism Act 2006).[11] Characteristic of these offences is that activities that are not harmful *an sich* are seen – in combination with circumstances and a degree of interpretation about intent – as carrying enough risk for harm as to warrant

[11] Although, as Ashworth and Zedner (2014) note, the offence of 'meeting a child following sexual grooming' in English law can be seen as a pre-inchoate offence. It penalises a person who intentionally meets or travels to meet a minor with the intention of doing something that would constitute the commission of an offence (s 15 of the Sexual Offences Act 2003).

severe punishment (the maximum penalty for the preparatory activities under the Terrorism Act 2006 is life imprisonment). This fits with a shift from post-crime to pre-crime (Zedner 2007), whereby criminal justice resources and responses are increasingly oriented towards the pre-emption of crime rather than the reaction to crime. Such a criminalisation of risk obscures assumptions about risk factors and how they are related to actual harm: the problem of imperfect predictive validity is completely disregarded when behaviour indicative of a high risk of harm is itself illegal.

Similarly, technological advancements raise new questions about fairness, even though they may improve the accuracy of predictions. There are two particularly noteworthy developments in relation to the technology of risk prediction: machine learning algorithms and neurological assessments. Machine learning techniques have enabled the search for instruments that can detect more complex patterns than traditional regression-based instruments (Berk and Bleich 2013; Berk et al 2009). This means that the algorithm that turns input information into a risk score is highly complex (a 'black box'), and consequently cannot be used to inform interventions and monitor progress in the way that third- and fourth-generation instruments can be used. There is not yet agreement on whether machine learning techniques are more accurate at predicting recidivism (Berk and Bleich 2013; Tollenaar and van der Heijden 2013; for a discussion of the impact of machine learning on the predictive fairness of risk assessment, see Hannah-Moffat, Chapter 10 in this volume).

A second development is the potential of neurological assessment to inform assessments of dangerousness. While the study of brain function in relation to offending is still in its infancy and has not yet widely penetrated the court room (although see Catley and Claydon 2016; Denno 2015; Gaudet and Marchant 2016), recent brain imaging developments could potentially be used for the purpose of 'neuropredicting' violence and offending more generally (Aggarwal 2009; Gkotsi and Gasser 2016; Glenn and Raine 2014; Nadelhoffer and Sinnot-Armstrong 2012). For example, reduced functioning in the frontal lobe is associated with antisocial and violent behaviour (Yang and Raine 2009). While most evidence is cross-sectional in nature, there are some studies that have successfully used neuro-assessment to predict re-arrest and violent offending (Aharoni et al 2013; Pardini et al 2014). Nevertheless, the brain is a product of complex biosocial interactions and there is a danger of reductionism and stigmatisation if we rely on 'brain data' to predict future offending (Gkotsi and Gasser 2016). So far, however, research suggests that neurological evidence of brain abnormalities has mostly been interpreted as diminished culpability in sentencing decisions rather than as an indication of future risk (Catley and Claydon 2016; Denno 2015). This, again, suggests that the *discretionary* use of risk assessment does not at this time have a uniformly 'aggravating' impact on sentencing decisions. Yet, given the volatile nature and political sensitivity of 'risk', the future may not be kind to such discretion.

References

Aggarwal, NK (2009) 'Neuroimaging, Culture, and Forensic Psychiatry' 37 *Journal of the American Academy of Psychiatry and the Law* 239.

Aharoni, E, Vincent, GM, Harenski, CL, Calhoun, VD, Sinnott-Armstrong, W, Gazzaniga, M S and Kiehl, KA (2013) 'Neuroprediction of Future Rearrest' 110 *Proceedings of the National Academy of Sciences* 6223.

Andrews, DA and Bonta, J (1995) *The Level of Supervision Inventory – Revised* (Toronto, Multi-Health Systems).

——. (2010) *The Psychology of Criminal Conduct*, 5th edn (Cincinnati, Anderson Publishing Company).

Andrews, DA, Bonta, J and Wormith, JS (2004) *The Level of Service/Case Management Inventory (LS/CMI)* (Toronto, Multi-Health Systems).

——. (2006) 'The Recent Past and Near Future of Risk and/or Need Assessment' 52 *Crime & Delinquency* 7.

Angwin, J, Larson, J, Mattu, S and Kirchner, L (2016) 'Machine Bias: There's Software Used across the Country to Predict Future Criminals. And it's Biased against Blacks', *ProPublica*, www.propublica.org/article/machine-bias-risk-assessments-in-criminal-sentencing.

Ashworth, A and Zedner, L (2014) *Preventive Justice* (Oxford, Oxford University Press).

Auerhahn, K (1999) 'Selective Incapacitation and the Problem of Prediction' 37 *Criminology* 703.

Austin, J, Coleman, D, Peyton, J and Johnson, KD (2003) *Reliability and Validity Study of the LSI-R Risk Assessment Instrument* (Washington DC, Institute on Crime, Justice, and Corrections at the George Washington University).

Bagaric, M (2001) *Punishment and Sentencing: A Rational Approach* (London, Cavendish Publishing).

Baird, C (2009) *A Question of the Evidence: A Critique of Risk Assessment Models Used in the Justice System* (Madison, WI, National Council on Crime and Delinquency).

Beck, U (1992) *Risk Society: Towards a New Modernity* (London, Sage).

Berk, RA and Bleich, J (2013) 'Statistical Procedures for Forecasting Criminal Behavior' 12 *Criminology & Public Policy* 513.

Berk, R, Sherman, L, Barnes, G, Kurtz, E and Ahlman, L (2009) 'Forecasting Murder within a Population of Probationers and Parolees: A High Stakes Application of Statistical Learning' 172 *Journal of the Royal Statistical Society: Series A (Statistics in Society)* 191.

Beyens, K and Scheirs, V (2010) 'Encounters of a Different Kind: Social Enquiry and Sentencing in Belgium' 12 *Punishment & Society* 309.

Blokland, AA and Nieuwbeerta, P (2007) 'Selectively Incapacitating Frequent Offenders: Costs and Benefits of Various Penal Scenarios' 23 *Journal of Quantitative Criminology* 327.

Casey, PM, Warren, RK and Elek JK (2011) *Using Offender Risk and Needs Assessment Information at Sentencing: Guidance for Courts from a National Working Group* (Williamsburg, VA, National Center for State Courts).
Catley, P and Claydon, L (2016) 'The Use of Neuroscientific Evidence in the Courtroom by Those Accused of Criminal Offenses in England and Wales' 2 *Journal of Law and the Biosciences* 510.
Caudy, MS, Durso, JM and Taxman, FS (2013) 'How Well Do Dynamic Needs Predict Recidivism? Implications for Risk Assessment and Risk Reduction' 41 *Journal of Criminal Justice* 458.
Chouldechova, A (2017) 'Fair Prediction with Disparate Impact: A Study of Bias in Recidivism Prediction Instruments' 5 *Big Data* 153.
De Keijser, JW (2011) 'Never Mind the Pain; It's a Measure! Justifying Measures as Part of the Dutch Bifurcated System of Sanctions' in M Tonry (ed), *Retributivism Has a Past: Has it a Future?* (Oxford, Oxford University Press).
Denno, DW (2015) 'The Myth of the Double-Edged Sword: An Empirical Study of Neuroscience Evidence in Criminal Cases' 56 *Boston College Law Review* 493.
Dowdy, ER, Lacy, MG and Unnithan, NP (2002) 'Correctional Prediction and the Level of Supervision Inventory' 30 *Journal of Criminal Justice* 29.
Dressel, J and Farid, H (2018) 'The Accuracy, Fairness, and Limits of Predicting Recidivism' 4 *Science Advances* eaao5580.
Duguid, S (2000) *Can Prisons Work? The Prisoner as Object and Subject in Modern Corrections* (Toronto, University of Toronto Press).
Durnescu, I (2011) 'Pains of Probation: Effective Practice and Human Rights' 55 *International Journal of Offender Therapy and Comparative Criminology* 530.
Elek, JK, Warren, RK and Casey, PM (2015) *Using Risk and Needs Assessment Information at Sentencing: Observations from Ten Jurisdictions* (Williamsburg, VA, National Center for State Courts).
Fazel, S, Singh, JP, Doll, H and Grann, M (2012) 'Use of Risk Assessment Instruments to Predict Violence and Antisocial Behaviour in 73 Samples Involving 24,827 People: Systematic Review and Meta-analysis' 345 *British Medical Journal* e4692.
Feeley, MM and Simon, J (1992) 'The New Penology: Notes on the Emerging Strategy of Corrections and its Implications' 30 *Criminology* 449.
——. (1994) 'Actuarial Justice: The Emerging New Criminal Law' in D Nelken (ed), *The Futures of Criminology* (London, Sage).
Flores, AW, Bechtel, K and Lowenkamp, CT (2016) 'False Positives, False Negatives, and False Analyses: A Rejoinder to "Machine Bias: There's Software Used Across the Country to Predict Future Criminals. And it's Biased against Blacks"' 80 *Federal Probation* 38.
Frase, RS and Hester, R (2015) 'Magnitude of Criminal History Enhancements' in RS Frase et al, *Criminal History Enhancements Sourcebook* (Minneapolis, Robina Institute of Criminal Law and Criminal Justice).
Garland, D (2001) *The Culture of Control* (Oxford, Oxford University Press).

Garrett, BL, Jakubow, A and Monahan, J (2018) *Nonviolent Risk Assessment in Virginia Sentencing: The Sentencing Commission Data* (University of Virginia School of Law).

Gaudet, LM and Marchant, GE (2016) 'Under the Radar: Neuroimaging Evidence in the Criminal Courtroom' 64 *Drake Law Review* 577.

Gendreau, P, Little, T and Goggin, C (1996) 'A Meta-analysis of the Predictors of Adult Offender Recidivism: What Works!' 34 *Criminology* 575.

Giddens, A (1990) *The Consequences of Modernity* (Stanford, Stanford University Press).

Gkotsi, GM and Gasser, J (2016) 'Neuroscience in Forensic Psychiatry: From Responsibility to Dangerousness. Ethical and Legal Implications of Using Neuroscience for Dangerousness Assessments' 46 *International Journal of Law and Psychiatry* 58.

Glenn, AL and Raine, A (2014) 'Neurocriminology: Implications for the Punishment, Prediction and Prevention of Criminal Behaviour' 15 *Nature Reviews Neuroscience* 54.

Gottfredson, SD and Moriarty, LJ (2006) 'Statistical Risk Assessment: Old Problems and New Applications' 52 *Crime & Delinquency* 178.

Greenwood, PW and Abrahamse, AF (1982) *Selective Incapacitation* (Santa Monica, RAND Corporation).

Hannah-Moffat, K (2005) 'Criminogenic Needs and the Transformative Risk Subject: Hybridizations of Risk/Need in Penality' 7 *Punishment & Society* 29.

——. (2016) 'A Conceptual Kaleidoscope: Contemplating "Dynamic Structural Risk" and an Uncoupling of Risk from Need' 22 *Psychology, Crime & Law* 33.

Hannah-Moffat, K and Maurutto, P (2010) 'Re-contextualizing Pre-sentence Reports: Risk and Race' 12 *Punishment & Society* 262.

Hanson, RK and Morton-Bourgon, KE (2009) 'The Accuracy of Recidivism Risk Assessments for Sexual Offenders: A Meta-analysis of 118 Prediction Studies' 21 *Psychological Assessment* 1.

Hanson, RK and Thornton, D (1999) *Static 99: Improving Actuarial Risk Assessments for Sex Offenders*, vol 2 (Ottawa, Solicitor General Canada).

Harcourt, BE (2007) *Against Prediction: Profiling, Policing and Punishing in the Actuarial Age* (Chicago, University of Chicago Press).

Hart, HLA (1968) *Punishment and Responsibility* (Oxford, Oxford University Press).

Hart, SD, Michie, C and Cooke, DJ (2007) 'Precision of Actuarial Risk Assessment Instruments: Evaluating the 'Margins of Error' of Group versus Individual Predictions of Violence' *British Journal of Psychiatry* 190(49), 60.

HMCIP (2008) *The Indeterminate Sentence for Public Protection: A Thematic Review* (London, HMCIP).

Holtfreter, K, Reisig, MD and Morash, M (2004) 'Poverty, State Capital, and Recidivism among Women Offenders' 3 *Criminology & Public Policy* 185.

Jacobson, J and Hough, M (2010) *Unjust Deserts: Imprisonment for Public Protection* (London, Prison Reform Trust).

Kleinig, J (1973) *Punishment and Desert* (The Hague, Martinus Nijhoff).
Labrecque, RM, Smith, P, Lovins, BK and Latessa, EJ (2014) 'The Importance of Reassessment: How Changes in the LSI-R Risk Score Can Improve the Prediction of Recidivism' 53 *Journal of Offender Rehabilitation* 116.
Lee, Y (2010) 'Repeat Offenders and the Question of Desert' in JV Roberts and A von Hirsch (eds), *Previous Convictions at Sentencing: Theoretical and Applied Perspectives* (Oxford, Hart Publishing).
McNeill, F, Burns, N, Halliday, S, Hutton, N and Tata, C. (2009) 'Risk, Responsibility and Reconfiguration: Penal Adaptation and Misadaptation' 11 *Punishment & Society* 419.
Ministry of Justice (2018) *Offender Management Statistics Quarterly, England and Wales. Quarter: July to September 2017, Prison Population: 31 December 2017* (London, Ministry of Justice).
Monahan, J (1981) *The Clinical Prediction of Violent Behavior* (Northvale, NJ, Jason J Aronson).
Monahan, J, Metz, AL and Garrett, BL (2018) *Nonviolent Risk Assessment in Virginia Sentencing, Report 2: A Survey of Circuit Court Judges* (University of Virginia School of Law).
Nadelhoffer, T and Sinnott-Armstrong, W (2012) 'Neurolaw and Neuroprediction: Potential Promises and Perils' 7 *Philosophy Compass* 631.
Netter, B (2007) 'Using Group Statistics to Sentence Individual Criminals: An Ethical and Statistical Critique of the Virginia Risk Assessment Program' 97 *Journal of Criminal Law and Criminology* 699.
O'Malley, P (1999) *The Risk Society: Implications for Justice and Beyond* (Victoria, Department of Justice).
Ostrom, BJ and Kauder, NB (2012) 'The Evolution of Offender Risk Assessment in Virginia' 25 *Federal Sentencing Reporter* 161.
Pardini, DA, Raine, A, Erickson, K and Loeber, R (2014) 'Lower Amygdala Volume in Men is Associated with Childhood Aggression, Early Psychopathic Traits, and Future Violence' 75 *Biological Psychiatry* 73.
Persson, A and Svensson, K (2012) 'Shades of Professionalism: Risk Assessment in Pre-sentence Reports in Sweden' 9 *European Journal of Criminolog* 176.
Phelps, MS (2011) 'Rehabilitation in the Punitive Era: The Gap between Rhetoric and Reality in US Prison Programs' 45 *Law & Society Review* 33.
Pratt, J (1995) 'Dangerousness, Risk and Technologies of Power' 28 *Australian & New Zealand Journal of Criminology* 3.
Raynor, P and Lewis, S (2011) 'Risk-Need Assessment, Sentencing and Minority Ethnic Offenders in Britain' 41 *British Journal of Social Work* 1357.
Robinson, G (2017) 'Stand-Down and Deliver: Pre-sentence Reports, Quality and the New Culture of Speed' 64 *Probation Journal* 337.
Rothschild-Elyassi, G, Koehler, J and Simon J (in press) 'Actuarial Justice' in M Deflem (ed), *The Handbook of Social Control* (Malden, MA, Wiley-Blackwell).

Ryberg, J (2019) 'Risk and Retribution: On the Possibility of Reconciling Considerations of Dangerousness and Desert' in JW de Keijser, JV Roberts and J Ryberg (eds), *Predictive Sentencing: Normative and Empirical Perspectives* (Oxford, Hart Publishing).

Singh, JP, Desmarais, SL and van Dorn, RA (2013) 'Measurement of Predictive Validity in Violence Risk Assessment Studies: A Second-Order Systematic Review' 31 *Behavioral Sciences & the Law* 55.

Singh, JP, Grann, M and Fazel, S (2011) 'A Comparative Study of Violence Risk Assessment Tools: A Systematic Review and Metaregression Analysis of 68 Studies Involving 25,980 Participants' 31 *Clinical Psychology Review* 499.

Skeem, JL and Lowenkamp, CT (2016) 'Risk, Race, and Recidivism: Predictive Bias and Disparate Impact' 54 *Criminology* 680.

Skeem, JL and Monahan, J (2011) 'Current Directions in Violence Risk Assessment' 20 *Current Directions in Psychological Science* 38.

Skeem, JL Monahan, J and Lowenkamp, C (2016) 'Gender, Risk Assessment, and Sanctioning: The Cost of Treating Women Like Men' 40 *Law and Human Behavior* 580.

Slobogin, C (2012) 'Risk Assessment' in J Petersilia and KR Reitz (eds), *The Oxford Handbook of Sentencing and Corrections* (Oxford, Oxford University Press).

Starr, SB (2014) 'Evidence-Based Sentencing and the Scientific Rationalization of Discrimination' 66 *Stanford Law Review* 803.

Tollenaar, N and van der Heijden, PGM (2013) 'Which Method Predicts Recidivism Best? A Comparison of Statistical, Machine Learning and Data Mining Predictive Models' 176 *Journal of the Royal Statistical Society: Series A (Statistics in Society)* 565.

Tollenaar, N, van der Laan, AM and van der Heijden, PGM (2014) 'Effectiveness of a Prolonged Incarceration and Rehabilitation Measure for High-Frequency Offenders' 10 *Journal of Experimental Criminology* 29.

——. (2018). 'Correction to: Effectiveness of a Prolonged Incarceration and Rehabilitation Measure for High-Frequency Offenders' 14 *Journal of Experimental Criminology* 121.

Tonry, M (2014) 'Legal and Ethical Issues in the Prediction of Recidivism' 26 *Federal Sentencing Reporter* 167.

Van der Wolf, MJ and Herzog-Evans, M (2015) 'Mandatory Measures: "Safety Measures". Supervision and Detention of Dangerous Offenders in France and the Netherlands: A Comparative and Human Rights' Perspective' in M Herzog-Evans (ed), *Offender Release and Supervision: The Role of Courts and the Use of Discretion* (Nijmegen, Wolf Legal Publishers).

Van Eijk, G (2017) 'Socioeconomic Marginality in Sentencing: The Built-in Bias in Risk Assessment Tools and the Reproduction of Social Inequality' 19 *Punishment & Society* 463.

Van Ginneken, EFJC and Hayes, D (2017) '"Just" Punishment? Offenders' Views on the Meaning and Severity of Punishment' 17 *Criminology & Criminal Justice* 62.

van Voorhis, P, Wright, EM, Salisbury, E and Bauman, A (2010) 'Women's Risk Factors and Their Contributions to Existing Risk/Needs Assessment: The Current Status of a Gender-Responsive Supplement' 37 *Criminal Justice and Behavior* 261.

van Wingerden, S, Van Wilsem, J and Moerings, M (2014) 'Pre-sentence Reports and Punishment: A Quasi-experiment Assessing the Effects of Risk-Based Pre-sentence Reports on Sentencing' 11 *European Journal of Criminology* 723.

Vera Institute of Justice (2011) *Risk and Needs Assessments*, Memorandum to the Delaware Justice Reinvestment Task Force, available at: www.ma4jr.org/wp-content/uploads/2014/10/vera-institute-memo-on-risk-assessment-for-delaware-2011.pdf.

Virginia Criminal Sentencing Commission (2001) *Annual Report* (Richmond, VA, Virginia Criminal Sentencing Commission).

Von Hirsch, A (1976) *Doing Justice: The Choice of Punishments* (New York, Hill and Wang).

——. (2010) 'Proportionality and the Progressive Loss of Mitigation: Some Further Reflections' in JV Roberts and A von Hirsch (eds), *Previous Convictions at Sentencing: Theoretical and Applied Perspectives* (Oxford, Hart Publishing).

Vose, B, Cullen, FT and Smith, P (2008) 'The Empirical Status of the Level of Service Inventory' 72 *Federal Probation* 22.

Wandall, RH (2010) 'Resisting Risk Assessment? Pre-sentence Reports and Individualized Sentencing in Denmark' 12 *Punishment & Society* 329.

Wolfgang, M, Figlio, R and Sellin, T (1972) *Delinquency in a Birth Cohort* (Chicago, University of Chicago Press).

Yang, Y and Raine, A (2009) 'Prefrontal Structural and Functional Brain Imaging Findings in Antisocial, Violent, and Psychopathic Individuals: A Meta-analysis' 174 *Psychiatry Research: Neuroimaging* 81.

Yang, M, Wong, SC and Coid, J (2010) 'The Efficacy of Violence Prediction: A Meta-analytic Comparison of Nine Risk Assessment Tools' 136 *Psychological Bulletin* 740.

Zedner, L (2007) 'Pre-crime and Post-criminology?' 11 *Theoretical Criminology* 261.

3

Why Legal Philosophers (Including Retributivists) Should Be Less Resistant to Risk-Based Sentencing

DOUGLAS HUSAK

I. Introduction

I respond to two of the grounds on which I believe risk-based sentencing (RBS) is controversial among legal theorists. First, it seemingly triggers a deontological constraint against harmfully discriminating against one person to minimise the risk of harm to another. In the next section, I point out how countless social and economic practices seemingly implicate this same 'means principle'. These practices do not attract much opposition; it is hard to see why they *should* be changed even if they *could*. Second, RBS is said to be incompatible with retributivism – the dominant penal philosophy of our era. In the second part of my chapter, I try to show how this alleged inconsistency stems from a misunderstanding of the nature of retributivism. A better account of retributivism dissolves the apparent inconsistency with risk-based sentencing. If these difficulties are overcome, I will have succeeded in removing two of the most trenchant barriers to the use of risked-based sentencing. Unless other objections emerge, I conclude that risk-based sentencing should be employed if it accomplishes a net balance of good objectives.

II. Risk-Based Sentencing and the Impermissible Use of Persons

I begin my discussion of RBS by placing the issue in a broader context. Any such exercise is often useful on its own merits, and I hope my efforts are valuable for that reason as well. But the larger framework I will construct is especially significant for the topic at hand. I gather that the use of risk-analysis in sentencing decisions is thought to be controversial for at least two reasons, one of which is that it implicates a principle that has proved difficult to justify: *we may inflict actual harms on one person (those who are sentenced) in order to reduce the risks of harm that might befall others (those who would be victimised if the risks materialise).* This principle, in turn, is controversial because it seemingly transgresses a Kantian deontological constraint against using people as a mere means. Exactly how the Kantian 'means principle' should be formulated, how it might be circumvented, and whether it should be accepted at all, are deep matters that have spawned a huge literature I will not explicitly discuss here.[1]

Superficially, at least, RBS is worrisome because it implicates the foregoing principle – although this supposition has been challenged, and I will return to it later. But if the rationale for using projections about future risks at sentencing is to harm one to minimise the occurrence of subsequent harms to another, it is worthwhile to be reminded that such practices are surprisingly common throughout our society and usually attract little scrutiny. If I am correct, a promising way to approach the present topic is to examine whether there are any *special* difficulties in using risk assessments in the criminal law generally or as a factor in sentencing in particular. Perhaps such difficulties exist, but the case must be made rather than assumed. In other words, we might ask: if efforts to prevent the likelihood of future harms to others are routinely invoked to support a wide variety of practices that impose present harms on individuals, why might RBS encounter *more* opposition than these other practices?

Thus, I begin my examination of RBS by calling attention to the pervasiveness of practices that seemingly implicate the foregoing principle. My point of departure is that such practices are far more common than moral, political and legal philosophers have tended to acknowledge. Both states and private institutions harm one agent to prevent the occurrence of subsequent harms to other agents far more casually than many commentators seem to appreciate. As long as we think such practices are rare or extraordinary, we are apt to demand a special justification for them. And I believe that quite a few moral and legal philosophers *do* tend to regard instances of preventive harming as exceptional. Philosophers who specialise in the justifiability of preventive harming typically focus on cases of war or self-defence. These topics are obviously important and raise countless complex moral issues, yet few of us are likely to encounter them in our ordinary lives. I trust I am not unusual in never having taken part in a war or had the need to exercise real (or even putative) self-defence. Thus, I propose to set aside the foregoing well-worn but statistically unusual topics. Instead, quite a few of the examples on which I will focus are mundane and can easily escape our notice. The realisation that practices that harm one person today to prevent harm to a different person tomorrow are so common helps to shine a new normative light on the topic at hand. The social and legal practices I will discuss probably

[1] See the many perspectives defended in the special issue of *Criminal Law and Philosophy*: (2016) 10 *Criminal Law and Philosophy* 741–863.

cannot and presumably *should* not be altered so easily. If harms are seemingly justified for preventive purposes in the contexts I mention, we might ask whether or for what reason they should be deemed especially controversial when used at sentencing.

The most obvious instance of a state measure that harms offenders is punishment itself, whether or not it involves incarceration. As long as we include sentences that do *not* include jail or prison, some seven million people in the US are undergoing punishment at any given time. In the opinion of quite a few legal philosophers, including myself, the actual imposition of punishment is at least partly justified by its special and general deterrent effects. Commentators disagree, sometimes bitterly, about the number of crimes that punishment prevents. We need not wade into this morass to agree that the number is probably significant. However, in most of the remainder of this section, I discuss additional state practices and policies that (presumably) do not involve punishment, but nonetheless harm persons in order to reduce the risk of subsequent harm to others. *Ceteris paribus*, I would suppose that practices that impose present harms on persons to prevent later harms that involve punishment are inferior to practices that impose present harms on persons to prevent later harms, but do *not* involve punishment. If this supposition is correct and if some modes of punishment are justifiable – which few legal philosophers contest – many of the practices and policies I will examine are likely to be justifiable as well.

Quite a few of the mandatory or discretionary measures that harm offenders take place *after* the defendant's 'official punishment' has ended. Most of the practices and policies I have in mind can be called *collateral consequences* (Hoskins 2018). This term lacks a standard definition; I adopt a very expansive understanding of it. In what follows, I understand a collateral consequence as any harm suffered by a person caused by his interaction with the criminal justice system (other than whatever constitutes his official punishment). Notice that this (admittedly vague) definition does not require that the harm be imposed by the *state* or that anyone is ever actually *punished. Any* harm suffered by a person as a result of her interaction with the criminal justice system can suffice. The important point is that a vast array of harms are inflicted as a result such interactions and, when these harms are designed to prevent future harms to others, they form the topic of my examination because they seemingly implement the same principle that leads to anxiety about RBS.

Systems of criminal justice are blaming institutions. To understand them, we need to understand blame. To understand blame, we need to grasp its role in our everyday social lives (Strawson 1962). Thus, my general background assumption is that we can learn a great deal about the normative status of state practices of preventive harming (of which RBS is an instance) by understanding how they are similar to practices that are familiar to us as private individuals who interact with one another on a daily basis. Efforts to minimise risks are among the most salient features of these interactions. I will invoke this background assumption throughout my discussion of collateral consequences.

To be sure, the most well-known collateral consequences are imposed by the state. Restrictions on *employment* constitute the most widely used of such measures. Some of these practices seem punitive and are not designed to prevent subsequent harms. More typically, however, these restrictions are intended to ban persons from a particular job in which they are thought to pose an elevated risk of causing harm – especially when the persons who are most prone to be victimised comprise a vulnerable group. Although laws restricting employment opportunities for convicted offenders vary from place to place, I offer a few illustrations: in many states, those convicted of drug or sex offences are barred permanently from obtaining a teaching licence. Other vocations restricted under various state statutes include accountant, beautician, chiropractor, police officer, architect, barber, roofer, plumber, interior designer, land surveyor, and farm labour contractor. Similar disqualifications apply to fostering or adopting children, obtaining driver's licences, serving on juries, possessing firearms or serving in the military.

The next most-common category of collateral consequences pertains to housing rather than employment. Federal regulations permit local authorities to evict tenants who engage in unlawful activity and to deny occupancy to applicants with criminal histories. Specifically, federal law allows housing authorities to obtain criminal background checks on applicants, requires them to deny residence to those convicted of specified offences and permits them to withhold housing from anyone who has, during a reasonable time prior to admission, engaged in violent, drug-related or other illegal conduct that might threaten health or safety. The interpretation of these vague terms (eg, 'reasonable time') is left to the discretion of the local authorities, who have an incentive to make full use of the latitude they are afforded in light of the high demand for the limited stock of public housing. As a result, many communities deny public housing to persons with criminal records.

But the more far-reaching class of collateral consequences on which I propose to focus do not require the person to be *convicted* or even *charged* with an offence. Instead, they are triggered by a mere *arrest* – permitted when the police have *probable cause* to believe that a person is engaged in criminal activity. The total impact of these collateral consequences dwarf those predicated on conviction. Deprivations that require a mere arrest affect astounding numbers of people; approximately 25 per cent of the adult population of the US have an arrest record for actual or alleged conduct not involving a traffic offence. Easily accessed criminal intelligence databases are filled with information about people who may be monitored because of the risk they are thought to pose. Thus, some 70 million Americans are potentially affected by adverse collateral consequences that result from their interaction with the criminal justice system. For perhaps the majority of arrestees, the most worrying consequence of this is not the threat of conviction and punishment, but the ensuing criminal record. The collateral consequences that result from an arrest are both formal (de jure) and informal (de facto) (Logan 2013). In his seminal book on criminal records, James Jacobs alleges that the need to balance the goal of preventing crime with the civil liberties of persons who interact with the criminal justice system is 'one of the greatest law enforcement challenges of our time' (Jacobs 2015: 30).

I hope to have given a brief glimpse of the broad range of collateral consequences that are triggered simply by an interaction with the criminal justice system. A more complete description of these measures is well beyond the scope of this chapter, but is easily accessed from a number of comprehensive websites.[2] Instead, I propose to address some of the philosophical questions raised by the examples I have presented.

First, I have persistently characterised these collateral consequences as *harms*. I believe this characterisation is appropriate; these results qualify as harms according to any respectable comparative account (Hanser 2008). All comparative accounts of harming involve a *worsening*, and most of the examples I have described involve a worsening of *opportunities* needed to secure an autonomous life. When opportunities are worsened, harms result in the same way that discrimination is harmful – even when a particular instance of discrimination is justified. Various comparative accounts employ a different baseline to identify whether a worsening has occurred. According to counterfactual comparative accounts, harm is suffered when one is made to be worse off than he otherwise would have been. According to temporal comparative accounts, harm is suffered when one is made worse off than he had previously been. I believe the cases I have described qualify as harms under each of these comparative accounts – although perhaps not under *non*-comparative accounts. Even though the states of affairs caused by these practices may not be especially severe, they should be counted as harms nonetheless. Second, it is even clearer that many of the practices I have described are intended to be *preventive*. As I understand it, preventive action (whether harmful or not) is designed to reduce the probability that something bad will happen in the future. Many but not all of the bad things we want not to happen involve conduct that would amount to a *crime*. However, the important point is that my examples implicate the means principle with which I began: actual harms are inflicted on one person in order to reduce a risk of harm that might befall another.

Collateral consequences have a bad reputation among legal theorists. For a number of reasons, quite a few reformers who are appalled by the size and scale of the criminal justice system in the US have called for an end to most or all of the collateral consequences I have described. This recommendation is motivated by humane concerns. Re-entry of prisoners into society is incredibly difficult, and these difficulties need not be exacerbated by additional barriers. Some have gone so far as to recommend the enactment of laws to outlaw some of the kinds of discrimination I have described, in much the same way as we ban discrimination of grounds of race or religion (Chin 2018). And if the case for not allowing *conviction* to reduce employment and housing prospects is compelling, the argument for

[2] See Justice Center, National Inventory of the Collateral Consequences of Conviction, https://niccc.csgjusticecenter.org.

not allowing a mere *arrest* to do so is even stronger. As I have suggested, a quarter of the adult population of the US is subject to the harms that can result from a mere arrest, and no one seriously disputes that persons with an arrest record are treated more harshly than those without such a record at each stage of the criminal justice process (Jacobs 2015). More importantly for my purposes, *private* parties respond similarly to arrestees. A total of 92 per cent of private employers who replied to a survey say they require a background check for some or all jobs and admit to drawing a negative inference from a negative finding (Jacobs 2015). To add insult to injury, it is apparent that these practices place an especially heavy burden on minorities, thereby raising protests from liberals and prioritarians alike (Temkin 2016). From a procedural point of view, it seems outrageous that a single police officer has the de facto power to place an individual at a lifelong disability in employment and housing (Jacobs 2015: 277 and 291). For these reasons alone, it is surprising that those philosophers who are worried about the justifiability of preventive harming generally have tended to overlook the significance of the collateral consequences of arrest.

Despite these legitimate concerns, it is crucial to appreciate the difficulties of categorically rejecting the permissibility of many of the collateral consequences I have described. Reflection about the nature of our relationships with one another in our capacity as private agents is helpful to illustrate the problems we would face if we tried to eliminate these practices from our everyday lives. Inasmuch as three-year recidivism rates are as high as 68 per cent, no one should be too quick to fault persons for treating a conviction as predictive of future criminality. As John Monahan observes: 'It has long been axiomatic in the field of risk assessment that past crime is the best predictor of future crime. All actuarial risk assessment instruments reflect this empirical truism' (2018: 87–88). In short, past crime is the least controversial risk factor used to predict future criminality. In addition, it is hard to see how anyone could realistically hope to *preclude* anyone from drawing these negative inferences.

Indeed, even when predicated on a mere arrest, what mechanism could possibly be put into place to prevent anyone from reaching these conclusions? More importantly for normative purposes, are we so certain that these negative inferences should *not* be drawn? Job seekers with a spotless record might have a valid complaint against a government policy requiring private employers to treat a criminal record as irrelevant (Jacobs 2015: 282). And should state or private elementary schools be criticised for refusing to hire a teacher who had been arrested for child abuse? Would we be paranoid to discharge a housekeeper we learned had been arrested for stealing from his former employer? In our interactions with other persons, we often disassociate ourselves from those we believe to have committed acts we judge to be dangerous or blameworthy. The rationale that underlies the foregoing examples of preventive harming is deeply embedded in our social life.

Can any of these problems be alleviated if they cannot be solved altogether? Arguably, the discriminatory practices of employers and housing authorities might be narrowly tailored to target only those persons who present a specific kind of risk. Child molesters might well be barred from leading the Boy Scouts, but why should tax evaders be disqualified from public housing? Tempting though this argument may be, criminological research tends to show that many individuals who engage in illegal conduct are generalists and opportunists. Today's burglar has a higher probability of emerging as tomorrow's drug dealer (Jacobs 2015: 284). If I am correct thus far, the case for allowing various kinds of harmful discrimination based on an arrest seems stronger than many legal theorists appear to acknowledge.

Of course, one might continue to challenge my supposition that any of the social and economic practices I have discussed are permissible. If they are objectionable, they cannot form the basis of an analogy to reduce opposition to RBS. It is tempting to condemn these practices because, in quite a few instances, the harm to be prevented would not have taken place; its occurrence is simply a matter of fallible prediction. Of course, *all* practices that depend on future contingencies are vulnerable to this same worry; persons who use deadly force in self-defence or in war cannot be certain that their victims would have made good on their threats. By the same token, a prospective employer cannot have much confidence that the applicant he rejects would have committed a future crime. Many legal philosophers (van Ginneken, Chapter 2 in this volume) lament the imprecision in risk-prevention instruments. Obviously, ordinary persons would prefer to have a more accurate indication than a mere arrest to identify those persons who pose elevated risks of future harm. Proceeding on the basis of such imperfect information clearly introduces a host of problems (Roberts forthcoming). However, in the absence of better data, it is rational to act on the best evidence available. Nothing approximating certainty can be required for *subjective permissibility* – that part of moral philosophy that governs how rational persons are allowed to behave on the basis of the evidence they possess. A prospective employer should not be made to need 'proof beyond a reasonable doubt' or to treat arrestees as 'innocent until proven guilty' of future misbehaviour. Surely nothing comparable to these demanding legal standards must be satisfied when persons engage in the social and economic practices I have discussed.

To underscore these claims, consider some of the other reasons that job applicants, for example, are turned away. An employer can refuse to hire someone because of a poor recommendation from his previous boss. He can decline to interview someone after an examination of her Facebook page reveals something unsavory. In fact, he can fail to select someone simply because she supports the wrong football team. If these reasons permit discrimination against job candidates, why shouldn't employers be allowed to reject an applicant because a policeman has determined there to be probable cause that she has committed a crime? This latter reason is at least as good as the former three. Moreover, it would be nearly impossible to monitor employers and preclude them from making decisions for any of these reasons. But should we even *aspire* to do so? Freedom of contract and association are core constitutional and political values with which we should be reluctant to tamper.

Finally, one might dispute these analogies by questioning whether RBS really implicates the means principle in the first place. In other words, is it obvious that RBS *must* be used to inflict actual harm on one person in order to prevent various risks of harm that might befall others? I confess I am unsure on this point. Perhaps predictions of risk *could* be invoked at sentencing only to *reduce* the harms that would otherwise be imposed on defendants. Some enthusiasts of RBS seem to understand the practice in this way and cite evidence about how a number of states actually use these instruments (Monahan 2018). If this understanding is accurate, quite a few (but not all) of the normative objections to RBS would dissipate. Expressed somewhat differently, the case for or against RBS depends on what we *do* with it. Might it be used exclusively to achieve positive effects? In this context, the most important such positive effect is to help reduce the epidemic of mass incarceration from which nearly everyone agrees that Western states, and the US in particular, presently suffer. Can RBS be used to achieve this important goal without harming anyone?

This way of conceptualising the practice *seems* disingenuous. If RBS is employed to *decrease* the severity of the sentence on an individual who does *not* pose a strong risk of causing future harms by re-offending, it seems inevitable that it must also be employed *not* to decrease the severity of the sentence on an individual who *does* pose such a risk. From the perspective of the latter defendants, their punishments are increased relative to those whose punishments are reduced by applications of RBS. But is this appearance correct? In other words, is it coherent to suppose that RBS can be used only to reduce some sentences without simultaneously increasing others? In order to resolve this matter, it becomes clear that an assessment of RBS cannot proceed without an answer to a fundamental and basic question that is too seldom raised. If we want to determine whether RBS can be used solely to *reduce* the harms that would *otherwise* be imposed, to what does the word *otherwise* refer? In other words, we need to know: *RBS as opposed to what?* This question casts debates about the notorious imprecision of RBS in an entirely new light. Persons convicted of crimes will be sentenced pursuant to *some* set of standards. If estimates of future risk are *not* a factor in sentencing, how *else* should sentences be calculated? In many (but not all) jurisdictions throughout the US, *sentencing guidelines* or *judicial hunches* provide the answer to this question. Unfortunately, these alternatives have contributed greatly to the epidemic of mass incarceration. If our choices are to use RBS, the existing sentencing guidelines, or to rely on judicial hunches, the case in favour of the former appears considerably more powerful than when RBS is evaluated in isolation. The judicious use of RBS may represent a significant improvement over the status quo, and we should not be too quick to resist progress even if we would like to do even better.

If I am correct that a host of familiar social and economic practices implicate the means principle with which I began, I believe we should conclude that this principle does not create an especially formidable obstacle to RBS; that is, measures that harm one person to reduce the risk of harm to another are not quite as worrisome on moral grounds as many moral and legal philosophers tend to suppose. I will not attempt to undertake the difficult and controversial task of showing what might be correct and might be incorrect about the means principle, or how it could be reformulated to provide a plausible barrier to morally problematic social practices. My goal is more modest. I conclude only that this principle should not simply be trotted out as though it constitutes a fatal objection to the use of RBS.

III. Does Risk-Based Sentencing Contradict Retributivism?

Once we recognise the extent of discriminatory harm inflicted on persons as a result of their interaction with the criminal justice system, we come to appreciate the broad range of state practices that implement the controversial 'means principle' with which I began. But many (although of course not all) of the collateral consequences I have described result from decisions by private parties. Suppose we agree that many such harms are imposed permissibly. Might the use of RBS be *more* objectionable than these other social and economic responses because it involves *state action* through *law* – and the *criminal* law in particular? In what follows, I try to defend only *one* of several reasons why a negative answer might be given. The most trenchant worry, I believe, is that RBS is incompatible with the philosophy of *retributivism* that governs the state practice of punishment. If it is true that RBS cannot co-exist with retributivism, we cannot accept the former without rejecting the latter. This is a price that I, for one, would be unwilling to pay – although others would accept it gladly. Fortunately, however, RBS and retributivism are able to cohere comfortably within our sentencing practices. In my judgement, the supposed incompatibility between retributivism and RBS derives from an excessively narrow and implausible conception of what retributivism *is*.

The alleged conflict between RBS and retributivism presupposes a particular conception of the nature of retributivism. According to this train of thought, retributivism categorically rejects the relevance of any consequentialist factor that recommends a punishment for offenders because it is expected to achieve a future good. Admittedly, some prominent retributivists have characterised their theory so that consequences *are* utterly immaterial to the quantum of punishment that should be imposed. Michael Moore, for example, is frequently quoted as providing the canonical definition. According to Moore, retributivism 'is the view that punishment is justified by the desert of the offender. The good that is achieved by punishing, on this view, has nothing to do with future states of affairs, such as the prevention of crime or the maintenance of social cohesion. Rather, the good that punishment achieves is that someone who deserves it gets it. Punishment of the guilty is thus for the retributivist an *intrinsic* good, not merely the *instrumental* good that it may be to the utilitarian' (Moore 1997: 87–88, emphasis in original). He famously concludes: '[T]he distinctive aspect of retributivism is that the moral desert of an offender is a *sufficient* reason to punish him or her' (Moore 1997: 88, emphasis in original). This particular account of the nature of retributivism has been attacked more often than it has been defended. In the absence of further clarification, I fear it is an easy target. Despite his stature as the most influential philosopher of criminal law in the US and the most well-known retributivist anywhere, Moore's work may have had the perverse effect of making retributivism *less* popular than it should be. Critics of this tradition borrow the above definition and suppose that all retributivists believe desert is all that is needed to justify punishment. By showing that desert cannot possibly perform this function, these critics conclude that retributivism itself must be rejected. If desert need not play the role Moore assigns to it in a retributive penal philosophy, these objections miss their target.

Critics are correct to respond that desert cannot possibly suffice to justify punishment. In response to their objections, Moore claims to have been misunderstood. He replies: '"Sufficiency" is like "qualitatively identical" in that we almost never use such words or phrases literally. When we say that one condition was sufficient for another … we mean that within some limited set of conditions that one by itself was sufficient. Other conditions outside that set … are invariably *necessary* even while we idiomatically describe a condition within that set as "sufficient" … It would be a crude caricature of the retributivist to make him monomaniacally focused on the achievement of retributive justice. The retributivist like anyone else can admit that there are other intrinsic goods … The retributivist can also admit that sometimes some of these [other] rights will trump the achieving of retributive justice' (Moore 1997: 172–73). These remarks are instructive. However, without further clarification, they obfuscate as much as they illuminate. We now know that Moore denies that desert *literally* suffices to justify punishment; it is sufficient only 'within some limited set of conditions'. However, we do *not* know exactly *what* these conditions encompass. Are they trivial and satisfied most *everywhere* in the real world? Even, say, in Syria and North Korea? Or are they stringent and never actually satisfied *anywhere*? More to the point, are they satisfied throughout developed countries such as the US and the UK in the twenty-first century?

A better definition is needed. On my view, retributivism is not the name of a particular theory, but rather the name of a *kind* or *type* of theory. It is no easier to specify what all theories of this type share in common than, for example, to identify the defining characteristics of liberalism or conservativism. Perhaps all we can say with confidence is that all such theories award a prominent and indispensable place to desert in their justifications of punishment (Bedau 1978). Retributivists can and do disagree about any number of questions about desert. Most notably, they can disagree about the exact role it plays in the justification of punishment

(Husak 2016). As might be anticipated, desert plays a more central role in some theories than in others. Thus, I hold the relatively novel position that whether a theory qualifies as retributive turns out to be a matter of degree; some theories are *more* retributive than others. What makes one theory more retributive than another is not that it recommends more severe punishments across the board, but that it affords a more central role to desert.

RBS proves easier to reconcile with this more nuanced understanding of retributivism. Perhaps the simplest and most familiar way to make consequentialist ends compatible with retributivism is to adopt what has long been called *limiting retributivism* (Morris 1974). Although this label has somewhat different meanings for those who use it, I construe it to emerge from the inevitable imprecision that infects judgements of cardinal proportionality. According to my preferred version of the principle of proportionality, *the severity of a punishment should,* ceteris paribus, *be a function of the seriousness of a crime.* However, try as we might, no theorist has succeeded in specifying the exact quantum of punishment that is deserved by a person who commits a given crime. It is hard even to agree upon the *metric* of punishment severity (Husak 2019). Because of this intractable uncertainty, some retributivists urge that their theory should be construed only to rule out a range of punishments that are *undeserved.* A punishment can be undeserved because it is too lenient or too severe in light of the seriousness of the offence for which it is imposed. Within these upper and lower boundaries, limiting retributivists allows other factors – such as crime prevention – to operate. Of course, RBS is designed to do just that. Thus, room is made for RBS within a penal philosophy of retributivism, as long as the latter is construed to enact boundaries rather than to identify a precise quantum of punishment that is deserved.

Limiting retributivism is plausible. But even though the difficulties in specifying cardinal proportionality are very real, I do not think limiting retributivism succeeds in avoiding them. The very same problems in identifying a quantum of deserved punishment resurface when we recommend the *range* of punishment that is deserved. For example, we will continue to disagree about whether a six-month sentence for first-time rapists is inside or outside that range. Thus, the case for limiting retributivism is somewhat problematic. Fortunately, however, we need not accept limiting retributivism in order to create room for RBS. To my mind, the supposed imprecision and vagueness of cardinal judgements of desert is not the best and certainly not the only ground on which to remove obstacles to RBS.

A better approach is as follows: even if we *could* be precise about the exact punishment a defendant deserves for committing a given offence, retributivism would not require that we actually inflict it (Husak 2011a). No one should think desert need be the *only* relevant factor in deciding what sentence the state should impose. A sensible formulation of the principle of proportionality – including my preferred version above – includes a *ceteris paribus* clause. This clause does important work in a theory of sentencing. Quite a few of the morally relevant considerations that should affect the punishment that ought to be imposed are almost certainly *extrinsic* to desert and proportionality. Suppose the punishment an offender deserves would be hugely expensive to inflict. For example, imagine the perpetrator has fled to some remote locale. It would be ludicrous to hold that anyone (retributivists or otherwise) must be indifferent to this fact. The obvious resistance among retributivists to a punishment that would strain the treasury necessitates a resort to principles outside of their theory. Moreover, even if retributivists (Ryberg, Chapter 4 in this volume) *could* specify a uniquely correct *degree* of punishment, they still would have little to say about the *mode* or *type* this punishment should take. Consequentialist considerations should govern here (Husak 2018a). Such considerations demonstrate that it is no objection to retributivism that it needs to be supplemented by non-desert considerations.

Variables that cannot be derived from desert have always been invoked to justify sentences of unequal severity when offenders commit the same offence with the identical level of culpability. Different criminal histories provide the most familiar reason to impose different punishments on such persons. Few theorists contest the intuition that first-time and repeat offenders should be punished with unequal severity, although the nearly-universal policy that reflects this intuition has proved difficult to justify (Roberts and von Hirsch 2010). I doubt that this policy can be explained in terms of desert at all, but may be justifiable nonetheless. In any event, this probable exception to proportionality is not a minor aberration. In addition to the familiar problems of identifying the cardinal desert of a typical shoplifter or burglar, sentencing authorities must also wrestle with the fact that nearly all of the few concerted efforts to identify the punishment that is deserved apply to first-time offenders who commit a single crime. But many and perhaps most actual offenders commit multiple offences (Tonry 2018). In any event, factors that are even more clearly immaterial to desert than criminal history or multiple offences are routinely invoked to justify disparate sentences. Suppose a defendant is terminally ill, for example, or old and infirm. Or suppose an offender has been seriously injured and permanently incapacitated in the very crime he perpetrated. Or suppose he has evaded capture for decades and has shown himself to be able to live respectably in the interim. It is overly formalistic to insist that these factors *must* be immaterial to sentencing because they are virtually impossible to square with desert.

To my mind, we can recognise these exceptions without abandoning retributivism as I have conceptualised it. Instead, retributivists should preserve the role of desert while weakening its strength. The weight of a factor, as I understand it, is a function of how easily it is outweighed when it competes with other factors (Lord and Maguire 2016). As I hope the above discussion demonstrates, no one should assume that our judgements of desert are especially weighty in our all-things-considered moral judgements of how people should be treated. We can preserve proportionality, but allow exceptions when we have a good rationale for them. My position, then, is to retain desert while recognising deviations from it. Proportionality continues to be significant because it remains the default position in the absence of a special ground to depart from it. But if proportionality can be outweighed without too much difficulty, a space for RBS is opened. If we have good reason to inflict different amounts of punishment on two offenders who have committed equally serious crimes, we should not be worried that our decision does not preserve proportionality. A rationale in favour of this disparity might be sufficient to outweigh the considerations of desert inherent in proportionality. My position is sometimes derided as *mixed*, but I prefer to soften resistance to it by characterising it as *pluralistic*. For some reason, pluralistic theories that have received a warm reception elsewhere in moral and political philosophy tend to be viewed with undue suspicion when applied by penal theorists. Admittedly, the results produced by pluralists are messy; sentencing, like morality more generally, is not governed by an algorithm. However, after several decades, no one has begun to show how a position that is *not* messy can possibly succeed in producing sensible results. Any attempt to formulate an algorithm or set of easily applied principles has been subjected to devastating criticisms. In any event, regardless of how my position should be labelled, I hold that sentencing theorists can appeal to consequentialist factors without abandoning retributivism.

The recent history of sentencing drug offenders illustrates the strategy I have in mind. Since the introduction of drug courts, some defendants have been diverted to treatment programmes, while others have not – despite committing the same offence. At one point, I questioned how this disparity could possibly be justifiable in light of the fact that the treatment programme mandated by a drug court and the punishment imposed by a traditional court are bound to differ radically in terms of their severity. Drug court enthusiasts have been sensitive to this difficulty and have felt enormous pressure to ensure that treatment programmes are onerous so that they do not deviate from proportionality (Husak 2011b). But a different response to this disparity is not to ratchet up the severity of treatment regimes, but to acknowledge the relative weakness of the principle of proportionality. A reasonable belief that different offenders respond to different sanctions may be all that is needed to warrant a deviation. For this reason, it would be misguided, for example, to impose the same quantum of punishment on perpetrators whose violence is or is not fuelled by alcohol. If incarceration should be reserved for those who cannot be released safely, the difference in their circumstances (which need not be construed as a difference in their desert) may be all that is needed to justify their differential sentence. In light of such factors, we should not be overly rigid in ensuring that equally severe punishments are inflicted. Different strategies about how to prevent repetition of the offence may be all that is needed to outweigh the desert considerations inherent in proportionality.

Although desert is indispensable in any theory of punishment that merits the label of *retributivism*, the supposition that desert should be the sole or even the most important factor in sentencing is further undermined by considering the strength played by desert in other, non-legal human institutions and relations. In everyday affairs, we all recognise many instances in which we have powerful all-things-considered reasons not to treat others as they deserve. Practices that withhold blame from persons who are blameworthy (or responsible) may prove to be more effective in achieving valuable ends – such as maintaining friendships or rehabilitating deviants. Again, I use drug policy as an illustration of what I have in mind. If our primary objective is to help drug addicts to overcome their destructive behaviours, it is a contingent (and probably erroneous) supposition that blaming them is the most effective strategy. However, it does not follow that addicts are *not* (often) blameworthy, either because they foresaw the consequences of their drug experimentation before they became addicted or because they failed to seek treatment at moments when they were lucid and their craving had subsided. What *does* follow is that there may be decisive all-things-considered reasons not to blame the blameworthy (Pickard 2017). More generally, someone who elects to ignore an affront from his friend in order to preserve their valuable relationship would find it odd to be criticised on the ground that she had failed to treat her friend as he deserved.

If desert plays so small a role elsewhere in human affairs, the unanswered question is *why do so many penal theorists apparently believe it should play a dominant role in punishment*? What could be the rationale for singling out a given institution and requiring that desert alone, to the exclusion of any other normative factor, should dictate the outcome? And even if desert *should* be the sole factor in sentencing, why not *whole-life* desert? What is the rationale for carving out a particular aspect of a life – a person's criminal activity on a given occasion – and attaching such immense importance to desert here? I am unaware of a persuasive answer to these fundamental questions. In the law of sentencing, as elsewhere in human affairs, desert is only *one* consideration that is relevant to how we ought to behave all-things-considered.

Still, it is hard to dislodge the intuition that there is a special difficulty in using predictions of future risk in criminal justice. How might this intuition be weakened? In a strategy that replicates that used earlier in this chapter, I point out that the inclusion of predictive factors has long been a staple of the substantive penal law. Since I have discussed elsewhere how the substantive criminal law is appropriately used to prevent future risks (Husak 2011 and 2013; but see Ryberg, Chapter 4 in this volume), I only mention *one* familiar means by which this objective is achieved. Crimes of ulterior intent are presumably designed to reduce the risk of future harm (Horder 1996). For example, the crime of illicit drug possession with intent to distribute is a different and more serious offence than mere possession. Why is this so? *One* answer is that the intent to distribute increases the risk of subsequent distribution. If an act accompanied by an intent to do an additional wrong is more serious because its commission increases the probability that the subsequent wrong will occur (although see Tadros 2016), offences of ulterior intent are more wrongful than offences without ulterior intent. If I am correct, the criminal law has been used to minimise the likelihood of future risks for as long as it has included crimes of ulterior intent. The fact that a given practice (viz RBS) is so controversial while offences within the substantive criminal law (eg, offences of ulterior intent) have flown beneath the radar screen is an indication of the confusion many theorists suffer about the legitimacy of risk prevention in penal justice. As now should be clear, I believe that the general hostility among legal theorists towards risk prevention generally and to RBS in particular tends to be overblown.

IV. Conclusion: *Should* Risk-Based Sentencing Be Used?

I conclude that the two primary objections to the use of RBS can be surmounted. The Kantian means principle that is implicated by RBS is less sacrosanct than we are likely to suppose. Moreover, RBS can be shown to be compatible with a retributive theory of sentencing. It does not follow, of course, that RBS *should* be employed. Removing obstacles to a practice is not tantamount to endorsing it. Whether RBS should be used depends on whether it helps to accomplish good ends – ends that are independently worthwhile. In order to determine whether RBS is capable of achieving good ends, we need criteria to identify which ends are good. Without much argument, I mention only *one* objective shared by a great many legal philosophers and commentators from all points along the political spectrum: a reduction in mass incarceration (Garland 2018). Since both the extent of incarceration and the problems associated with it have been extensively documented elsewhere (Pfaff 2016), I leave them aside here. But we should be receptive to any means at our disposal with the potential to make a dent in our unacceptable rate of incarceration. If RBS can help to do so – as I believe it can – legal philosophers should be enthusiastic about it (Monahan 2018).

However, I anticipate that my conclusion will still encounter stiff resistance. I am aware that RBS has a bad reputation among many academics, and opposition to its implementation derives not only from the two sources I have addressed above. A recurrent worry is that some of the factors that might be used to predict risk include *race*. Even though a given risk analysis rarely if ever includes race among its explicit factors, many theorists warn that some of the factors that *are* included are mere *proxies* for race (Angwin et al 2016). In our heightened sensitivity to racial injustice, any practice that threatens to exacerbate racial inequality is disqualified from serious discussion, whatever its other merits might be. I take no position on whether the factors used in risk analysis *are* proxies for race or whether RBS should be abandoned even if these factors *are* such proxies. Again, whether RBS increases or decreases racial discrimination depends on the alternative with which it is contrasted. Perhaps rival sentencing schemes are worse on this score; the status quo, after all, is what led to these racial disparities in the first place. But if these fears are trenchant and a given form of RBS produces an unacceptable degree of racial disparity, we should be careful not to throw out the baby with the bath water. In my judgement, scrapping RBS altogether because it can produce racial injustice is too hasty (Richardson 2017). It is akin to abandoning stop, question and frisk because it is infected by implicit bias and used disproportionately against persons of colour (Husak 2018b). The better solution would be to explicitly bar the use of race (or any proxy for race) as a risk factor (Frase 2014). This simple step would allow us to gain the advantages of RBS in reducing rates of incarceration without simultaneously perpetuating racial injustice.

References

Angwin, J et al (2016) 'Machine Bias: There's Software Used across the Country to Predict Future Criminals, and it's Biased against Blacks' *ProPublica*, 23 May.

Bedau, H (1978) 'Retribution and the Theory of Punishment' 75 *Journal of Philosophy* 601.

Chin, GJ (2018) 'Collateral Consequences of Criminal Conviction' in E Luna (ed), *Academy for Justice: A Report on Scholarship and Criminal Justice Reform.*

Frase, RS (2014) 'Recurring Policy Issues of Guidelines (and Non-guidelines) Sentencing: Risk Assessments, Criminal History Enhancements, and the Enforcement of Release Conditions' 26 *Federal Sentencing Reporter* 145.

Garland, D (2018) 'Theoretical Advances and Problems in the Sociology of Punishment' 20 *Punishment & Society* 8.

Hanser, M (2008) 'The Metaphysics of Harm' LXXVII *Philosophy and Phenomenological Research* 421.

Horder, J (1996) 'Crimes of Ulterior Intent' in AP Simester and ATH Smith (eds), *Harm and Culpability* (Oxford, Oxford University Press).

Hoskins, Z (2018) *Beyond Punishment* (Oxford, Oxford University Press).

Husak, D (1992) 'Why Punish the Deserving?' 26 *Nous* 447.

——. (2011a) 'Lifting the Cloak: Preventive Detention as Punishment' 48 *San Diego Law Review* 1173.

——. (2011b) 'Retributivism, Proportionality, and the Challenge of the Drug Court Movement' in M Tonry (ed), *Retributivism Has a Past: Has It a Future?* (Oxford, Oxford University Press,).

——. (2013) 'Preventive Detention as Punishment? Some Possible Reservations' in A Ashworth, L Zedner, and P Tomlin (eds), *Prevention and the Limits of the Criminal Law* (Oxford, Oxford University Press).

——. (2016) 'What Do Criminals Deserve?' in K Ferzan and S Morse (eds), *Legal, Moral, and Metaphysical Truths: The Philosophy of Michael S Moore* (New York, Oxford University Press).

——. (2018a) 'Kinds of Punishment' in H Hurd (ed), *The Work of Larry Alexander* (New York, Oxford University Press).

——. (2018b) 'Policing and Racial Discrimination: Throwing out the Baby with the Bath Water' in M Gardner and M Webber et al (eds), *The Ethics of Policing and Imprisonment* (London, Palgrave Macmillan).

——. (2019) 'The Metric of Punishment Severity: A Puzzle about the Principle of Proportionality'. in M Tonry (ed), *Proportionality, Punishment, and Justice – Making the Punishment Fit the Crime* (Oxford, Oxford University Press).

Jacobs, J (2015) *The Eternal Criminal Record* (Cambridge, MA, Harvard University Press).

Logan, W (2013) 'Informal Collateral Consequences' 88 *Washington Law Review* 1103.

Lord, E and Maguire, B (eds) (2016) *Weighing Reasons* (Oxford, Oxford University Press).

Monahan, J (2018) 'Risk Assessment in Sentencing' in E Luna (ed), *Academy for Justice: A Report on Scholarship and Criminal Justice Reform.*

Moore, MS (1997) *Placing Blame* (Oxford, Clarendon Press).

Morris, N (1974) *The Future of Imprisonment* (Chicago, University of Chicago Press).

Pfaff, J (2016) *Locked in: The True Causes of Mass Incarceration – and How to Achieve Real Reform* (New York, Basic Books).

Pickard, H (2017) 'Responsibility without Blame for Addiction' 10 *Neuroethics* 169.

Richardson, L (2017) 'Implicit Racial Bias and Racial Anxiety: Implications for Stops and Frisks' 15 *Ohio State Journal of Criminal Law* 73.

Roberts, A (forthcoming) 'Arrests as Guilt' *Alabama Law Review.*

Roberts, JV and von Hirsch, A (eds) (2010) *Previous Convictions at Sentencing* (Oxford, Hart Publishing).

Strawson, P (1962) 'Freedom and Resentment' 48 *Proceedings of the British Academy* 1.

Tadros, V (2016) *Wrongs and Crimes* (Oxford, Oxford University Press).

Temkin, L (2016) 'Equality as Comparative Fairness' 34 *Journal of Applied Philosophy* 43.

Tonry, M (2018) 'Punishment and Human Dignity: Sentencing Principles for Twenty-First-Century America' 47 *Crime and Justice* 119.

4

Risk and Retribution

On the Possibility of Reconciling Considerations of Dangerousness and Desert

JESPER RYBERG

I. Introduction

The assessment of the risk of future criminal behaviour influences decisions on how the criminal justice system punitively reacts to the misdeeds of criminal offenders in various ways. In recent decades, many countries have developed risk assessment methods with a corresponding increasing use of such assessments in sentencing (see van Ginneken, Chapter 2 in this volume). However, even though this development has been interpreted as reflecting reasonable aims, such as the prevention of recidivism and a reduction in prison populations, the use of risk assessment in sentencing is also highly controversial. Risk-informed sentencing has given rise to two types of considerations.

First, it has been asked whether the prediction of future criminal activity can be achieved with any reasonable degree of accuracy. When it comes to the prediction of future crimes in individual offenders, some critics have gone so far as to dismiss such forecasts as 'virtually meaningless' (Hart et al 2007: 263). Other theorists have expressed more confidence in the use of risk assessments (see, eg, Faigman et al 2014; Monahan and Skeem 2014, 2016). Second, some have questioned whether risk of re-offending should play any role in sentencing. This question is logically prior to the first in the sense that if the second is answered in the negative, then it does not matter whether risk assessments are currently invalid or whether it will in the future be possible to develop more accurate methods.[1] Such assessments will simply be irrelevant when seen from the perspective of a proper moral theory

[1] Needless to say, risk assessments could still be relevant to other questions than those concerning sentencing. But it is the use of risk assessments in relation to sentencing that is considered in this chapter.

of sentencing. Conversely, if it is answered in the affirmative, then there is reason to engage with all the technicalities and more detailed normative issues associated with risk assessments. This chapter is devoted exclusively to considerations of the second question.

As a point of departure, it should be underlined that the question as to whether risk assessments should have any role to play in sentencing must be answered in the affirmative. At least it can be convincingly argued so, I believe. The conclusion follows from the premises that: first, if consequences should play a role in sentencing, then the way in which sentencing affects future criminal behaviour should be taken into account; second, if the way in which sentencing affects future criminal behaviour should be taken into account, then risk assessments should have a role to play; and, third: that any plausible theory of sentencing implies that consequences should play a role.

The first two premises are uncontroversial. If one subscribes to the view that consequences matter morally, then it is implausible to contend that the effects which a sentence will have upon the lives and property of future victims fall outside the scope of the consequences that have moral significance. Surely the harm caused to individuals constitutes a standard instance of what matters from a moral perspective. Furthermore, it is obvious that if future harms should be taken into account, then one should consider risk. The third premise may seem more controversial.[2] However, it is easy to see that this should not be the case. Needless to say, consequences play a role if one follows a consequentialist approach to sentencing. The same is the case if one adopts some sort of mixed theory. If one subscribes either to a negative retributivist point of view, which sets upper proportionality constraints on proper sentencing, or a limiting retributivist theory, according to which there exists a range of deserved punishments for a certain crime, then consequences will be regarded as crucial for the determination of the proper sentence within those constraints. But what then if one subscribes to a full-blown retributivist theory of sentencing? What if one holds, as does Moore, that the 'desert of an offender is a sufficient reason to punish him' (Moore 1997: 88)? Does it then follow, as Moore contends, that any reference to 'consequences is simply beside the point' (1997: 111)?

The answer is in the negative. Even if desert constitutes a sufficient justification and if the precise proportionate sentencing for a particular crime has been determined, this does not answer the question as to what *type* of punishment should be inflicted on the offender. As long as the severity of the sentence fully reflects the gravity of the crime, there will still be room for allowing consequentialist considerations in the question as to which type of punishment one should impose. In many cases, it will be possible to impose either one or another type while still

[2] Several theorists have argued that risk assessments do not play a role in retributivist theories of punishment. For instance, Monahan and Skeem hold that: 'Risk assessment is relevant to utilitarian (crime control), but not retributive (just deserts), sentencing concerns' (2016: 508).

preserving the 'penal bite' of the punishment, that is, without compromising proportionality.[3] To hold that one should in such cases not take into consideration the consequences that the different types of substitutable sentences will have would commit one to the view that *everything else being equal*, it does not matter whether a sentence will prevent harm. However, this is a highly implausible view. If the *ceteris partibus* clause is satisfied, that is, if the offender receives a precisely proportionate punishment, then it would be morally absurd to hold that it does not matter at all morally whether future harms of individuals could be prevented by imposing one form of punishment rather than another.[4] Therefore, regardless of whether one subscribes to a consequentialist theory of sentencing, a mixed theory or a full-blown retributivist theory, one will have to accept that consequences matter morally and, consequently, that risk assessments should have *some* role to play in sentencing (see also Husak, Chapter 3 in this volume).

However, even if this conclusion is correct – that is, even if, contrary to what has often been asserted, the assessment of the risk of future crimes should play a role in all theories of sentencing – this does not demonstrate that the problem that has fuelled the discussion of how the criminal justice system should deal with dangerous offenders has been properly resolved. It might still be maintained that the basic tension that constitutes the crux of the discussion – namely, that between, on the one hand, the possibility of appropriately accounting for dangerousness in sentencing decisions and, on the other, the observance of retributivist proportionality constraints – remains intact, even if risk assessment, as argued above, plays some role within all sentencing theories. Two reasons could be held in favour of this contention. First, if one subscribes to a mixed theory or a full-blown retributivist theory and if it is the case, say, that proportionality dictates that an offender should receive no more than one year in prison for a particular crime, and, furthermore, if it is the case that the offender after a year behind bars is considered to be highly dangerous, then one will still have to release the offender after he or she has served his time. Second, there may be cases, even if these are rare, where a person is highly dangerous (and fully competent), but has not (yet) committed any crime (eg, a potential terrorist). Both types of case indicate that dangerousness constitutes a challenge even if it is true that risk assessments should, according to all theoretical penal positions, play a role in sentencing decisions. How should this challenge be addressed? For the retributively minded theorist, there are two ways to proceed.

The first possibility is to maintain that dangerousness in these cases is simply not something that the criminal justice system should deal with. If justice is the

[3] For a theory of the substitutability of punishments of the same degree of severity, see von Hirsch et al (1989). See also Morris and Miller (1985); and Husak (2018).

[4] Note also that the view that the retributivist should *ceteris paribus* take consequences into account, that is, that consequences should count as long as justice has been observed, accords with the modern standard idea of deontology as an ethical theory characterised by the existence of constraints and *pro tanto* reasons to promote the good, see, eg, Kagan (1998).

main concern, then there will of course be cases in which one will have to accept that the criminal justice system should not react, even if not doing so will have dreadful consequences. The other possibility is to reconsider whether there are ways in which dangerousness can somehow be incorporated into a retributivist framework to an extent that reaches beyond the more modest room that, as argued above, is otherwise left for risk assessments. But how could this be done? To contend that one subscribes to a threshold position, according to which proportionality constraints can be overruled if enough is at stake, is not sufficient. If the threshold is set at a low level, then the retributivists will become vulnerable to precisely the same counter-arguments which traditionally (and repeatedly) have been directed against the consequentialist approach to sentencing (such as the 'punishment of the innocent' objection). If, alternatively, the threshold is set at a much higher level – such as is the case if one subscribes to the more traditional general deontological view that constraints can be overridden only in catastrophic cases where an evil of 'enormous magnitude' can be prevented – then there will be no room for genuinely dealing with the predictable crimes of dangerous individuals. Thus, a threshold retributivist approach, even if this is more plausible than absolutist accounts, is insufficient to meet the challenge of dangerousness.[5] Another possibility could be to account for dangerousness in the type of punishment that is imposed on offenders. For instance, Walen (2011) has suggested that a punishment can consist in the loss of the benefit of the presumption that a person is law-abiding and that this loss opens up the possibility of preventively detaining dangerous offenders. Yet another possibility has been to defend the idea of pre-punishment as a way of dealing with dangerousness within a retributivist framework (see, eg, New 1992, 1995; Statman 1997). I will not comment further on these proposals.[6] There is, however, a final possibility, namely, to hold that dangerousness can in itself, under certain conditions, be something that warrants deserved punitive reactions. The purpose in the following is to more thoroughly examine this possibility.

More precisely, the chapter proceeds as follows. In section II, I briefly outline the content of theories which hold that dangerousness can warrant desert claims. It will be shown how this approach has the potential for dealing more adequately with the above-mentioned challenges that dangerousness raises for standard accounts of retributivism. However, sections III–VII identify a number of challenges to the idea that dangerousness can give rise to deserved punitive reactions. It is argued, first, that contrary to that which adherents to the two models seem to believe (namely, that they will only have consequences in a few cases involving individuals who constitute a present and very high risk), the more accurate picture

[5] For a discussion of how some types of crime constitute a challenge to the threshold retributivist, see Ryberg (2010), in which retributivism in relation to mass atrocities is discussed.

[6] For a critical discussion of some of the attempts at reconciling dangerousness and desert, see Lippke (2008).

is that the models end up having consequences for many. In short, large groups of citizens will face deserved punishment. Second, it is suggested that though there are reasons to be cautious in terms of drawing conclusions, several of the challenges question the plausibility of the models. Finally, section VIII summarises and concludes. Therefore, the overall upshot will be that the discussion points in the direction of the traditionally acknowledged theoretical divide; namely, that one will either have to adhere to some sort of retributivist position, but bite the bullet and admit that retributivism has only limited resources for dealing with dangerousness, or one will have to move in a more traditional consequentialist direction.

II. Deserved Punishment for Dangerousness

An analysis of the concept of desert opens up various questions. In general terms, desert claims can be said to ascribe desert to someone or something on the ground of characteristics possessed or actions taken by the person or thing. Therefore, a more precise discussion must address the questions as to what can figure as the deserving part, on what grounds, and what one can possibly deserve (see, eg, Kleinig 1973; Ryberg 2004). Although there is disagreement regarding the answers to these questions, the overall structure of desert claims is widely accepted, namely, that someone A deserves something B on the ground of C. Insofar as one wishes to defend the suggestion that dangerousness can warrant desert claims, one will thus have to establish that dangerousness somehow manifests itself in a set of characteristics that can properly fit into the base of desert. Merely pointing to something that is likely to take place in the future is not in itself sufficient to establish a desert base that can justify punishment. But how can the risk of future harms be incorporated into a currently existing base of desert?

The answer is that this can be done in different ways. One possibility is to adopt the position that the existence of risk factors should figure in the desert base – a view defended by Husak. Husak does not commit himself to any particular view on the contents of these characteristics (he simply refers to such traits as x, y and z), but his point is that there is nothing that prevents the criminalisation of the possession of these traits or the possibility that a person can deserve a punishment in virtue of possessing such traits. As Husak is of course fully aware, the idea of deserving a punishment merely by virtue of the possession of characteristics that predict future wrongdoing may seem to violate what is standardly referred to as the 'act-requirement' of the criminal law. However, as he has argued in several writings, this requirement should be rejected in favour of a control requirement, namely, that '[n]o one should be punished for what is beyond their control' (Husak 2011: 1195). Thus, characteristics that predict future wrongdoing but that are under the individual's control should figure in the desert base.

Another possibility is to hold that an individual deserves punishment not only for possessing risk characteristics, but also on the ground of his way of dealing with such characteristics. More precisely, it could be held that a person deserves punishment for not taking steps to lower this risk. A view along these lines has been proposed by Morse, who has suggested that if a person is aware of an extremely high risk that he or she will cause harm, then she has 'a moral duty to avoid unjustifiable harmdoing by taking preventive action' and, furthermore, that '[o]mitting to take appropriate action under the circumstances is a culpable moral failure that imperils others and fairly justifies criminalization and punishment' (1996: 152). A slightly different approach could be to contend that one is deserving of punishment insofar as one has contributed to the development or existence of characteristics that predict future crimes. However, to specify precisely which initiatives have contributed to making someone dangerous raises many problems.[7] Therefore, in the following, I will not consider this approach any further.

Thus, while the base of desert on the first approach consists in the mere possession of risk characteristics, the second bases punitive desert on the failure to react to such characteristics. Let us, for reasons of ease in exposition, refer to these two models respectively as the 'possession model' and the 'omission model'. It is clear that both models succeed in overcoming the repeatedly made claim that one must distinguish sharply between punishment which is for past crimes and dangerousness which concerns future crimes. By incorporating considerations of dangerousness into the desert base in either way, it is clear that dangerous offenders will be punishable on purely retributive grounds. Such offenders would be punishable for the crime of risk. Furthermore, it is clear that both models deal with the challenges that dangerousness prompts for retributivism. If an offender at the end of a prison term is considered dangerous, then the models provide a rationale for further incarceration. And if an individual is highly dangerous, but has not engaged in criminal activity, then both models also provide sufficient reasons to justify a punitive response. Thus, there is a good starting point for considering more thoroughly whether the two models can stand further scrutiny. This is what we will do in the ensuing sections.

III. The Specification Challenge

The first question that confronts theories that seek to retributively account for the existence of risk factors is what kind of predictors of future crime should be regarded as relevant for the imposition of punishment. From a consequentialist point of view, there are per se no restrictions on which risk factors should figure in the determination of what constitutes a proper punishment. All characteristics that can contribute to providing a valid assessment of the risk of future crimes

[7] Moreover, this theory would be vulnerable to all the same challenges that will be presented against the other theories in this chapter.

and, hence, of the crimes that may be preventable through some sort of intervention must be regarded as relevant. But what happens if the question is considered from a retributivist perspective? Will there be restrictions on which risk factors the possession model can plausibly incorporate into the desert base or on which factors merit just deserts if they are not appropriately addressed according to the omission model? This question is important, both because an answer is necessary in order for the models to provide genuine action guidance in penal practice, but also because it is crucial for the moral assessment of full-fledged versions of the two models.

Seen from the perspective of the omission model, it is clear that there is an overall restriction on which predictors of future crime should be regarded as relevant. Only risk factors which an individual could have addressed should be included in the determination of what the person deserves from his or her inaction. In the same way, there are also restrictions on what should count as the relevant risk factors from a possession account. The ascription of desert only seems to make sense in relation to factors over which a person has some control. As indicated above, in his exposition of the possession model, Husak explicitly underlines control as a necessary condition for desert. Thus, notwithstanding their predictive power, he holds that characteristics such as gender, race and age cannot be among the elements that warrant deserved punishment. This view has intuitive appeal. However, on closer scrutiny, it is less obvious how this conclusion is reached. The crucial question is what it means to possess control over a certain risk factor.

Suppose, as a first possibility, that someone has control of characteristics x, y and z if he or she can prevent these characteristics manifesting themselves in actual behaviour. On this account, what matters is the extent to which a person is able to influence the degree to which a certain trait constitutes a risk. For instance, if a person has a certain strong paedophilic preference and if it is possible for this person to somehow eliminate this preference, reduce its strength or restrain its influence in other ways, then the preference should be regarded as controllable. However, as this indicates, there are several ways in which the manifestations of a certain trait can be prevented. The decision to take measures to eliminate the trait is only one possibility. Another would be to place oneself under circumstances where the trait cannot result in behaviour. For instance, the paedophile can take the requisite precautions not to place himself or herself in a particular circumstance with children. But if this is what it takes to be in control, then there seem to be no limits as to which risk factors could be incorporated into the desert base. If gender, age and race constitute reliable predictors of future crime, then a person who, as a result of these variables, would be a high-risk individual could influence the risk in various ways, for instance, by staying inside, moving to a deserted area or taking other such initiatives to place himself or herself under circumstances that make it impossible for these risk factors to result in wrongful behaviour. In other words, on this account of control, it seems to follow – contrary to what Husak suggests – that people could be punished for being a certain age, gender or race. But is this unacceptable or is it simply something that one will have to accept if one subscribes to the possession model or the omission model?[8]

I cannot engage here in a comprehensive discussion of this question, but it seems to me that the retributivists who are willing to accept that such risk factors (if reliable) should be incorporated into the desert base will have to answer difficult questions. Briefly put, if a characteristic such as race constitutes a risk factor, and if this is the result of various sorts of discrimination built into societal structures, can it then possibly be morally acceptable to talk of just deserts on the ground of such a risk factor? In more general terms, if it follows from the concept of control that all risk factors could be incorporated into the base of desert, then one is faced with a version of the traditional 'justice in an unjust society' question concerning the preconditions for a system of just deserts. It seems fair to say that there is no consensus on how this question should be answered within a retributivist framework. But it seems reasonable to believe that a broad interpretation of the control requirement cannot in itself (ie, in the absence of proper answers to other moral challenges) provide a complete specification of which characteristics warrant deserved punishments. However, perhaps one need not accept the broad interpretation.

Another possibility would be to contend that the control condition must be interpreted much more narrowly. More precisely, it could be held that what matters is not whether a person has control over the manifestations of a certain trait, but rather whether one possesses direct control over the trait itself. Roughly, it could be said that a person possesses control over a certain trait if it lies within this person's power to eliminate the trait. Thus, on this account, the possibility of circumventing the influence of a risk factor by placing oneself in particular circumstances does not count as an exercise of control in the relevant sense if the trait itself is unaffected. Something along these lines is probably what Husak has in mind when he underlines that age, gender and race cannot satisfy the control condition. Some commentators have questioned whether there are any risk factors which can properly be said to lie within a person's control in this narrower sense.[9] However, in my view, there is another problem facing this interpretation, namely, whether it actually suffices to restrict the number of risk factors for which one can deserve punishment. In short, it is always possible to eliminate the existence of a certain trait if it is possible to eliminate the individual. But this means that a person ultimately always has control over characteristics such as age, gender and race in the simple sense that the person can always decide to commit suicide. Now, I assume that many will feel that this cannot possibly be part of what it means to be in control of a certain trait. But the interesting question then is how

[8] Of course, on the omission model, it would be the person's culpable failure to respond to these risk traits that make the him or her deserving of punishment.

[9] For a discussion of the significance of control, see, eg, Lippke (2008).

this implication can be blocked. There are two ways to proceed. Either one will have to present a definition of control which implies that this particular way of eliminating a trait does not suffice to regard the trait as controllable. Whether such a definition can be given is an open question. Alternatively, one can stick to a definition of control according to which the possibility of eliminating oneself implies that one possesses control, while at the same time holding that this way of being in control is too demanding; that is, on this account, other moral considerations overrule the control condition. But this means that one will have to engage in considerations of why and when a certain trait, even if strictly speaking it is controllable, nevertheless does not warrant a deserved punishment. What such considerations of the significance of demandingness more generally imply for the question as to which traits are punishable is hard to say (but it does not seem unlikely that it will often be quite demanding to change risk factors; see also Clearwater (2017)).

What the previous considerations establish is obviously not that there are reasons to reject the possession model or the omission model. Rather, the point has been to show that the questions of what it means to be in possession of controllable risk traits or to fail to take appropriate action to prevent the risk of future wrongdoing provoke a number of theoretical challenges. The moral evaluation and the possibility of operationalising the models into genuine action guidance hinge on whether these questions can be properly answered.

IV. The Proportionality Challenge

The idea of accounting for the risk of future wrongdoing within a retributivist framework naturally raises the question as to how the particular crimes that an offender commits by being dangerous – that is, either by possessing certain risk traits or by not taking appropriate action to counter the risk – fit into a retributivist scheme of punishment. More precisely, one of the questions that has been discussed is whether there will be a conflict between, on the one hand, the severity of the punishment that is proportionate to the crime of possessing risk traits or of not reacting to them and, on the other, the dangerousness of the person who is being punished. For instance, it could be the case that the time of incarceration which is necessary in order to fully account for the dangerousness of a person does not coincide with the severity of the punishment which this person deserves for being dangerous (see Clearwater 2017). In short, it could be the case that a person is still dangerous when he or she is about to be released after having served the punishment he or she deserved for initially being dangerous. The answers that have been given to this challenge have consisted in pointing out that in practice, the punishments which a dangerous person deserves will be rather severe, which means that the person will be incarcerated for a long period of time and, furthermore, that if a person is still dangerous at the end of the period for which he or she deserves to be imprisoned, then this could in itself be regarded as the ground for imposing a new deserved punishment on the person. More precisely, following the possession model, if the person still possesses characteristics x, y and z, then he or she could be regarded as having perpetrated a new offence and would therefore deserve a new punishment after the previous one (Husak 2011: 1199). Likewise, according to the omission model, if the person has not shown any signs of taking appropriate action to deal with his or her dangerousness while in prison, this would constitute an instance of an omission that warrants a new deserved punishment (Morse 1996: 152). Whether these arguments are sufficient to deal with a possible conflict between proportionate sentencing and the prevention of future crimes is not an issue that will be pursued here. In my view, there is a more basic problem related to the way in which the models may satisfy the proportionality requirement.

If dangerousness can warrant deserved punishment in either of the outlined ways, then we need to know how severely a dangerous offender should be punished. More precisely, we need to know the seriousness of the crime that someone has committed by possessing traits that predict future wrongdoing or by not taking appropriate action to counter such traits. The standard retributivist answer is that the gravity of the crime is determined on the ground of harm and culpability. But what harm is involved in the mere possession of risk factors or the failure to address such factors? The straightforward answer is that no harm is involved in either case. Harm is only caused when a risk materialises in actual behaviour. The obvious way to get around this problem would be to contend that what matters for the determination of the gravity of these crimes is not the actual harm, but rather the risk-adjusted harm. In fact, this answer is precisely what has been suggested in relation to other traditional types of crime such as the crime of criminal attempt (see Husak 1994; von Hirsch and Jareborg 1991). However, this answer provokes several serious challenges. For instance, if what matters in the computation of the seriousness of such dangerousness crimes is harm x risk, then why should this not be the case for all traditional types of crime? After all, the risk-adjusted harm of a certain crime is the same independently whether or not the risk materialises itself in actual harm. It seems arbitrary to hold that it is the actual harm that counts for some crimes (namely, those where the risk materialises itself in actual harm), but not for other crimes (namely, those where the risk is not materialised in actual harm) (see Ryberg 2004, 2019). However, be that as it may, there is another problem related specifically to the type of dangerousness-crime we are considering here.

Suppose that we accept that the seriousness of such crimes should be determined on the basis of risk-adjusted harm: how should one determine the degree of harm? The fact that a person is dangerous in the relevant sense (ie, possesses certain risk characteristics or fails to react to such characteristics) does not show precisely what sort of future wrongdoing he or she is at risk of committing. Even if a person possesses a combination of actuarial risk factors which makes it very likely that he or she will engage in future criminal activity, it will often be impossible to tell precisely which crime he or she will in fact commit.[10] For instance, a psychopath with a comprehensive criminal record may be highly dangerous, but it may at the same time be almost impossible to forecast which crime this person will commit in the future; he or she may engage in various sorts of property crimes, violent crimes, murder or still other types of crime. Furthermore, even an offender who has a narrower risk profile, such as a paedophile sex offender, may engage in very different sorts of crime in the future, ranging from voyeurism, the production and distribution of pornographic photographs, to child abuse and rape. In more general terms, while a person can be highly dangerous, it may be impossible to know which crime he or she is likely to commit in the future.[11] But if, for this reason, it is (often) impossible to estimate the harm of the future crime, then the idea of determining crime gravity on the ground of risk-adjusted harm falls apart. Thus, in my view, the main challenge in relation to the observance of the principle of proportionality does not pertain to the possible conflict between continued dangerousness and proportionate sentences. Rather, it concerns the more basic problem that both the possession model and the omission model face serious trouble when it comes to devising viable answers as to how the seriousness of the alleged dangerousness-crimes should be determined. In the absence of an answer, the allocation of the appropriate quantum of deserved punishment will not be possible; that is, the observance of the proportionality principle becomes illusionary.

V. The Scope Challenge

The task of developing a way of reacting to dangerousness becomes more urgent the more dangerous the potential perpetrator. If the probability that an individual will engage in future criminal activity is low, or if there are reasons to believe that this activity will only amount to minor crimes, then it seems less important for the criminal justice system to provide a procedure to address the risk.[12] From a standard consequentialist point of view, there may be a point below which the

[10] Obviously, there may be some cases in which it is possible to predict that an offender will commit a particular type of crime; in fact, this is precisely what some risk assessments instrument aim to achieve. However, it should be noted that even crimes of the same type may differ significantly in terms of the harm they cause.

[11] The omission model might suggest it is possible that a dangerous person may know which act he or she is about to perform just before it takes place, and that it is the failure to take action to prevent this behaviour that constitutes the ground for the determination of the seriousness of the omission. However, if the wrong a person does by not taking appropriate action is limited in this way, then the possibility of dealing with dangerousness by incarcerating dangerous individuals will be lost. There will be no ground for incarcerating a very dangerous person as long as it is not yet clear for this person which harmful act he or she is about to commit.

[12] For a discussion of how such cases are dealt with in criminal justice practice, see van Ginneken, ch 2 in this volume; or de Keijser (2011).

benefit of countering the risk of future crimes no longer outweighs the cost of the remedy. For instance, preventively detaining a person who may, with a very low probability, commit a serious crime in the future or, alternatively, someone who with a higher probability will commit a minor crime (say, petty theft) is unlikely to be cost-efficient.[13] But what if the point of imposing punishment is not the prevention of future crime, but rather to impose a deserved punishment for the possession of risk factors or for the failure to take appropriate action regarding these factors? If one adopts a purely retrospectively oriented approach to punishment, then when does a risk become too small to warrant a punitive response?

Adherents of both the possession model and the omission model have clearly underlined that it is only when a *serious* risk is involved that a person deserves to be punished. For instance, Husak seems to believe that imposing deserved punishment for the possession of risk characteristics x, y and z is relevant only when there is a risk of crimes that are 'incredibly serious' (Husak 2011: 1198). In the same vein, Morse contends that a person deserves punishment when he or she fails to take action, but 'only when the risk of harm is extraordinarily high' (Morse 1996: 153). However, very little is said to justify these contentions. Obviously, one cannot resort to the more general principle that punishment is only deserved in a case of very serious wrongdoing. To my knowledge, all retributivists – even those who believe that we are currently facing serious problems of overcriminalisation – subscribe to the view that there are many less serious crimes that justify a deserved punishment. Thus, how can the two models avoid the implication that even more moderate risks may result in deserved punishments?

The significance of this question is easy to grasp. If one cannot explain why a more moderate risk does not call for a deserved punitive response – although of course one that is more lenient than in high-risk cases – then the number of citizens that will be deserving of punishment, even though they have not committed any traditional crimes, will rise significantly. What we are considering is no longer a measure that is reserved for a particular group of potentially high-risk offenders (such as a few terrorists and psychopaths). Many people are at some risk of committing some future crime. In this respect, it is quite sobering to recall the study by Farrington showing that more than 90 per cent of males in London admitted to having committed at least one crime (Farrington 2002). It might perhaps be objected that it would be absurd if the possession and omission models were to imply that the criminal justice system should start imposing punishments on a large proportion of the populace and that this is precisely why punishment is warranted only in high-risk cases. However, in the absence of a justification, this seems ad hoc. If the two models cannot justify the claim that deserved punishment is reserved only for the highest-risk cases and not for cases involving more

[13] The picture might of cause change if the offender would commit many instances of less serious crimes.

moderate risks, then, insofar as there is absurdity involved in the implications of punishing risks more broadly, this is something that relates to how the theories should be morally assessed.

VI. The Challenge of the Past

As noted earlier, the main motivation behind the models we are considering here is that there seem to be very strong moral reasons in favour of intervening if there are valid reasons to believe that an individual is about to cause harm to others. However, if one tries to account for this type of moral reason by incorporating considerations of dangerousness into the ground for which an individual deserves a punishment, then one has totally changed the temporal perspective of the justification of punishment. From what at first seems to constitute a forward-looking reason in favour of intervening with some sort of punishment, one has to move to a retrospectively oriented type of justification. Obviously, the theoretical ability of accounting for dangerousness within the framework of a backward-looking justification is precisely what adherents of such retributivist theories would claim constitutes the theoretical elegance of the models. But this temporal shift in the justificatory orientation has an important implication to which I shall now turn.

Suppose that an individual at time t_1 possesses all the characteristics that constitute the most reliable predictors of future wrongful behaviour, or that this individual is recklessly endangering others by failing to take appropriate action to limit his or her dangerousness. Moreover, suppose that at a later point in time t_2, it happens to be the case that the same individual no longer possesses these characteristics – that is, the person no longer possesses traits x, y, and z that, according to the possession model, warrant a deserved punishment and therefore cannot fail to take the sort of proper actions which the omission model regards as crucial for the imposition of deserved punishment. An adherent of the latter model might at this point object that if the person no longer constitutes a danger to others, then this indicates that the person has taken the requisite initiatives to counter the risk. However, obviously this is not necessarily the case. Let us simply assume that the risk has been eliminated for reasons that have nothing to do with the person's own initiative to avoid the risk (eg, a person who is very dangerous at t_1 may perhaps become ill, may undergo neurological changes that reduce the risk as he or she matures, or may for various other reasons be deprived of the circumstances that are necessary to turn the risk into actual wrongdoing). Now, given these (not unlikely) assumptions, how should the criminal justice system react to this person after t_2? Do the changes which this person has undergone have any significance as to whether he or she should be punished?

Few theorists have addressed this question. Husak, for his part, seems to believe that it does make a difference when an individual possesses the risk characteristics: 'persons can be deserving of punishment in virtue of *presently* possessing the characteristics that predict future dangerousness' (Husak 2011: 1197, emphasis added). Apparently, this indicates that the person would not be deserving of punishment at t_2. However, it seems to me that this contention is basically unjustified. If the possession of x, y and z or the failure to take action to counter the influence of these characteristics in itself constitutes a crime that warrants a deserved punitive reaction, then all that matters from a desert-theoretical perspective is that the person has at some time possessed these characteristics or has failed to react to them. This would be sufficient for the person to be deserving of punishment. Whether the person at a later stage ceases to be dangerous is totally irrelevant. The 'crime', so to speak, has already been committed. To insist that deserved punishment presupposes some sort of simultaneity condition in the sense that one can only deserve a punishment if the sentence and the crime somehow temporally coincide is clearly absurd. Surely, a burglar can deserve a sentence today for the offence he or she committed yesterday. Such a condition would rule out the possibility of imposing deserved sentences on perpetrators *tout court*. And it would constitute a misinterpretation of what constitutes the main idea of desert, namely, that you can currently deserve a punishment for a crime you have committed in the past.

But this seems to establish that, on the ground of both the possession model and the omission model, the person in our hypothetical case would deserve a sentence at t_2. In other words, even if a person has never committed a traditional crime – that is, the risk was not materialised in harmful behaviour – and even though he or she is currently not at all dangerous, the mere fact that the person did constitute a risk at some point earlier in history is sufficient to warrant that he or she is now being punished. Moreover, it is also worth noting that *ceteris paribus*, it makes absolutely no difference whether, in the comparison of two persons, the first person was dangerous for a brief period three years ago while the second is dangerous now; they both deserve the same punishment. To object that it seems absurd to punish someone for being dangerous if this person no longer constitutes risk is precisely to misconceive or conflate the significance of the different temporal directions in forward-looking and backward-looking justifications of punishment. From a forward-looking point of view, it would *ceteris paribus* be tantamount to the loss of reason to punish a person if he or she is no longer dangerous, that is, if no future crime will be prevented by imposing the punishment. However, from a backward-looking perspective, the possession of risk characteristics, or the failure to react to these characteristics, in itself constitutes a completed crime sufficient to make the person deserving of punishment independently of the person's present risk profile. As a final illustration, we can image a person who is a member of a notorious criminal gang and who, on all risk parameters, must be regarded as dangerous; in contrast to him or her, let us imagine a person who was a member of the same gang and who used to be equally dangerous, but who has now successfully been through an exit programme and is spending time helping others escape such an environment. On the retributivist models we are considering here, risk considerations provide equally good reasons for punishing both.[14] I must admit that I find this implication somewhat hard to accept.

VII. The Additional Punishment Challenge

A final implication of the possession model and the omission model concerns the simple question as to who should be punished for being dangerous. The obvious answer is that it is those individuals who are (or have been) dangerous who deserve punishment. Insofar as it is possible to determine sufficiently reliable risk factors, the answer to the question seems straightforward. It is nevertheless worth taking a closer look at the individuals who may comprise this group of risk-offenders.

As noted above, the retrospective orientation of retributivist theories implies that, *ceteris paribus*, it makes no difference whether an individual was or currently is dangerous; the reason for imposing deserved punishment would in both cases be the same. But this means that when it comes to the identification of those who deserve to be punished for risk-offences, there is one group of individuals who naturally fall into this category, namely, those who have committed other 'traditional' crimes. If a person has committed a murder and if he or she was dangerous just before the murder took place, then he or she is punishable not only for the murder but also for the dangerousness. The same will of course be the outcome in relation to many other types of crime. Therefore, the answer to the above question is that a significant proportion of those who should be punished for risk-offences are those who are being punished for other crimes.

To object that a person need not be dangerous at the time just before he or she committed a certain crime will not alter the picture. Insofar as it is possible to identify reliable risk factors, it must be the very type of factors which a person possessed before he or she committed a crime. If this were not the case, then how could risk factors possibly predict crime? Thus, even if we can imagine some cases where a person committed a crime without being dangerous prior to the crime, the general picture must be that those who commit crimes – and, in particular, more serious crimes – are dangerous just before the misdeeds are perpetrated. In other words, both the possession model and the omission model seem to imply that murderers, rapists and those who have committed other serious violent crimes should usually be punished for two crimes: the crime itself and the crime of being dangerous just before it took place. Another way to put it is that all those who are now serving time for such crimes or who have been released after having served

[14] On the ground of the possession model, the latter person would be deserving for having at some point possessed the relevant risk characteristics, while, according to the omission model, he or she would be deserving for having at an earlier point been dangerous without reacting to this (and this would be the case even if he or she eventually did react and succeed in finding a way out of the environment).

the time they deserved, should have been given an extra punishment for the fact that they also, at some point before the crimes were committed, were dangerous. In my view, this is a dubious implication.

VIII. Conclusion

This chapter has addressed what several theorists regard as an 'unresolved dilemma' in penal theory, namely, that between, on the one hand, the existence of proportionality constraints on how offenders should be punished and, on the other, the fact that there seem to be strong reasons for the criminal justice system to undertake procedures that will prevent future crimes being committed by dangerous offenders or, in some cases, by individuals who are dangerous but not (yet) offenders.

What I have argued is that, contrary to what has often been upheld, there is room for taking the risks of future crimes into consideration, regardless of the theory of punishment to which one subscribes – that is, even if one holds that a retributivist theory provides sufficient justification for punishment and for the determination of how severely different crimes should be punished. In fact, not only is there theoretical room within all theories for paying some attention to the consequences of punishment, but it would be wrong on all accounts *not* to take consequences into consideration. This conclusion is important, not only because it counters the view that consequences matter if you are a consequentialist but not if you are a retributivist, but also because it implies that there is a theoretical foundation for taking steps into the comprehensive discussion of whether reliable risk factors can be determined and, if so, how these factors should be used. However, as we have also seen, the role which consequences play within penal theory gradually diminishes as we move from pure consequentialist theories, through mixed theories, to full-blown retributivist theories of punishment. On the latter type of theories, considerations of risk were limited to questions on which type of punishment should be imposed on offenders. But this meant that, at least according to some theorists, there is still a tension between observing retributivist proportionality constraints and the possibility of initiating more comprehensive measures to prevent criminal activity by dangerous persons. This led to the discussion of two versions of the idea that risk considerations can be incorporated into the ground for which persons become deserving of punishment. The examination of this attempt of reconciling dangerousness and desert has led to two conclusions.

First, it has been argued that if one adopts such an approach, then one easily ends up with a penal scheme that will affect many people. Despite the contention that desert presupposes control, there are reasons to believe that many types of risk factors should (if reliable) be taken into account. Furthermore, and more importantly, there may be many people who should be punished because they possess certain risk characteristics, and the theories seem to imply that all people should be punished if they at some point in the past were dangerous, despite the fact that this is no longer the case, and that many people who are being punished for traditional crimes should also be punished for risk-crimes. Thus, even though there has been a tendency amongst theorists to underline that such theories would apply only to a few extreme cases (say, terrorists), the more accurate picture seems to be that such schemes will have comprehensive consequences for large groups of citizens. Second, it has been suggested that the two models are both confronted with theoretical challenges and that both have several morally questionable implications. Thus, even though I do not want to suggest that the above considerations constitute anything close to conclusive arguments, I believe, more modestly, that they point in the direction of the conclusion that although there is some appeal in pursuing justice and in preventing future crimes, you cannot completely achieve both.

References

Clearwater, D (2017) 'If the Cloak Doesn't Fit, You Must Acquit: Retributivist Models of Preventive Detention and the Problem of Coextensiveness' 11 *Criminal Law and Philosophy* 49.

Davis, M (1996) 'Preventive Detention, Corado, and Me' 13 *Criminal Justice Ethics* 13.

De Keijser, JW (2011) 'Never Mind the Pain, it's a Measure: Justifying Measures as Part of the Dutch Bifurcated System of Sanctions' in M Tonry (ed), *Retributivism Has a Part: Has it a Future?* (New York, Oxford University Press).

Faigman, DL et al (2014) 'Group to Individual (G2i) Inference in Scientific Expert Testimony' 81 *University of Chicago Law Review* 417.

Farrington, DP (2002) 'Key Results from the First 40 Years of the Cambridge Study in Delinquent Development' in TP Thornberry and M Krohn (eds), *Taking Stock of Delinquency* (New York, Kluwer/Plenum).

Hart, SD et al (2017) 'Precision of Actuarial Risk Assessment Instruments: Evaluating the Margins of Error of Group v Individual Predictions of Violence' 190 *British Journal of Psychiatry* 60.

Husak, D (1994) 'Is Drunk Driving a Serious Offence?' 23 *Philosophy and Public Affairs* 52.

——. (2007) 'Rethinking the Act Requirement' 28 *Cardozo Law Review* 2437.

——. (2011) 'Lifting the Cloak: Preventive Detention as Punishment' 48 *San Diego Law Review* 1173.

——. (2018) 'Kinds of Punishment' in H Hurd (ed), *Moral Puzzles and Legal Perplexities* (Oxford, Oxford University Press).

Kagan, S (1998) *Normative Ethics* (Boulder, CO, Westview Press).

Kleinig, J (1973) *Punishment and Desert* (The Hague, Martinus Nijhoff).

Lippke, RL (2008) 'No Easy Way out: Dangerous Offenders and Preventive Detention' 27 *Law and Philosophy* 383.

Monahan, J and Skeem, JL (2014) 'Risk Redux: The Resurgence of Risk Assessment in Criminal Sentencing' 26 *Federal Sentencing Report* 391.
——. (2016) 'Risk Assessment in Criminal Sentencing' 12 *Annual Review of Clinical Psychology* 489.
Moore, M (1997) *Placing Blame* (Oxford, Clarendon Press).
Morse, SJ (1996) 'Blame and Danger: An Essay on Preventive Detention' 76 *Boston University Law Review* 113.
Morris, N and Miller, M (1985) 'Predictions of Dangerousness' 6 *Crime and Justice: An Annual Review of Research* 1.
New, C (1992) 'Time and Punishment' 52 *Analysis* 35.
——. (1995) 'Punishing Times: A Reply to Smilansky' 55 *Analysis* 60.
Robinson, PH (2001) 'Punishing Dangerousness: Cloaking Preventive Detention as Criminal Justice' 114 *Harvard Law Review* 1429.
Ryberg, J (2004) *The Ethics of Proportionate Punishment: A Critical Investigation* (Dordrecht, Kluwer Academic Publishers).
——. (2010) 'Mass Atrocities, Retributivism, and the Threshold Challenge' 16 *Res Publica* 169.
——. (forthcoming 2019) 'Proportionality and the Seriousness of Crime' in M Tonry (ed) *Proportionality, Punishment and Sentencing* (New York: Oxford University Press.
Schoman, S (1979) 'On Incapacitating the Dangerous' 16 *American Philosophical Quarterly* 27.
Slobogin, C (2003) 'A Jurisprudence of Dangerousness' 98 *Northwestern University Law Review* 1.
Statman, D (1997) 'The Time to Punish and the Problem of Moral Luck' 14 *Journal of Applied Philosophy* 129.
Von Hirsch, A and Jareborg, N (1991) 'Gauging Criminal Harm: A Living-Standard Analysis' 11 *Oxford Journal of Legal Studies* 1.
Von Hirsch, A et al (1989) 'Punishments in the Community and the Principle of Desert' 20 *Rutgers Law Journal* 595.
Walen, A (2011) 'A Unified Theory of Detention, with Application to Preventive Detention for Suspected Terrorists' 70 *Maryland Law Review* 871.

5

Is Preventive Detention Morally Worse than Quarantine?[1]

THOMAS DOUGLAS

I. Introduction

In some jurisdictions, the institutions of criminal justice may subject individuals who have committed crimes to *preventive detention*. By this, I mean detention of criminal offenders: (i) who have already been punished to (or beyond) the point that no further punishment can be justified on general deterrent, retributive, restitutory, communicative or other backward-looking grounds; and (ii) for preventive purposes – that is, for the purposes of preventing the detained individual from engaging in further criminal or otherwise socially costly conduct.

Preventive detention, thus understood, shares many features with the quarantine measures sometimes employed in the context of infectious disease control.[2] Both interventions involve imposing (usually severe) constraints on freedom of movement and association. Both interventions are standardly undeserved: in quarantine, the detained individual deserves no detention (or so I will, for the moment, assume), and in preventive detention, the individual has already endured any detention that can be justified by reference to desert. Both interventions are, in contrast to civil commitment under mental health legislation, normally imposed on more or less fully autonomous individuals. And both interventions are intended to reduce the risk that the constrained individual poses to the public.

Yet despite these similarities, preventive detention and quarantine have received rather different moral report cards. Preventive detention and the assessments of forensic risk that it necessitates have been subject to frequent and diverse moral objections (eg, Corrado 1996a: 778; Duff 2007; Kitai-Sangero 2009;

[1] I would like to thank Jesper Ryberg and audiences in Oxford and Utrecht for comments on an earlier version of this chapter. I also thank Areti Theofilopoulou for her research assistance.

[2] I use the term 'quarantine' to refer to what would more properly be called 'isolation or quarantine'. 'Isolation' standardly refers to the separation from others of individuals infected with an infectious agent, while 'quarantine' refers to the separation of individuals merely at risk of being infected. I use the term 'quarantine' to refer to both.

Morse 2011; Harcourt 2012). By contrast, quarantine is relatively well accepted by those who might be thought most likely to offer a moral critique of it: scholars of public health ethics and public health law. It also appears to be accepted by many of the very same scholars who object to preventive detention. Despite the obvious parallels between preventive detention and quarantine, these scholars have typically remained silent on quarantine.[3] Indeed, when theorists of criminal justice have mentioned quarantine, they have often done so precisely because it seems to them to be morally justified. For example, Gregg Caruso and Derek Pereboom seek to defend preventive detention in part by drawing parallels between it and quarantine (Caruso 2016; Pereboom 2014: 156–74).[4]

Why the comparative critical silence on quarantine, as compared to preventive detention? Several candidate explanations are available. It could be, for example, that moral objections to quarantine are comparatively rare because most potential commentators regard it as so morally problematic as to not be worth discussing; because quarantine itself is rare (Meyerson 2009: 510); or because the ethical analysis of quarantine has fallen down the disciplinary cracks between healthcare ethics and political philosophy. However, it is plausible that at least part of the explanation lies in widespread implicit acceptance that there is a genuine moral difference between these practices – that preventive detention *is* more morally problematic than quarantine.[5] A soft version of this view would hold that:

Soft Moral Difference: preventive detention is *typically* in at least one respect more morally problematic than quarantine.

A harder version of the view would posit a universal moral difference between the two practices:

Hard Moral Difference: preventive detention is *always* in at least one respect more morally problematic than quarantine.

I believe that both of these views warrant attention. Unfortunately, though, as a philosopher, I am not well qualified to assess the former. Whether preventive detention is *typically* more problematic than quarantine will depend heavily on the facts about how these two practices are typically imposed and what effects they normally have on those subject to them, on those whom they are intended to protect and on those required to fund them. These are empirical questions that cannot be addressed through philosophical methods. I thus focus here purely on the latter view.

The primary purpose of this chapter is to challenge Hard Moral Difference. I seek to advance this challenge by considering and rejecting six attempts to justify

[3] For exceptions, see Ashworth and Zedner, ch 8 in this volume; Meyerson (2009: 510).

[4] For other discussions of preventive detention that also touch on quarantine, see Ashworth and Zedner, ch 8 in this volume; Slobogin (2011).

[5] This view has sometimes been explicitly or implicitly endorsed by critics of preventive detention (Gavaghan, Snelling and McMillan 2014: 82–83).

it, beginning with four attempts that I think can be easily dismissed, and proceeding to consider in more detail two attempts that are more resilient to criticism. Ultimately, I argue that all six attempts fail: preventive detention is *not* always more problematic, in one respect, than quarantine – at least not if my survey is exhaustive and my arguments are persuasive. I conclude by drawing out some implications of my argument.

Of course, it does not follow from my argument that preventive detention is not *in some cases* more problematic than quarantine. Perhaps it is even *typically* more problematic, as Soft Moral Difference asserts. A secondary purpose of this chapter, pursued in parallel to the first, is to identify the considerations that determine whether and when preventive detention is indeed in some respect more problematic.

II. Preliminaries

However, before beginning to pursue either of these purposes, I must offer two preliminary comments and introduce three significant assumptions.

The first preliminary comment concerns the relationship between preventive detention and predictive sentencing, which is the topic of this volume. Preventive detention, as I have defined it, can occur after completion of a criminal sentence: offenders are transferred to preventive detention when or after their sentences expire. But preventive detention can also occur within the confines of a sentence (Ashworth and Zedner, Chapter 8 in this volume; van Ginneken, Chapter 2 in this volume). Suppose an offender is sentenced to a period of 10 years in prison, with a minimum tariff of five years. Suppose that the initial five years of imprisonment are intended to realise general deterrent and/or backward-looking goals, with any further detention being subject to risk assessment and intended to prevent the individual from committing further offences. Finally, suppose that five years is indeed the maximum period of detention that can be justified on non-preventive grounds. In this case, if the offender is detained beyond five years, the portion of detention that extends beyond the five-year mark will qualify as preventive detention, as I have defined it. We will thus have an instance of *within sentence* preventive detention. In such cases, the preventive element of the sentence will normally (and, I would say, should) be made contingent on a predictive risk assessment, or series of risk assessments, and we will thus have an instance of *predictive sentencing*.

Thus, preventive detention can, but need not, be an upshot of predictive sentencing.[6] In the remainder of this chapter, I focus on preventive detention rather than predictive sentencing, since I believe the issues I raise apply also to

[6] That preventive detention can occur either within or outside a criminal sentence is not an idiosyncratic implication of my way of understanding of preventive detention. See also Slobogin (2011: 1128–29, 1140).

post-sentence preventive detention. However, everything I will say applies a fortiori to predictive sentencing.

The second preliminary comment is a note about what I will not cover. I will not have anything to say about objections to preventive detention that, I think, clearly apply equally to quarantine. In this category are objections appealing to a Kantian requirement never to treat individuals merely as means (Husak, Chapter 3 in this volume) and objections to treating some individuals less favourably than others on the basis of statistical generalisations about groups (Meyerson 2009: 514–15).

Now for the three assumptions. I assume, first, that we are comparing only forms of preventive detention and quarantine that are actually used, or are likely to be used in the future. I take it that the proponent of Hard Moral Difference is making a claim about these actual or likely practices, not about hypothetical, ideal versions of them. Thus, it is compatible with Hard Moral Difference that some idealised forms of preventive detention would be in no way more morally problematic than quarantine.

Second, I assume throughout that preventive detention is imposed by the institutions of criminal justice under the provisions of criminal law and that quarantine is imposed by public health authorities under the provisions of public health law.[7] This allows me to exclude from both categories, and thus set aside, some rather institutionally messy and ethically complex detention practices, including the civil commitment of psychiatric patients deemed to pose a risk to self or others (for a discussion of these, see Slobogin (2011)).

Third, I grant the proponent of Hard Moral Difference that those subjected to preventive detention are *no more liable* to the harms and intrusions that it involves than are those subjected to quarantine. Though preventively detained individuals do not positively deserve their detention, it could be held that they have, in committing a crime, made themselves (more) liable to it; they have forfeited some of the rights that would ordinarily be infringed by such detention, or caused those rights to lose some of their normal force or scope. By contrast, it might be held that those subjected to quarantine retain all of their normal rights, with their normal force and normal scope. These views could be used to diffuse some arguments for Hard Moral Difference; for instance, some might hold that even if preventive detention *seems* to involve some rights infringements that quarantine does not, this turns out to not to be so, since criminal offenders have in fact forfeited the rights in question. I exclude this possibility by assuming that preventively detained individuals are no more liable to the constraints they face than are quarantined individuals; both groups possess the same relevant rights, and those rights have the same force and the same scope.

With these assumptions in hand, let me turn to the task of assessing Hard Moral Difference.

[7] This stipulation precludes quarantine from qualifying as a *kind* of preventive detention. For a contrasting view, see Slobogin (2011).

III. Four Preliminary Arguments

I begin by assessing four arguments for Hard Moral Difference that can, I think, be dismissed easily and in similar ways.

The first of these arguments holds that preventive detention is more morally problematic than quarantine in the sense that the expected benefits of preventive detention, in the form of public protection, are smaller than those of quarantine, so, all other things being equal, are less likely to outweigh the moral costs. The underlying thought here is that those with the sorts of infectious diseases that trigger quarantine procedures pose a greater risk to the public than those subjected to preventive detention (Smilansky 2017: 597–98).

The second argument adverts to the putatively self-fulfilling nature of the risk assessments necessitated by preventive detention. It has been argued that when individuals are deemed to be high risk in the context of criminal justice, this judgement, and the interventions that follow from it, in fact *increase* the risk that the individual will re-offend (Sidhu 2015). It might be argued that this effect does not occur, or at least is weaker, in the context of infectious disease control. After all, the mechanism via which criminal justice risk assessments become self-fulfilling is often supposed to be partly psychological: those deemed to be high risk come to see themselves as such, and this makes them less psychologically resilient to crime-promoting environments. It may seem doubtful that any such process could occur in the case of infectious disease.

A third argument holds that the declarations of high forensic risk necessitated by preventive detention are more stigmatising than the declarations of high infectious risk necessitated by quarantine. Individuals deemed to be high risk in the context of criminal justice may not only be subjected to longer periods of detention than their 'low-risk' contemporaries, but may also become the object of significant social disapproval, which may be intrinsically harmful and lead to myriad other forms of disadvantage (Silver and Miller 2002; von Hirsch 1972: 743). It might be argued that this effect does not occur, or at least is weaker, when individuals are deemed to be 'high risk' in the context of infectious disease control.

Finally, the fourth argument holds that the risk assessments necessitated by preventive detention are more *inegalitarian* than those necessitated by quarantine. Risk assessments will tend to exacerbate social inequality when: (i) those deemed high risk are on average more disadvantaged than others (on whatever metric is relevant to the moral assessment of social equality); and (ii) the assessments, or interventions that follow from them, tend to increase that disadvantage (Gavaghan, Snelling and McMillan 2014: 25; Sidhu 2015). It can plausibly be argued that both (i) and (ii) hold in relation to assessments of forensic risk: disadvantaged groups are overrepresented among those deemed to be high risk by commonly used forensic risk assessment tools, and it is plausible that both the longer periods of incarceration and the stigmatisation endured by these individuals tend to increase levels of disadvantage (Hannah-Moffat and Struthers Montford,

Chapter 10 in this volume). It might be argued that the risk assessments employed in infectious disease control are less strongly associated with prior disadvantage and are less liable to produce further disadvantage (for example, because they are less stigmatising).

I believe that all of these arguments face the same problem: they do not apply universally. Thus, though they may support Soft Moral Difference, they do not support Hard Moral Difference; they do not show that preventive detention is *always* in one respect more problematic than quarantine.[8] This is true even when we limit ourselves to actual and likely preventive detention and quarantine practices.

Consider first the claim that preventive detention has smaller benefits than risk-based quarantine. This may be true of many pairwise comparisons between the two kinds of intervention, but it is not true of all. Some prevailing forms of quarantine can be expected to have rather small benefits. Consider quarantine procedures that involve restraining individuals who live in an area where a pandemic is thriving, but who have had no close personal contact with infected individuals and whose individual risk of being infected thus remains low. The containment of any one individual in such cases has a very low expected benefit. There are also some prevailing forms of preventive detention that probably have large expected benefits. These may include the detention of those who have perpetrated major terrorist attacks and appear to be 'unreformed'. The detention of these individuals plausibly has greater expected benefits than many instances of quarantine.

Consider next the claim that preventive detention is more problematic than quarantine because forensic risk assessments are self-fulfilling in a way that infectious disease risk assessments are not. Again, this claim does not hold universally. Though forensic risk assessments can have a self-fulfilling effect, infectious disease risk assessments can also be self-fulfilling, for example, because individuals who are deemed to be at a high risk of being infected, but are in fact uninfected, are quarantined alongside individuals who are indeed infected. Such quarantine procedures can significantly increase one's risk of becoming infected.

Similar points can be made in relation to the claim that the declarations of high forensic risk necessitated by preventive detention are more stigmatising than the declarations of high infectious risk necessitated by quarantine. It is true that there is often a very strong negative stigma associated with criminality. However, there is also a strong negative stigma associated with some infectious diseases, with HIV being the most obvious example (van Brakel 2006; Whittle et al 2017). It thus seems plausible that at least some declarations of high forensic risk are no more negatively stigmatising than some declarations of high infectious risk.

[8] Though I do not have the space to argue it here, I think the same point holds in relation to three other reasons that might be given for thinking that preventive detention is more problematic than quarantine: the conditions of preventive detention are harsher than those of quarantine, forensic risk is more difficult to accurately predict than infectious risk, and preventive detention can more easily be replaced with less restrictive alternatives than can quarantine.

In response, it might be argued that the negative stigma associated with declarations of high forensic risk is different in kind from that associated with declarations of high infectious risk. The former typically has a moral character, whereas the latter typically does not. Those declared to pose a high forensic risk are not merely stigmatised as dangerous, like those deemed to pose a high infectious risk, but are also deemed to be morally flawed, perhaps in part because the imposition of preventive detention is itself sometimes mistakenly taken as an official expression of moral condemnation rather than as a purely preventive measure.[9] However, even this difference is not universal. Some infectious diseases are associated with heavily moralised behaviours, such as illicit drug use and homosexual or unprotected sex, and these diseases frequently carry a stigma that is moral in nature. Quarantine measures may help to reinforce that stigma. Moreover, even if there is a difference in the *kind* of stigma associated with high forensic risk and high infectious risk, it does not clearly follow that preventive detention is always more problematic than quarantine. After all, it is plausible that stigma matters only insofar as it diminishes the wellbeing of the stigmatised individual, and even if forensic risk assessments produce a different – and perhaps more serious – kind of stigma than infectious risk assessments, it may be that the overall effect on wellbeing produced by these two different kinds of stigma is similar. Alternatively, it may be that, even if there is a greater *stigma-related* loss of wellbeing in the case of preventive detention than in quarantine, this is in some cases offset by countervailing effects on wellbeing (eg, the greater risk of acquiring a disease associated with certain forms of quarantine).

Finally, the claim that forensic risk assessments are more inegalitarian than infectious disease risk assessments also does not hold universally. Because a person's being deemed to pose a high infectious risk can lead to both negative stigma and an increased risk of becoming infected, such assignments of risk can contribute substantially to disadvantage. Moreover, in some cases, the assignment of high infectious disease risk can be expected to track pre-existing disadvantage, because acquisition of some infectious diseases is correlated with prior disadvantage. For example, within Europe alone, there is evidence that meningococcal meningitis and hepatitis A are associated with low socio-economic status (Hrivniaková, Sláčiková and Kolcunová 2009; Twisselmann 2000; Williams et al 2004), Methicillin-resistant Staphylococcus aureus infection is associated with social deprivation (Bagger, Zindrou and Taylor 2004) and tuberculosis disproportionately afflicts persons from a range of frequently disadvantaged populations, including immigrants, homeless people, substance abusers, prisoners and HIV-positive persons (European Centre for Disease Prevention and Control/World Health Organization Regional Office for Europe 2013; Klinkenberg et al 2009; Semenza and Giesecke 2008).

[9] I thank Jesper Ryberg for pointing this out to me.

IV. Desert

Let us turn to consider a more promising argument for Hard Moral Difference. This argument invokes a desert-based constraint on detention within the context of criminal justice.

Many object to preventive detention on the basis that it flaunts the requirement that the institutions of criminal justice not impose more harm or intrusion than an individual deserves or, as I take to be equivalent, that they not impose harm or intrusion that is *disproportionately severe* relative to the individual's culpability (Gavaghan, Snelling and McMillan 2014: 75; Morse 2011). (This is often called the 'negative retributivist constraint.') By contrast, considerations of culpability and desert are seldom raised in discussions of the ethics of quarantine, and I am not aware of anyone having defended an analogue of the negative retributivist constraint in relation to quarantine and other public health practices.[10] Perhaps, then, preventive detention is more morally problematic than quarantine by virtue of the undeserved harm or intrusions that it imposes.

An initial problem with this suggestion is that quarantine also imposes underserved harm and intrusions: I have been assuming throughout that individuals subjected to quarantine are not at all culpable, and that the harm and intrusions that they suffer are thus underserved. It seems clear that this assumption holds in at least some cases of quarantine. There may be cases in which quarantined individuals are culpable for the infectious risk that they pose; for example, they may have acquired the infectious condition through unsafe sexual practices or through violating the conditions of a previously imposed quarantine, or they may have negligently failed to take steps to have the infection treated. However, there are clearly also cases in which quarantined individuals are not at all culpable, and even in cases where they are culpable, it is in most cases not plausible that their culpability rises to the level that they deserve the severe constraints imposed by quarantine.

However, it might be argued that the institutions of public health are not bound by the same desert-based moral constraints as those of criminal justice; that is, it might be argued that public health institutions fall under no analogue of the negative retributivist constraint. Thus, even if both preventive detention and quarantine impose undeserved harm and intrusions, this may violate a moral constraint in the case of preventive detention, but not in that of quarantine. The difference between them lies not in whether they impose underserved harm or intrusions, but in whether, in doing so, they violate a moral constraint.

[10] Considerations of *proportionality* are sometimes raised in relation to public health (Childress et al 2002: 173). However, the concern here is not with proportionality *to* desert or culpability; it is not that public health interventions might impose more harm or intrusion than the targeted individuals deserve, but that they might impose more harm or intrusion than can be justified by the objective threat that the targeted individuals pose.

The question then becomes: why think that institutions of public health are free from the sort of desert-based moral constraints that apply to institutions of criminal justice? Why not accept an analogue of the negative retributivist constraint in public health? After all, the negative retributivist constraint plausibly derives from a more general requirement that the state and its agents not impose more suffering on individuals than they deserve, and this more general requirement would also apply to the individuals and institutions responsible for quarantine.

An initial answer to these questions would appeal to the different goals of criminal justice and public health. Inflicting deserved harm or intrusions is part of the *purpose* of criminal justice, but not part of the purpose of public health. Perhaps this explains why desert-based *constraints* apply in criminal justice, but not in public health.

In the absence of further elucidation, this suggestion is unconvincing; it is not clear why desert-based constraints should be connected to desert-based purposes. After all, within penal theory, the two sometimes come apart: some accept the negative retributivist constraint while denying that punishment serves any desert-related purpose (Hart 1968: Chapter 1). More importantly, the sorts of considerations typically mentioned in favour of the negative retributivist constraint do not presuppose a desert-based purpose of punishment. The chief motivation for accepting the constraint is that it is otherwise difficult to rule out the punishment of innocents and the imposition of harsh punishments on the perpetrators of minor wrongs (McCloskey 1972: 127; Pereboom 2014: 164). These concerns are consistent with non-desert-based accounts of the purposes of punishment, and indeed are frequently illustrated by reference to 'scapegoating' punishments administered for a forward-looking, general deterrent purpose. If the justification of desert-based constraints within criminal justice is independent of the purposes of criminal justice, it is unclear why the justification for desert-based constraints in *public health* should be undermined by the fact that public health has no desert-based purpose.

However, perhaps there are other grounds for thinking that desert-based constraints apply in criminal justice, but not in public health. It might be argued that there are reasons, pertaining to the costs of assessing individual desert, for adopting different desert-based constraints in the two domains. Individual desert is difficult to assess, and the institutions of public health are not well set up to conduct such assessments. It may be that the costs of reforming public health institutions to accurately assess desert would outweigh the benefits, and it may be that any attempt to assess individual desert without such reforms would be unacceptably prone to errors. However, the institutions of criminal justice are arguably far better placed to assess desert. For instance, they include trial-based procedures for identifying and appraising the intentions of individual criminal offenders. Perhaps, then, the costs of accurately assessing desert are acceptable in the context of criminal justice, but unacceptable in the context of public health. And perhaps it follows that public health institutions are free from any desert-based constraints, though the institutions of criminal justice are not.

This argument is unpersuasive. It assumes that if assessing desert would be unacceptably costly for some institutions, then those institutions fall under no desert-based constraints. In effect, they are free to ignore considerations of desert. But this is implausible. More plausible is that if assessing individual desert is too costly for some institutions, those institutions should still seek to avoid inflicting underserved harm or intrusions, though they should rely on reasonable assumptions about who deserves what, rather than individualised assessments of desert. (In the case of the public health institutions that administer quarantine, the most reasonable assumption to make would surely be that all individuals subjected to quarantine do *not* deserve the harms and intrusions that this entails, since, for almost all quarantined individuals, this will be true.)

Another argument for rejecting a desert-based constraint within public health would appeal to the idea of an efficient division of moral labour. This is the idea that, in some cases, different moral obligations and permissions should be assigned to different agents because this heterogeneous distribution of moral considerations more efficiently realises some moral objective than would a uniform distribution. Rawls famously held that social justice is best achieved by adopting stringent requirements of justice in relation to the design of a society's basic institutions, while individuals acting within this institutional structure are for the most part left free to set aside justice and pursue their own good (Murphy 1999; Nagel 1995; Rawls 1993: 268–69; Scheffler 2005). Similarly, it has been suggested that the goal of socially beneficial scientific progress is best realised by ascribing to scientists an obligation only to pursue their curiosity, while science regulators and funders ought to nudge the direction of science towards social benefit and away from social harm.[11]

In the present context, it might be argued that the goal of matching suffering to desert is most efficiently realised by leaving this task to the institutions of criminal justice, while other institutions – including those of public health – are left free to ignore considerations of desert.

However, the difficulty is that the institutions of criminal justice seem woefully inadequate for the task of ensuring, in general, that people suffer no more or less than they deserve. One reason for this is that they correct for the effects of other institutions only in one direction; though they may sometimes impose deserved suffering when other institutions have failed to do so, they do nothing to negate or compensate for the imposition of undeserved suffering by other parties or institutions. For instance, they do nothing to correct for the imposition of undeserved suffering through quarantine. It is thus difficult to see how one could plausibly claim that public health institutions may permissibly ignore considerations of desert on the basis that criminal justice institutions will efficiently negate or compensate for any underserved suffering that they might impose. Moreover, it is

[11] For a discussion of this view, see Douglas (2014).

doubtful that any other institutions *do* efficiently negate or compensate such undeserved suffering. It is thus difficult to see how an appeal to an efficient division of moral labour could get the public health institutions 'off the hook' with respect to desert.

V. Respect

A sixth argument for Hard Moral Difference holds that preventive detention violates a requirement to treat people with respect, whereas quarantine does not.[12]

The risk that individuals subjected to preventive detention pose to the public is a risk that arises from their own rational agency: the risk is that they will choose to exercise their rational agency in harmful ways. It might be thought that in cases where an individual poses such a risk, one must seek to mitigate the risk *through engaging the rational capacities of those individuals*, for example, through engaging them in forms of 'talking therapy' that help them to appreciate their reasons to refrain from harmful conduct. Yet preventive detention does not seek to engage rational capacities. It thus arguably fails to respect the detained individuals' by treating them *as if* they were not rational agents – as if, in Von Hirsch's words, they were 'beasts in a circus … beings that must be restrained, intimidated, or conditioned into submission because they are incapable of understanding that harmful conduct is wrong' (von Hirsch 1992: 67).

Of course, quarantine also does not engage the rational capacities of the detained individual, but in this case, it might seem that there is no failure of respect, since the risk that the individual poses is in any case not a rationality-based risk: it is not that we fear that the (possibly) infected individual might choose to exercise her rational agency in ways that cause harm to the public.[13] True, quarantine treats the risky individual as if she were simply a dangerous 'beast', but, *with regard to her infectiousness*, she *is* like a dangerous beast, so perhaps there is nothing disrespectful about failing to engage rational capacities in this case.[14]

[12] For the claim that preventive detention fails to respect agency, see Corrado (1996a; 779); Duff (2007: 165); Morse (2011); and Smilansky (1994: 52–53). For similar objections to other criminal justice practices, see Hoskins (2013); and Zedner (2010: 25).

[13] In some cases, rational agency *does* play a role in mediating the infectious risk that the quarantined individual poses to others. It may be, for example, that the individual will infect others only if she chooses to engage in unsafe sexual practices or fails to respect voluntary constraints on free movement. Still, it seems plausible that rational agency plays a more central role in generating forensic risks than it does in generating infectious ones, and perhaps this is all the present argument requires.

[14] Denise Meyerson's (2009: 527–28) statement of this argument is the most complete I have been able to find. She holds that: 'Some predictions of dangerousness are not inconsistent with respect for a person's autonomy. As Barbara D Underwood points out, when "the predicted fact is not subject to individual control, then predicting that fact is less threatening to the value of respect for autonomy. For example, prediction of violent behavior by the mentally ill … is seldom characterized as a threat to the autonomy of the mentally ill." The same could be said about isolating someone who has a highly infectious disease, since spreading the disease is not under their control. It is very different, however, when

One worry about this argument relates to the suggestion that we need not engage a person's rational capacities in seeking to mitigate her infectious risk, since that risk does not *arise from* the quarantined individual's rational agency. We might wonder why the *source* of a risk should matter for how we should seek to mitigate it. An alternative view would hold that whenever a risk can be mitigated through means that engage rational capacities, it ought to be so mitigated, regardless of its source. What matters for respect is not whether a risk arises from rational agency, but whether it can be *effectively mitigated* through means that engage it.

I will not pursue this worry; I will take it as given that quarantine involves no failure of respect. Instead, I focus my attention on the other half of the present argument for Hard Moral Difference: the claim that preventive detention always fails to respect the detained individual. To assess this claim, we need to be clearer about what exactly respect requires. In what follows, I will try to show that it is difficult to formulate this requirement in such a way that it is strong enough to rule out all cases of preventive detention, but weak enough to avoid implying that seemingly innocuous forms of treatment are disrespectful.

One understanding of the respect requirement is suggested by the claim – alluded to above – that failing to engage an individual's agency involves treating her *as if she were a non-agent*. On a straightforward interpretation, the thought here is that, for *A* to respect *B*, *A*'s actual treatment of *B* must differ from the treatment that *A* would have given to *B* had *B* not been a rational agent. *B*'s rational agency must have made a difference to how *A* treated her.

The problem with this formulation is that it leaves the respect requirement demanding far too much. We often treat people in ways that are no different from how we would also have treated comparable non-rational animals, and in many cases, this seems morally innocuous. Consider the installation of centre barriers intended to prevent head-on collisions on highways. This seems to treat drivers precisely as we might treat equivalently dangerous non-rational animals, yet it does not seem disrespectful.

To avoid this problem, one might hold that, in determining whether *A* respects *B*, we should look not at individual forms of treatment that *A* gives to *B*, but at *A*'s treatment of *B* considered globally. (Perhaps we should also consider how *A* *would have* treated *B* in certain counterfactual circumstances.) Suppose the state installs central barriers on highways, but *also* employs rationality-engaging measures to prevent head-on collisions – for example, it also presents drivers with reasons to take frequent breaks to avoid sleepiness. In that case, it might seem that,

someone is deprived of their liberty when the threat they pose is under their control. In cases such as this, preventive measures assume that people who are capable of choosing not to cause harm will cause harm, thereby denying them the opportunity to choose differently. They are treated as "predictable objects", or "dangerous animals", rather than as individuals with the capacity for free choice.' The argument entertained by Meyerson here differs from the one I am considering only in invoking the narrower 'respect for autonomy' rather than my preferred, more generic 'respect'.

considered globally, the state is treating drivers differently from how it would treat non-rational animals, so the respect requirement is satisfied.

However, if we take this more global perspective, then it is not clear why preventive detention must involve any failure of respect. To avoid such a failure, it would, on the present understanding, be enough to combine preventive detention with other, rationality-engaging interventions, as is often done.

Let us turn, then, to consider two further interpretations of the respect requirement. On the first of these interpretations, the requirement demands that *A* not express a (certain kind of) objectionable negative appraisal of *B* – it is a requirement not to send the wrong kind of message. On the second interpretation, it demands that *A* not act on the basis of a (certain kind of) objectionable negative judgement about *B* – it is a requirement not to act on the wrong kind of judgement. On the first of these two understandings, what matters is the meaning expressed ('message sent') by the putatively disrespectful treatment (let us call this the 'expressivist' interpretation); on the second, what matters is the set of judgements that played a part in motivating it (let us call this the 'motivationist' interpretation).

These two understandings of the respect requirement are closely related, since the message sent by, for example, preventively detaining an individual plausibly depends on the judgements that played a part in motivating the imposition of that detention. However, the meaning expressed by preventive detention could also depend on other factors, such as mere social conventions regarding what different actions mean, so it is possible that the expressivist and motivationist interpretations could come apart. In what follows, I will take the motivationist interpretation as my target, though, as it happens, I believe that everything I will say about the motivationist interpretation of the respect requirement applies to the expressivist interpretation as well.

On the motivationist interpretation of the respect requirement, whether preventive detention is disrespectful depends on whether there is some objectionable moral judgement that always plays a role in motivating the imposition of preventive detention. What might that judgement be?

Here is an initial suggestion: the objectionable judgement is the judgement that the detained individual *is not a rational agent*. On this view, the disrespectfulness of preventive detention derives from an underlying failure, on the part of the detaining agents,[15] to *recognise* the rational agency of the detained individual.

This suggestion faces an obvious problem as a basis for Hard Moral Difference: there is no reason to suppose that the agents responsible for imposing preventive detention must make any such judgement. Indeed, in cases where the detaining

[15] I use the term 'detaining agent' because I wish to remain silent on who, precisely, is responsible for imposing detention. Plausible candidates would include the state, the various institutions of criminal justice and particular individuals within those institutions (such as judges, jurors and parole board members).

agents couple preventive detention with rationality-engaging interventions, such as talking therapies, we have clear reasons not to impute any such judgement; in such cases, the detaining agents clearly take the detained individual to be a rational agent. Suppose that Arama, who is deemed to pose a risk of criminal offending, is subjected to a package of interventions which include a short period of preventive detention, but also rationality-engaging interventions, such as talking therapies, which extend over a longer period. The most credible explanation for why the detaining agents treat Arama in this way would be that they believe Arama to be a *somewhat morally deficient* rational agent; they believe her to be an agent who is somewhat capable of responding to moral reasons, but who sometimes fails to do so, either because she is subject to non-rational forces, such as strong brute urges, or because she sometimes fails to recognise or chooses to ignore her moral reasons. The detaining agents thus employ a multifaceted risk reduction strategy that seeks both to engage Arama's rational agency and to erect brute barriers to offending in case these appeals to her rationality fail.

Let us turn, then, to a proposal that is more promising, as a basis for Hard Moral Difference, and is suggested by the case of Arama. Perhaps the objectionable judgement underpinning preventive detention is the judgement that the detained individual is a *morally deficient* rational agent, which I will gloss here as the judgement that the detained individual is *less responsive to moral reasons than most*.

Again, it might seem doubtful that the detaining agents *always* make such a judgement. It might seem that the detaining agents could deem that detainees are 'dangerous' or 'risky' without subjecting them to any moral appraisal – indeed, without thinking about morality at all.

However, perhaps it could be maintained that the detaining agents always, at least *implicitly*, endorse the judgement that detainees are morally deficient. After all, they plausibly believe that: (i) the detainees are unusually dangerous; and (ii) their dangerousness derives from the way in which they tend to exercise their rational agency. These propositions might seem to jointly entail that the detained individual is less responsive to moral reasons than most.

In fact, it is not clear to me that even such an implicit judgement can be attributed to the detaining agents. An individual might be subjected to preventive detention on the basis of the judgement that she is morally normal, though at high risk of recidivism due, say, to the especially challenging social circumstances that she faces. But let us concede, for the sake of argument, that preventive detention is invariably motivated in part by the judgement that the detained individual is morally deficient. The question then becomes: what is wrong with that? Why think that the respect requirement rules out acting on the basis of such a judgement?

One answer to this question would appeal to the epistemic status of the judgement. Acting on the judgement that a person is morally deficient may be disrespectful if and when that person is not in fact morally deficient, or not *as* deficient as one's judgement maintains, or when one's judgement has no good evidential basis. In such cases, we might say that one acts on an *overestimation* of the individual's moral failings. However, there seems little reason to suppose that imposing preventive detention will always be motivated in part by such an overestimation.

A second answer would hold that acting on the basis of a judgement of moral deficiency is disrespectful not because the judgement is false or epistemically unjustified, but because that judgement is at odds with moral equality. Perhaps respect requires that we treat one another as rough moral equals, in the sense of being roughly equally responsive to moral reasons, regardless of whether this is in fact the case. However, more would need to be said about *when* it is disrespectful to act on the basis of a judgement that a person is morally deficient, for intuitively, we often act on the basis of such judgements without violating any moral requirement.

Consider criminal punishments – including detention – that are intended to realise backward-looking objectives, such as retribution, restitution or the communication of social censure. Those who administer such punishments plausibly act on the basis of a judgement – implicit or explicit – that the punished individual is (or at least was) morally deficient. Yet many, including many opponents of preventive detention, accept backward-looking punishment as compatible with respect.

To avoid committing ourselves to the rejection of backward-looking punishment, we could distinguish between acting on the judgement that an individual *has* exhibited a moral deficiency in the past and acting on the judgement that she *will* exhibit moral deficiencies in the future. Perhaps respect requires only that we not act on *predictions* of moral failure – it requires us to take an optimistic stance regarding a person's future moral agency, but not to take a rosy view of their past moral agency.

However, even this view has implausible implications. Suppose that very rich individuals tend to commit more tax fraud than other individuals, partly because they normally have a strong prudential interest in evading taxation, partly because their wealth can often buy them good access to tax evasion strategies and partly because they often became wealthy in part through unscrupulousness that also disposes them to a willingness to evade taxes. For all of these reasons, very rich individuals tend to be less responsive to moral reasons than others when it comes to the payment of taxes. Suppose further that, being aware of this, the state focuses its anti-tax-evasion measures on very rich individuals. Some of these measures seek to engage the rational agency of the very rich – for example, through persuading them to pay their taxes – but others merely seek to exclude certain available routes to tax evasion. In this case, the agents who implement the anti-tax-evasion policy clearly act on the basis of a prediction of moral failure. Yet it is not clear that they disrespect the very rich.

Perhaps it could be said that this targeting of taxation enforcement efforts is consistent with respect because the underlying prediction is narrow in scope – those who implement the targeting predict that the very rich will be morally deficient only in a narrow domain, namely, with respect to tax evasion. Perhaps it is only acting on predictions of *global* moral failure that fall foul of the respect requirement.

However, if this is how we should understand the respect requirement, it is not clear that preventive detention always fails to meet it. Preventive detention may also be imposed on the basis of a predicted *narrow* moral failure. It might, for example, be imposed on the basis that an individual is deemed to be poorly responsive to moral reasons within the realm of sexual conduct.

Alternatively, we could hold that acting on the basis of predicted moral failure is disrespectful only when the prediction is based on factors for which the object of the prediction is not responsible (in such cases, we might aptly characterise the prediction as *unfair*). The predictions that underpin typical cases of preventive detention are often unfair in this sense. They are often based in part on demographic variables, such as age and sex, for which the detained individual is not responsible. By contrast, the prediction that is operant in the tax evasion case is based on a factor – being very rich – for which people generally *are* responsible. Perhaps this explains why there is not disrespect in the tax evasion case.

However, if our ultimate worry is with acting on the basis of *unfair* predictions of moral failure, then there is again no reason to suppose that preventive detention will *always* raise the worry. Whether it does will depend on the particular case. In some cases, preventive detention is grounded on factors such as past conduct or declared plans, for which the detained individual is responsible.

Finally, yet another suggestion would be that acting on the basis of a prediction of moral failure is disrespectful only when it also seriously harms or intrudes upon the person in whom the moral failure is predicted. Preventive detention plausibly involves serious harms and intrusions; anti-tax-evasion strategies may involve neither.

The problem with this suggestion, it seems to me, it is that it is simply not clear why the degree of harm or intrusion should be relevant to whether acting on the basis of a prediction of moral failure is disrespectful. The understanding of disrespect that I have been exploring is one in which disrespect arises from the judgements that motivate an action. Disrespectful treatment is disrespectful because of the motivations it manifests. It is not clear why, on this sort of view, the severity of the effects of the action should matter.

Perhaps there is some way of accommodating the intuition that the tax evasion case satisfies the respect requirement, despite the prediction of moral failure that it involves, without also generating the result that preventive detention also, at least in some cases, satisfies the requirement. However, I am at a loss as to how this might be done. I thus provisionally conclude that the appeal to the respect requirement, at least on the formulations of it that I have considered here, is unable to establish Hard Moral Difference.

VI. Concluding Thoughts

I have considered six arguments for Hard Moral Difference. I have argued that none succeed in sustaining that view and have sought thereby to undermine, or at least diminish the credibility of, Hard Moral Difference.

Still, several of the arguments that I have considered might, either independently or jointly, support a restricted version of Hard Moral Difference. For example, they might support Soft Moral Difference, according to which preventive detention is *typically* more problematic, in some respects, than quarantine. The interesting question then becomes: when is it more problematic and in what respects exactly? My discussion suggests a number of considerations that will be relevant here. First, there are those considerations surveyed briefly in section III above. Preventive detention may in some cases produce smaller social benefits than quarantine, or be more stigmatising, self-fulfilling or inequality-promoting. Second, there are the factors discussed in section V. In some cases, predictive detention may be disrespectful, in a way that quarantine is not, because it is based on an overestimation of the detainee's moral failings or on a prediction of moral failure that is unfair in the sense that it is based on factors for which the detained individual is not responsible.

What is the practical payoff of my discussion? Insofar as I have succeeded in clarifying the moral differences and similarities between preventive detention and quarantine, I hope that my discussion may point to ways in which the ethical assessment of preventive detention could be fruitfully informed by existing discussions of quarantine. With a few notable exceptions, discussions of the ethics of quarantine and the ethics of preventive detention have, so far as I can see, taken largely separate courses. My discussion suggests that there might be benefits to bringing them closer together.

More specifically, my arguments may, if successful, pose a substantive challenge to opponents of preventive detention, though showing as much is beyond the scope of this chapter. If I have succeeded in undermining Hard Moral Difference, this may support attempts to extrapolate arguments for quarantine into the sphere of criminal justice, so as to generate arguments in favour of preventive detention. But even if it turns out that Hard Moral Difference holds – for example, because I have missed some argument that might be invoked in its defence – my discussion may put pressure on some particular arguments against preventive detention. For example, it may suggest that some desert-based arguments against preventive detention also count equally strongly against intuitively permissible forms of quarantine. This may present the proponents of these arguments with a dilemma: either drop the arguments or accept a counter-intuitive position on quarantine.

My arguments may also suggest that conclusions regarding *when* and *how* quarantine ought to be imposed will carry over to preventive detention. For example, it would normally be thought that quarantine should be implemented in the least harmful and intrusive manner possible (Gostin 2001: 68) and that it should be coupled with treatments for medical conditions by virtue of which the individual poses a risk to the public (Slobogin 2011: 1139–40). Some would also hold that quarantined individuals should be compensated for the harms and restrictions imposed on them (Corrado 1996b: 3, 11; Schoeman 1981: 175, 181). My argument suggests that similar measures might be justified in the case of preventive detention.[16] However, my argument does not on its own establish this, for, as I noted above, it could be held that those subjected to preventive detention have, through their past offending, rendered themselves liable to certain intrusions in a way that those subjected to quarantine have not.

References

Bagger, JP, Zindrou D, and Taylor KM (2004) 'Postoperative Infection with Meticillin-Resistant Staphylococcus Aureus and Socioeconomic Background' 363 *The Lancet* 706.

Caruso, GD (2016) 'Free Will Skepticism and Criminal Behavior: A Public Health-Quarantine Model' 32 *Southwest Philosophy Review* 25.

Childress, JF, Faden, RR, Gaare, RD, Gostin, LO, Kahn, J, Bonnie, RJ, Kass, NE, Mastroianni, AC, Moreno, JD and Nieburg, P (2002) 'Public Health Ethics: Mapping the Terrain' 30 *Journal of Law, Medicine & Ethics* 170.

Corrado, ML (1996a) 'Punishment and the Wild Beast of Prey: The Problem of Preventive Detention' 86 *Journal of Criminal Law and Criminology* 778.

——. (1996b) 'Punishment, Quarantine, and Preventive Detention' 15 *Criminal Justice Ethics* 3.

Douglas, T (2014) 'The Dual-Use Problem, Scientific Isolationism and the Division of Moral Labour' 32 *Monash Bioethics Review* 86.

Duff, RA (2007) *Answering for Crime: Responsibility and Liability in the Criminal Law* (Oxford, Hart Publishing).

European Centre for Disease Prevention and Control (ECDC)/World Health Organization Regional Office for Europe (2013) *Tuberculosis Surveillance and Monitoring in Europe 2013* (Stockholm, ECDC).

Schoeman, FD (1981) 'On Incapacitating the Dangerous' in H Gross and A von Hirsch (eds), *Sentencing* (Oxford, Oxford University Press).

Gavaghan, C, Snelling, J and McMillan, J (2014) *Better and Better and Better? A Legal and Ethical Analysis of Preventive Detention in New Zealand: Report for the New Zealand Law Foundation* (Dunedin, University of Otago).

[16] For an example of how such an argument might go, see Ashworth and Zedner's discussion in ch 8 of this volume of how the case in favour of minimising the harmfulness of quarantine might carry over to the case of preventive detention. For an argument that preventively detained individuals ought to be offered treatment, see Slobogin (2011: 1139–40).

Gostin, LO (2001) *Public Health Law: Power, Duty, Restraint* (Berkeley, University of California Press).
Harcourt, BE (2012) 'Punitive Preventive Justice: A Critique' *Coase-Sandor Working Paper Series in Law and Economics* 599.
Hart, HLA (1968) *Punishment and Responsibility: Essays in the Philosophy of Law* (Oxford, Oxford University Press).
Hoskins, Z (2013) 'Punishment, Contempt, and the Prospect of Moral Reform' 32 *Criminal Justice Ethics*, 1.
Hrivniaková, L, Sláčiková, M and Kolcunová, S (2009) 'Hepatitis A Outbreak in a Roma Village in Eastern Slovakia' *Eurosurveillance* 14.
Kitai-Sangero, R (2009) 'The Limits of Preventive Detention' 40 *McGeorge Law Review* 903.
Klinkenberg, E, Manissero, D, Semenza, JC and Verver, S (2009) 'Migrant Tuberculosis Screening in the EU/EEA: Yield, Coverage and Limitations' 34 *European Respiratory Journal* 1180.
McCloskey, HJ (1972) 'A Non-utilitarian Approach to Punishment' in G Ezorsky (ed), *Philosophical Perspectives on Punishment* (Albany, University of New York Press).
Meyerson, D (2009) 'Risks, Rights, Statistics and Compulsory Measures' 31 *Sydney Law Review* 507.
Morse, SJ (2011) 'Protecting Liberty and Autonomy: Desert/Disease Jurisprudence' 48 *San Diego Law Review* 1077.
Murphy, LB (1999) 'Institutions and the Demands of Justice' 27 *Philosophy & Public Affairs* 251.
Nagel, T (1995) *Equality and Partiality* (New York, Oxford University Press).
Pereboom, D (2014) *Free Will, Agency, and Meaning in Life* (Oxford, Oxford University Press).
Rawls, J (1993) *Political Liberalism* (New York, Columbia University Press).
Scheffler, S (2005) 'Egalitarian Liberalism as Moral Pluralism' 79 *Aristotelian Society Supplementary Volume* 229.
Semenza, JC, Giesecke, J (2008) 'Intervening to Reduce Inequalities in Infections in Europe' 98 *American Journal of Public Health* 787.
Sidhu, DS (2015) 'Moneyball Sentencing' 671 *Boston College Law Review* 672.
Silver, E and Miller, LL (2002) 'A Cautionary Note on the Use of Actuarial Risk Assessment Tools for Social Control' 48 *Crime & Delinquency* 138.
Slobogin, C (2011) 'Prevention as the Primary Goal of Sentencing: The Modern Case for Indeterminate Dispositions in Criminal Cases' 48 *San Diego Law Review* 1127.
Smilansky, S (1994) 'The Time to Punish' 54 *Analysis* 50.
——. (2017) 'Pereboom on Punishment: Funishment, Innocence, Motivation, and Other Difficulties' 11 *Criminal Law and Philosophy* 591.
Twisselmann, B (2000) 'Risk Factors for Meningococcal Disease in Children in the Czech Republic' 4 *Eurosurveillance*.

Van Brakel, WH (2006) 'Measuring Health-Related Stigma: A Literature Review' 11 *Psychology, Health & Medicine* 307.
Von Hirsch, A (1972) 'Prediction of Criminal Conduct and Preventive Confinement of Convicted Persons' 21 *Buffalo Law Review* 717.
——. (1992) 'Proportionality in the Philosophy of Punishment' 16 *Crime and Justice* 55.
Whittle, HJ, Palar, K, Ranadive, NA, Turan, JM, Kushel, M and Weiser, SD (2017) '"The Land of the Sick and the Land of the Healthy": Disability, Bureaucracy, and Stigma Among People Living with Poverty and Chronic Illness in the United States' 190 *Social Science & Medicine* 181.
Williams, CJ, Willocks, LJ, Lake, IR, Hunter, PR (2004) 'Geographic Correlation between Deprivation and Risk of Meningococcal Disease: An Ecological Study' 4 *BMC Public Health*.
Zedner, L (2010) 'Pre-crime and Pre-punishment: A Health Warning' 81 *Criminal Justice Matters* 24.

6

Against Incapacitative Punishment

ZACHARY HOSKINS

I. Introduction

Risk assessment is a widely accepted consideration in criminal sentencing. Many legal systems incorporate assessments of offender riskiness into their sentencing guidelines. The rationale for such assessments is generally grounded in the frequently asserted punitive aim of incapacitation, whereby punishment aims to help reduce the risk of future criminal wrongdoing by removing supposedly dangerous individuals from situations in which they might be a threat to others. In this chapter, I argue that punishing to incapacitate people based on assessments of their riskiness is unjustified. The argument I defend has been gestured at elsewhere (see, eg, Robinson 2001: 1446–47), although as far as I know, it has not been given the extended treatment it receives here. More importantly, to my knowledge the objection has never been successfully answered, which is troubling given the prevalence of risk-based sentencing grounded in the logic of incapacitation.

It is worth highlighting at the outset that my target in this chapter is risk assessment in the service of sentencing, for which incapacitation is the rationale. Considerations of risk reduction may play other roles in criminal punishment; namely, punishment might help to reduce the risk of future criminal offending by serving as a credible deterrent threat to potential offenders, by reinforcing social norms or by helping to reform offenders (see, respectively, Bentham 1996 [1789]: Chapters 13–14; Ewing 1927; Hampton 1984). In each of these cases, punishment aims to reduce the risk of crime and protect public safety by providing compelling reasons for people not to offend (or re-offend): deterrence aims to provide a prudential reason, namely, the onerousness of punishment; norm reinforcement and offender reform instead operate in the currency of moral reasons. The logic of incapacitation, by contrast, does not involve any appeal to reasons, whether prudential or moral; rather than aiming to provide some reason not to θ, incapacitation aims simply to remove θ from the set of options among which the agent is free to choose. For reasons that will become apparent, the argument considered here does not apply to deterrence or, on some accounts, norm reinforcement or offender reform as rationales for punishment. Also, we might accept as a constraining principle that sentences should not be so severe that they tend to increase the risks of future criminal wrongdoing. The argument in this chapter does not address this sort of risk-based constraint.

In what follows, I first set the stage by briefly discussing some common lines of objection to incapacitative sentencing, based on the imprecise nature of risk-assessment tools and the perceived tensions between risk reduction and retributivism. Next, I set out a different argument against incapacitative punishment, one that in my view cuts more deeply than arguments based on concerns about risk-assessment tools or retributivism. After setting out the case against incapacitative punishment, I consider and respond to potential responses that defenders of the practice might offer. Ultimately, I conclude that all but one of these defences is unsuccessful and that the remaining defence succeeds to such a limited extent as to be likely unsatisfying for proponents of incapacitative punishment.

II. Standard Objections

Challenges to incapacitative punishment have commonly taken two general forms. First, many have objected to incapacitative sentencing on the ground that risk assessment is, to say the least, an imperfect science (see, eg, Dubber 1995: 710–11, Zimring and Hawkins 1995: Chapter 5; and Fazel, Chapter 11 in this volume). Historically, risk assessment tools have tended to overpredict the risk of recidivism by a significant margin. For example, a 2012 meta-analysis of 68 studies of commonly used risk-assessment tools found that 59 per cent of people judged to be at moderate or high risk by violence risk-assessment tools did not go on to violently offend; 77 per cent judged to be at moderate or high risk by sexual risk-assessment tools did not go on to sexually offend; and 48 per cent of those rated moderate or high risk by generic risk-assessment tools did not subsequently commit any offence (Fazel et al 2012; see also Fazel, Chapter 11 in this volume; Cohen 1984: especially 270–71; Monahan 1981: 73–80, 101–04; but see Lieb, Quinsey and Berliner 1998: especially 94–100). Setting sentencing levels according to risk-assessment tools that so drastically overpredict riskiness appears unjust, in that it will lead to many offenders' serving sentences longer than the actual risks warrant. However, my focus in this chapter is not on the imperfect science of risk assessment; instead, I focus on the in-principle case against incapacitative sentencing. This line of objection would hold even if, counter-factually, risk-assessment tools were perfectly accurate.

The other most common line of objection to incapacitative punishment focuses on the apparent tensions between *punishment* as a response to prior wrongdoing and *prevention* as concerned with averting future wrongdoing. This general worry manifests in various ways: some critics claim that the concept of incapacitative punishment is incoherent and that punishment cannot be incapacitative because punishment is for a past crime, whereas incapacitative detention or other measures are concerned solely with preventing future wrongdoing (see, eg, Robinson 2001: 1432; Slobogin 2003: 12). This objection essentially aims to define away the problem, a move Hart (1959–60: 5) termed the 'definitional stop'. But as Hart recognised, we should be wary of attempts to settle normative debates by appeals to definition (1959–60: 5–6). The argument I offer below is not that incapacitative treatment cannot *constitute* punishment; rather, I contend that the rationale of incapacitation cannot *justify* punishment.

Others object that the aim of incapacitation will often prescribe sentences that violate the commonly accepted desert-based proportionality constraint – that sentences should be no more (and perhaps, no less) severe than is deserved given the seriousness of the crime and the offender's culpability (see, eg, Robinson 2001: 1438–41; and Ryberg, Chapter 4 in this volume). Again, the worry here is that the rationale of incapacitation is purely forward-looking, whereas the desert-based proportionality principle is concerned with the relationship of the sentence to the prior crime to which it responds. And although it is of course possible that an offender might suddenly cease being dangerous at just the same time that he completes a deserved term of punishment, this would be merely a coincidence. When concerns of dangerousness and desert do not align, the rationale of incapacitation will prescribe apparent violations of the desert-based proportionality principle.

This worry is, I think, less problematic than it might at first appear. Hybrid theorists, at least, have a number of responses available. They might regard desert-based proportionality as asymmetrical, setting an upper limit, but not a lower limit on sentencing severity (see, eg, Armstrong 1961: 486–87; Corlett 2001: 78). Beneath the ceiling set by desert, sentences could then vary depending on considerations of risk. Alternatively, they might endorse 'limiting retributivism', according to which there is not a specific deserved sentence for each crime, but rather a range of not clearly undeserved sentences (see, eg, Frase 2013; Morris 1974; Morris and Tonry 1990). Within this range of not clearly undeserved sentencing options, considerations of incapacitation might play a role in determining precise sentence levels. Or there might be other ways of reconciling considerations of incapacitation and desert. For those who believe, as I do, that any successful justificatory account of punishment will need to incorporate various moral values, there will always be questions of how to resolve potential tensions among these values. The devil is in the detail, of course, and we must assess pluralistic accounts as we find them, but in my view, the inevitable existence of such tensions does not pose an insurmountable challenge to hybrid theories generally or, in particular, to theories that integrate considerations of incapacitation and retribution. At any rate, the argument that follows is not grounded in the challenges of integrating forward-looking and backward-looking elements into a unified theory.

III. The Case against Incapacitative Punishment

A justificatory theory of punishment must answer a number of questions, but among the most crucial are these two: why is punishment justifiable in principle and what sentences are justified in particular cases? The answers to these questions will vary depending on what rationale we cite for the practice and on what constraining principles we endorse. As Hart wrote, 'in relation to any social institution, after stating what general aim or value its maintenance fosters we should enquire whether there are any and if so what principles limiting the unqualified pursuit of that aim or value' (Hart 1959–60: 8).[1] I want to focus on the question of punishment's rationale. A compelling rationale is a necessary condition, albeit not a sufficient one, of punishment's justification. Essentially, the case against incapacitation as a rationale for punishment is that it is unable either to ground an answer to the question of punishment's in-principle justification or to provide appropriate guidance about sentence severity in particular cases.

First, consider the question of why punishment is justifiable in principle. Importantly, in order to answer this question, we need to be clear about what we are aiming to justify. Criminal punishment, on common characterisations, is a burdensome response to criminal wrongdoing, imposed by a legal authority on the supposed perpetrator of the wrongdoing. But punishment is not merely burdensome, it is also *intentionally* burdensome. In this respect, punishment is distinctive as a state institution. Other state practices, such as taxation, licensing fees, or the construction of airports or major highways near residential areas, will often be burdensome. But typically, it is not the aim of such practices to burden those subject to them. This is not to say that legislators might not levy a new tax with the intention of harming those subject to it, but the standard purpose of taxation, to generate revenue to fund public goods, does not require that those subject to taxation are burdened by this. The same is true of licensing fees or major building projects near residential areas.

Punishment, however, is different. Punishment's burdensomeness is not merely incidental to the practice; it is essential to it (Benn 1985: 8). This conceptual point has important normative implications, as it helps to illuminate the distinctive moral challenge presented by punishment. As David Boonin writes:

> It is one thing to justify the claim that it is morally permissible for the state to act in various ways while foreseeing that so acting will cause some of its citizens to suffer

[1] Hart referred to what I have termed punishment's rationale as its 'general justifying aim'. I think his phrasing is unfortunate in two respects. First, the term 'aim' may seem to privilege consequentialist rather than retributivist answers to this question, whereas in fact punishment's compelling rationale may be a retributivist one. Second, characterising the aim as 'justifying' may suggest that the aim itself is sufficient to justify the practice, whereas in fact, whether punishment is justified will depend not only on there being a compelling rationale for the practice, but also on punishment's not violating the rights of those punished or whatever other constraints we take to govern the practice.

> (eg, changing the speed limit, modifying air pollution standards, imposing new regulations, raising taxes, or conscripting soldiers, all of which cause harm to a significant number of people). It is quite another to justify the claim that it is morally permissible for the state to act in various ways *in order that* some of its citizens will suffer. Yet, this is precisely what must be justified in order to justify punishment. (Boonin 2008: 16)

A normative account of punishment, then, is not merely an attempt to justify burdensome state treatment of some of its members; it is an attempt to justify *intentionally* burdensome treatment. And as I have discussed before, a necessary condition in the justification of such treatment is that there is some sufficiently compelling rationale.[2]

Deterrence, retribution and, on some accounts, norm reinforcement or offender reform are rationales geared towards justifying intentionally burdensome treatment of offenders. The logic of deterrence requires that punishment be onerous, so that the threat of punishment may be effective at dissuading potential offenders from carrying out their crimes (but see Hanna 2014).[3] Meting out retribution for wrongdoing also requires that punishment be burdensome, as retributivists believe offenders deserve some form of hard treatment (or deserve censure that is communicated by hard treatment). And on at least some norm reinforcement or offender reform accounts, the onerousness of punishment plays a crucial role in spurring the community or the offender himself to consider the wrongfulness of the offender's conduct (on punishment's role in societal norm reinforcement, see Andenaes (1974); on its role in spurring offender reflection and reform, see, eg, Duff (2001): especially 106–12; or Hampton (1984)). In each of these cases, the burdensomeness of punishment is necessary to its achieving its ends. And as Kant reminds us, to intend some end rationally commits us to intending the necessary means to that end (Kant 1996 [1785]: 70). Thus, insofar as we set, say, deterrence as our end, we are rationally committed to intending the burdensome means necessary to achieve that end. The same is true of retribution and some norm reinforcement or offender reform accounts. And if setting these ends rationally commits us to intending the burdensome means necessary to achieving them, then these ends are at least the right kinds of rationales to figure in a justification

[2] It is important to distinguish the task of justifying a state's intentionally acting in burdensome ways from the task of justifying its acting in intentionally burdensome ways. The distinction matters, as a state may intentionally act in ways that are only foreseeably burdensome to its members (eg, through taxation or licensing fees). But what is distinctive about punishment is that it is not just the state's act that is intended, but also the burdensomeness of the act.

[3] One might argue that the burdensomeness needed for deterrence is not intended, but merely foreseeable. After all, if the deterrent threat were perfectly effective, no punishment would ever be imposed; it is only when the deterrent threat is not perfectly effective that punishment will foreseeably be inflicted. Thus, the burdens associated with punishment are foreseen but not intended. I have previously endorsed this line of argument (Hoskins 2011: 372–73, drawing on Benn 1958: 330). However, I now believe this was a mistake. Even if, in issuing a deterrent threat, the state does not intend the burdens that ultimately befall those who do not heed the threat, it remains the case that in actually imposing the sentences themselves, the state intends these to be burdensome so that they will function to maintain the credible deterrent threat.

of punishment as an intentionally burdensome practice. This is not to say that any of these ends is ultimately successful as a rationale for punishment, just that each is at least the right kind of rationale for the job, given the nature of what they aim to justify.

The rationale of incapacitating supposedly dangerous individuals, by contrast, is not the right sort of rationale to serve in a justification of punishment. This is because setting incapacitation as an end does not rationally commit us to intending that the means of incapacitation be burdensome. Confinement of a dangerous person, for example, is not made possible, or even more effective, by its being burdensome. The state could in principle incapacitate people effectively, even if the conditions of confinement were so pleasant that neither offenders nor members of the public generally viewed being confined as burdensome. Of course, in practice, incapacitation typically will be burdensome. But as with taxation or licensing fees, the aim of incapacitating dangerous people does not require that this be burdensome for them. Thus, the rationale of incapacitation, unlike the rationales of deterrence or retribution, does not justify intending that the measures be burdensome. Although incapacitation is the right kind of rationale to serve as part of a justification of foreseeably burdensome involuntary confinement or other liberty restrictions, it is not the right kind of rationale to justify *intentionally* burdensome treatment, ie, punishment.

Perhaps, though, incapacitation could still function as an important consideration in sentencing, even if punishment's in-principle permissibility is supported by some other rationales – desert, deterrence, norm reinforcement, offender reform or something else – that are suitable as justifications of intentionally burdensome treatment. In other words, perhaps we can separate the question of whether (and why) punishment is permissible from the question of how (or how severely) we may punish in particular cases, and considerations of incapacitation can figure in our answer to the second question. Hart (1959–60), Rawls (1955), Ross (1930: 56–64) and others (see, eg, Byrd 1989; Scheid 1997) have offered hybrid theories of punishment that distinguish various questions and answer them according to different moral or political considerations. If we accept a hybrid theory of punishment along the lines of those endorsed by these scholars, then considerations of incapacitation may yet have a role to play in sentencing.

In my view, a hybrid approach is the most promising strategy for developing a satisfactory justification of punishment (see Hoskins 2018: 88–92). But such a strategy does not pave the way for legitimate appeal to considerations of incapacitation in sentencing. To see why, suppose our answer to the second question above – of how severely we may punish in particular cases – is to appeal to a version of limiting retributivism, so that within the range of not clearly undeserved sentences available in a given case, we are free to appeal to other considerations in setting precise sentencing levels. Suppose also that there are two offenders, Stan and Oliver, who have been found guilty of the same type of conduct, with the same degree of culpability, and thus their cases fall within the same range of not clearly undeserved sentences. Our best risk-assessment models suggest that Oliver is more dangerous than Stan, and so we sentence Oliver on the high end and Stan on the low end of the range of not clearly undeserved sentences. When Oliver complains about this state of affairs, we first try to appease him by pointing out that his sentence is at least not clearly undeserved. However, his concern is with why he is being punished more severely than Stan. We explain to him that we regard him as a greater risk than Stan. 'No, no', Oliver responds. 'You've misunderstood the question. I'm not asking why I'm being confined for longer than Stan. I'm asking why I'm being *punished* for longer.'

Oliver recognises, as we have seen, that punishment is not merely burdensome treatment, but *intentionally* burdensome treatment, and he is asking what justifies our inflicting this additional intentionally burdensome treatment on him, but not on Stan. Even if neither his nor Stan's sentence is clearly undeserved, we might still expect (as Oliver might reasonably expect) some explanation of what justifies the discrepancy in the severity of intentionally burdensome treatment in the two cases. Incapacitation is poorly suited as an answer to this question, because the rationale of incapacitation cannot justify the infliction of intended burdens.

By contrast, considerations of deterrence would be the right sorts of considerations to ground sentencing disparities within the not clearly undeserved range recommended in particular cases by limiting retributivism. Suppose Oliver is punished somewhat more severely than Stan (within the not clearly undeserved range) because, unlike Oliver, Stan is no serious threat to re-offend and thus is not in need of specific deterrence, or perhaps because Oliver's case is a higher-profile case and has more potential for general deterrent impact. Setting aside whether such sentencing disparities would be justified, my point is just that deterrence is the right sort of consideration to justify what needs to be justified here; namely, a disparity in intentionally burdensome measures. Because maintaining a credible deterrent threat requires that there be some undesirable consequence to offending and because intending the ends rationally commits us to intending the necessary means, the rationale of deterrence is at least the right sort of consideration to appeal to in answering Oliver's question about why he receives more severe intentionally burdensome treatment than does Stan. The same is true of the rationale of retribution and, at least on some accounts, norm reinforcement or offender reform.

The relevant point is that the objection that incapacitation is not a proper rationale for punishment cannot be met by answering the in-principle justification question with some other consideration (desert, rights forfeiture, deterrence etc) and then integrating the rationale of incapacitation into the sentencing scheme. Whatever work this rationale does within such a scheme to differentiate sentences in various cases will be unjustified because, as we have seen, incapacitation cannot justify intentionally burdensome treatment. Notice, too, that this objection cannot be avoided by characterising incapacitation as a *constraining* consideration rather than as a positive rationale, on sentencing within the not clearly undeserved range (ie, sentences should be no less severe than is necessary to incapacitate). To the extent that such a constraining principle ever actually has the effect of ruling out less severe sentences in favour of more severe sentences – that is, insofar as the principle has any bite at all – the state will thereby be inflicting a degree of intentionally burdensome treatment on people without any justification for intending that the treatment be burdensome.

The rationale of incapacitation is thus unsuited as an answer to the question of whether punishment is justified in principle, and it fares no better as a basis for sentencing guidance in particular cases. I conclude, then, that incapacitative punishment, driven by assessments of an offender's riskiness going forward, is unjustifiable. In the next section, I consider various possible responses to the line of objection I have developed here.

IV. Defences of Incapacitative Punishment

Given the objection to incapacitative punishment offered in the previous section, what might be said in defence of the rationale of incapacitation? In this section, I consider various possibilities. First, one might object that rather than characterising punishment as involving burdens, we should instead think of it as involving restrictions of liberty. The rationale of incapacitation may not require burdensome treatment (and thus cannot justify intended burdens), but it does require restrictions of certain liberties: the freedoms of movement and association, for example. Thus incapacitation does appear to be the right kind of rationale to justify punishment characterised as an intentionally liberty-restricting practice. The problem with this objection is that although criminal sentences typically involve restrictions of liberty, it is by virtue of their being burdensome that these restrictions constitute punishment. If the state's response to crime was to restrict liberties in a way that no one regarded as burdensome (perhaps because the liberties were highly unlikely to be exercised anyway or because the restrictions were offset by generous forms of compensation), then it seems unlikely that we would regard such a response as punishment. By contrast, if the state's response to crime was to inflict burdensome treatment so quickly or suddenly (perhaps an unexpected punch to an offender's abdomen) that we could not construe this to restrict the offender's liberty in any way, then this nonetheless intuitively would seem to constitute punishment. I conclude, then, that although actual state impositions of punishment will typically restrict liberties and be burdensome, it is by virtue of the burdensomeness, not the liberty restrictions, that they constitute punishment. Thus, the objection that punishment is about liberty restrictions, not burdensome treatment, and that incapacitation is the right sort of rationale to figure in a justification of liberty-restricting treatment fails.

One might instead maintain, contrary to what I have said above, that punishment is not *intentionally* burdensome. If justifying punishment merely requires justifying a burdensome legal response to crime rather than an intentionally burdensome response, then perhaps the rationale of incapacitation is fit for the job after all. It is difficult to know exactly what to say in response to this objection.

I could point out that acceptance of the intentionality feature is widespread among punishment theorists. To take just a few examples, Burgh (1982: 193) writes that punishment involves 'the deliberate and intentional infliction of suffering'. Lucas (1968: 207) states: 'Punishments … not only are unwelcome but are intended to be, and would lose their point if they were not.' Boonin (2008: 14) writes that 'the punisher intends to harm the recipient of the punishment and does not merely foresee it'. Stephenson (1990: 229) states that an intention of punishment is 'to make [the offender] suffer for having broken the law'. Duff (2001: xiv) describes the typical case of punishment as 'something intended to be burdensome or painful'. And Husak (2011: 1189) writes that 'state sanctions do not qualify as punishments because they *happen* to impose deprivations and stigmatize their recipients. The very *purpose* of a punitive state sanction is to inflict a stigmatizing deprivation on the offender'. But if someone nevertheless contends that this common conception of punishment is the wrong one and that the accurate conception does not involve the intendedness of the burdens, what may be said in response?

I could perhaps also point out that the intentionality feature is crucial to distinguishing punishment from other possible burdensome legal responses to criminal wrongdoing. For example, a state might respond to a burglary by confiscating the offender's ill-gotten goods and returning them to their rightful owner. Or if the goods could not be returned, it might require the offender to offer material compensation to his victim in some other way. The state might also commit the offender to a course of rehabilitative treatment. Any of these legal responses to the burglary would be burdensome. However, it seems intuitively clear that the state could respond in these ways without thereby punishing the offender. The reason is that the burdens associated with these responses, although they may be foreseeable, are not essential to the respective rationales. Thus intending to return ill-gotten goods to their owners, to require offenders to make restitution to their victims or to rehabilitate offenders does not rationally commit us to intending that these measures be burdensome.

I maintain, then, that punishment is intended to be burdensome and that recognising this feature of punishment allows us to distinguish the practice from other types of burdensome legal responses to crime. A critic might respond, I suppose, that punishment is neither intentionally burdensome nor distinct from these other types of responses, because these responses in fact constitute forms of punishment.[4] Alternatively, he might insist that punishment is not intentionally burdensome and that some other feature of punishment distinguishes it from other burdensome legal responses to crime. The most obvious other feature to cite is that punishment is intended to express societal condemnation or censure

[4] For an argument that compulsory victim restitution constitutes punishment, see Cholbi (2010: especially 89–92). A full response to Cholbi's account is beyond the scope of this chapter, but it is worth noting that his most plausible argument for his thesis is that compulsory victim restitution *is* in fact intentionally burdensome. This argument concedes the intentionality feature of punishment.

(see Feinberg 1970). One problem with citing this alternative feature as the basis for distinguishing punishment from other responses is that many accounts that endorse this expressivist feature regard punishment's burdensomeness as necessary to convey adequately the censure. M Margaret Falls offers an explanation typical of expressivist accounts:

> Just as calmly telling a friend she ought not to have lied to us communicates neither the pain she has caused nor our unqualified insistence that we not be so treated, so the state's verbal or written reprimand with attached explanation would be inadequate … Thus, subjection to 'hard treatment' (Feinberg's term), whether it be temporary exclusion from a close friendship or isolation from society, is in no way incidental to holding persons accountable. (Falls 1987: 42–43; see also, eg, Duff 2001: 29–30; and Hampton 1992: 12; but see Hanna 2008)

Insofar as some sort of onerous treatment is necessary to convey the condemnatory message, then intending to convey the censure rationally commits the state to intending that the treatment be onerous. It is possible, of course, that other accounts might endorse condemnatory responses to crime that are not intentionally burdensome. I am sceptical that such responses would much resemble common conceptions of punishment. But I readily concede that my argument in this chapter would have no purchase against a legal practice of condemnation that is not intentionally burdensome.

Another possible response to my objection to incapacitative punishment would be to accept that punishment is intentionally burdensome, but then to argue that incapacitation *is* at least in some cases intentionally burdensome. If this is the case, then the rationale of incapacitation may after all be the right sort of rationale to justify intentionally burdensome treatment. Doug Husak contends that at least with respect to the prevention of serious crimes such as terrorism, it is reasonable to think that incapacitative detention is intended to be onerous. For persons 'who pose dangers of megaterrorism', he writes: 'Surely the state *has* a punitive intention in preventively detaining these individuals. Few of us would be receptive to a device to prevent megaterrorists from causing enormous destruction that spares them from both deprivation and stigma' (Husak 2011: 1190).

A couple of things are worth noting in response to Husak's argument here. First, notice that his use of the term 'megaterrorist' is unhelpful insofar as it suggests someone who is already guilty of terrorism on a massive scale rather than someone who might commit terrorist acts in the future. Just as a person is not a murderer until he murders someone, a person is not a megaterrorist until he commits acts of large-scale terrorism. Insofar as Husak's example evokes the intuition he has in mind, namely that the megaterrorist's detention would be intended as burdensome and stigmatising, we should ask whether this intention is tied to the incapacitative aim or whether another, retributive intuition is lurking here as well: his detention should be onerous because he is a megaterrorist, and megaterrorists do not deserve a light touch. If this is the case, then the detention in Husak's example is not merely preventive but also retributive, and it seems that it is more likely the retributivism rather than the incapacitative aim that is responsible for the intended burdensomeness. This would be consistent with maintaining that mere incapacitation is not a punitive rationale, because incapacitation does not require burdensome treatment.[5]

However, suppose that incapacitation can be a punitive aim insofar as merely incapacitative detention may be intended to be burdensome. My argument above does not depend on the claim that incapacitation cannot be intentionally burdensome and thus constitute punishment. Rather, whereas Husak in the cited passage is offering an argument about whether incapacitative detention fits within our conception of punishment, my thesis is normative rather than conceptual: the rationale of incapacitation is not the right sort of rationale to justify intentionally burdensome treatment. So even if confinement with the central (or sole) aim of incapacitation is in some cases intentionally burdensome, this fact does not undermine my contention that this intentionally burdensome treatment will not be justified as incapacitation. Again, the rationale of incapacitation may be able to justify confining someone, but it cannot justify intentionally making the confinement burdensome.

Still, one might object that I have employed exactly the strategy I criticised earlier, namely, appeal to the so-called 'definitional stop'.[6] Essentially, this strategy is an attempt to settle normative debate by definitional stipulation. Hart (1959–60) critiques the use of the definitional stop as a response to the objection that utilitarian accounts of punishment might not be able to rule out punishment of the innocent. Some scholars (eg, Quinton 1954; and Benn 1958: 332) responded to this objection by insisting that punishment, by definition, is only of the guilty; thus, punishment of the innocent would be, by definition, impossible. Hart writes that 'here the wrong reply is: That, by definition, would not be "punishment" and it is the justification of punishment which is in issue' (1959–60: 5). One might object that my argument similarly attempts to resolve a normative question through definitional fiat. After all, I have defended the normative claim that incapacitation is not a legitimate aim of punishment by appeal to a particular element of the definition of punishment (that punishment is intentionally burdensome). Is my argument thus similarly guilty of the definitional stop?

Note that objections to the definitional stop, if they are to have any force, cannot merely be objections to appeals to definition in the context of normative discourse. In particular, if our question is whether some practice is justified, it is surely important to be clear about what it is that we are seeking to justify. The distinctive features of the practice are thus relevant. Instead, the definitional stop, as used in response to the punishing-the-innocent objection, is problematic in two respects. First, many theorists dispute the claim that punishment is only of the guilty (see, eg, Champlin 1976: 85; and Ten 1987: 16). Rather than merely

[5] I argue for this view in Hoskins (forthcoming: ch 2).

[6] In particular, I thank Jesper Ryberg for pushing me on this point.

stipulating this point, it is one that must be supported by arguments. Second, even if punishment is only of the guilty, this does not save utilitarian accounts from the objection that they may permit (or even require) onerous legal treatment of innocent people in the wake of crimes, but under some other name. In other words, if the challenge to utilitarian views is that they might permit unjust burdensome treatment of innocent individuals if the benefits (in terms of deterrence, for example) were sufficiently great, it is hardly a satisfactory response to assert that such treatment would not properly be labelled 'punishment' (see Boonin 2008: 44).

My objection to incapacitative punishment, as I have said, is not that incapacitation cannot constitute punishment, but rather that the rationale of incapacitation cannot justify punishment. It is true that my central argument trades on a particular feature of punishment: not that it is only of the guilty, but that it is intentionally burdensome. But I do not claim that incapacitation cannot be intentionally burdensome; rather, I contend that we cannot rely on the aim of incapacitation as justification for imposing onerous legal measures with the intention that they be onerous. I have defended what I take to be the commonly held notion that punishment is intended to be burdensome. But if others want to insist that this is not so, my thesis can be restated this way: intentionally burdensome state responses to crime cannot be justified by appeal to the rationale of incapacitation.

Another sort of argument in favour of incapacitative punishment might appeal to practical, public safety concerns. Protecting members of the public from dangerous offenders requires that we integrate risk assessments into sentencing practices. This is essentially to appeal to necessity: incapacitative punishment is a necessary means to securing the valuable public safety ends. Necessity here might be construed in different ways. Understood as the claim that incapacitative punishment is the *only* way to achieve the public safety ends, the claim is straightforwardly false. Non-punitive incapacitation is another means of achieving the same ends. Construing the necessity claim instead as holding that incapacitative punishment is the *most effective* way to achieve the public safety ends fares no better. There is no plausible reason to believe that incapacitation is more effective insofar as it is intended to be burdensome. Some theorists, particularly in the just war literature, instead construe the necessity condition as a requirement that there be *no less burdensome means* available to secure a given aim (see McMahan 2013–14: 2–3).[7] The claim that incapacitation through punishment is necessary for public safety clearly fails on this construal of necessity too, unless one is prepared to argue that, *ceteris paribus*, intentionally burdensome treatment will typically be less burdensome than unintentionally burdensome treatment. In fact, exactly the opposite appears more likely to be the case: if the state imposes burdensome treatment intending it to be burdensome, we should expect such

[7] This least-burdensome-means principle is essentially equivalent to the principle of parsimony, which is often cited by sentencing scholars: see, eg, Frase (2013: especially 32).

treatment to be, *ceteris paribus*, more burdensome than treatment imposed without this intention. I conclude, then, that even if certain forms of offender confinement or other restrictive measures are needed to keep supposedly dangerous people away from vulnerable members of the public, such measures need not be intentionally burdensome to serve this end – that is, they need not constitute punishment.

Perhaps, though, relying on non-punitive measures such as civil confinement rather than incapacitative punishment would lead to abuses, as the state could subject citizens to long periods of confinement or other burdensome restrictions without being constrained by due process protections that limit the scope of criminal punishment. As an illustration of this concern, Sexually Violent Predator (SVP) laws in many US states allow for the extended incapacitative detention of people well after they have completed their formal sentences. Courts have tended to defer to legislative claims that these measures are civil rather than criminal measures. As a result, those subject to SVP laws have been denied certain legal protections that are afforded to individuals subject to criminal prosecution and punishment. To give one example, whereas criminal defendants considering a guilty plea have a legal right to be notified of the range of criminal sentences they could face as a result, they are not legally entitled to be informed of the additional, potentially permanent civil confinement they may also face due to SVP laws (see, eg, Janus 2013; and Roberts 2008). If we take seriously concerns about non-punitive incapacitation's potential to sprawl in terms of its duration or scope with inadequate legal constraints on its implementation, then maybe incapacitative punishment is after all a less burdensome means of protecting public safety.

The problem with this line of argument is that it creates a false dichotomy between, on the one hand, civil incapacitative measures as they are often administered in current legal practice and, on the other hand, incapacitative punishment. Although incapacitative measures in current practice are often inadequately constrained by various due process protections, things need not be this way. Protections such as the notification requirement could be extended to apply to civil incapacitative measures as well as to criminal sentences. In my view, such civil measures would be a less burdensome means than incapacitative punishment of achieving the public safety ends.

A related argument claims that integrating incapacitation into punishment allows for retributivist, desert-based proportionality considerations to constrain the duration and severity of incapacitative measures. One might be tempted to respond to this concern in the same way as to the concern about notification requirements or other due process protections: we could simply incorporate retributivist proportionality constraints into civil incapacitative measures as well as criminal sentences. However, I think we should reject this response with respect to retributivist proportionality constraints. Retributivist proportionality is concerned with the relationship between sentence severity and the seriousness of the prior offence and one's degree of culpability. The rationale of incapacitation suggests a different proportionality consideration; namely, the restrictiveness of the incapacitative measure should be proportionate to the degree of harm it is likely to avert. Thus, retributivist proportionality is the wrong sort of proportionality to govern risk-reductive incapacitative measures. Besides, considerations of retributivist desert can cut both ways: they might help to protect against excessively severe incapacitative civil measures, but they might instead motivate incapacitative civil measures that are harsher than would be required to achieve the incapacitative aims. Thus, I suggest that we should keep considerations of retributivist desert out of incapacitative civil measures.

Finally, one might respond to my argument that there is still a role for the rationale of incapacitation to play in determining the appropriate mode of punishment, if not the appropriate severity. Sentencing theorists typically focus on how to determine what severity of sentence is appropriate in particular cases. Much less attention has been paid to the question of what mode, or form, that punishment should take. Here, rather than asking whether one year or 20 years in prison is the appropriate term of punishment, we should ask whether prison is the right form of punishment at all rather than, say, fines, community service or something else. Perhaps in considering two candidate sentences of (as best we can determine) roughly equal severity but different modes – for example, a short jail term or a very heavy financial penalty – incapacitative interests might provide a justification for choosing the mode of punishment more likely to keep the supposedly dangerous person away from vulnerable populations.

Here, I think, we have at last a permissible role for considerations of incapacitation within sentencing decisions. I have argued throughout that the rationale of incapacitation cannot justify the infliction of intended burdens. But in the case at hand, incapacitation is not playing this role. Rather, the intentionally burdensome treatment must be justified entirely on other grounds; incapacitation is only giving us a reason to choose this otherwise-justified form of treatment over that otherwise-justified form of treatment. A justification of the choice of one intentionally burdensome form of treatment over another intentionally (and equally) burdensome form of treatment is not itself a justification of intentionally burdensome treatment. Thus, appeal to incapacitative interests in this way does not run afoul of the argument I have defended in this chapter. It also does not, as far as I can tell, run afoul of the other objections to incapacitative punishment that I briefly canvassed at the start of the chapter.

However, I should stress how limited a space this carves out for considerations of incapacitation in sentencing decisions. Incapacitation is only appropriate as, essentially, a tie-breaker between multiple approximately equally severe modes of punishment. It cannot justify a prison term instead of a fine when the prison term is, by our best estimates, clearly more severe than the fine. This would be to subject the offender to a higher quantum of intentionally burdensome treatment based on a rationale unsuited to justifying intentionally burdensome treatment. For proponents of incapacitative punishment, the admission of considerations of incapacitation into sentencing only to decide between multiple equally severe modes of punishment will probably seem an insufficient role for incapacitation to play in sentencing. But any role beyond this is, I contend, unjustifiable.

V. Conclusion

One question raised by the preceding account is whether it is enough that incapacitative measures are not intended to be burdensome or whether they should also be intended not to be burdensome. In other words, could non-punitive incapacitation be justified if it was imposed with indifference to the foreseeable burdens it would create? Adherence to the least-burdensome-alternative principle discussed earlier would seem to suggest that these measures should be intended to be no more burdensome than is required by their incapacitative rationale, insofar as incapacitative measures that are intended to be no more burdensome than their end requires are more likely *actually to be* no more burdensome than is required. One way, of course, to reduce the inevitable burdensomeness of incapacitative measures would be to compensate those subject to them in various ways. Determining whether compensation is appropriate for supposedly dangerous people who are incapacitated, and if so what form the compensation should take and what degree of compensation is justifiable, is beyond the scope of this chapter (see de Keijser 2011: 202–03). Here I merely gesture at this issue as worthy of further consideration.

I have contended that incapacitative punishment is unjustifiable because the rationale of incapacitation is the wrong sort of consideration to justify the infliction of intended burdens. Thus, the rationale of incapacitation is unsuited to justifying the institution of punishment in general and also unsuited to grounding sentencing decisions in particular cases. Instead, incapacitative measures should be treated separately, as foreseeably but not intentionally burdensome civil measures aimed at protecting members of the public.

References

Andenaes, J (1974) *Punishment and Deterrence* (Ann Arbor, University of Michigan Press).

Armstrong, KG (1961) 'The Retributivist Hits Back' 70 *Mind* 471.

Benn, SI (1958) 'An Approach to the Problems of Punishment' 33 *Philosophy* 325.

——. (1985) 'Punishment' in J Murphy (ed), *Punishment and Rehabilitation*, 2nd edn (Belmont, Wadsworth).

Bentham, J (1996 [1789]) *An Introduction to the Principles of Morals and Legislation*. Reprinted in JH Burns and HLA Hart (eds), *The Collected Works of Jeremy Bentham: An Introduction to the Principles of Morals and Legislation* (Oxford, Clarendon Press).

Boonin, D (2008) *The Problem of Punishment* (New York, Cambridge University Press).

Burgh, R (1982) 'Do the Guilty Deserve Punishment?' 79 *Journal of Philosophy* 193.

Byrd, BS (1989) 'Kant's Theory of Punishment: Deterrence in its Threat, Retribution in its Execution' 8 *Law and Philosophy* 151.

Champlin, TS (1976) 'Punishment without Offence' 13 *American Philosophical Quarterly* 85.

Cholbi, M (2010) 'Compulsory Victim Restitution is Punishment: A Reply to Boonin' 2 *Public Reason* 85.

Cohen, J (1984) 'Selective Incapacitation: An Assessment' 2 *University of Illinois Law Review*: 253.

Corlett, JA (2001) 'Making Sense of Retributivism' 76 *Philosophy* 77.

De Keijser, JW (2011) 'Never Mind the Pain, It's a Measure! Justifying Measures as Part of the Dutch Bifurcated System of Sanctions' in M Tonry (ed), *Retributivism Has a Past: Has it a Future?* (Oxford, Oxford University Press).

Dubber, MD (1995) 'Recidivist Statutes as Arational Punishment' 43 *Buffalo Law Review* 689.

Duff, RA (2001) *Punishment, Communication, and Community* (Oxford, Oxford University Press).

Ewing, AC (1927) 'Punishment as Moral Agency: An Attempt to Reconcile the Retributive and the Utilitarian View' 36 *Mind* 292.

Falls, MM (1987) 'Retribution, Reciprocity, and Respect for Persons' 6 *Law and Philosophy* 25.

Fazel, S, Singh, JP, Doll, H and Grann, M (2012) 'Use of Risk Assessment Instruments to Predict Violence and Antisocial Behaviour in 73 Samples Involving 24,827 People: Systematic Review and Meta-analysis' 345 *British Medical Journal* 1.

Feinberg, J (1970) 'The Expressive Function of Punishment' in *Doing and Deserving: Essays in the Theory of Responsibility* (Princeton, Princeton University Press).

Frase, RS (2013) *Just Sentencing: Principles and Procedures for a Workable System* (Oxford, Oxford University Press).

Hampton, J (1984) 'The Moral Education Theory of Punishment' 13 *Philosophy and Public Affairs* 208.

——. (1992) 'An Expressive Theory of Retribution' in W Cragg (ed), *Retributivism and its Critics* (Stuttgart, Franz Steiner).

Hanna, N (2008) 'Say What? A Critique of Expressive Retributivism' 27 *Law and Philosophy* 123.

——. (2014) 'Facing the Consequences' 8 *Criminal Law and Philosophy* 589.

Hart, HLA (1959–60) 'Prolegomenon to the Principles of Punishment' 60 *Proceedings of the Aristotelian Society* 1.

Hoskins, Z (2011) 'Deterrent Punishment and Respect for Persons' 8 *Ohio State Journal of Criminal Law* 369.

——. (2018) 'Multiple-Offense Sentencing Discounts: Score One for Hybrid Accounts of Punishment' in J Ryberg, JV Roberts and JW de Keijser (eds), *Sentencing Multiple Crimes* (New York, Oxford University Press).
——. (forthcoming) *Beyond Punishment? A Normative Account of the Collateral Legal Consequences of Conviction* (New York, Oxford University Press).
Husak, D (2011) 'Lifting the Cloak: Preventive Detention as Punishment' 48 *San Diego Law Review* 1173.
Janus, ES (2013) 'Preventive Detention of Sex Offenders: The American Experience Versus International Human Rights Norms' 31 *Behavioral Sciences and the Law* 328.
Kant, I (1996 [1785]) 'Groundwork of the Metaphysics of Morals' in M Gregor (trans and ed), *The Cambridge Edition of the Works of Immanuel Kant: Practical Philosophy* (Cambridge, Cambridge University Press).
Lieb, R, Quinsey, V and Berliner, L (1998) 'Sexual Predators and Social Policy' 23 *Crime and Justice* 43.
Lucas, JR (1968) 'Or Else' 69 *Proceedings of the Aristotelian Society* 207.
McMahan, J (2013–14) 'Proportionate Defense' 23 *Journal of Transnational Law and Policy* 1.
Monahan, J (1981) *Predicting Violent Behavior: An Assessment of Clinical Techniques* (Beverly Hills, Sage).
Morris, N (1974) *The Future of Imprisonment* (Chicago, University of Chicago Press).
Morris, N and Tonry, M (1990) *Between Prison and Probation: Intermediate Punishments in a Rational Sentencing System* (New York, Oxford University Press).
Quinton, A (1954) 'On Punishment' 14 *Analysis* 33.
Rawls, J (1955) 'Two Concepts of Rules' 64 *Philosophical Review* 3.
Roberts, J (2008) 'The Mythical Divide between Collateral and Direct Consequences of Criminal Convictions: Involuntary Commitment of "Sexually Violent Predators"' 93 *Minnesota Law Review* 670.
Robinson, P (2001) 'Punishing Dangerousness: Cloaking Preventive Detention as Criminal Justice' 144 *Harvard Law Review* 1429.
Ross, WD (1930) *The Right and the Good* (Oxford, Oxford University Press).
Scheid, DE (1997) 'Constructing a Theory of Punishment, Desert, and the Distribution of Punishments' 10 *Canadian Journal of Law and Jurisprudence* 441.
Slobogin, C (2003) 'A Jurisprudence of Dangerousness' 98 *Northwestern University Law Review* 1.
Stephenson, W (1990) 'Fingarette and Johnson on Retributive Punishment' 24 *Journal of Value Inquiry* 227.
Ten, CL (1987) *Crime, Guilt, and Punishment: A Philosophical Introduction* (Oxford, Clarendon Press).
Zimring, FE and Hawkins, G (1995) *Incapacitation: Penal Confinement and the Restraint of Crime* (Oxford, Oxford University Press).

7

A Defence of Modern Risk-Based Sentencing

CHRISTOPHER SLOBOGIN*

I. Introduction

The story of sentencing over the past half-century is well known (see van Ginneken, Chapter 2 in this volume). Throughout the 1960s, the sentencing regimes in most American and European jurisdictions were indeterminate, with broad sentencing ranges within which judges and parole boards determined sentence length, based on an amalgam of retributive, deterrent, incapacitative and rehabilitative considerations. Beginning in the 1970s, a sentencing revolution took hold, with many jurisdictions in the US and several European countries moving towards determinate sentenced based predominately, and occasionally entirely, on a desert philosophy (von Hirsch and Ashworth 2012). Many American states eliminated parole boards, and even those that retained them vastly reduced their discretion (Petersilia 2001: 4).

The impetus for this revolution came from many directions. Indeterminate sentences were viewed as unfair because they were not necessarily proportionate to desert and because people who committed the same crime might receive seriously disparate sentences (von Hirsch and Ashworth 2012: 4–9). The calculations necessary to determine dangerousness and treatability were rightly perceived to be primarily guesswork, and parole boards were rightly castigated as inept at their job (Monahan and Ruggiero 1980; Jacobi et al 2014). In some quarters, indeterminate sentences determined by judges and parole boards were also seen as too lenient, a concern that legislatures sought to redress through mandatory minima, truth-in-sentencing requirements and three-strikes laws (Slobogin 2015: 311).

However, criminal justice dispositions based in whole or in part on assessments of re-offence risk have not disappeared. Many jurisdictions rely on such

* The author would like to thank the participants of the Predictive Sentencing Seminar at Oxford University, faculty members at workshops at the University of Utah SJ Quinney Law School, the University of Washington Law School and Vanderbilt University, and the participants at the 2018 Crimfest conference for their comments on earlier versions of this work.

assessments as one means of determining dispositions, allocating resources and reducing prison populations. In an effort to increase the reliability of these assessments, a number of American and European jurisdictions have in the past decade or so been experimenting with an approach to sentencing and corrections that has come to be called 'evidence-based' (Klingele 2016: 566–67). While governments have tried to structure risk assessment for some time (Simon 2005), a central characteristic of this newer type of dispositional decision making is the use of risk assessment instruments (RAIs) that rely on statistical or actuarial algorithms to assess an offender's relative risk of re-offending.

RAIs are generally thought to be more accurate and nuanced than the type of seat-of-the-pants and offence-dominated risk assessment in which judges and parole boards have traditionally engaged. But RAIs bring with them their own set of controversies (van Ginneken, Chapter 2 in this volume). First, despite their improved accuracy, they still generate a high number of false positives (non-recidivists identified as recidivists) and false negatives (recidivists identified as non-recidivists). Second, most RAIs include risk factors that have nothing to do with criminal conduct and may be related to race and class or both, characteristics that have made their fairness a major point of contention. Third, even sufficiently accurate RAIs that are based on criminal conduct might be resisted on the ground that punishment meted out to individuals should not be grounded on statistics about groups, because doing so dehumanises and quantifies the individual while stigmatising the group.

This chapter mounts a defence of both RAIs as a sentencing tool and the underlying predicate that risk assessment is a legitimate consideration at sentencing. Section II sets out the pragmatic case for making risk assessment a significant aspect of sentencing analysis, based on the assumption that effective risk assessment is possible. Section III explores the plausibility of that assumption by briefly describing RAIs and other means of assessing risk and then setting forth three principles that ought to govern when RAIs may be used in fashioning criminal dispositions. Sections IV and V advance the position that, limited by the principles in section III, release decision making based on risk assessments can be reconciled with desert-norms and should not be considered illegitimate or unethical.

II. The Policy Argument for Risk Assessment

The type of risk-based sentencing defended in this chapter is a version of 'limiting retributivism', which is meant to limit sentences based on risk assessment to a dispositional range determined by retributive considerations (Frase 2012; Morris 1974). Limiting retributivism ensures that no sentence will be grossly disproportionate to blameworthiness by establishing sentence ranges based on desert. These ranges can be broad or narrow. For instance, the original

Model Penal Code recommended fairly broad sentence ranges (eg, 1–20 years for first-degree felonies, 1–10 years for second-degree felonies, and 1–5 years for third-degree felonies) (American Law Institute, 1962, alternate § 6.06). The recent revision of the Code, in contrast, calls for a significantly greater number of sentencing categories and for ranges that are significantly narrower in scope (American Law Institute, 2017, §6.06).[1] The important point for the present purposes is that the type of limiting retributivism described here would set the upper and lower limits of punishment in each case, while risk assessment using RAIs would determine, or help determine, whether imprisonment occurs and, if it does, when release should occur.

Assume now that we can differentiate high-risk offenders from low-risk offenders. On that assumption, policy makers might well want to adopt a sentencing regime that implements risk-informed limiting retributivism. In an effort to reduce costs, legislation might, depending on the crime, direct that low-risk offenders receive less prison time or no prison at all, or that they be released earlier than high-risk offenders convicted of the same crime. Within the prison system, low-risk prisoners would be sent to cheaper low-security facilities. Overall, the impact of energetically incorporating risk assessment into sentencing might be a significant reduction in the prison population, which, in the US at least, has burgeoned to alarming proportions (Slobogin 2015: 307). To the extent that prison is criminogenic (see Bales and Piquero 2012: 98; Pritkin 2008: 1082), such policies might also reduce the overall crime rate by exposing fewer offenders to prison's ill effects and by facilitating identification of causal risk factors that can be the focus of rehabilitation efforts, many of which can and should take place outside of prison (Slobogin and Fondacaro 2011: 80–93).

In practice, limiting retributivism of this type is still relatively popular. The revised Model Penal Code and several commentators have cautiously endorsed use of RAIs to help set the precise sentence (eg, American Law Institute 2017, App A: 133–35; Frase 2013: 35–38). So have a number of states with ostensibly determinate sentencing regimes, as have many states that have retained indeterminate sentencing and allow parole boards to make release decisions (Frase 2012: 144–46; Klingele 2016). In most of these jurisdictions, it is difficult to discern whether the above-theorised benefits of risk assessment have been realised, because the extent to which the relevant judicial and parole board decisions are based on risk as opposed to an amalgam of risk and desert, desert alone or something else entirely is not clear (see, eg, Reitz 2006; Stemen and Rengifo 2011: 174–77; Zhang, Zhang and Vaughn 2009). Nonetheless, a few states have moved in the direction

[1] However, in contrast to the original Code, the revised Code abolishes parole, meaning that sentences, including any adjustments based on a risk assessment, are set at the front end rather than being left to a back-end decision by a parole board (American Law Institute, § 6.06(10) and commentary). For reasons that should become clear in this chapter, I do not think that determining sentence length at the front end makes sense in a regime that considers risk.

of evidence-based sentencing that is *explicitly* focused on risk assessment and that typically relies on RAIs. Preliminary research in Virginia suggests that use of RAIs can substantially reduce the proportion of non-violent prisoners in prison, while minimising re-conviction rates (Virginia Criminal Sentencing Commission 2009). The Justice Research Institute has estimated that the evidence-based sentencing programmes now in existence, focused on risk rather than desert, will reap about $4.6 billion in savings in the next 10 years (National Association of State Budget Officers 2013).

As a matter of cost-effective protection of the public, then, risk assessment within a limiting retributivist sentencing framework may be a good investment. But as a matter of criminal justice theory, risk assessments have increasingly been subject to attack, particularly in their evidence-based form. To the traditional complaints – that predictions of recidivism generate too many false positives (and false negatives) and that sentences based on them violate basic notions of desert – have been added charges that RAIs are discriminatory and dehumanising (eg, Starr 2014: 806). After describing RAIs in more detail, the following discussion evaluates these concerns.

III. Risk Assessment and Three Principles that Might Govern it

Today there are a huge number of RAIs, some developed by government and some by researchers at universities or private companies (Douglas et al 2016). These instruments usually consist of statistically derived algorithms that rely on risk factors (factors found to correlative positively with recidivism) and occasionally also protective factors (factors found to correlate negatively with recidivism). RAIs can include fewer than 10 and as many as 130 such factors (compare Hanson and Thornton (2000), describing the STATIC-99R, with Correctional Offender Management Profiling for Alternative Sanctions (2011), describing the COMPAS). The most sophisticated RAIs assign weights to the presence of each risk or protective factor; others simply assign a score of 1 if the factor is present (eg, Pennsylvania Commission on Sentencing 2012).

Every RAI includes antisocial behaviour as a risk factor. In this category, some RAIs include only convictions, others include convictions and arrests, and others include those factors plus elementary school misconduct, parole violations and the like (see, eg, Harris et al (2002), describing the Violence Risk Appraisal Guide or VRAG). These historical risk factors are called 'static' because they cannot be changed through decisions made by the offender or through treatment interventions. Additional static risk factors sometimes found in RAIs include gender (maleness), age (youth), victim injury, gender of victim, absence of parents in the home at age 16, and various other aspects of social history, such as past relationship, psychological and employment instability (see, eg, Harris (2002); and

Fazel et al (2016), describing the Oxford Risk of Recidivism Tool). RAIs are also increasingly including 'dynamic' risk factors (factors that can be changed through offender decisions or treatment), such as diagnoses (eg, substance abuse disorders), lack of insight, negative attitudes, active symptoms of major mental illness, impulsivity, lack of personal support or employment, non-compliance with remediation attempts, and degree of stress (eg, Douglas and Webster (1999), describing the HCR-20).

In a previous piece, I assumed that risk assessment is a legitimate consideration at sentencing, and developed three principles that should apply to that endeavour, whether pursued through RAIs or other means (here the focus will be RAIs, although alternative types of risk assessment are briefly discussed below) (Slobogin 2018). The *fit principle* posits that RAIs ought to address the precise legal question at issue. The *validity principle* requires that RAIs do what they purport to do. The *fairness principle* calls for balancing the incremental validity of each risk and protective factor against the extent to which it undermines the autonomy and dignity values that undergird the criminal justice system. The three principles are briefly summarised here.

A. The Fit Principle

With respect to fit, I set forth normative reasons as to why courts or policy makers should ensure that RAIs provide the following information: (1) specific probability estimates, (2) about the commission of serious crime, (3) within a short timeframe (eg, one or two years), as well as (4) information about interventions short of imprisonment that might achieve the state's preventive goal. RAIs that merely produce a conclusion that a person is 'high', 'medium' or 'low' risk, without specifying a precise probability or probability range (see, eg, Douglas et al (2010), describing the HCR-20), would not be consistent with this principle. Nor would RAIs based on validation studies that use as an outcome measure the commission of *any* criminal act or a criminal act within a prolonged period, as in the case of one well-known RAI that labels a person a recidivist if he or she committed a simple assault within seven years (Harris et al (2002: 385), describing the VRAG); otherwise, detention decisions might be based on predictions of trivial crime in the far-distant future.

Finally, a risk assessment that does not provide information about potentially successful interventions short of prison is close to useless in those situations in which the law has authorised community dispositions. Prison is not the only way, and certainly not the most effective way, of preventing or reducing re-offending. Risk management alternatives involving treatment, counselling, job training and surveillance can curtail recidivism (Chettiar 2017: 142–43; Cullen and Jonson 2011), and a good risk assessment can help judges or parole boards fashion suspended sentence or parole supervision provisions that take advantage of them.

B. The Validity Principle

The validity principle would require that RAIs have sound psychometric properties. One way to ensure that RAIs meet this requirement is by adapting the requirements of *Daubert v Dow Chemical*,[2] the US Supreme Court's seminal decision on the admissibility of expert testimony at trial, to the sentencing setting. As applied to risk assessment, *Daubert* would require a demonstration that an RAI's statistical techniques are appropriate for the task and that its validation samples reflect the relevant population (Hopkinson 2018).

Carried out rigorously, *Daubert* analysis would raise several difficult issues. One is whether an arrest should count as 'recidivism' in constructing an RAI and in determining how accurate an RAI is (Eaglin 2017: 75–79). The answer may well be 'sometimes'. While many RAIs equate an arrest with the commission of a crime, a significant subset of these do not consider arrests for drug crimes, perhaps because such arrests are less likely to result in conviction or because they can be disproportionately inflated by racially biased policing (but see Skeem and Lowenkamp 2016). Another validity issue, frequently neglected, is the nature of the reference population on which the RAI was validated (Bechman 2001). A risk assessment of a property offender should not rely on an RAI normed on sex offenders. An RAI normed in an urban locale probably should not be used in a rural area. An instrument validated on violent offenders in Virginia may not be appropriate for assessing the risk of violent offenders in Pennsylvania. A third validity issue that should be resolved is how good an RAI must be at distinguishing high-risk and low-risk offenders (to be distinguished from the fit issue of how one defines a 'high' risk sufficient to warrant detention). Based on American constitutional jurisprudence, I have suggested a batting average of approximately 75 per cent (Slobogin 2018).

C. The Fairness Principle

The fairness principle requires a more detailed summary. The concept of 'fairness' can encompass the fitness and validity principles, and incorporate procedural concerns as well. But as I use the term, the fairness principle is meant to address only the concern that risk assessment is insufficiently cognisant of the traditional tenet that criminal justice dispositions be based on blameworthy conduct. That concern was well put by the Supreme Court in its recent decision *Buck v Davis* when it stated – in the course of holding that race may never be an explicit risk factor – that 'a basic premise of our criminal justice system [is that it] punishes people for what they do, not who they are'.[3]

[2] *Daubert v Dow Chemical* (1993) 509 US 579.
[3] *Buck v Davis* (2017) 137 S Ct 759, 778.

Taken literally, that sentiment would prohibit reliance not only on race, but also on risk factors such as gender and age, and probably on factors such as current mental state (eg, impulsivity and lack of insight) as well, since none of these variables involves conduct. It should be noted, however, that the Supreme Court has, on several occasions, upheld even death sentences imposed on the ground that the offender is 'dangerous' (*Jurek v Texas*),[4] including when dangerousness was predicated on a diagnosis (*Barefoot v Estelle*).[5] Thus, the *Davis* decision is probably more accurately described as a prohibition on the use of race in sentencing rather than as a wholesale rejection of punishment based on status.

Nonetheless, at the very least, *Davis* raises a serious question about the legitimacy of relying on many commonly used risk factors in fashioning criminal justice dispositions. Furthermore, many commentators have argued for a position even less friendly to RAIs than the quoted language in *Davis* by endorsing the notion, put succinctly by Andrew von Hirsch, that: 'Unless the person actually made the wrongful choice he was predicted to make, he ought not to be condemned for that choice – and hence should not suffer punishment for it' (von Hirsch 1985: 11). That view might permit punishment based on prior crimes as well as the crime of conviction. But it would prohibit not only risk factors that do not consist of conduct, but also risk factors based on conduct that is non-blameworthy, such as choices about residence, marriage and employment.

In short, one version of the fairness principle might prohibit any type of risk assessment that is not based on criminal history. However, so limited, both the validity and fit principles would be threatened. Removal of all non-crime factors from an RAI is likely to substantially reduce accuracy. For instance, removal from an RAI of gender and age, perhaps the worst offenders under this view of fairness, would substantially reduce predictive validity, given the impact of maleness and youth on risk (Skeem, Monahan and Lowencamp 2016; Monahan, Skeem and Lowencamp 2017). As a result, it would also make adherence to the requirements imposed by the fit principle much more difficult.

More importantly, removal from RAIs of factors like gender and age, along with other non-criminal factors such as psychiatric diagnosis, would lead to inaccurate *discrimination*. A young male with psychopathic tendencies and one prior crime represents a much higher risk than an older female suffering from schizophrenia who has committed the same crime, yet, under von Hirsch's approach, both would be treated identically. The claim that RAIs are discriminatory because they make distinctions based on membership in 'protected' groups, or based on proxies for such membership (such as neighbourhood), ignores the unfair impact removal of those variables would have on other protected groups.[6]

[4] *Jurek v Texas* (1976) 428 US 262.

[5] *Barefoot v Estelle* (1983) 463 US 880.

[6] Elsewhere, I have discussed why use of these factors does not violate the equal protection clause (Slobogin 2012: 203–06; see also Hamilton 2015).

Given these concerns, I have argued for a more nuanced approach that balances the incremental validity of a given risk factor with fairness concerns. Race, in isolation, is a poor predictor (Kubrin, Squires and Stewart 2016: 27), and in any event was declared off-limits by *Davis*. In contrast, as noted above, gender and age significantly improve predictive accuracy. The same may not be true of marital, employment or residential status. The important point is that data is needed to carry out the necessary balancing analysis. In addition, the fairness principle would require RAIs to include as many useful dynamic factors as possible because these are factors that can be changed through individual choice (and are also most relevant to risk management issues that the fit principle urges RAIs to address). Finally, offenders should always be permitted to introduce evidence of protective factors that were not considered in the development of the RAI (Slobogin 2007: 125–29). These might include treatment successes, recent changes in circumstances, or aspects of criminal history (including a wrongful arrest or cooperation with the police or prosecution) that suggest reduced risk.

Note that the type of inquiry mandated by this interpretation of fairness requires transparency about the risk factors that go into the RAI calculus and their relative weights (and also means that those RAIs that do not weight items are problematic). Some developers of RAIs claim that their source codes and algorithmic analysis are proprietary products that they should not have to disclose, an argument that at least one court has accepted (see *Wisconsin v Loomis*).[7] However, where sentences involving deprivations of liberty are concerned, courts and policy makers should demand, at a minimum, the opportunity to examine the instruments in camera (Edwards and Veale forthcoming). Otherwise implementation of the fairness principle will be impossible.

IV. Implications of the Principles

Taken seriously, the fit, validity and fairness principles are very difficult to meet. Probably no RAI currently in existence does so. One can imagine at least three responses to this fact.

First, the principles could be treated as aspirations. Under this option, RAIs that do not meet the requisites of each principle would not be categorically rejected; rather courts would determine how close they come to doing so. A judicial decision that hints at this approach but that ultimately fails at it is *Wisconsin v Loomis*, one of the few American appellate cases to analyse the admissibility of risk assessments based on an RAI. To its credit, the Wisconsin Supreme Court noted that the RAI in question (the COMPAS) was not normed on a local population, could possibly misclassify minority offenders and could not be carefully analysed because the company that created it would not reveal the basis of its

[7] *Wisconsin v Loomis* (2016) 881 NW 2d 749, 761 (Wisconsin).

algorithm.[8] But rather than demanding such information so that fit, validity and fairness could be analysed, the court lamely concluded that trial courts could continue to use the COMPAS in connection with sentencing as long as judges are cognisant of these limitations and do not make the risk score so produced determinative of whether the offender is incarcerated or receives an enhanced sentence.[9]

If the aspirational approach is viewed as unsatisfactory, a second response to the fact that RAIs have difficulty meeting the three principles is to revert back to the type of risk assessment that preceded RAIs, an approach usually called 'clinical risk assessment'. This type of assessment involves a subjective judgment by the sentencing court or the parole board, perhaps aided by an expert and sometimes structured through the use of assessment instruments (Slobogin 2007: 101–04). Such assessments can easily achieve what might be called 'facial fit'; the judge or parole board can assert, for instance, that the expert evidence shows there is a substantial probability the offender will commit a violent offence within the next year if not confined. But such judgments quickly run afoul of the validity and fairness principles. Although clinical experts can often perform better than chance, research consistently shows that clinical judgment is inferior to actuarial judgment in the violence prediction context (Hilton, Harris and Rice 2006; but see Dressel 2017). And while the explicit explanation for a particular clinical judgment may recount only legitimate risk factors such as prior crimes, the influence (conscious or otherwise) of illegitimate or suspect factors, including race, cannot be discounted. In contrast, the risk factors considered when an RAI is used are apparent on the face of the instrument and, assuming that the same RAI is used throughout the jurisdiction, will promote more consistent judgments. Reinforcing these points is a study that found that while, in the abstract, lay subjects preferred clinical to actuarial judgment, their preferences were reversed when they were informed that the algorithm was more accurate, and they were even more likely to prefer algorithms when the factors used to construct them were made transparent (Wang forthcoming). Both of these conditions would exist under the regime proposed here.

Despite its problems, clinical prediction might nonetheless be preferred over an RAI-based prediction on the separate ground it is more 'individualised'. Because RAIs reflect group tendencies, some scholars have argued that they cannot say anything meaningful about an individual (Cooke and Michie 2010). That argument has been debunked as a statistical matter (Imrey and Dawid 2015). Just as importantly, it proves too much. Ultimately, all risk assessment – indeed, all expert testimony – is based on stereotyping. Experts who claim they believe that an offender will re-offend are basing that assertion on factors that they have come to believe are correlated with risk, based on their experience with, or on their reading

[8] ibid 769.
[9] ibid.

or hearing about, other people. There is no way to avoid what I and my co-authors have called the G2i (general-to-individual) challenge in expert testimony (Faigman, Monahan and Slobogin 2014).

If neither of the two foregoing responses to the difficulty of carrying out risk assessment in a principled manner is satisfactory, there is, of course, a third response: elimination of risk assessment as a factor in sentencing. Indeed, some would choose this response even if the fiscal benefits of risk assessment noted in section II are assumed, and even if the principles outlined in section III were *fully* achieved. Section V addresses these challenges to risk-based sentencing by comparing it to its principal alternative.

V. A Comparison of Risk-Based and Desert-Based Sentencing

Many have argued that no amount of regulation will sufficiently reduce either the inaccuracy of risk assessment or its unfairness. Both arguments are powerful. There is no dispute that eradicating false positives is impossible. Given the current state of knowledge, even a reduction of the false positive rate below 30 or 40 per cent is unlikely, at least for the general offender population (as opposed, perhaps, to certain subsets of it). Further, as section III has noted, most RAIs clearly rely on risk factors that have nothing to do with blameworthy conduct, and the same can probably be said for clinical risk assessment.

However, before declaring that these facts doom risk-based sentencing as a normative matter, the worthiness of this type of sentencing should be compared to sentences based on backward-looking culpability assessments.[10] If the former is no worse than the latter with respect to either accuracy or fairness considerations, then perhaps the criticisms of risk-based sentencing ought to be reconsidered. In what follows, I suggest reasons why desert-based sentencing may be just as rife with error and unfairness as risk-based sentencing. And I suggest that risk-based sentencing may not be as antithetical to desert as is commonly thought.

A. The Accuracy of Desert

One reason for doing away with or significantly minimising risk as a consideration in the criminal justice system is concern about inaccuracy. But the alternative – sentences based solely on desert – is likely no better, for a number of reasons.

[10] Of course, retribution is not the only alternative basis for sentencing. But general deterrence, while a significant reason for having a criminal justice system, is not a good basis for differentiating between individuals (see Tonry 2006: 28), and goals such as rehabilitation and specific deterrence are easily subsumed in a regime based on risk assessments (see Slobogin 2014: 382).

First, of course, despite hundreds of years of deliberation, we still have not reached a consensus about relative blameworthiness in a large number of important, commonly occurring criminal scenarios. Should negligent conduct be criminalised and, if so, should negligence be judged on an objective or individualised standard? Is felony murder as culpable as intentional killing? Is a reckless killer always less blameworthy than a premediated killer? When, if ever, should an accomplice receive the same sentence as the principal, and is knowing facilitation the same as purposeful aiding and abetting? Should a person who engages in the same act repeatedly (eg, acquiring multiple pornographic pictures) be punished for each? And, perhaps most relevant to sentencing, should criminal history be considered in assessing desert and, if so, should the length of time between offences be relevant? The debates are endless, as those of us who have taught or taken criminal law classes know.

Second, even if we can agree on these points, to the extent that punishment depends on evaluations of internal mental states, such as purpose, recklessness or negligence, obtaining accurate information about the relevant facts is extremely difficult. Even defendants who are honest have trouble recounting their mental state at the time of the offence. As I argued in my book *Proving the Unprovable*, evidence about past mental states is at root simply narrative, not objective fact (Slobogin 2007: 43–44).

Third, even if we can reach a consensus on blameworthiness concepts and even if the true mental state of the defendant can be discerned, jurors might not be able to accurately label that mental state. A number of recent studies indicate that laypeople, even when given clear descriptions of the relevant mens rea terms, have trouble differentiating between purpose and negligence, much less recklessness and knowledge (Beatty and Fondacaro 2018; Shen et al 2011: 1347–48). Yet significant sentencing differentials can rest on such determinations.

Finally, and most importantly, even if we could nail down the relative gravity of a person's blameworthiness and his or her precise mens rea, devising a sentence that 'accurately' reflects desert is, to put it bluntly, an exercise in futility, given the absence of a clear outcome measure. Does a thief who stole £1,000 deserve two years, two months or two days? Does a premeditated murderer deserve the death penalty (as a number of jurisdictions in the US have declared), 15 years (the practical maximum in much of Europe) or five years, as von Hirsch once suggested (von Hirsch 1976: 139)?Any of these answers, and many more, could be 'correct'. In a study I conducted with Lauren Brinkley-Rubinstein, subjects were asked to look at 12 crime scenarios describing only the actus reus and mens rea for the crime, and then indicate appropriate punishment on a 13-point scale (Slobogin and Brinkley-Rubinstein 2013: 94–96). For both groups, the standard deviations were huge. And the range of sentences was also very broad, even when the extreme dispositions beyond two standard deviations were thrown out. Further, in only the least and most serious crime scenarios did more than 25 per cent of the sample choose the same punishment. Thus, while consensus on the ordinal ranking of crimes might be possible, the maximum 'anchor' point for the most serious crime and the proper spacing between offences is open to serious dispute (cf. von Hirsch and Ashworth 2012: 141–43).

Compare risk assessments. Because research on such assessments has a concrete outcome measure – whether a person predicted to re-offend in fact recidivated – risk assessment can be associated with true and false positive rates. In contrast, it is impossible to generate true and false positive rates with respect to desert, because there is no definitive stance on what a positive finding is. Indeed, from the scientific perspective, talk about the 'accuracy' of desert-based punishment does not make sense.

A cynic might conclude that it is this absence of an outcome measure that explains many people's preference for culpability-based sentencing: we can tell ourselves we are right without fear of contradiction by any objective referent. In contrast, risk-based sentencing is shunned because it flaunts in our face how often we are wrong. However, in fact, the 'error rate' associated with desert-based sentences is both likely to be high and impossible to know. If risk-based assessment is rejected, it should not be on the ground that it is less accurate than the alternative.

B. Desert and Fairness

A retributive theorist might respond that even if desert-based sentences are unfalsifiable, they are fairer, both objectively and in appearance. The fairness challenge to risk assessment at sentencing consists of both a concern about disparity and a claim that it is an affront to human dignity. Desert-based sentencing is fairer, its proponents claim, both because it minimises divergent sentences between similarly situated offenders and because it honours autonomy by basing punishment solely on blameworthy choices.

i. Desert and Disparity

There is no doubt that a major goal of offence-based determinate sentencing is to avoid disparity between offenders (O'Hear 2006: 773, 791–93). However, as a practical matter, it has failed miserably. First, of course, sentences for the same crime can vary radically from state to state and between the states and the federal government. Second, as many have pointed out, prosecutors' charging decisions and judicial sentencing decisions in determinate regimes manipulate the relevant criteria in ways that have routinely produced disparate racial and other unjustifiable impacts (Baron-Evans and Stith 2012: 1689; Hamilton 2017: 9, 37–38).

But even if these causes of inconsistency could be eliminated, the indecipherability of desert, noted above in the discussion of inaccuracy, undermines the goal of consistency as well. That is because desert, even when focused exclusively on blameworthy conduct and mental state,[11] is infinitely nuanced. Sentencing commissions and sentencers understandably have a very difficult time distinguishing between different versions of the same crime. Take armed robbery: an armed robber can be young or old, a leader or a follower, the one with the gun or the getaway car driver, a person who really needs the money or one who robs for fun. Disagreement as to whether, or the extent to which, these types of variables should be reflected in sentencing guidelines is very likely. This disagreement, in turn, can result in the perception on the part of both offenders and the public that the 'deserved' sentences have been miscalibrated. In contrast, even different RAIs tend to arrive at similar results on the metric of interest, ie, risk (Kroner, Mills and Reddon 2005).

Even more fundamentally, as I have noted elsewhere, 'disparity is in the eye of beholder' (Slobogin 2005: 154–55). Some might be most concerned about ensuring that all armed robbers receive the same sentence, while others might be more bothered if those people convicted of robbery who have demonstrated an ability to participate in civil society nonetheless continue to be confined as long as robbers who are incorrigible. As a general matter, consistency across offences is likely to result in inconsistency across risk or treatability levels, and vice versa. The justification for insisting on one form of consistency over another reduces to whether one prefers desert or risk as the basis of disposition.

That preference, once one accepts the argument in the previous section that accuracy concerns at best cancel each other out, is likely to be driven by the importance one ascribes to blameworthiness as a basis for punishment.

ii. Desert and Blameworthiness

The bulk of antipathy towards risk-based sentencing probably stems not from concerns about inaccuracy or disparity, but rather a belief that it undermines the complex of values having to do with autonomy, choice and dignity to which section III alluded, a belief that, for desert theorists at least, probably lingers even if the fairness principle described there is implemented. Again, however, these concerns about risk-based sentencing diminish when honestly compared to analogous concerns about desert-based sentencing. Three brief observations are offered in this regard: one made here and two in the next section.

First, desert-based sentencing has its own moral dilemmas with respect to autonomy and choice. As the RAIs described in this chapter indicate, most criminal offenders are poor, unemployed, single and male, come from a broken family, have a serious mental disorder or live in a bad neighbourhood. Solid arguments have been made that these circumstances make them less deserving of punishment,

[11] Of course, desert *could* be conceptualised as much more than this (see Robinson and Jacowitz 2012).

on the ground that any criminal conduct they have committed is not the product of unfettered choice, but rather is, at least in part, situationally or biologically constrained (see generally Symposium 2011). Yet the law generally does not mitigate based on these types of considerations because it assumes that offenders are fully culpable for any harmful conduct they voluntarily carry out with the relevant mens rea. For both practical and philosophical reasons (not the least of which is its tendency to be most lenient towards those who are most dangerous), the 'whole life' view of moral desert has very few defenders (Ryberg 2004: 18–19) and even mitigation schemes several steps short of that view have been very cautious (Von Hirsch and Ashworth 2012: 62–74).

One does not have to be a determinist to question this stance. For instance, Chad Flanders has asked, in dissecting Rawls' position on this issue, why criminal justice is retributive (as Rawls suggested) rather than distributive (as Rawls asserted in virtually every other context) (Flanders 2016: 86). Yet, it is not my objective to wade into this age-old debate. The only point made here is that the desert alternative to sentencing should not automatically triumph because it is assumed to have few difficulties arriving at 'fair' results respectful of human autonomy.

C. The Blameworthiness of Risk

However, let us assume that, contrary to the argument just made, crime committed with the requisite actus reus and mens rea (in the absence of serious mental impairment) is the product of unconstrained choice and thus can justly be morally condemned. Even if we take blameworthy conduct, so defined, to be the linchpin of just punishment, risk-based sentencing is not necessarily unjust. It is true that risk assessment is orthogonal to culpability assessment in a number of ways. It is forward-looking rather than backward-looking; its use of criminal behaviour as a sentence enhancement is based on a different rationale; and, as just described, non-criminal factors that could mitigate in a strict offence-based regime might instead aggravate punishment in a risk-based regime. But risk assessments are still closely associated with blameworthy choices, in two ways.

First, one can plausibly say that, contrary to the literal interpretation of the Supreme Court's decision in *Buck v Davis*,[12] risk-based sentences are not predicated simply on what a person is, but rather on what he or she has chosen to do. That is because risk assessment can be, in essence, an evaluation of one's character, which on many accounts is directly relevant to desert, especially at the sentencing stage (Arenella 1990; Huigens 2000; Whitman 2014). The Supreme Court

[12] *Buck v Davis* (n 3).

itself has made the connection when it stated in *Deck v Missouri* that 'character and propensities of the defendant are part of a "unique, individualized judgment regarding the punishment that a particular person deserves"'.[13] Character is an amalgam of choices – choices not only about whether to engage in antisocial conduct, but also choices about one's friends, family life, education and work; the places one frequents; the amount of drugs or alcohol one ingests; and whether to seek treatment for emotional problems such as anger and impulsivity, all of which are examples of precisely the types of activities captured in the most sophisticated RAIs. If most choices are unconstrained – as one must assume in order to avoid the Pandora's Box described in the previous section – and if they combine to make one's character high risk, they could be said to be blameworthy, even if they do not involve criminal activity (Husak 2011: 1195).

Indeed, a risk-based sentence can even be linked to *criminally* blameworthy choices, specifically, choices to commit crime *in the future*. Concededly, risk factors such as employment status, neighbourhood or diagnosis are not blameworthy in and of themselves, but they are not the *reason* for an offender's sentence. Rather, they are merely evidence of what a person will decide to do in the future, in the same way that a finding of blameworthy choice in the past may rely on various pieces of circumstantial evidence that are not culpable in themselves, like being married to the victim, presence near the scene of the crime or possession of a weapon. Risk assessments at sentencing could be said to predict future culpable choices, just as at trials we try to postdict culpable choices.

Combining the foregoing observations and keeping in mind that it would function within a limiting retributivism framework, the conclusion is easily reached that risk-based sentencing has a significant association with blameworthiness. Risk is not pristine desert, but it is not some soulless mechanical assessment of humans-as-machines either. The debate on this score has been more hyperbolic than productive.

VI. Conclusion

The use of risk assessment instruments at sentencing is justifiably controversial. Courts should carefully monitor whether such instruments address the precise legal issue at stake, meet rigorous threshold validity requirements and avoid risk factors that unfairly discriminate on the basis of race or offer little incremental validity. However, if these requirements are substantially met, risk assessment can play a significant role at sentencing without undermining a commitment to desert, choice and dignity as important goals of the criminal justice system.

[13] *Deck v Missouri* (2005) 544 US 622, 633.

References

American Law Institute (1962) Model Penal Code, www.ali.org/publications/show/model-penal-code.

——. (2017) Model Penal Code, www.ali.org/publications/show/sentencing.

Arenella, P (1990) 'Character, Choice and Moral Agency: The Relevance of Character to Our Moral Culpability Judgments' 2 *Social Philosophy & Policy* 59.

Bales, WD and Piquero, AR (2012) 'Assessing the Impact of Imprisonment on Recidivism' 8 *Journal of Experimental Criminology* 71.

Baron-Evans, A and Stith, K (2012) 'Sentencing Law: Rhetoric and Reality' 160 *University of Pennsylvania Law Review* 1631.

Beatty, RA and Fondacaro, MR (2018) 'The Misjudgment of Criminal Responsibility' 36 *Behavioral Sciences and the Law* 457.

Bechman, DC (2001) 'Sex Offender Civil Commitments' 16 *Criminal Justice* 24.

Chettiar, I (2017) 'How Many Americans are Unnecessarily Incarcerated?' 29 *Federal Sentencing Reporter* 140.

Cooke, DJ and Michie, C (2010) 'Limitations of Diagnostic Precision and Predictive Utility in the Individual Case: A Challenge for Forensic Practice' 34 *Law and Human Behavior* 259.

Correctional Offender Management Profiling for Alternative Sanctions (2011), www.documentcloud.org/documents/2702103-Sample-Risk-Assessment-COMPAS-CORE.html.

Cullen, F and Jonson, CL (2011) 'Rehabilitation and Treatment Programs' in JQ Wilson and J Peterslia (eds), *Crime and Public Policy* (Oxford: Oxford University Press).

Douglas, K et al (2010) 'HCR-20 Violence Risk Assessment Scheme: Overview and Annotated Bibliography', kdouglas.files.wordpress.com/2007/10/hcr-20-annotated-biblio-sept-2010.pdf.

Douglas, KS and Webster, CD (1999) 'The HCR-20 Violence Risk Assessment Scheme: Concurrent Validity in a Sample of Incarcerated Offenders' 26 *Criminal Justice and Behavior* 19.

Douglas, T et al (2016) 'Risk Assessment Tools in Criminal Justice and Forensic Psychiatry: The Need for Better Data' 42 *European Psychiatry* 137, http://dx.doi.org/10.1016/j.eurpsy.2016.12.009.

Dressel, JJ (2017) 'Accuracy and Racial Biases of Recidivism Prediction Instruments', 1–78 https://www.cs.dartmouth.edu/farid/downloads/publications/jdthesis17.pdf.

Eaglin, JM (2017) 'Constructing Recidivism Risk' 67 *Emory Law Journal* 122.

Edwards, L and Veale, M (forthcoming) 'Enslaving the Algorithm: From a "Right to an Explanation" to a "Right to Better Decisions"', *IEEE Security and Privacy*, 1–15, ssrn.com/abstract=3052831.

Faigman, DL, Monahan, J and Slobogin, C (2014) 'Group to Individual Inference in Expert Scientific Testimony' *81 University of Chicago Law Review* 417.

Fazel, S et al (2016) 'Prediction of Violent Reoffending on Release from Prison: Derivation and External Validation of a Scalable Tool' 3 *Lancet Psychiatry* 535.
Flanders, C (2016) 'Criminals behind the Veil: Political Philosophy and Punishment' 31 *Brigham Young University Journal of Public Law* 83.
Frase, RS (2012) 'Theories of Proportionality and Desert' in K Reitz and J Petersilia (eds), *The Oxford Handbook of Sentencing and Corrections* (New York, Oxford University Press).
——. (2013) *Just Sentencing: Principles and Procedures for a Workable System* (Oxford, Oxford University Press).
Hamilton, M (2015) 'Risk-Needs Assessment: Constitutional and Ethical Issues' 42 *American Criminal Law Review* 231.
——. (2017) 'Sentencing Disparities' 6 *British Journal of American Legal Studies* 177.
Hanson, RK and Thornton, D (2000) 'Improving Risk Assessments for Sex Offenders: A Comparison of Three Actuarial Scales' 24 *Law and Human Behavior* 119.
Harris, GT et al (2002) 'Prospective Replication of the Violence Risk Appraisal Guide in Predicting Violent Recidivism among Forensic Patients' 26 *Law and Human Behavior* 377.
Hilton, NZ, Harris, GT and Rice, ME (2006) 'Sixty-Six Years of Research on the Clinical Versus Actuarial Prediction of Violence' 34 *Counseling Psychologist* 400.
Hopkinson, C (2018) 'Using *Daubert* to Evaluate Evidence-Based Sentencing' 103 *Cornell Law Review* 723.
Huigens, K (2000) 'The End of Deterrence and Beyond' 41 *William & Mary Law Review* 943.
Husak, D (2011) 'Lifting the Cloak: Preventive Detention as Punishment' 48 *San Diego Law Review* 1173.
Hyatt, JM and Chanenson, SL (2017) 'The Use of Risk Assessment at Sentencing: Implications for Research and Policy' ssrn.com/abstract=2961288.
Imrey, PB and Dawid, AP (2015) 'A Commentary on Statistical Assessment of Violence Recidivism Risk' 2 *Statistics and Public Policy* 1.
Jacobi, T, et al (2014) 'The Attrition of Rights under Parole' 87 *Southern California Law Review* 887.
Klingele, C (2016) 'The Promises and Perils of Evidence-Based Corrections' 91 *Notre Law Review* 537.
Kroner, DG, Mills, JF and Reddon, JF (2005) 'A Coffee Can, Factor Analysis, and Prediction of Antisocial Behavior: The Structure of Criminal Risk' 28 *International Journal of Law and Psychiatry* 360.
Kubrin, C, Squires, GD and Stewart (2016) 'Neighborhoods, Race and Recidivism: The Community Reoffending Nexus and Its Implications for African-Americans' 32 *Sage Race Relations Abstracts* 7.
Monahan, J and Ruggiero, M (1980) 'Psychological and Psychiatric Aspects of Determinate Criminal Sentencing' 3 *International Journal of Law and Psychiatry* 143.

Monahan, J, Skeem, J and Lowencamp, C (2017) 'Age and Risk Assessment, and Sanctioning: Overestimating the Old, Underestimating the Young' 41 *Law and Human Behavior* 191.

Morris, N (1974) *The Future of Imprisonmen*t (Chicago, University of Chicago Press).

National Association of State Budget Officers (2013) 'State Spending for Corrections: Long-Term Trends and Recent Criminal Justice Policy Reforms', higherlogicdownload.s3.amazonaws.com/NASBO/0f09ced0-449d-4c11-b787-10505cd90bb9/UploadedImages/Issue%20Briefs%20/State%20Spending%20for%20Corrections.pdf.

O'Hear, MM (2006) 'The Original Intent of Uniformity in Federal Sentencing' 74 *University of Cincinnati Law Review* 749.

Pennsylvania Commission on Sentencing (2012) Risk/Needs Assessment Project: Interim Report 4: Development of Risk Assessment Scale, hominid.psu.edu/specialty_programs/pacs/publications-and-research/risk-assessment/phase-i-reports/interim-report-4-development-of-risk-assessment-scale/view.

Petersilia, J (2001) 'When Prisoners Return to Communities: Political, Economic, and Social Consequences' 65 *Federal Probation* 3.

Pritkin, MH (2008) 'Is Prison Increasing Crime?' 6 *Wisconsin Law Review* 1049.

Reitz, KR (2006) 'Don't Blame Determinacy: US Incarceration Growth Has Been Driven by Other Factors' 84 *Texas Law Review* 1787.

Robinson, PH and Jacowitz, S (2012) 'Extralegal Punishment Factors: A Study of Forgiveness, Hardship, Good Deeds, Apology, Remorse and Other Such Discretionary Factors in Assessing Criminal Punishment' 65 *Vanderbilt Law Review* 737.

Ryberg, J (2004) *The Ethics of Proportionate Punishment: A Critical Investigation* (Dordrecht, Kluwer Academic Press).

Shen, FX et al (2011) 'Sorting Guilty Minds' 84 *New York University Law Review* 1306.

Simon, J (2005) 'Reversal of Fortune: The Resurgence of Individual Risk Assessment in Criminal Justice' *1 Annual Review of Law & Social Science* 397.

Skeem, J and Lowenkamp, CT (2016) 'Risk, Race, & Recidivism: Predictive Bias and Disparate Impact', papers.ssrn.com/sol3/papers.cfm?abstract_id=2687339.

Skeem, J, Monahan, J and Lowencamp, C (2016) 'Gender, Risk Assessment and Sanctioning: The Cost of Treating Women like Men', ssrn.com/abstract=2718460.

Slobogin, C (2005) 'The Civilization of the Criminal Law' 58 *Vanderbilt Law Review* 121.

——. (2007) *Proving the Unprovable: The Role of Law, Science, and Speculation in Adjudicating Culpability and Dangerousness* (Oxford, Oxford University Press).

——. (2012) 'Risk Assessment' in K Reitz and J Petersilia (eds), *The Oxford Handbook of Sentencing and Corrections* (New York, Oxford University Press).

——. (2014) 'Empirical Desert and Preventive Justice: A Comment' 17 *New Criminal Law Review* 376.

——. (2015) 'How Changes in American Culture Triggered Hyper-incarceration: Variations on the Tazian View' *58 Howard Law Journal* 305.

——. (2018) 'Principles of Risk Assessment: Sentencing and Policing' 15 *Ohio State Journal of Criminal Law* 583.

Slobogin, C and Brinkley-Rubinstein, L (2013) 'Putting Desert in its Place' 65 *Stanford Law Review* 77.

Slobogin, C and Fondacaro, M (2011) *Juveniles at Risk: A Plea for Preventive Justice* (Oxford, Oxford University Press).

Starr, SB (2014) 'Evidence-Based Sentencing and the Scientific Rationalization of Sentencing' 66 *Stanford Law Review* 803.

Stemen, D and Rengifo, A.F (2011) 'Policies and Imprisonment: The Impact of Structured Sentencing and Determinate Sentencing on State Incarceration Rates, 1978–2004' 28 *Justice Quarterly* 174.

Symposium (2011) '"Rotten Social Background" Twenty-Five Years Later: Should the Criminal Law Recognise a Defence of Severe Environmental Deprivation?' 2 *Alabama Civil Rights and Civil Liberties Review* 1.

Tonry, MJ (2006) 'Purposes and Functions of Sentencing' 34 *Crime & Justice* 1.

Virginia Criminal Sentencing Commission (2009) Annual Reports 2001–2009, www.vcsc.virginia.gov/reports.html.

Von Hirsch, A (1976) *Doing Justice* (Boston, Northeastern University Press).

——. (1985) *Past or Future Crimes: Deservedness and Dangerousness in the Sentencing of Criminals* (Manchester, Manchester University Press).

Von Hirsch, A and Ashworth, A (2012) *Proportionate Sentencing: Exploring the Principles* (Oxford, Oxford University Press).

Wang, AJ (forthcoming) 'Procedural Justice and Risk Assessment Algorithms', https://ssrn.com/abstract=3170136.

Whitman, JQ (2014) 'The Case for Penal Modernism: Beyond Utility and Desert' 1 *Critical Analysis of the Law* 143.

Zhang, Y, Zhang, L and Vaughn, MS (2009) 'Indeterminate and Determinate Sentencing Models: A State-Specific Analysis of Their Effects on Recidivism' 60 *Crime and Delinquency* 693.

8

Some Dilemmas of Indeterminate Sentences

Risk and Uncertainty, Dignity and Hope

ANDREW ASHWORTH AND LUCIA ZEDNER

I. Introduction

The predictive element in sentencing, resulting in the imposition of indeterminate sentences, rests upon the foundational role of the state to protect the public from risk of harm. What public protection is deemed to require depends on differing perceptions of threat that vary according to time and place, on the political climate in which risk assessments are made and on the penal culture that shapes the sentences that follow (Maurutto and Hannah-Moffat 2006). Debates about what level of security the state owes the public and what the public have a right to expect by way of protection against those judged to pose a serious risk of significant harm prompt news headlines and hostile questions in parliament, particularly when grave harms eventuate. They are less often subject to dispassionate public deliberation about the ethical problems of taking away liberty on preventive grounds (Ashworth and Zedner 2014: Chapters 6, 7 and 9; Meyerson 2009) or about the predictive limits of risk assessment instruments, although these are clearly acknowledged in the academic literature (see, eg, Dressel and Farid 2018). As Douglas and colleagues observe: 'Existing data suggest that most risk assessment tools have poor to moderate accuracy in most applications. Typically, more than half of individuals judged by tools as high risk are incorrectly classified – they will not go on to offend' (Douglas et al 2017: 135). Decisions to impose indeterminate sentences are fraught with difficulties arising from the methodological and ethical problems inherent in risk assessment, its application in the criminal court and its implications for those consequently sentenced on predictive grounds.

In public debate about predictive sentencing, it is commonly assumed that protection is owed only to those 'law-abiding' citizens that such sentences are designed to keep safe. What protections are owed to those considered sufficiently risky to require extended or indeterminate sentences and what residual rights they should enjoy in prison are less commonly topics for public debate, though such questions do attract serious legal and academic attention (Drenkhahn, Morgenstern, and van Zyl Smit 2012; Lazarus 2004, 2006). Only in the case of particularly egregious measures such as the sentence of Imprisonment for Public Protection (IPP)[1] are the general public and politicians roused to protest the overreach of state power.[2] This chapter considers the legitimate expectations of those sentenced on grounds of predicted risk and asks what the state owes to those it deems dangerous. It does so by examining important recent jurisprudence of domestic courts in Europe and of the European Court of Human Rights (ECtHR) on the rights of those subject to indeterminate sentences. It explores the contention that a fundamental precondition of respect for human dignity is that an offender who is imprisoned indefinitely should 'not be turned into an object of crime prevention', but should retain their basic rights.[3] For those subject to indeterminate detention, this includes 'a right a hope', which can be met only by ensuring a real prospect of release. The argument that a 'right to hope' is owed to all, even to those who have committed the most serious offences or who pose the gravest risk of harm, has proven contentious because of its profound implications for predictive sentencing. The right to hope also acknowledges the offender's autonomy and capacity for change, which raise challenging issues for risk assessments and the predictive sentences based upon them that this chapter seeks to address.

II. Overview

This chapter focusses on central questions relating to the use of prediction in sentencing, namely what level of probability and seriousness of predicted harm justify the imposition of indeterminate sentences, and also what are and what should be the structure and conditions of sentences imposed as a result. The chapter begins by examining three issues in predictive sentencing: the time at which the prediction of future behaviour should be made, the practices of risk assessment, and the court's decision-making in the face of uncertainty. We address the consequences of risk prediction by considering the human rights implications of the indeterminate sentences that follow, in particular of Life without Parole

[1] Introduced under the Criminal Justice Act 2003, the IPP was designed to protect the public in cases that did not merit a life sentence, but where the offender had been convicted of a specified offence and the court was of the view that there was 'a significant risk of serious harm' (s 229(1) of the Criminal Justice Act 2003). The sentence of IPP imposed a tariff term of imprisonment followed by indefinite detention on preventive grounds. Offenders are detained until the Parole Board determine that the risk posed is sufficiently reduced that the offender no longer needs to be detained for public protection. See further Annison 2015; Ramsay 2012b; Rose 2012.

[2] The IPP sentence was repealed in 2012 following extensive legal challenges and political protest.

[3] The view of the Federal Constitutional Court of Germany discussed in *Vinter v UK* (Grand Chamber, 2013: Application Nos 66069/09, 130/10 and 3896/10) [69]. See also Tonry (2016).

(LWOP) sentences in the US and 'whole-life' minimum terms in the UK. We explore the dignity principle and examine the contention that it gives rise to a 'right to hope' for those subject to indeterminate sentences. We then turn to civil preventive detention, asking whether the same or different principles should apply to it. We ask whether there is an inconsistency between holding an individual to be responsible at the point of conviction and sentencing, yet non-responsible for the purposes of civil commitment. In the final section, we examine what implications the principle of dignity and the right to hope have for the conditions of detention, whether civil or criminal. We conclude by calling into question the legitimacy of indeterminate sentencing on the grounds of predicted risk.

III. Risk Assessment and the Dilemmas of Predictive Sentencing

Predictive sentencing rests on the premise that it is possible for the criminal court to assess an offender's risk of re-offending. Much of the literature on criminal risk assessment has focused on technical questions of validity (Ashworth and Zedner 2014: Chapter 6; Monahan and Skeem 2016; see also van Ginneken, Chapter 2 in this volume), but there are many further questions of timing, fit and fairness that need to be brought into view (Slobogin 2018; Tonry 2014). In terms of timing, there are three relevant points – the time of the offence, the time of conviction and sentence, and the time of consideration for release. Below we consider the important question of whether a court when imposing an indeterminate sentence should be expected to make a prediction of an offender's dangerousness at the prospective time of release. There is also the question of consistency in relation to the offender's responsibility. To attribute responsibility for wrongdoing is to recognise that the individual in question is autonomous and has the capacity for moral choice (Lacey 2016: 27–33). Where an individual has been found to have chosen to do wrong, the acknowledgement of that capacity for choice implies a capacity to choose to do otherwise and thus that the offender has the potential to change. Moreover, the attribution of responsibility and acknowledgement of individual autonomy at the point of conviction raise difficult questions about what risk assessment is measuring. If risk assessment is to be a valid basis for sentencing, the question arises as to whether it necessarily entails a denial or downplaying of individual autonomy and capacity for change (see Douglas on the 'disrespectfulness of preventive detention' and Slobogin on the 'difficulties in arriving at "fair" results respectful of human autonomy' in Chapters 5 and 7 in this volume respectively). Addressing this dilemma requires that further thought be given to the relevant timeframe at or over which risk is assessed, the means by which it is assessed and the degree of certainty that should be required before an indefinite sentence is imposed on the grounds of risk. The UK courts have struggled with all three.

IV. Timing of the Determination of Risk

First, the temporal aspect: a fundamental question is whether the risk to be assessed is that at the time of sentencing or a predictive estimation of future risk (Harris and Walker 2018a). In the controversial case of *R v Smith* (2011), the UK Supreme Court held that the court was not making a predictive judgment about the risk the offender would pose at the end of the minimum period of imprisonment on the grounds that to try to see so far into the future 'places an unrealistic burden on the sentencing judge'.[4] Rather, the Court held that the risk must be assessed 'on the premise that the defendant is at large. It is at the moment that he imposes the sentence that the judge must decide whether, on that premise, the defendant poses a significant risk of causing serious harm to members of the public'.[5] However, subsequent judgments have rejected the idea that the risk to be assessed is the 'present risk'; in *Sturnham*, it was stated that '[t]here is nothing unrealistic about asking a sentencing judge to assess whether an offender presents a risk for a period which cannot reliably be estimated and may well continue after the tariff period'[6] and in *Bryant* that 'the consistent practice of this court has been to consider the dangers that the offender will present on eventual release'.[7]

The underlying premise in these cases is that the court must make a risk assessment that is sufficient to justify the imposition of an extended or indeterminate sentence (for critical discussion, see Wasik (2012)). In one sense, to require the court to attempt to predict the offender's risk at the point of release is to usurp the role of the Parole Board. Moreover, to compel the court to calculate the offender's risk so far in the future assumes that the assessment is enduring: it must not be capable of being invalidated by the impact of long-term incarceration, the availability or absence of risk reductive programmes, or the offender's own capacity or willingness to change. The development of dynamic risk assessment has moved assessment tools beyond their earlier reliance on static factors (such as background, sex and criminal history) to take into account attributes that can be changed through risk-reductive interventions (eg, rehabilitation or drug programmes) or life choices (eg, concerning friends and family relationships) (Hannah-Moffat 2013: 274–77). This raises the question whether a prediction of risk at the point of release is capable of allowing for the possibility that an individual might in the future reform to such a degree as to bear little resemblance to the risky person in the dock. If it does not, is this not a denial of the offender's capacity for moral choice, which is difficult to reconcile with ideas of individual autonomy and respect for human dignity?

[4] *R v Smith* [2011] UKSC 37 [15].

[5] ibid.

[6] *R (on the Application of Sturnham) (Appellant) v The Parole Board of England and Wales and Another (Respondents) (No 2)* [2013] UKSC 47 [36].

[7] *R v Bryant* [2017] EWCA Crim 1662 [8].

V. Validity of Predictive Sentencing Tools

Second, although risk assessment tools are more sophisticated and more reliable than was once the case (on the history of risk assessment, see Simon 2005; van Ginneken, Chapter 2 in this volume), their capacity to assess risk accurately remains contested. The criminal court is not a scientific laboratory, and risk of offending cannot be measured, assessed and applied systematically and precisely. The practice of criminal risk assessment is constrained by limited resources and informed by larger political concerns, not least those arising in a precautionary environment committed to public protection from serious harm, and the avoidance of blame by public officials (Hood 2011; Lomell 2012). Whatever claims to accuracy may be made for risk assessment instruments in theory (for a critique, see Dressel and Farid (2018: 3)), the manner in which they are used at sentencing depends on the exercise of discretion by court officials and, especially, judges. In North America, other factors have been shown to influence sentencing practice, including judicial commitment to adhere to sentencing guidelines, judicial education, statistical competence and understanding of probability, and judicial willingness (or reluctance) to privilege risk assessment instruments over their own professional judgement (Hannah-Moffat 2013; Monahan, Metz and Garrett 2018). English judges questioned about their practices of risk assessment admit to relying upon 'instinct', 'intuition', 'common sense' and 'gut reaction' to assess risk, as well as on their personal perception of the risk posed by offenders before them in court. Judicial responses such as 'they stare out at you' or 'you've watched them in the witness box, and you've seen the person and felt the presence – and you know' (Prison Reform Trust 2010: 29) suggest that formal risk assessments may be mediated in practice by judicial preconceptions and beliefs in their personal ability to assess risk.

VI. Predicting the Future in a State of Uncertainty

Finally, and more problematic still, is the question of how predictive sentencing decisions are to be reached not when judges know (or think they know) the risk, but when they plainly do not, namely in conditions of uncertainty. The question of the appropriate sentencing approach in cases of acknowledged uncertainty arose in the English case of *Attorney General's Reference (Smith)*.[8] The trial court was faced with a single historic offence of violent sexual assault on a 14-year-old girl by a defendant with no prior or subsequent criminal history.[9] At sentencing, the

[8] *Attorney General's Reference (Smith)* [2017] EWCA Crim 252.

[9] The case came to trial some six years after the offence as a result of DNA tests; ibid [5].

trial judge considered the question of dangerousness and concluded: 'Other than the facts of the case … there is no evidence upon which I can make a finding of dangerousness and I decline to do so.'[10] Accordingly, he imposed a sentence of 12 years' imprisonment, along with a restraining order and a sexual harm prevention order of indefinite duration.[11] The Attorney General sought leave to refer the case to the Court of Appeal,[12] which considered whether an extended sentence should have been imposed on the grounds of dangerousness. The Court noted that in the earlier case of *Troninas*, it was held that because the cause of the offence was 'a mystery, no one has any idea what is the level of danger that it may recur'[13] and that 'where the risk is of that nature, then, as it seems to us, the only correct conclusion is an indeterminate sentence'.[14] In light of this decision, the Court of Appeal in *Attorney General's Reference (Smith)* held that: 'In circumstances where the court has no idea as to why these very serious offences were committed or what triggered them there cannot be confidence that another serious event might not occur in the future.' Given this uncertainty, it concluded that a lengthy determinate sentence was inappropriate and an indeterminate sentence should have been passed.[15]

The decision in *Attorney General's Reference (Smith)* appears to adopt the view, as Harris and Kelly observe, that 'sentencing courts should abstain from a finding of dangerousness only if confident another offence will not occur' (Harris and Kelly 2018). They regard such a 'presumption of dangerousness' in the face of uncertainty as objectionable on several grounds, not least that it ignores the fact that the statutory scheme set out in section 229(3) of the Criminal Justice Act 2003 for Imprisonment for Public Protection, which required the courts to presume dangerousness, had been repealed by section 17 of the Criminal Justice and Immigration Act 2008 on the grounds that it denied the courts the ability to exercise discretion (Zedner 2012: 223–24). It is also the case that to presume dangerousness in cases such as *Smith* is to disregard the well-established 'presumption of harmlessness'. Thus, the Floud Report argued that every person should be presumed to be free of harmful intentions, but that the presumption is lost once a person has manifested, by committing a serious crime, the capacity to harm others (Floud and Young 1981: Chapters 3 and 4). A weak version of this presumption is said to apply only to those who have yet to offend (as was the case with *Smith*)

[10] ibid [13].

[11] ibid [2].

[12] Under a provision for referral of 'unduly lenient sentences' (ss 35–36 of the Criminal Justice Act 1998), which approximates to systems of prosecution appeals in some other jurisdictions.

[13] *Attorney General's Reference (No 5 of 2011) (Troninas)* [2012] 1 Cr App R (S) 103, quoted in *Attorney General's Reference (Smith)* (n 8) [20].

[14] *Troninas* (n 13).

[15] ibid [26]. The Court therefore quashed the determinate sentence of 12 years and replaced it with an extended determinate sentence of 17 years, comprising a custodial term of 12 years and an extended licence period of five years (at [27]). For a similarly problematic case, see *R v Emile Cilliers* (2018), https://www.judiciary.uk/wp-content/uploads/2018/06/r-v-cilliers-mr-justice-sweeney-sentencing-remarks-winchester-crown-court-15-june-2018.pdf.

and the presumption is lost on conviction. Nigel Walker argued that: 'someone who has harmed, or tried to harm, another person, can hardly claim a right to the presumption of harmlessness: he has forfeited that right, and given society the right to interfere in his life' (Walker 1996: 7). On this view, it is justifiable to redistribute the risk of future harms by protecting potential victims and by burdening the known offender, who has lost the benefit of the presumption of harmlessness.

A stronger version holds that the fact that the offender has been proven to have intended harm on one occasion cannot ground future claims as to harmfulness (Ashworth and Zedner 2014: 130; for a different view, see Husak, Chapter 3 in this volume: 38). This stronger version better accords with the presumption of innocence, which requires the defendant to be deemed innocent unless and until their guilt is proven.[16] By contrast, a positive presumption of dangerousness in the face of uncertainty abandons both strong and weak versions of the presumption of harmlessness. For the judges in *Attorney General's Reference (Smith)* to conclude that uncertainty as to the cause of a serious offence should lead the court to presume dangerousness and thus to impose an indeterminate sentence goes against the fundamental principles of criminal justice.

This approach to decision making in the face of uncertainty may be influenced by the 'precautionary principle', which informs many areas of public policy concerning the risk of serious harm (Hebenton and Seddon 2009). Developed originally in relation to environmental risk (Fisher 2002), the precautionary principle states that 'where there are threats of serious or irreversible damage, lack of full scientific certainty shall not be used as a reason for postponing cost-effective measures'.[17] Recognising that absence of clear evidence is not the same as absence of threat, it holds that where the prospective harm is grave, uncertainty should not be treated as a sufficient ground for inaction. A precautionary approach may make sense in respect of global warming, construction hazards and the drug industry, where risks are widespread and potentially catastrophic, but its application to long or indeterminate sentences is more problematic in that it is liable to result in prolonged deprivation of an individual's liberty and a denial of autonomy (Ramsay 2012b; however, see also Stacey 2017). It is to this interaction between indeterminate sentences and human rights that the discussion now moves.

VII. Indeterminate Sentences and Human Rights

In English law, life imprisonment is the mandatory sentence for murder (see below), but there are also two other forms of life imprisonment (see van Ginneken,

[16] Article 6(2) of the European Convention on Human Rights provides that: 'Everyone charged with a criminal offence shall be presumed innocent until proved guilty according to law.'

[17] Principle 15 of the UN Rio Declaration on Environment and Development.

Chapter 2 in this volume). One is also expressed as mandatory (according to section 225 of the Criminal Justice Act 2003), which means that a court must impose a sentence of life imprisonment if there is a significant risk of serious harm to members of the public and the seriousness of the offence(s) is such as to justify the imposition of imprisonment for life.[18] The other form of life sentence was introduced by the Legal Aid, Sentencing and Punishment of Offenders Act 2012, and once again it is mandatory if two conditions are fulfilled: if a court would have imposed a sentence of 10 years or longer but for this provision; and if the offender had previously been convicted of a listed offence and sentenced either to life imprisonment or to a prison sentence of 10 years or more.[19] Whenever any form of life imprisonment is imposed, the judge must specify a 'minimum term', this being the minimum number of years proportionate to the relative gravity of the crime(s). After that term has expired, the offender remains in prison until the Parole Board decides that it is no longer necessary for the protection of the public that he or she should be imprisoned (Padfield 2016). Release is then on licence, with liability to recall (Appleton 2010). Thus, the effect of the sentencing decision is to fix the minimum number of years to be served and to reach a judgment that the offender is dangerous enough that release should be determined by the Parole Board, but the predictive part of the life sentence is not engaged until the minimum term has been served. From then on, the matter is in the hands of the Parole Board. More frequently imposed since 2012 are 'extended determinate sentences' (EDS), which may be imposed upon those the court deems to be dangerous. EDS comprise an ordinary determinate term and an extended licence period for such time as the court considers necessary to protect the public from serious harm, which together must not exceed the maximum length for the offence (Saunders 2017: 942–43). The detailed legislation has changed a few times, but in essence EDS may be relatively severe because release from the custodial part comes at or after the two-thirds point (not one-half as with other prison sentences), as determined by the Parole Board, and release is on licence, with liability to recall.[20]

As for the mandatory sentence of life imprisonment for murder, Schedule 21 to the Criminal Justice Act 2003 (as amended) provides statutory starting points for minimum terms: a general starting point of 15 years; 25 years for murder with a knife or other weapon taken to the scene; 30 years for murders of police or prison officers, murders involving firearms and other aggravating factors; and a whole-life minimum term for exceptionally serious cases, such as premeditated killings of two or more people, sexual or sadistic child murders, political

[18] For a fuller discussion of the relevant English law, see Harris and Walker (2018b); and Ashworth (2015: 237–48). It seems that a discretionary life sentence may also be imposed at common law: *Saunders* [2013] *Crim LR* 930.

[19] The sentence is not absolutely mandatory: a court may pass a different sentence if it decides that there are 'particular circumstances' that would make it 'unjust' to impose the life sentence.

[20] See, eg, *R (on the Application of Stott) v Secretary of State for Justice* [2017] EWHC 214 (Admin).

murders and second murders (Appleton and Grover 2007). The question arises as to whether a whole-life term (or its US equivalent, LWOP) is compatible with the human rights of the offender.

VIII. Whole-Life Sentences in Europe

In England and Wales, the answer to this question has been the subject of a lengthy contest of judicial ping-pong between the Court of Appeal and the ECtHR. Our concern here is not to chart the positions taken by the courts or to attempt to interpret the politics of the various exchanges; rather, it is to identify and examine their treatment of the fundamental right (declared in Article 3 of the European Convention on Human Rights (ECHR)) not to be subjected to 'inhuman or degrading treatment or punishment'. This right is regarded as a manifestation of the principle of human dignity: the International Covenant on Civil and Political Rights declares that its rights 'derive from the inherent dignity of the human person'[21] and the same principle is recognised as underpinning the whole of the ECHR. The Grand Chamber of the ECtHR in *Vinter v UK* held that these rights are not violated if an offender is in fact detained for life, nor are they violated if an offender is sentenced to imprisonment for his or her whole life.[22] However, it held that in order to satisfy Article 3, there must be both the possibility of review and the prospect of release (see the analysis in Snacken (2016: 53–55)). Without a real prospect of release, a whole-life sentence would be 'irreducible' and it would be incompatible with human dignity for the state to deprive a person of his or her freedom without some opportunity to regain it.[23] The key issue, according to the ECtHR, is that:

> A whole life prisoner is entitled to know, at the outset of his sentence, what he must do to be considered for release and under what conditions, including when a review of his sentence will take place or will be sought.[24]

There must be a mechanism for review, which should take the form of:

> [A] review which allows the domestic authorities to consider whether any changes in the life prisoner are so significant, and such progress has been made in the course of the sentence, as to mean that continued detention can no longer be justified on legitimate penological grounds.[25]

Where the domestic law fails to provide any mechanism or possibility for review of a whole-life sentence, the incompatibility with Article 3 on this ground arises

[21] www.ohchr.org/en/professionalinterest/pages/ccpr.aspx.
[22] *Vinter v UK* (n 3) [110].
[23] ibid [113].
[24] ibid [122].
[25] ibid [119]. For further discussion of this point, see van Zyl Smit, Weatherby and Creighton (2014).

at the moment of the imposition of the whole-life sentence, a point confirmed in the concurring judgment of Judge Mahoney in *Vinter*: 'if it can be said that there is in Article 3 a prohibition on irreducible life sentences, this in itself is a preventive requirement that should logically come into play at the moment of sentencing and not later'.[26] Having regard to the margin of appreciation,[27] the Court does not seek to prescribe the form or timing of the review.[28] However, the essential disagreement between the Strasbourg judges in *Vinter* and the English judges in *Attorney General's Reference No 69 of 2013 (McLoughlin)*[29] is whether English law provides such a review mechanism. The ECtHR in *Vinter* held that the possibility of release by the Home Secretary on 'compassionate grounds' provided by section 30(1) of the Crime (Sentences) Act 1997 was not sufficient to satisfy the review requirement, either in substance or clarity. The Court of Appeal in *McLoughlin* held that the section 30 power does provide a mechanism for review and release, even though it is statutorily confined to 'compassionate grounds' rather than to rehabilitative progress. While reiterating the *Vinter* principles, the Grand Chamber in *Hutchinson v UK*[30] accepted the analysis of the Court of Appeal and concluded that English law is compliant with Article 3. The reason given in *Vinter* for insisting on a mechanism for review is that the penal aims of a sentence may shift in the course of the sentence if the risk posed by the prisoner reduces and therefore review is necessary in order to 'determine whether imprisonment remains justified'.[31] In particular, the Grand Chamber pointed to the wide European and international support for the principle that all prisoners must be offered the possibility of rehabilitation, release and re-integration.[32] To deprive an offender who is subject to a whole-life tariff of the possibility of release is contrary to the principle of human dignity, respect for which is 'the very essence' of the Convention.[33] It is this that Judge Power-Forde, in her concurring judgment in *Vinter*, described as 'the right to hope' deriving from the principle of human dignity of all individuals, no matter how grave their wrongs. Judge Power-Forde elaborated:

> [H]ope is an important and constitutive aspect of the human person. Those who commit the most abhorrent and egregious of acts and who inflict untold suffering upon others, nevertheless retain their fundamental humanity and carry within themselves the capacity to change … To deny them the experience of hope would be to deny a fundamental aspect of their humanity and, to do that, would be degrading.[34]

[26] *Vinter v UK* (n 22) [7].

[27] That is, the margin of discretion allowed to states signatory to the ECHR that is used by ECtHR when determining if a Member State has breached the Convention.

[28] *Vinter v UK* (n 22) [120].

[29] *Attorney General's Reference No 69 of 2013 (McLoughlin)* [2014] 2 Cr App R (S) 321.

[30] *Hutchinson v UK* (2015) ECHR 239.

[31] *Vinter v UK* (n 22) [47].

[32] ibid [114].

[33] ibid [113].

[34] *Vinter v UK* (n 22); see also the analysis in Vannier (2016: 192).

IX. Developments in the US

At the same time as these European developments, the US Supreme Court has begun to 'row back' from the widespread imposition of LWOP sentences (Kirby 2011; Ristroph 2010). In *Graham v Florida*,[35] the Supreme Court held that the LWOP sentence was a 'cruel and unusual' punishment, contrary to the US Constitution, if imposed on a juvenile (under 18) for a non-homicide offence: 'Life in prison without the possibility of parole gives no chance for fulfilment outside prison walls, no chance for reconciliation with society, no hope.'[36] In *Miller v Alabama*[37] the Supreme Court held that LWOP violated the 'cruel and unusual' clause if it was mandatory for a juvenile. Whatever the offence of conviction, it was essential to allow room for a court sentencing a juvenile to take account of mitigating circumstances. And in *Montgomery v Louisiana*,[38] it was held that the two previous decisions apply retrospectively to young people already sentenced. The animating reasons for these US developments include the principle of respect for the human attributes of all individuals, even those who have committed very serious crimes; opposition to the 'denial of hope' integral to a sentence that means that endeavours to rehabilitate the offender are immaterial; and the principle of proportionality, which is violated if a sentence as absolute as LWOP is imposed for non-homicide offences or for homicide offences that might involve significant mitigating factors. Although the focus in the Supreme Court judgments is upon the developmental aspects of juvenile characters, some of the above arguments would apply equally to the imposition of LWOP on adults. However, the Supreme Court has not yet applied the 'cruel and unusual' clause to LWOP more generally or confronted the argument that if LWOP aims to protect society from offenders who pose the greatest risk, then it should be used more selectively (for further discussion, see Ogletree and Sarat (2013); van Zyl Smit and Appleton (2016)).

X. Indeterminacy, Hope and Human Dignity

The argument in favour of recognising the 'right to hope' in all court sentences, including those imposed for extremely serious offences, is clearly related to the principle of human dignity. Indeed, it is arguable that the ECtHR has placed hope, human dignity and access to rehabilitation at the heart of a decent penal system. In so doing, it spawned a complex jurisprudence that centres on the 'right

[35] *Graham v Florida* 130 S Ct 2011 (2010).
[36] ibid per Kennedy J at 2032.
[37] *Miller v Alabama* 132 S Ct 2455 (2012).
[38] *Montgomery v Louisiana* 136 S Ct 718 (2016).

to hope', but which, in the contrary view taken by the UK court in *Hutchinson*, has also thrown it into question.[39] Although some now doubt whether the right to hope persists and suggest that it is 'too soon to hope for a Convention right to hope' (Simonsen 2015), the concept of hope has become a topic of larger political debate in the UK about the role of penal institutions.[40] However, the prospects for the promotion of hope as a penal value are uncertain in a precautionary climate dominated by demands for public protection. Despite the avowed political commitment to hope made by successive governments in England and Wales,[41] current penal practices, based as they are on a precautionary approach committed to risk assessment and indeterminate sentencing, sit uneasily alongside the promise of hope.

A commitment to hope requires that capacity for moral choice is acknowledged and that sentences imposed even on those deemed dangerous have, built within them, the means to enable, assess and act on signs of change. Furthermore, it is not sufficient for the sentence merely to prescribe or be premised on an architecture of risk-reductive intervention, risk assessment, provision for review and, where appropriate, release. If, in practice, risk management or rehabilitative programmes within prisons are scarce, inaccessible or inadequate, the result will be to deny hope to those sentenced to indeterminate terms. Much of the critical commentary on the risk-based sentence of IPP (see, eg, van Ginneken, Chapter 2 in this volume) focused on its scope and structure, including the dubious statutory formulation of dangerousness, the problematic measures of risk adopted and the fact that seriously disproportionate indefinite sentences could be imposed on those eligible for IPP (Ashworth and Zedner 2014: 150–51). Arguably an equally important flaw lay in its implementation, as inadequate planning and resources meant that the availability of rehabilitative or risk-management programmes was so poor that IPP prisoners were effectively consigned to an enduring state of hopelessness. Denied access to risk management programmes (often available only in other prisons to which transfer was impossible) and therefore the means to reduce their individual risk, they had very little hope of persuading the Parole Board they no longer posed a significant risk of serious harm to the public. The abolition of IPP in 2012 saw a manifestly unfair sentencing regime overturned: its abolition

[39] See the developments summarised in the previous paragraph and http://echrblog.blogspot.co.uk/2015/02/hutchinson-v-uk-right-to-hope-revisited.html on the 'retreat from *Vinter*'.

[40] In 2016, Michael Gove, the then UK Justice Secretary, set out a new agenda for prisons in which he insisted that 'we must offer chances to change; that for those trying hard to turn themselves around, we should offer hope; that in a compassionate country, we should help those who've made mistakes to find their way back onto the right path': https://www.gov.uk/government/news/prime-minister-outlines-plan-for-reform-of-prisons. See also M Gove 'Hope is at the Heart of My Prisons Reform' *The Telegraph* (18 May 2016), https://www.telegraph.co.uk/news/2016/05/18/hope-is-at-the-heart-of-my-prisons-reform.

[41] The promotion of hope as a penal value initiated by Gove was continued by his successor as Justice Secretary, Liz Truss, and has been revived by the Justice Secretary, David Gauke: 'Prisons Reform Speech', 6 March 2018, https://www.gov.uk/government/speeches/prisons-reform-speech.

was held to be a victory by many critics, but for those 'left behind' (Annison 2015: 167–73),[42] the continuing difficulty of securing access to risk-reductive programmes means that the prospect of release remains a vain hope for many. This sense of hopelessness is sadly evidenced by statistics on the risk of harm suffered by IPP prisoners, who are significantly more likely to self-harm than those on life or determinate sentences.[43] This sad history demonstrates the need to promote the right to hope for all those subject to indeterminate sentences. The ECtHR was right in its *Vinter* judgment that even if, as a result of predictive sentence, a prisoner had to 'spend the rest of his or her life in detention because he or she remained a risk to the community',[44] human dignity requires that there be periodic review and a real prospect of release.

XI. The Scope of Civil Preventive Detention

Earlier we noted the possible inconsistency between holding a person to be an autonomous moral agent at the point of conviction and yet relying, at the sentencing stage, on an assessment of his or her future risk that seemed to deny his or her capacity for change. A further dilemma is the apparent inconsistency between holding a person responsible at trial for the purposes of punishment and yet non-responsible (mentally disordered) at a later stage for the purposes of civil preventive detention. For example, the German system provides for the imposition of civil preventive detention after the end of a sentence. In several judgments starting with *M v Germany*,[45] the ECtHR held that this form of post-sentence detention was in substance a 'penalty' within Article 7 ECHR and therefore could not be imposed retrospectively. German law was then changed, and in *Ilnseher v Germany* (2017),[46] the ECtHR held that the new form of post-sentence civil detention may be imposed retrospectively if it is imposed for 'therapeutic purposes', in order to address the individual's mental disorder. One of the arguments put to the Grand Chamber in the *Ilnseher* case was that it is inconsistent to

[42] In 2017, 3,162 people remained in prison on IPP of whom 2,718 (86%) had already served their tariff period. Over two-thirds had a tariff of 4 years or less. The Parole Board predicts that, without legislation, there will still be 1,500 people in prison serving an IPP by 2020. http://www.prisonreformtrust.org.uk/Portals/0/Documents/Bromley%20Briefings/Autumn%202017%20factfile.pdf 28-29.

[43] The 2016 Ministry of Justice *Safety in Custody* statistics reported 719 incidents of self-harm per 1,000 IPP prisoners as compared to 393 incidents per 1,000 determinate sentence prisoners and 313 incidents per 1,000 life sentenced prisoners in England and Wales. Source: http://www.prisonreformtrust.org.uk/Portals/0/Documents/Bromley%20Briefings/Autumn%202017%20factfile.pdf 29.

[44] *Vinter v United Kingdom* (Grand Chamber, 2013: Application Nos. 66069/09, 130/10 and 3896/10), (99).

[45] *M v Germany* (2010) 51 EHRR 976.

[46] *Ilnseher v Germany* (2017), Section, 2 February 2017: Application Nos 10211/12 and 27505/14. See also the earlier judgment in *Bergmann v Germany* (2016) 63 EHRR 991.

sentence a person as an autonomous actor and then subsequently to impose civil detention on the grounds of mental disorder; the Grand Chamber's judgment is awaited.

This line of argument has not met with success in the United States. Thus, in the leading case of *Kansas v Hendricks*,[47] the US Supreme Court upheld the legality of post-conviction civil confinement, adopting the argument that the purpose of the detention was preventive and protective of the public, not punitive, and that the detention was therefore correctly classified as civil.[48] Several commentators have criticised the alleged inconsistency between finding the individual not to be mentally disordered at the point of conviction and sentence, and yet finding the individual to be suffering from a form of personality disorder sufficient to render him or her so dangerous as to require indefinite commitment. Thus, Janus argues that 'civil commitment as a means to violence-control produces the contradictory holding that a criminal can be at the same time held responsible and yet be unable to control their behaviour' (Janus 2000: 82). Morse criticizes the *Hendricks* decision strongly:

> It is utterly paradoxical to claim that a sexually violent predator is sufficiently responsible to deserve the stigma and punishment of criminal incarceration, but that the predator is not sufficiently responsible to be permitted the usual freedom from involuntary civil commitment that even the very predictably dangerous but responsible agents retain because our society wishes to maximise the liberty and dignity of all citizens. (Morse 1998: 259)

However, Morse does enter a caveat ('even if the standards for responsibility in the two systems need not be symmetrical') that complicates matters. It is quite common for the criminal law's defence of insanity to be drawn narrowly, whereas at the sentencing stage, a more expansive definition of mental disorder may be adopted. Thus, in order to sustain Morse's critique, we must be satisfied that the position adopted, for example, by English law is 'utterly paradoxical'.

Returning to the judgment in *Hendricks*, Steiker is surely right to argue that it 'failed to use the case as an opportunity to clarify important issues regarding whether and what limits exist on the non-punitive use of civil confinement to deal with dangerous individuals' (Steiker 1998: 791–92). In *Kansas v Crane*,[49] the US Supreme Court went on to define mental abnormality for the purposes of civil detention as 'serious difficulty in controlling behaviour', a most unsatisfactory designation, since it goes well beyond the clinical definitions of mental disorder and could apply widely to persons convicted of sexual and violent offences (Janus 2004). The looseness of this definition, rather than the alleged paradox to which Morse points, is surely the strongest critique of the US position.

[47] *Kansas v Hendricks* 521 US 346 (1997).

[48] By contrast, Husak has challenged the idea that preventive detention is conceptually distinct and has championed the idea that preventive detention should be understood and justified as punishment (Husak 2011; Husak 2013: 178–93).

[49] *Kansas v Crane* 534 US 407 (2002).

XII. Public Protection and the Conditions of Detention

As we acknowledged at the outset, we take it as generally accepted that the state has a duty to protect people from harm or, alternatively put, to prevent harm. Whether this 'duty to protect' is regarded (after Hobbes) as reciprocal to the citizen's duty to obey the law or whether we adopt Blackstone's more pragmatic statement that 'preventive justice is, upon every principle of reason, of humanity, and of sound policy, preferable in all respects to punishing justice' (Ashworth and Zedner 2014: 7–10), it may be regarded as a fundamental plank of liberal political philosophy. Even if we are completely satisfied with this foundation, it remains to decide on the form that the 'duty to protect' may take, the deprivations it may inflict and the limits that should be placed on its pursuit. Thus, having earlier explored the justifications for imposing indeterminate sentences and civil detention on predictive grounds, we now move on to consider the conditions in which those so detained should be held.

Article 5(1) ECHR declares the right to liberty and then states that a person may be deprived of liberty in certain circumstances, of which one is '(e) the lawful detention of persons for the prevention of the spreading of infectious diseases, of persons of unsound mind, alcoholics or drug addicts or vagrants'. This is one of the least satisfactory provisions in the ECHR: even if one sets aside the controversies surrounding the list of qualifying conditions (most obviously 'vagrants'), what is remarkable about this provision is that it implies that simply having that condition, eg, being mentally disordered ('unsound mind'), is enough in itself to justify deprivation of liberty. This is surely wrong in principle. Article 5(1) should be qualified by some such requirement as 'necessary for the prevention of serious harm' in order to provide a justification for the detention. There is an element of this in relation to compulsory isolation or quarantine, which is only permissible 'for the prevention of the spreading of infectious diseases' (Gable and Gostin 2010: 129–30). Fortunately, the ECtHR has imposed tighter conditions on detention for this purpose, stating that the key questions are:

> [W]hether the spreading of infectious disease is dangerous for public health or safety, and whether detention of the person infected is the last resort in order to prevent the spreading of the disease, because less severe measures have been considered and found to be insufficient to safeguard the public interest.[50]

In effect, these are the requirements developed by the ECtHR and known as the principles of proportionality and necessity. The principle of proportionality calls for a balance to be struck between the individual's fundamental rights and the general interest of the community. The 'last resort' requirement is an application

[50] *Enhorn v Sweden* (2005) 41 EHRR 643) [44].

of the principle of necessity. It applies not only to the decision to impose detention or restrictions, but also to release, so that the individual must be released when the point is reached at which some lesser measure would be sufficient. It is important to recall that individuals detained under this power are being deprived of their liberty to prevent harm to the public. This is an exercise of the state's duty to protect, but one that calls for justification, since it impinges on the fundamental right to liberty (Meyerson 2009: 522–26). In principle, therefore, the conditions of the detention should be as close as possible to normal life, in terms of accommodation, food and facilities.

A similar argument can be made in relation to the civil detention of mentally disordered people. In English law, the criteria for detention in hospital are that the mental condition 'warrants' such detention or that it is 'appropriate', both rather vague and falling well below a requirement of necessity. Similarly vague criteria were read into Article 5(1)(e) by the ECtHR in *Winterwerp v The Netherlands*.[51] However, insofar as these mentally disordered persons are detained for the protection of the public (some are detained, at least in part, to protect them from themselves), the same principle ought surely to apply as to detention to prevent the spread of infectious diseases. Should not the conditions of detention be as close as possible to normal life, in terms of accommodation, food and facilities?

When the compulsory detention of a mentally disordered person arises from a criminal conviction, or a finding in criminal proceedings of unfitness to plead or insanity, the argument for normalisation of the conditions of detention is more contestable. The rationale for the detention is linked to the state's duty to protect, but it is also linked to the element of criminality. Where a mentally disordered person is detained under a hospital order with a restriction order (or the equivalent), release must be ordered if a tribunal is satisfied that the patient is no longer suffering from a mental disorder of a nature or degree that warrants detention (Ashworth and Zedner 2014: 210–12).

Returning to life imprisonment and other indeterminate sentences, can it be argued that, since the offender is detained after the expiry of the minimum term for the purpose of public protection, that portion of the sentence should be served in 'normalised' conditions (Wood 1988)? The ECtHR has certainly insisted that the conditions of detention of indeterminate sentence prisoners must offer facilities for rehabilitation. This principle was stated in relation to the English sentence of IPP, which is structured so as to have a minimum term and then indeterminate detention for public protection, and it also applies to any detention during the extended licence period of an extended determinate sentence.[52] Thus, rehabilitation was said to be 'a necessary element of any part of the detention which is to be

[51] *Winterwerp v The Netherlands* (1979) 2 EHRR 387.

[52] See the UK Supreme Court in *Brown v Parole Board for Scotland* [2017] UKSC 69, overruling its own decision in *R (Kaiyam) v Secretary of State for Justice* [2014] UKSC 66, which had supported a general duty to provide rehabilitative opportunities to all prisoners under sentence.

justified solely by reference to public protection'.[53] And, as we have already noted, if post-sentence detention in Germany (*Sicherungsverwahrung*) is to qualify as prevention rather than punishment, it must have 'a clear therapeutic orientation' designed to reduce the dangerousness of the offender.[54]

If the provision of rehabilitative facilities is now regarded as part of the state's 'duty to protect' – achieving the dual aims of protecting the public and enabling the offender to work towards release from detention – should this be taken further by insisting that the conditions of any detention for public protection should be 'normalised', as is the case for quarantine and isolation (for discussion, see Douglas, Chapter 5 in this volume; 'those subjected to quarantine retain all of their normal rights')? It was argued above that although detention in these cases is for the purpose of public protection, it originated in a criminal conviction for a serious offence.[55] This may be said to distinguish prisoners serving indeterminate sentences from persons subjected to isolation or quarantine to prevent the spread of an infectious disease, who are not detained because of any criminal wrong, past or prospective. While there may be good reasons for the prison authorities to devise a more relaxed regime for indeterminate prisoners, it is doubtful whether there is a strong enough argument for the normalisation of the conditions of their detention or, indeed, whether in the present penal climate, it would be politically plausible to do so.

XIII. Conclusion

This chapter has sought to address some difficult dilemmas arising from risk assessment, prediction and indeterminate sentencing. We began by discussing three problems of principle and practice arising from legislation and judicial decisions on indeterminate sentences in England and Wales – whether the risk assessment should relate to the time of sentencing or should be projected to the end of the minimum term of detention; how risk assessments may operate in practice; and the proper approach when there is uncertainty about the prediction. Underlying several of the relevant issues is the question whether current procedures respect the autonomy of the individual and the capacity to change. This is crucial to our discussion of the human rights challenge to indeterminate sentences, where the

[53] *James, Wells and Lee v UK* (2013) 56 EHRR 399 [209].

[54] *Ilnseher v Germany* (n 45). For an insightful discussion of rehabilitation in US preventive detention, see Slobogin (2011: 1165–68).

[55] This cannot be said of offenders still held in prison under IPP, whose offence(s) (particularly if sentenced before 2008) may not have been particularly serious. According to evidence given by the Parole Board, prior to the 2008 reform of IPP, half of IPP prisoners received a tariff sentence of 20 months or less, while 20 per cent received a tariff of less than 18 months (HC Justice Committee 2008: 21). See https://www.publications.parliament.uk/pa/cm200708/cmselect/cmjust/184/184.pdf.

argument for a right to hope is founded on respect for human dignity. The final sections of the chapter examined the boundary between imprisonment and civil detention, and the consequential question of the appropriate conditions for those detained on risk predictive grounds 'for the protection of the public'.

There are no easy or right answers to the dilemmas addressed in this chapter. To the extent that the spread of indeterminate sentences and their predictive drivers are fuelled by the demands of a fearful public for protection against risk of harm, it is tempting to think that there is an optimal equilibrium to be achieved between fear and hope. But as Krygier observes:

> There are no all-purpose bright line guides to the exact mix of fear and hope that our institutions should respect and reflect; no political and institutional recipes, stable and apt for every time and circumstance, which we should follow without deviation (Krygier 1997).

Krygier suggests that 'we should be prepared to hazard more improvement, temper fear with hope' (1997). The implication is that hope is owed not only to those we incarcerate indefinitely, but also to ourselves – that we, the fearful public, should be willing to fear a little less and hope a little more. In the US, concession to public anxiety and the tendency towards 'harsh justice' has resulted in too ready resort to sentences of LWOP (Whitman 2003), whereas in Europe, this is tempered by an approach to penal policy constrained by 'milder' penal values, a culture of regard for human rights and a continuing faith in the rehabilitative potential, even of those who seem most hopeless (Snacken 2010). As Duff has argued, in contrast to the US, in Europe 'the idea that offenders and prisoners must be accorded the respect and dignity that is still their due remains central to the rhetoric and aspirations of penal policy' (Duff 2005: 143). We applaud Duff's suggestion that 'we can develop a morally plausible conception of liberal citizenship that portrays it not as a set of rights whose retention depends on good behaviour, but as a status that cannot be lost by the commission of even serious crimes' (Duff 2005: 154–55; also Meyerson 2009).[56] Accepting the contention that prisoners should be accorded fundamental rights, respect and dignity calls into question the legitimacy of predictive risk assessment which results in indeterminate sentencing regimes that tend to deny all these.

References

Annison, H (2015) *Dangerous Politics: Risk, Political Vulnerability and Penal Policy* (Oxford, Oxford University Press).

Appleton, C (2010) *Life after Life Imprisonment* (Oxford, Oxford University Press).

[56] We might query Duff's reliance on 'citizenship' here for its apparent failure to accord equal value and protection to those who are non-citizens; see Zedner (2013: 40–57).

Appleton, C and Grover, B (2007) 'The Pros and Cons of Life without Parole' 47 *British Journal of Criminology* 597.

Ashworth, A (2015) *Sentencing and Criminal Justice*, 6th edn (Cambridge, Cambridge University Press).

Ashworth, A and Zedner, L (2014) *Preventive Justice* (Oxford, Oxford University Press).

Douglas, T et al (2017) 'Risk Assessment Tools in Criminal Justice and Forensic Psychiatry: The Need for Better Data' 42 *European Psychiatry* 134.

Drenkhahn, K, Morgenstern, C, and van Zyl Smit, D (2012) 'Preventive Detention in Germany in the Shadow of European Human Rights Law' 3 *Criminal Law Review* 167.

Dressel, J and Farid, H (2018) 'The Accuracy, Fairness, and Limits of Predicting Recidivism' 4 *Science Advances* 1.

Duff, RA (2005) 'Punishment, Dignity and Degradation' 25 *Oxford Journal of Legal Studies* 141.

Fisher, E (2002) 'Precaution, Precaution Everywhere: Developing a "Common Understanding" of the Precautionary Principle in the European Community' 9 *Maastricht Journal of European and Comparative Law* 7.

Floud, J and Young, W (1981) *Dangerousness and Criminal Justice* (London, Heinemann).

Gable, L and Gostin, LO (2010) 'Human Rights of Persons with Mental Disabilities: The European Convention on Human Rights' in LO Gostin et al. (eds), *Principles of Mental Health Law and Policy* (Oxford, Oxford University Press).

Hannah-Moffat, K (2013) 'Actuarial Sentencing: An "Unsettled" Proposition' 30 *Justice Quarterly* 270.

Harris, L and Walker, S (2018a) 'Difficulties with Dangerousness: (1) The Timing of Assessment of Risk' *Criminal Law Review* 695.

——. (2018b) 'Difficulties with Dangerousness: (2) Determining the Appropriate Sentence', *Criminal Law Review* 792.

Harris, L and Kelly, R (2018) 'A Dangerous Presumption for Risk-Based Sentencing?' 134 *Law Quarterly Review* 353.

Hebenton, B and Seddon, T (2009) 'From Dangerousness to Precaution: Managing Sexual and Violent Offenders in an Insecure and Uncertain Age' 49 *British Journal of Criminology* 343.

Hood, C (2011) 'Risk and Government: The Architectonics of Blame-Avoidance' in L Skinns, M Scott and T Cox (eds), *Risk* (Cambridge, Cambridge University Press).

House of Commons Justice Committee (2008) *Towards Effective Sentencing* (London, The Stationery Office), https://www.publications.parliament.uk/pa/cm200708/cmselect/cmjust/184/184.pdf.

Husak, D (2011), 'Lifting the Cloak: Preventive Detention as Punishment' 48 *San Diego Law Review* 1173.

——. (2013) 'Preventive Detention as Punishment? Some Possible Obstacles' in A Ashworth, L Zedner and P Tomlin (eds), *Prevention and the Limits of the Criminal Law* (Oxford, Oxford University Press).

Janus, E (2000) 'Civil Commitment as Social Control' in M Brown and J Pratt (eds), *Dangerous Offenders: Punishment and Social Order* (London, Routledge).
——. (2004) 'The Preventive State, Terrorists and Sexual Predators: Countering the Threat of a New Outsider Jurisprudence' 40 *Criminal Law Bulletin* 576.
Kirby, JM (2011) 'Graham, Miller, & the Right to Hope' 15 *City University of New York Law Review* 149.
Krygier, M (1997) 'Between Fear and Hope', ABC Boyer Lecture, www.abc.net.au/radionational/programs/boyerlectures/lecture-2-between-fear-and-hope/3460226#transcript.
Lacey, N (2016) *In Search of Criminal Responsibility: Ideas, Interests, and Institutions* (Oxford, Oxford University Press).
Lazarus, L (2004) *Contrasting Prisoners' Rights* (Oxford, Oxford University Press).
——. (2006) 'Conceptions of Liberty Deprivation' 69 *Modern Law Review* 738.
Lomell, HM (2012) 'Punishing the Uncommitted Crime: Prevention, Pre-emption, Precaution and the Transformation of the Criminal Law' in B Hudson and S Ugelvik (eds), *Justice and Security in the 21st Century: Risks, Rights and the Rule of Law* (London, Routledge).
Maurutto, P and Hannah-Moffat, K (2006) 'Assembling Risk and the Restructuring of Penal Control' 46 *British Journal of Criminology* 438.
Meyerson, D (2009), 'Risks, Rights, Statistics and Compulsory Measures' 31 *Sydney Law Review* 507.
Monahan, J and Skeem, JL (2016) 'Risk Assessment in Criminal Sentencing' 12 *Annual Review of Clinical Psychology* 489.
Monahan, J, Metz, AL and Garrett, BL (2018) 'Judicial Appraisals of Risk Assessment in Sentencing' University of Virginia School of Law Public Law and Legal Theory Research Paper Series, https://ssrn.com/abstract=3168644.
Morse, SJ (1998) 'Fear of Danger, Flight from Culpability' 4 *Psychology, Public Policy, and Law* 250.
Ogletree, C and Sarat, A (2013) *Life without Parole: America's New Death Penalty?* (New York, New York University Press).
Padfield, N (2016) 'Justifying Indefinite Detention: On What Grounds?' 11 *Criminal Law Review* 797.
Prison Reform Trust (2010) *Unjust Deserts: Imprisonment for Public Protection* (London, PRT).
Ramsay, P (2012a) *The Insecurity State: Vulnerable Autonomy and the Right to Security in the Criminal Law* (Oxford, Oxford University Press).
——. (2012b) 'Imprisonment under the Precautionary Principle' in GR Sullivan and I Dennis (eds) *Seeking Security: Pre-empting the Commission of Criminal Harms* (Oxford, Hart Publishing).
Ristroph, A (2010) 'Hope, Imprisonment, and the Constitution' 23 *Federal Sentencing Reporter* 75.
Rose, C (2012) 'RIP the IPP: A Look Back at the Sentence of Imprisonment for Public Protection' 76 *Journal of Criminal Law* 303.

Saunders, J (2017) 'The Extended Determinate Sentence: Is it a Just and Fair Sentence?' 12 *Criminal Law Review* 940.

Simon, J (2005), 'Reversal of Fortune: The Resurgence of Individual Risk Assessment in Criminal Justice' 1 *Annual Review of Law and Social Science* 397.

Simonsen, N (2015) 'Too Soon for the Right to Hope? Whole Life Sentences and the Strasbourg Court's Decision in *Hutchinson v UK*', *European Journal of International Law Blog*, https://www.ejiltalk.org/too-soon-for-the-right-to-hope-whole-life-sentences-and-the-strasbourg-courts-decision-in-hutchinson-v-uk.

Slobogin, C (2011) 'Prevention as the Primary Goal of Sentencing: The Modern Case for Indeterminate Dispositions in Criminal Cases' 48 *San Diego Law Review* 1127.

——. (2018) 'Principles of Risk Assessment: Sentencing and Policing' 15 *Ohio State Journal of Criminal Law* 583.

Snacken, S (2010) 'Resisting Punitiveness in Europe?' 14 *Theoretical Criminology* 273.

——. (2016) 'Punishment, Legitimacy and the Role of the State: Reimagining More Moderate Penal Policies' in S Farrall et al (eds), *Justice and Penal Reform: Re-shaping the Penal Landscape* (London, Routledge).

Stacey, J (2017) 'Preventive Justice, the Precautionary Principle and the Rule of Law' in T Tulich et al (eds), *Regulating Preventive Justice* (London: Routledge).

Steiker, C (1998) 'The Limits of the Preventive State' 88 *Journal of Criminal Law and Criminology* 771.

Tonry, M (2014) 'Legal and Ethical Issues in the Prediction of Recidivism' 26 *Federal Sentencing Reporter* 167.

——. (2016) 'Equality and Human Dignity: The Missing Ingredients in American Sentencing' 45 *Crime and Justice: A Review of Research* 459.

Vannier, M (2016) 'A Right to Hope? Life Imprisonment in France' in D van Zyl Smit and C Appleton (eds), *Life Imprisonment and Human Rights* (Oxford, Hart Publishing).

van Zyl Smit, D and Appleton, C (eds) (2016) *Life Imprisonment and Human Rights* (Oxford, Hart Publishing).

van Zyl Smit, D, Weatherby, P and Creighton, S (2014) 'Whole Life Sentences and the Tide of European Human Rights Jurisprudence' 14 *Human Rights Law Review* 59.

Walker, N (1996) 'Ethical and Other Problems' in N Walker (ed), *Dangerous People* (London, Blackstone).

Wasik M (2012) 'The Test for Dangerousness' in GR Sullivan and I Dennis (eds), *Seeking Security* (Oxford, Hart Publishing).

Whitman, J (2003) *Harsh Justice: Criminal Punishment and the Widening Divide between America and Europe* (Oxford, Oxford University Press).

Wood, D (1988) 'Dangerous Offenders, and the Morality of Protective Sentencing' *Criminal Law Review* 424.

Zedner, L (2012) 'Erring on the Side of Safety: Risk Assessment, Expert Knowledge, and the Criminal Court' in I Dennis and GR Sullivan (eds), *Seeking Security: Pre-empting the Commission of Criminal Harms* (Oxford, Hart Publishing).

——. (2013) 'Is the Criminal Law Only for Citizens? A Problem at the Borders of Punishment' in K Franko Aas and M Bosworth (eds), *The Borders of Punishment: Migration, Citizenship, and Social Exclusion* (Oxford, Oxford University Press).

9

The Problematic Role of Prior Record Enhancements in Predictive Sentencing

JULIAN V ROBERTS AND RICHARD S FRASE

Predictive sentencing assumes that courts can reliably predict which offenders are likely to re-offend. The range of potential predictors is vast, including factors relating to the offence, the offender and circumstances external to both. Some predictors are simply correlates of future offending, while others are directly causal. Of all the potential predictors, one stands above the rest in terms of its intuitive appeal and predictive ability: an offender's criminal history. For centuries, courts have used an offender's past to help determine the nature of the sentence. This usually means imposing a harsher sentence in order to prevent the offender from re-offending.

Sentence enhancements based on the offender's prior record of convictions are a universal feature of contemporary sentencing regimes in Western countries (Roberts 1997). They play a particularly important role in numerical guidelines systems, such as those found in several American state and federal jurisdictions; these systems incorporate prior record into 'criminal history' formulas that strongly determine the form and severity of recommended punishment (Frase et al 2015). Prior record sentencing enhancements are justified in part by the assumed higher recidivism risk of offenders with prior convictions, and in that sense these rules represent an important example of predictive sentencing. But such enhancements have attracted little attention from researchers and practitioners interested in risk assessment. This surprising neglect may be based on the assumption that prior record sentence enhancements are independently justified by retributive punishment goals, that is, by the heightened culpability of repeat offenders – elevated offender desert is assumed to justify enhanced punishment of such offenders, regardless of their actual degree of risk.

This chapter argues that all of these assumptions are incorrect and that prior record enhancements merit attention and scrutiny by anyone interested in predictive sentencing. First, as we will show, the retributive justifications are overstated, and prior record enhancements often greatly exceed the offender's deserved punishment; thus, retributive goals cannot provide an adequate and independent rationale. Second, most prior record enhancements, especially the formulas found in American guidelines, cannot be justified on crime-control grounds because they have not been validated to ensure that they accurately predict the probability and seriousness of future offending. Third, given the substantial costs and negative consequences of more severe punishment, it is also imperative to validate the actual crime-control benefits of these enhanced penalties. To date, no guidelines system has attempted such validation, and research on the effects of increased sanction severity suggests that most criminal history enhancements are ineffective crime-control measures.

Guidelines criminal history formulas also merit attention because they suggest promising avenues for research on and improvement of existing risk assessment tools. Such tools frequently lack limiting principles that are often incorporated into criminal history formulas – in particular, limits on the inclusion of older convictions, and rules that credit offenders for substantial crime-free periods. Moreover, the questions noted above that have not but should be asked about guidelines criminal history enhancements must be asked about *all* risk-based sentence enhancements, with or without guidelines – how accurately is recidivism risk predicted, and what is the seriousness of the predicted crimes? Are sentence enhancements based on elevated risk a cost-effective way to prevent future crime? And are any such reductions worth the substantial negative consequences of these enhancements? All too often, in predictive sentencing, such critical questions have been ignored.

I. Overview of the Chapter

Section II of this chapter examines the pervasiveness and importance of prior record as a factor at sentencing, with or without numerical guidelines. Section III exposes some weaknesses of current record-based sentencing enhancements, both in terms of offender desert (retributive justifications) and within a framework of predictive sentencing (crime control justification). We show that the common practice of mitigating punishment for first-time offenders has substantial support on both retributive and crime-control grounds, but that these rationales support only modest further increases in sanction severity as the number and seriousness of criminal history rises. Existing guidelines enhancements are often undeservedly severe, and do not faithfully reflect our knowledge of patterns of recidivism or the effectiveness of different sanctions. Section IV reconceptualises the use of criminal history in a predictive sentencing exercise.

II. The Universal Appeal and Substantial Impacts of Prior Record as a Sentencing Factor

While retributive rationales for prior record enhancements are conflicting and highly contested (as further discussed in section III), there is consensus that prior record has an important role to play in predictive sentencing. The latter aims to prevent offending by identifying the offender's likelihood of recidivism on the basis of risk factors and then crafting a sentence to address that level of risk. Criminogenic risk factors come in many forms; some are within the offender's control, some less so and some are factors over which the offender exercises no agency at all. Previous convictions fall into the first category[1] and unlike other risk factors, such as drug dependency, constitute an indirect measure of risk. Prior crimes predict future offending in the same way as cardiac episodes predict future cardiac incidents. In both contexts, the triggering incident (prior conviction or prior cardiac episode) serves as a proxy for some underlying dimension of risk (of criminal propensity or cardiac pathology). Drug dependency, for example, is a direct cause of offending; the need for a 'fix' triggers a robbery. Prior crimes are a symptom of underlying risk rather than a direct cause or facilitator of future crimes.

Of all the crime-related risk factors, prior offending is the most obvious and prior convictions are central to any discussion of predictive sentencing. For centuries, legislative sentencing provisions have prescribed recidivist premiums for a variety of offences. At the same time, courts have used prior convictions to help determine the nature and quantum of sentence for the current crime (see Roberts 2008: Chapter 1). In the modern era, previous convictions influence sentence directly and indirectly. Under US sentencing guidelines such as those operating in Minnesota and Pennsylvania, criminal history directly affects sentence outcomes as it constitutes one of the two dimensions of the sentencing grid.[2] In regimes without a sentencing grid or similar numerical formula, prior crimes affect sentencing through the use of risk-based scales (such as the LSI-Revised) or through prosecutorial submissions at sentencing.

Why is criminal history such a key component of contemporary sentencing regimes, particularly those with a predictive orientation? First, there is a powerful intuition that repeat offenders should receive harsher sentences, particularly when the prior offending is recent, similar to the current offence, or when both the prior and current offence involve serious violence. Members of the public ascribe

[1] We should not overlook the role that previous sentences play in contributing to re-offending. If an offender is sentenced to years in prison, this experience often impairs his life prospects upon release, increasing the likelihood of a return to crime. The state must assume some responsibility for the criminogenic effect of the prior conviction which resulted in imprisonment. In this way, the effects of a prior conviction are not wholly attributable to the offender.

[2] The Minnesota grid can be found at: http://mn.gov/msgc-stat/documents/2017Guidelines/2017StandardGrid.pdf.

higher risk of re-offending to and also impose harsher punishments upon offenders with previous convictions (for the relevant research on this, see Hester et al 2017; Roberts 2008: Chapters 8 and 9). Unlike factors such as gender, prior record resonates with popular (and some academic) conceptions of offender blameworthiness. Although female offenders as a category represent a lower risk than males convicted of the same crimes, no one regards women as less culpable for being female. Thus, at least on an intuitive reading of retribution, preventive and retributive justifications are in accord.

Support for some form of recidivist sentencing premium is also shared by most participants in the criminal justice system.[3] Second, since prior convictions are within the offender's control, prior record enhancements would seem to carry none of the normative problems associated with the use of other demographic risk factors such as gender or age (see, eg, Monahan and Skeem 2016; Starr 2015; Tonry 2014). On the other hand, recent research has shown that prior record enhancements have substantial disparate impacts on non-white offenders (see Frase et al 2015: Chapter 12; Frase and Roberts forthcoming: Chapter 7; see also Holder (2014), wherein US Attorney General Eric Holder raised concerns about the adverse racial impacts of all forms of risk-based sentencing).

Third, an offender's criminal history lends itself to quantification and is scalable. Prior crimes can be counted, weighted for various dimensions such as their recency or seriousness, and then converted into a prior record score. Under American guidelines, a higher score triggers a more severe recommended sentence and, in most cases, a more severe imposed sentence (Frase et al 2015; Frase and Roberts forthcoming). In addition, the quantifiable nature of criminal history means that it can easily be incorporated into risk assessment tools. Finally, unlike some other sentencing factors such as premeditation or remorse, prior offending is, as a general matter, demonstrably related to whether the offender is likely to re-offend. One of the most reliable empirical findings is that prior crimes predict re-offending; offenders with longer criminal records are more likely to re-offend than defendants with shorter criminal histories (Champion 1992; Frase and Roberts forthcoming: Chapter 2; US Sentencing Commission 2017).

The importance of criminal history to predictive sentencing (particularly in the US guidelines) can be demonstrated in many ways. Guidelines which articulate their objectives cite risk as one of the primary objectives. The Pennsylvania guidelines are a good example. The Guidelines 'recommend a range of minimum sentence based on the seriousness of the offense (Offense Gravity Score) and the prior criminal history (Prior Record Score) of the offender … an offender with a more serious and/or more extensive criminal history will have a more serious punishment recommended'.[4] Some US guidelines cite the enhanced

[3] Research conducted for the Home Office Sentencing Review (2001) in England demonstrated significant support for the recidivist premium among most practitioner groups.

[4] http://pcs.la.psu.edu/guidelines/sentencing.

blameworthiness of repeat offenders as a justification for record-based enhancements, but most systems rest on a preventive rationale (see Roberts 2015). Harsher sentences are imposed because the repeat offender is more likely to re-offend and the additional punishment is addressed at curbing that re-offending.

The emphasis on criminal history in guidelines rules results in prior convictions having a powerful effect upon sentencing outcomes. One measure is what we refer to as the 'durational enhancement'. This is a ratio of the recommended sentence length for offenders in the highest criminal history category to the recommended sentence for offenders with the lowest criminal history. The durational enhancement ratio on the main Minnesota grid ranges from 1.4 to 12.0, depending on the offence severity level, with an average ratio of 4.7. In other words, the recommended sentence length for offenders in the highest criminal history category is on average 4.7 times greater than the recommended sentence for offenders in the lowest criminal history category. And in many state guidelines systems, the magnitude of durational enhancement is even higher. In Washington and Arkansas, the average enhancement ratios are approximately 10:1, while in Kansas, the ratio is over 14:1 (for further discussion, see Frase and Roberts (forthcoming: Chapter 5)).

Another measure of the magnitude of prior record enhancements is the percentage of a sentencing grid's cells in which the offender's criminal history makes the difference between a recommended probation sentence and a recommended prison sentence – offenders who would otherwise be recommended for probation, due to the medium or low severity of their crimes, are pushed into the recommended prison zone of the grid because of their elevated criminal history scores. In half of American guidelines systems, the proportion of such 'push in' cells is 20–30 per cent, and in some states the proportion of offenders convicted in such cells is even higher – in the state of Washington, the figure is 40 per cent (Frase and Roberts forthcoming: Chapter 5).

A. The Contention

This chapter challenges the current use of prior convictions to enhance sentence severity. The core claims made in this chapter are as follows: (1) these enhancements exceed what can be justified by retributive punishment purposes; (2) with respect to predictive sentencing – in which predicting and preventing re-offending drive sentencing outcomes – prior record enhancements *as currently conceptualised and implemented* are also unjustifiable because they almost entirely lack empirical validation as predictors; indeed, as we shall demonstrate, criminal history enhancements depart in many ways from empirical findings relating to recidivism. If prior convictions are used to predictively sentence offenders, enhancements should reflect the degree to which criminal history actually *predicts* re-offending; and (3) current prior record enhancements also lack justification as predictive sentencing measures because they lack any validation as to the degree to which the enhancements actually succeed in efficiently preventing crime. These critiques are directed principally to prior record enhancements under American guidelines, where prior convictions carry the greatest weight at sentencing and where severity enhancements diverge most strongly from re-offending patterns. But many non-guidelines sentencing systems and risk assessment instruments also suffer from the problems identified in this chapter. Finally, the argument against current forms of repeat offender premiums is primarily empirical, although there is a normative critique of such enhancements (eg, Starr 2015; Tonry 2010).

III. Weaknesses of Current Prior Record Enhancements

A. Retributive Rationales

Guidelines drafters have often stated (with little if any elaboration) that criminal history enhancements are justified at least in part on the ground that repeat offenders are more blameworthy (Roberts 2015: Table 1.1), but retributive theorists are sharply divided on this question.[5] Some writers argue that past convictions should have no bearing on the deserved punishment for the current offence or offences, another group views the absence of prior convictions (or a minor record) as a mitigating factor, while a third group argues that prior convictions are an aggravating factor and that an offender's deserved punishment steadily increases as he acquires more and more convictions.

Any retributive rationale for prior record enhancements must be based on the view that prior convictions increase the offender's deserved punishment for the offence or offences now being sentenced. Offenders have already been punished for the crimes underlying their prior convictions and cannot be punished again for those crimes; indeed, to do so would violate constitutional and human rights principles (double jeopardy; *non bis in idem*). Most retributivists also agree that an offender's deserved punishment for his current crime depends on two factors: the harm(s) caused or threatened to be caused by the prohibited acts or omissions; and the offender's degree of culpability as measured by his intent or other mental state (mens rea) as well as his bad or good motives, role in the offence relative to co-defendants, situational pressures and reduced capacity to obey the law. Almost all retributivists agree that an offender's prior convictions rarely if ever increase the actual or threatened harms associated with the current offence, either for the victim or for society. But retributivists disagree strongly on whether and to what extent an offender's prior convictions affect his intent or other culpability factors, in a way that increases his blameworthiness and deserved punishment for the current offence(s).

[5] For further discussion of whether and how retributive principles might justify prior record enhancements, see Frase and Roberts (2019: Chapter 1); Hester et al (2018); and Roberts and von Hirsch (2010).

i. The 'Flat Rate' or 'Exclusionary' School

A number of writers (eg, Bagaric 2014; Dagger 2012; Fletcher 1978; Singer 1979; Tonry 2010) reject all of the mitigating-factor and aggravating-factor theories summarised below; these writers argue that prior convictions not only have no bearing on the harms associated with the current offence, but also have no bearing on culpability. Some writers (eg, Corlett 2012; Lippke 2015) further argue that many offenders with extensive prior records should be considered *less* culpable than offenders with few or no prior convictions: if an offender continues to offend, despite repeated punishment, it is likely that personal, family or community factors make compliance with the law very difficult for that offender. In such cases, the unfairness of prior record enhancements is compounded by the likelihood that the offender's compliance handicaps are the result of unjust social conditions or government policies and/or reflect the adverse, criminogenic effects of the offender's repeated prior punishments.

ii. The 'Mitigation' School: Lesser Desert of Offenders with Few or No Prior Convictions

Some writers have argued that we should view a first offence as out of character and likely to be due to excusing temporary or situational factors (or that, in any event, we should give a first-time offender the benefit of the doubt on that score and should also give him credit for his previous law-abiding life); we should not immediately and fully convert our condemnation of his illegal act into condemnation of the offender (see, eg, Ashworth 2005). Other writers (eg, von Hirsch 2010) go further, endorsing what has been called the theory of Progressive Loss of Mitigation: second-, third- and possibly even fourth-time offenders should receive a steadily declining degree of mitigation. The broadest versions of mitigation theory seem rather strained, especially when the offender is claiming that his third or fourth offence was still 'out of character' or otherwise excusable, or when a first-time offender has been convicted of a very serious crime lacking any apparent excusing factor, or a crime that required extensive advanced planning (Roberts 2010). However, subject to those caveats, there seems to be widespread agreement that most first-time offenders should be deemed less culpable and that they deserve less punishment than offenders with one or more prior convictions (O'Neill, Maxfield and Harer 2004).

iii. Prior Record as an Aggravating Desert-Based Factor

It has sometimes been argued, on varying grounds, that an offender's culpability and deserved punishment steadily increase as he acquires more and more prior convictions.[6] A common problem with all 'aggravated-desert' theories is that they

[6] For further discussion of these theories, see Lee (2009, 2010); and Frase (2010, 2013).

provide little support for automatic prior record sentence enhancements of the kind that courts impose, especially under guidelines. A further problem with most of these theories is that they lack any principled basis to decide by how much desert is increased; indeed, they seem to permit an open-ended escalation of punishment severity without regard to the seriousness of the offence being sentenced.

'Character' theories seem to assume that desert depends at least in part on some inner wickedness that is proportionate to prior record; however, a fundamental principle in common law legal systems is that people are convicted and punished for their criminal acts, not for who or what they are (Bagaric 2000; Tonry 2010). 'Notice' theories argue that prior convictions and penalties make repeat offenders more aware of the wrongfulness of their subsequent crimes. But this argument is very weak in the case of serious current crimes, or very different kinds of prior and current offending (Frase 2010; see also Ryberg and Petersen 2011). 'Defiance' theories view desert as enhanced by the repeat offender's apparent contempt for the law and previous judicial condemnations, but this rationale, like the character theory, risks punishing people for their bad thoughts or attitudes rather than their criminal acts. 'Omission' theories assume that previously convicted offenders are on notice of their criminal tendencies and have a heightened duty, especially as the number of their convictions rises, to change their lives or take other steps to ensure that they obey the law (Lee 2009). Again, this argument is weak when prior and current offences are very different. More fundamentally, the theory violates another core common law principle: that punishment based on an omission (rather than a prohibited act) requires a clear statement in advance, by statute or case law, of a legal duty to perform the specific act or acts that the defendant is charged with omitting to perform.

iv. Summary

Given the widely differing views summarised above, retributive punishment theory fails to supply a strong justification for prior record enhancements, especially of the kind applied in US guidelines systems. There is agreement among retributivists that first-time offenders are less blameworthy, but beyond that, the consensus breaks down; there is broad support for at most a modest increase in attributed blame and deserved punishment as offenders accumulate more and more prior convictions. In practice, however, penalty severity does not increase modestly, especially under US sentencing guidelines; as we noted earlier, high-criminal-history offenders receive very substantial penalty enhancements in most guidelines systems. The magnitudes of these enhancements violate core principles endorsed by all retributivists: that punishment should be at least roughly proportionate to the seriousness of the crime(s) being sentenced and that it is especially important to avoid inflicting penalties that exceed the offender's degree of desert (Frase 2013: Chapter 2). The latter point is critical: desert principles may not provide strong independent grounds for prior record enhancements, but offender desert is still a very important limiting factor, placing upper limits on the magnitude of enhancements based on offender risk and crime-prevention goals.

B. Crime-Prevention Rationales

The compelling risk-based explanations for prior record enhancements (summarised earlier) may have blinded many people to the very real problems of principle and practice which beset prior record enhancements. These problems can be briefly summarised as follows.[7] First, there is a logical problem in using the simple correlation between prior and future offending to justify severity enhancements. Several intervening assumptions need to be fulfilled and we will return to these later in the chapter. Second, advocates of the recidivist sentencing premium have overstated both the predictive utility of prior offending and the preventive efficacy of prior record enhancements. Prior convictions are not always a reliable predictor of recidivism and, as currently operationalised, severity premiums seldom generate the predicted decline in re-offending rates.

i. Inadequate Validation of Prior Record Enhancements: Three Prerequisites

The demonstrable aggregate relationship between previous and future crimes does not, in itself, justify the use of prior crimes within a predictive sentencing model. This rather obvious assertion seems to have eluded legislators, sentencing commissions and policy makers. Several assumptions need to be empirically verified in order to legitimise the recidivist premium as a cost-effective, risk-based method of preventing future offences.

Three principal prerequisites must be fulfilled to justify predictive, record-based sentencing enhancements.

a. Prior Offending Should Reliably Predict Future Offending

First, it must be verified that the prior offending in question is significantly predictive of future offending – that these repeat offenders constitute a distinct population in terms of the likelihood of re-offending. That repeat offenders generally have a higher risk of re-offending is a proposition that is well supported by research (Frase and Roberts forthcoming: Chapter 2). But very little research has examined the accuracy of particular criminal history formulas and formula

[7] For further discussion of many issues raised in this chapter, see Frase and Roberts (forthcoming); Frase et al (2015); Roberts (2008).

components to verify that they accurately and efficiently predict recidivism risk, including all available components that increase risk, and excluding components that add no predictive value.

b. Predicted Minor Future Offending Rarely Justifies Additional Punishment

Second, it must be established that the prior offending in question indicates a higher risk of re-offending seriousness enough to justify additional state punishment. Predictive sentencing should be sensitive to two components: not only the *likelihood* (and frequency) of further offending, but also the *seriousness* of re-offending if it occurs. The relationship between the probability and gravity of re-offending is multiplicative. If the likelihood of re-offending is close to zero, or the likely new offence will be at a low level of seriousness, enhancement is hard to justify. Yet validation research on criminal history and other risk assessment tools often ignores issues of frequency and seriousness of predicted recidivism, and only seeks to determine how well a given formula or tool predicts 'recidivism' – of any kind or frequency.

c. Prior Record Sentencing Enhancements Must Effectively Prevent Further Offending

Third, it must be verified that the record-based enhancement will actually reduce the offender's risk of re-offending by means of special deterrence and/or incapacitation.[8] If the remedy (an increase in severity) is ineffective, the preventive justification collapses.

These three prerequisites seem essential before an offender should be subject to an enhanced sentence due to his prior convictions. Unless these conditions are fulfilled, the state is imposing punishment without justification. In another publication, we propose additional requirements, namely that the enhancements apply only where there are no serious countervailing adverse consequences in terms of prison costs, minority overrepresentation or impacts on third parties such as dependants of the offender (Frase and Roberts forthcoming: Chapter 11). Below we focus on the third prerequisite and then we consider the broader implications of viewing prior record as a 'dynamic' risk factor.

[8] It might also be contended that prior record enhancements prevent crime by means of general deterrence – that other offenders will abstain from crime out of fear of receiving similar repeat-offender enhancements. We do not separately consider this argument because of the substantial body of research, from a variety of contexts, suggesting that increases in sentence severity have little if any demonstrable added general deterrent effects. For recent reviews of this literature, see Frase and Roberts (forthcoming); and Hester et al (2018). Likewise, we do not discuss the possibility that prior record enhancements prevent crime by facilitating offender rehabilitation, since research suggests that imprisonment, or an increased duration of imprisonment, either has no effect on recidivism or makes the offender more crime-prone (Hester et al 2018).

With regard to special deterrent effects, the recidivist sentencing premium affects offenders in two ways: an offender who otherwise would receive a community-based sentence is imprisoned as a result of his prior crimes – sanction enhancement. Alternatively, an offender convicted of a crime warranting custody receives a longer prison term due to his criminal antecedents. Both enhancement strategies are designed to reduce re-offending; neither receives much support from the relevant research.

Does imprisonment result in lower recidivism rate than a non-custodial sanction? Many systematic reviews of this literature have now been published, summarising research from many countries.[9] The general conclusion of this research is that prison is associated with higher recidivism rates than less severe penalties, principally community-based orders. For example, Villettaz et al (2006) reported that across the most stringent studies, imprisonment was associated with a five per cent *higher* rate of re-offending (compared to non-custodial sanctions). Aarten et al (2015) compared re-offending rates for two carefully matched samples of offenders, some of whom had received a custodial sentence, while others had received a suspended sentence. They found that offenders sentenced to prison were *more* likely to re-offend. The most recent tests of the hypothesis that 'custody specifically deters more effectively than community punishment' have employed sophisticated statistical controls which reduce the likelihood that variables other than the nature of the sentence may have caused the outcome. For example, researchers in the UK examined the recidivism rates of a large sample of offenders, some of whom had been incarcerated, while others had received a community order. Individuals in the incarcerated sample were more likely to subsequently commit another offence (Jolliffe and Hedderman 2015). The UK Ministry of Justice has published a series of studies comparing re-offending rates of offenders sentenced to custody with a control group sentenced to community-based sentences. After controlling for the background variables, these studies found higher rates of re-offending in the group sent to prison (Ministry of Justice 2015: Table 1). This research calls into question the structure of many sentencing grids whereby repeat offenders, convicted of medium- or low-severity crimes, are imprisoned on the basis of their prior convictions alone; at lower criminal history, they would have been recommended for a community sanction.

ii. *Preventive Effects of Increasing Sentence Length*

Even if a more severe form of sanctioning (prison) fails to deter re-offending more effectively than less severe sanctioning options (community-based punishments

[9] These include: Bales and Piquero (2012); Champion (1994); Cullen, Jonson and Nagin (2011); Jonson (2010); Kazemian (2010); Villettaz, Killias and Zoder (2006); Zara and Farrington (2016).

and suspended sentences), it remains possible that, among offenders sentenced to prison, the threat and imposition of more prison time for higher-record offenders might provide additional specific-deterrent effects. This assumption supports the architecture of criminal history enhancements, namely that the preventive benefit of incarceration is additive – longer prison terms deter more, and proportionately more, than shorter terms.[10]

As with the research on the preventive effectiveness of custody versus community sanctions, research offers little support for the second prior record enhancement prediction. Studies over the past 40 years have compared recidivism rates for offenders released after serving varying periods of imprisonment. A US Department of Justice study of offenders released in the mid-1970s concluded that 'no evidence was found to suggest that time served has any influence on subsequent offense severity, or to support hypotheses of specific deterrence' (1984: 4). Later research has sustained these conclusions. Andrews and Bonta (2003) in Canada, and Fink and Ducommun-Vaucher (2014) in Switzerland reported similar findings: recidivism rates were higher for offenders released after longer prison terms than after shorter terms.

The most recent and most rigorous studies incorporate a wider range of variables and more sophisticated statistical techniques to overcome the absence of random assignment of offenders to different sanctions. Wermink et al (2017) evaluated the relationship between time served in prison and subsequent recidivism, using a longitudinal and nationwide sample of Dutch offenders. Comparing the uncorrected recidivism rates of different groups revealed that re-offending rates declined as the length of time served increased, which was consistent with the underlying assumption of prior record enhancements. For example, the reconviction rate for the offenders who had served the longest time in prison was approximately half that of the group who had spent the shortest time in custody (see Wermink et al 2017: Table 3). Yet when the researchers introduced the appropriate statistical controls, these differences evaporated, and they concluded that there was 'no clear effect of length of imprisonment on recidivism' (Wermink et al 2017: 23). This conclusion is supported by a number of reviews of the literature (eg, Pew Center Review 2012). Put simply, more time (in prison) does not result in less crime.

Taken together, these two research traditions call into question the current ways in which criminal history enhances sentence severity in order to reduce re-offending by means of special deterrence. The lesson for predictive sentencing is that using this risk-related factor to reduce re-offending through the use of severity enhancements is unlikely to prove effective.

[10] As a Pew Center review of the issue noted, if increasing the length of sentence is beneficial in terms of crime prevention, then 'offenders serving more time in prison should have lower recidivism rates than those serving less time' (2012: 33).

a. Incapacitation

The theory of incapacitation seems plausible, at least superficially. First, offenders clearly cannot commit crimes (against the public) while they are incarcerated. Second, it may appear reasonable to assume that, in general, the higher an offender's risk of recidivism and the longer he is incarcerated, the more crimes will be prevented. But on closer inspection, the crime-preventive incapacitation effects of incarceration are limited and often not cost-effective.[11]

To some extent, these disappointing crime-control benefits are the inevitable result of problems we discussed above: it is difficult to accurately predict future criminal behaviour, especially violent or very serious crimes (low-probability events are harder to predict; 'high-rate' offenders are more likely to be property and low-level drug offenders); and most incapacitation-based sentencing regimes have failed to actually validate the accuracy of the risk-prediction tools or proxies being employed. Thus, in practice, even supposedly 'selective' incapacitation policies lead to incarceration of large numbers of offenders who would not, if left in the community, have offended or who would only have committed minor crimes the prevention of which does not justify the high costs and burdens of incarceration.

The marginal, crime-preventive benefits of an incapacitation sentencing strategy are further diminished by the fact that the highest-rate and most serious future offenders will usually already have been detained for other reasons – retribution, deterrence and/or a simple intuitive feeling that repeat offenders must receive more severe penalties. Incapacitation policies do not (and are unlikely to) replace other traditional rationales for incarceration, so any additional offenders who are sent to prison for reasons of incapacitation are likely to be lower risk in terms of the frequency and/or seriousness of their future crimes. The marginal benefits of an incapacitation strategy are particularly low in systems (including almost all systems in the US) that already have very high incarceration rates; in such a system, further increases in incarceration yield rapidly diminishing returns (Travis, Western and Redburn 2014).

But even if we could somehow limit incapacitation-based custody sentencing to offenders who would actually commit frequent and/or serious crimes if left free, the crime-control payoff will be severely limited by several additional factors:

- For some crimes, especially those involving highly desired illegal goods or services with substantial profit potential (eg, prohibited drugs or prostitution), the supply of willing producers and sellers of those goods and services is sufficiently robust that the incarcerated offender is likely to be promptly replaced by other producers and sellers (either those already in that business or those who see a profitable unmet demand and enter the business).

[11] For further discussion, see Frase and Roberts (forthcoming); and Hester et al (2018).

- In cases where the offender has committed his crime(s) with one or more other offenders, unless they are all locked up, it is likely that the criminal group will be able to continue without the offender or will be able recruit new members (especially in ghettos or other distressed areas with limited opportunities for lawful employment).
- Incarceration clearly makes some offenders worse – more likely to commit crime or more serious crime, or to have a longer criminal career before finally desisting. The reasons are not hard to identify: incarceration removes an offender from family and other pro-social influences and surrounds him with other criminals; it interrupts and at least postpones crime-preventive life course processes (eg, marriage and other longer-term partnerships, stable employment, reliable housing, and military service); and it creates serious legal and practical barriers to those processes, especially employment and housing.
- The benefits of using imprisonment and longer terms of imprisonment to incapacitate high-risk offenders are substantially undercut by the well-documented pattern of reduced offending, especially violent offending, as offenders grow older – the 'age-crime curve' (see, eg, Piquero, Farrington and Blumstein 2007). Giving an offender a lengthy prison term based on his past convictions and/or other static risk factors makes little sense if the offender is already past his peak offending years or if the prison term will last well into his middle age. Incapacitation policies often fail to take into account the offender's current, advancing age, and they almost always disregard the low-crime age brackets that the offender will enter and remain in before the enhanced prison term is completed.

In light of all of the problems summarised above, any strategy of incarceration to achieve incapacitation, based on prior record, is likely to have very meagre crime-control benefits that cannot be justified by their costs. To a great extent, the same will be true of any risk-based incarceration strategy, with or without an emphasis on prior convictions.

iii. Criminal History as a Dynamic Risk Factor

Sentencing guidelines, risk scale manuals and many scholars classify prior offending as a static rather than a dynamic risk factor, reflecting the reality that an offender cannot change the fact that he has acquired one or more criminal convictions.[12] However, prior convictions are more accurately classified as a dynamic risk factor,

[12] For example, the California Static Risk Assessment (CSRA) scale is heavily based on prior convictions (see Turner et al 2013). Commissions also assume that prior convictions are a static predictor (see, for example, Ministry of Justice 2014; Pennsylvania Commission on Sentencing 2011). Henning, Renauer and Feyerherm assert that 'many [risk-related] items are static – cannot change the fact of prior arrest' (2013: 13). The arrest cannot be changed, but its significance as a predictor of re-offending or its retributive value can (and does) evolve.

and this fact has implications for prior record enhancements – such enhancements must be imposed in a much more flexible manner than under current rules.

In most cases, the predictive power of a prior conviction declines as the offender ages out of offending; the consequence is that the risk of recidivism is dynamic not static. Practitioners and some scholars have recognised the declining significance of prior convictions over time (eg, Hillier 1997). Research by Kurlycheck, Brame and Bushway (2006, 2007) and Amirault and Lussier (2011) questions the static conceptualisation of prior record. If previous offending is a stable risk factor, it should exercise a constant influence. Yet risk of re-offending declines over time; indeed, when an offender remains crime-free for several years, his risk of a new offence is similar to that of an individual without a criminal record (Kurlycheck, Brame and Bushway 2006; see also Blumstein and Nakamura 2009; Ezell 2007). Simply put, a recent conviction is a much more reliable predictor of re-offending than an older conviction (eg, Kazemian 2010). An offender with prior convictions committed 10 years earlier is a lower risk than one with the same two previous convictions recorded a year ago. Some guidelines criminal history formulas recognise these dynamic effects, by means of 'decay' (also known as lapse, washout or look back) rules based solely on passage of time and/or 'gap' rules tied to periods of crime-free living, but these rules are much too limited; moreover, they are often entirely lacking in risk assessment scales and tools (Frase and Roberts 2019: Chapters 3 and 9).

The second reason why priors should be considered dynamic rather than statistic is that the predictive significance of a prior crime may diminish as a result of more than simply the passage of time. The offender's actions are relevant – for example, if the ex-offender succeeds in addressing the causes of that prior offending or makes changes to his living circumstances. If the offender lowers his risk of re-offending, he is effectively diminishing the predictive power of the prior crimes; previous offending is therefore not invariant, but potentially dynamic, with its significance changing in response to actions by the offender.

Two obvious examples involve substance abuse and marital status. If alcohol abuse contributed to an offender's previous crimes but he has now been abstinent for years, the predictive power of the previous conviction is no longer the same. Similarly, committing to a stable relationship may also reduce the probative value of the previous offence. Lifestyle changes caused by (or correlated with) a stable relationship include securing and maintaining steady employment, reducing time with criminogenic associates and reduced exposure to drugs or alcohol – all protective factors for criminal behaviour. Ezell (2007) and Kazemian and Farrington (2006) both report that lifestyle changes were better predictors of re-offending than criminal history scores.[13] One of the key lessons of the research

[13] On a retributive account, the offender who has addressed the cause of his offending has moved away from his prior self: the previous conviction therefore says less about the current individual and accordingly should carry less weight at sentencing. Classifying prior crimes as a static, unchanging risk factor is therefore inappropriate, although all common risk scales adopt this approach.

upon criminal careers and desistance is that these offending patterns are volatile; current prior record enhancements across the US assume a degree of stability which is belied by the research (see Kazemian 2010).

Finally, the actions of the state are also relevant to the evolving predictive value of prior crimes. Consider two offenders with the same two prior crimes. Offender A's priors occurred eight years ago and resulted in a lengthy (three-year) community sentence of intensive probation supervision and required treatment, which was completed successfully. Offender B received the same three-year community penalty, but without the intensive supervision and treatment, and re-offended three months into the order. The sentence imposed on Offender A was explicitly designed to reduce his risk of re-offending. To regard both offenders as equally likely to re-offend (they have the same prior and current convictions) and to assign the same recidivist premium assumes that the previous sentence had no effect. Yet that is what happens when a prior record enhancement is blind to the details of the prior sentence.

If previous convictions lose their predictive power over time, their weight in the sentencing equation should decline accordingly. This is another way in which the use of prior convictions is at odds with empirical research: most guidelines assign the same weight to prior crimes regardless of its recency (unless the prior is so old that it is excluded under decay rules); for example, in Minnesota, a 14-year-old felony carries the same weight as a one-year-old felony. Prior offending should not be regarded as carrying an unchanging risk-based punitive weight. Previous convictions should be treated as changing markers of re-offending. If a conviction has lost most or all of its predictive power, it should be disregarded. A prior record enhancement which was justified by predictions of re-offending would introduce 'look back' limits and 'gap' provisions; after a period of time, prior crimes would cease to aggravate sentence, and if the offender managed to achieve a substantial gap of crime-free living, any prior convictions would be down-weighted or ignored at subsequent sentencing decisions. Yet, as noted above, guidelines and risk assessment tools fail to incorporate adequate look-back limits and gap rules.

iv. Temporal Spacing of Prior Crimes

The temporal spacing of prior crimes is also likely to be related to risk of re-offending, in ways that a simple, 'static' conception of prior convictions fails to capture. Consider two offenders with the same multiple prior convictions. Offender A accumulated his within a 12-month period almost a decade ago, while Offender B's were spaced over the entire decade. The former offender appears to have passed through (and now left) a period of intense offending and should be seen as a lower risk than the other individual. Yet the guidelines do not generally distinguish between these two offender profiles, both of whom would receive the same criminal history score and the same degree of enhancement.

v. Failure to Match Sentencing Increments to Actual Increments in Offender Risk

US sentencing regimes impose regular increments of severity to reflect each prior crime, yet empirically, risk of re-offending does not operate in such a linear fashion. For example, the gap in re-offending between first-time offenders and those with one prior crime is much greater than the gap between offenders with three as opposed to four prior convictions. Recent recidivism data from the US Sentencing Commission illustrates this point. The greatest gap between adjacent criminal history categories was between the first-time offender group (Category I, zero or only one criminal history (CH) point) and Category II (two or three CH points): 34 per cent versus 54 per cent. This discrepancy is much greater than the average of six per cent between all other adjacent categories (see US Sentencing Commission 2017: Figure 2). Yet, perhaps for ease of application and consistency of treatment, the US schemes make the same magnitude of distinctions between offenders in different criminal history categories.[14] If risk-based sentencing is the orienting philosophy, prior record enhancements should track the trajectory of risk far more closely than at present.

vi. Failure to Recognise Interaction of Risk-Related Factors

Another weakness common to most guidelines and, indeed, non-guideline regimes is that they do not recognise the interaction of different risk factors. Offender age, for example, interacts with criminal history. An offender with a lengthy criminal history but who is over 60 is likely a lower risk of re-offending than one who has the same prior conviction profile and is in his thirties. In the older offender's case, age, a lower risk marker, is offsetting the high-risk factor of an extensive criminal history. For such cases, a truly predictive sentencing model would be sensitive to this interaction. However, most guidelines are not; prior record enhancements are applied uniformly across different profiles of offenders. The consequence is that older offenders with significant criminal records receive a sentence which is predictively disproportionate to their actual recidivism risk. A similar argument may be made for female offenders.[15]

[14] Recent research on several state guidelines systems has found similar failures to match sentencing increments with increased offender recidivism risk. See Hester (2018); and Laskorunsky (2017).

[15] 'Discounting' sentences for older offenders and female offenders on the basis that they constitute a lower aggregate risk of re-offending is of course problematic on normative grounds. We do not address this complex question here (but see the discussion in Frase 2015; Monahan and Skeem 2016; Starr 2015; and Tonry 2014). The only point we are making here is that a sentencing regime which purports to follow predictive sentencing should, viewed from that perspective, adjust prior-record enhancements to reflect these interacting risk factors.

vii. Summary

We can summarise the principal ways in which criminal history enhancements across the US diverge from empirical risk-related patterns with the following points. First, the structure of prior record enhancements, imposing steadily increasing penalties for each increment in criminal history, is inconsistent with what we know about how recidivism rates increase with increases in the number of prior convictions. Second, guidelines include prior crimes and other record-based variables with little or no predictive power in terms of re-offending (due to their remoteness in time or a lengthy gap between previous and current offending). For example, some schemes include crimes committed 30 years earlier, or petty misdemeanours, neither of which carries probative value in terms of future offending. Third, the enhancements increase the severity of imposed punishments in ways and magnitudes which are inconsistent with current knowledge of the effectiveness of different penal sanctions. These include imprisoning an offender to reflect his prior convictions when imprisonment results in higher, not lower rates of re-offending, and imposing longer prison terms when this is unlikely to reduce recidivism.

Imposing additional punishment for factors unrelated to risk or powerful enhancements for factors only weakly predictive of recidivism may be likened to an ill-conceived motor vehicle insurance scheme, where insurance premiums are only poorly correlated with accident risk. Under such a scheme, drivers receive heavy insurance premiums for traffic violations which are only weakly correlated with subsequent accident claims and pay higher premiums for characteristics which are unrelated to whether the driver will be responsible for an accident.

IV. Reconceptualising the Role of Previous Convictions at Sentencing

There is no denying the proposition that prior crimes often raise the offender's likelihood of re-offending. For this reason, predictive sentencing must incorporate prior crimes in the risk matrix and ignore the exclusionary approach advocated by some retributive scholars (see section III above). However, under current arrangements, prior convictions are poorly incorporated into the predictive sentencing equation. How then might prior crimes be more reasonably considered? A truly risk-based recidivist sentencing premium would look very different from current approaches.

First, the sentence imposed on the repeat offender would not necessarily entail harsher treatment than that imposed on first-time offenders convicted of the same offence. An alcohol-abusing recidivist might be subject to a rigorous community penalty, with mandatory treatment, abstinence requirements and mobility restrictions, rather than simply a longer prison term. The record-based enhanced sentence would be underpinned by an evidence-based justification. The simple assumption that increased severity carries preventive power would be rejected.

Second, the progressive, uniform increases in severity imposed for offenders convicted of imprisonable offences would be replaced by a more individualised approach to sentence enhancements. At present, grid-based enhancements impose the same, uniform increase in sentence severity between each category of criminal history. The court would have to confront two key questions: what does this prior record say about this individual's risk of re-offending, and what approach to enhancement is likely to prevent this particular offender from re-offending?

A. Threats to Consistency at Sentencing

This reconceptualised risk-based recidivist premium may undermine consistency and proportionality. As prior record enhancements become more individualised, comparability of treatment becomes harder to achieve and sentencing disparities increase. Similarly, wide variation in sentencing outcomes would also blur ordinal proportionality distinctions between offences of different seriousness; calibrating the sentence to the seriousness of the current offence will be more challenging. For these reasons, any prior record enhancements need to be relatively modest.[16] If the enhancements are powerful, retributive constraints will be breached. By keeping preventively justified enhancements modest, wide divergences of treatment are minimised, retaining the focus on the crime of current conviction. Second, courts or sentencing commissions need to develop scales of 'penal equivalents' to ensure that when a more individualised enhancement is imposed, it carries approximately the same weight as enhanced sentences for other repeat offenders for whom a different penal intervention seems more effective (for further discussion of such 'equivalency scales', see Morris and Tonry (1990)).

B. Considering the Offender's Perspective

Little research has been conducted into offender perceptions of the recidivist premium. Limited research in the UK found that most offenders regarded the premium as being a legitimate source of aggravation (Roberts 2008: Chapter 9). However, more research is needed to determine whether they regard the practice of imprisonment on record as being legitimate. Considering the offender's perspective would also suggest that the aggravating effect of previous crimes should be

[16] In Frase and Roberts (forthcoming), we propose that the sentence for the highest criminal history category should be no more than twice as long as the length of sentence for the lowest criminal history category. Tonry has proposed a similar, yet somewhat more restrictive rule, namely that the premium should be capped at 1.5 (see Tonry 2016: 244).

rebuttable. The risk register should be symmetrical, allowing the offender to claim credit for actions which mitigate his risk or which call his ascribed risk score into question. At sentencing, if the prosecutor advocates a harsher sentence because the crime was planned and premeditated, the defendant has a clear right of reply. Evidence of minimal preparation, it may be argued, is insufficient for a court to find 'planning and premeditation'. The defendant may concede the relevance of some preparatory acts but not others, or he may concede the relevance of all, yet still argue that the additional punishment demanded by the prosecutor is excessive. At present, prior convictions are seldom the subject of argument at sentencing hearings. The legitimacy of aggravation is established when the existence of the criminal history is entered into the record; argument about the enhancement begins and ends once the prior convictions are entered into the record. Offenders should be able to offset any ascribed higher risk with evidence that their actual risk level is lower due to steps they have taken to address the causes of their offending, maturation or other circumstances.

C. Explaining the Gap between Policy and Research

Our contention is that if preventive sentencing is the primary purpose underlying the US guidelines, prior record enhancements would be much more closely calibrated with empirical risk patterns. Why then has the use of prior convictions been conceptualised in a way that diverges from evidence-based findings relating to recidivism? Why, for example, did the early sentencing commissions such as those in Minnesota and Washington not tailor enhancements to more accurately reflect actual re-offending patterns?

One explanation is that most US-based enhancement regimes were created over 40 years ago when research into the causes of re-offending and the effectiveness of different sanctions was far less well developed. However, this is unlikely to be the whole story. Another explanation arises from the desire to achieve consistency and ease of application; commissions may have decided that the latter objectives outweighed the benefits of a more evidence-based approach to enhancements. In addition, the recommended sentences in many guidelines systems were strongly influenced by prior sentencing and parole-releasing practices that had given substantial weight to the offender's prior record. The final explanation is that another implicit rather than explicit model may underpin the enhancements. This latent model reflects a crude version of punitive retribution. On this view, repeat offenders deserve more punishment and the additional punishment should increase in direct response to the number of prior crimes, regardless of their timing or relation to the current offence. This approach is inconsistent with retributive accounts of prior offending (see section III above) and indifferent to the effects of the punitive enhancements on subsequent re-offending, hence the lack of fit between the architecture of prior record enhancements and research into patterns of recidivism and deterrent effects of punishments. We cannot exclude the possibility that this intuitive and punitive reaction to repeat offenders underpins the risk-based criminal history enhancements.

V. Conclusion

How would we be better off if recidivist sentencing premiums were re-conceptualised and restricted in the ways we advocate here? First, the degree of 'fit' between the enhancement and the risk of re-offending would be tighter; prior record enhancements would be more evidence-based. The state would be on firmer ground when imposing sentencing enhancements. Second, there would be greater transparency – the reason for enhancement and the ways in which prior crimes affect sentence severity would be clearer. Third, legitimacy, both perceived and actual, would be enhanced. Finally, the ability to contest the enhancement would both restore some adversarial integrity to this element of sentencing and promote defendants' perceptions that the system has treated them fairly based on an individualised assessment of their prior conduct; at present, the enhancement is categorical in nature.

References

Aarten, P, Denkers, A, Borgers, M and van der Laan, P (2015) 'Reconviction Rates after Suspended Sentences: Comparison of the Effects of Different Types of Suspended Sentences on Reconviction in the Netherlands' 59 *International Journal of Offender Therapy and Comparative Criminology* 143.

Amirault, J and Lussier, P (2011) 'Population Heterogeneity, State Dependence and Sexual Offender Recidivism: The Aging Process and the Lost Predictive Impact of Prior Criminal Charges over Time' 39 *Journal of Criminal Justice* 344.

Andrews, D and Bonta, J (2003) *The Psychology of Criminal Conduct*, 3rd edn (Cincinnati, Anderson).

Ashworth, A (2005) *Sentencing and Criminal Justice*, 4th edn (Cambridge, Cambridge University Press).

Bagaric, M (2000) 'Double Punishment and Punishing Character: The Unfairness of Prior Convictions' 19 *Criminal Justice Ethics* 10.

——. (2014) 'The Punishment Should Fit the Crime – Not the Prior Convictions of the Person That Committed the Crime: An Argument for Less Impact Being Accorded to Previous Convictions in Sentencing' 51 *San Diego Law Review* 343.

Bales, W and Piquero, A (2012) 'Assessing the Impact of Imprisonment on Recidivism' 8 *Journal of Experimental Criminology* 71.

Blumstein, A and Nakamura, K (2009) 'Redemption in the Presence of Widespread Criminal Background Checks' 47 *Criminology* 327.

Champion, D (1994) *Measuring Offender Risk: A Criminal Justice Sourcebook* (Westport, CT, Greenwood Publishing).

Corlett, A (2012) 'Retributivism and Recidivism' in C Tamburrini and J Ryberg (eds), *Recidivist Punishments: The Philosopher's View* (New York, Lexington Books).

Dagger, R (2012) 'Playing Fair with Recidivists' in C Tamburrini and J Ryberg (eds), *Recidivist Punishments: The Philosopher's View* (New York, Lexington Books).

Ezell, M (2007) 'Examining the Overall and Offense-Specific Criminal Career Lengths of a Sample of Serious Offenders' 53 *Crime & Delinquency* 3.

Fink, D and Ducommun-Vaucher, S (2014) 'Statistical Recidivism Analyses in Switzerland' in H-J Albrecht and J Jehle (eds), *National Reconviction Statistics and Studies in Europe* (Gottingen, University of Gottingen Press).

Fletcher, G (1978) *Rethinking Criminal Law* (Boston, Little, Brown & Company).

Frase, R (2010) 'Prior-Conviction Sentencing Enhancements: Rationales and Limits Based on Retributive and Utilitarian Proportionality Principles and Social Equality Goals' in JV Roberts and A von Hirsch (eds), *Previous Convictions at Sentencing: Theoretical and Applied Perspectives* (Oxford, Hart Publishing).

——. (2013) *Just Sentencing: Principles and Procedures for a Workable System* (New York, Oxford University Press).

——. (2015) 'The Relationship between Criminal History Scores and Recidivism Risk' in *Criminal History Enhancements Sourcebook* (Minneapolis, Robina Institute of Criminal Law and Criminal Justice). Available at https://robinainstitute.umn.edu/publications/criminal-history-enhancements-sourcebook.

Frase, R and Roberts, JV (forthcoming) *Paying for the Past: Prior Record Enhancements in the US Sentencing Guidelines* (New York, Oxford University Press).

Frase, R, Roberts, JV, Mitchell, K and Hester, R (2015) *Sourcebook of Criminal History Enhancements* (Minneapolis, Robina Institute of Criminal Law and Criminal Justice).

Henning, K, Renauer, B and Feyerherm, W (2013) 'Risk Assessment and the Public Safety Checklist' (Portland State University).

Hester, R (2018) 'Prior Record and Recidivism Risk' in *American Journal of Criminal Justice*, https://doi.org/10.1007/s12103-018-9460-8.

Hester, R, Frase, R, Roberts, JV and Mitchell, K (2018) 'Prior Record Enhancements at Sentencing: Unsettled Justifications and Unsettling Consequences' 47 *Crime and Justice: A Review of Research* 209.

Hester, R, Roberts, JV, Frase, R and Mitchell, K (2017) 'A Measure of Tolerance: Public Attitudes toward Sentencing Enhancements for Old and Juvenile Prior Records' *Corrections. Policy, Practice, and Research* 137.

Hillier, T (1997) 'Chapter Four: Time for an Overhaul, or a Tune-up' 9 *Federal Sentencing Reporter* 201.

Holder, E (2014) 'Justice News: Attorney General Eric Holder Speaks at the National Association of Criminal Defense Lawyers 57th Annual Meeting and 13th State Criminal Justice Network Conference, Philadelphia, PA, Friday, August 1, 2014', https://www.justice.gov/opa/speech/attorney-general-eric-holder-speaks-national-association-criminal-defense-lawyers-57th.

Home Office Sentencing Review (2001) *Making Punishments Work: A Review of the Sentencing Framework for England & Wales* (London, Home Office).

Jolliffe, D and Hedderman, C (2015) 'Investigating the Impact of Custody on Reoffending Using Propensity Scale Matching' 61 *Crime and Delinquency* 1051.

Jonson, C (2010) *The Impact of Imprisonment on Reoffending: A Meta-analysis* (Cincinnati, Department of Criminology, University of Cincinnati).

Kazemian, L (2010) 'Assessing the Impact of a Recidivist Sentencing Premium on Crime and Recidivism Rates' in JV Roberts and A von Hirsch (eds), *Previous Convictions at Sentencing: Theoretical and Applied Perspectives* (Oxford, Hart Publishing).

Kazemian, L and Farrington, D (2006) 'Exploring Residual Career Length and Residual Number of Offenses for Two Generations of Repeat Offenders' 43 *Journal of Research in Crime and Delinquency* 89.

Kurlycheck, M, Brame, M and Bushway, S (2006) 'Scarlet Letters and Recidivism: Does an Old Criminal Record Predict Future Offending?' 5 *Criminology & Public Policy* 483.

——. (2007) 'Enduring Risk? Old Criminal Records and Predictions of Future Criminal Involvement' 53 *Crime & Delinquency* 64.

Laskorunsky, J (2017) *The Predictive Validity of the Minnesota Sentencing Guidelines Criminal History Score* (Minneapolis, Robina Institute of Criminal Law and Criminal Justice).

Lee, Y (2009) 'Recidivism as Omission: A Relational Account' 87 *Texas Law Review* 571.

——. (2010) 'Repeat Offenders and the Question of Desert' in JV Roberts and A von Hirsch (eds), *The Role of Previous Convictions at Sentencing: Theoretical and Applied Perspective* (Oxford, Hart Publishing).

Lippke, R (2015) 'Elaborating Negative Retribution' *Philosophy and Public Issues* 57.

Ministry of Justice (2014) *Transforming Rehabilitation: A Summary of Evidence on Reducing Reoffending*, 2nd edn (London, Ministry of Justice).

Ministry of Justice (2015) *The Impact of Short Custodial Sentences, Community Orders and Suspended Sentence Orders on Re-offending* (London, Ministry of Justice).

Monahan, J and Skeem, J (2016) 'Risk Assessment in Criminal Sentencing' 12 *Annual Review of Clinical Psychology* 489.

Morris, N and Tonry, M (1990) *Between Prison and Probation: Intermediate Punishments in a Rational Sentencing System* (New York, Oxford University Press).

Nagin, D, Cullen, F, and Johnson, C (2009) 'Imprisonment and Reoffending' in M Tonry (ed), *Crime and Justice* (Chicago, University of Chicago Press).

O'Neill, M, Maxfield, L and Harer, M (2004) 'Past as Prologue: Reconciling Recidivism and Culpability' 73 *Fordham Law Review* 245.

Pennsylvania Commission on Sentencing (2011) *Risk/Needs Assessment Project: Factors that Predict Recidivism for Various Types of Offenders* (State College, Pennsylvania Commission on Sentencing).

Pew Center Review (2012) *Time Served: The High Cost, Low Return of Longer Prison Terms* (Washington DC, Pew Center on the States).

Piquero, A, Farrington, D and Blumstein, A (2007) *Key Issues in Criminal Career Research: New Analyses of the Cambridge Study in Delinquent Development* (Cambridge, Cambridge University Press).

Roberts, JV (1997) 'Paying for the Past: The Role of Criminal Record in the Sentencing Process' in M Tonry (ed), *Crime and Justice. A Review of Research*, vol 22 (Chicago, University of Chicago Press).

Roberts, JV (2008) *Punishing Persistent Offenders: Community and Offender Perspectives on the Recidivist Sentencing Premium* (Oxford, Oxford University Press).

——. (2010) 'Re-Examining First-time offender Discounts at Sentencing' in JV Roberts and A von Hirsch (eds), *Previous Convictions at Sentencing* (Oxford, Hart Publishing).

——. (2011) 'Past and Present Crimes: The Role of Previous Convictions at Sentencing' in C Tamburrini and J Ryberg (eds), *Recidivist Punishments: The Philosopher's View* (New York, Lexington Books).

——. (2015) 'Justifying Criminal History Enhancements at Sentencing' in *Sourcebook of Criminal History Enhancements* (Minneapolis, Robina Institute of Criminal Law and Criminal Justice).

Roberts, JV and von Hirsch, A (eds), (2010) *Previous Convictions at Sentencing: Theoretical and Applied Perspectives* (Oxford, Hart Publishing).

Ryberg, J and Petersen, TS (2011) 'Punishment, Criminal Recidivism and the Recidivist Premium' in C Tamburrini and J Ryberg (eds), *Recidivist Punishments: The Philosopher's View* (New York, Lexington Books).

Singer, R (1979) *Just Deserts: Sentencing Based on Equality and Desert* (Cambridge, MA, Ballinger Publishing).

Starr, S (2015) 'The New Profiling: Why Punishment Based on Poverty and Identity is Unconstitutional and Wrong' 27 *Federal Sentencing Reporter* 229.

Tonry, M (2010) 'The Questionable Relevance of Previous Convictions to Punishments for Later Crimes' in JV Roberts and A von Hirsch (eds), *Previous Convictions at Sentencing: Theoretical and Applied Perspectives* (Oxford: Hart Publishing).

——. (2014) 'Legal and Ethical Issues in the Prediction of Recidivism' 26 *Federal Sentencing Reporter* 167.

——. (2016) *Sentencing Fragments: Penal Reform in America 1975–2025* (New York, Oxford University Press).

Turner, S, Hess, J, Bradstreet, C, Chapman, S and Murphy, A (2013) *Development of the California Static Risk Assessment (CSRA): Recidivism Risk Prediction in the California Department of Corrections and Rehabilitation* (Irvine, Center for Evidence-Based Corrections).

Travis, J, Western, B and Redburn, S (2014) *The Growth of Incarceration in the United States: Exploring Causes and Consequences* (Washington DC, National Academies Press).

US Department of Justice (1984) *Time Served: Does it Relate to Patterns of Criminal Recidivism?* (Washington DC: Bureau of Justice Statistics).

US Sentencing Commission (2017) *The Past Predicts the Future: Criminal History and Recidivism of Federal Offenders* (Washington DC, US Sentencing Commission).

Villettaz, P, Killias, M and Zoder, I (2006) *The Effects of Custodial vs Non-custodial Sentences on Re-offending: A Systematic Review of the State of Knowledge* (Philadelphia, Campbell Collaboration Crime and Justice Group).

Von Hirsch, A (2010) 'Proportionality and the Progressive Loss of Mitigation: Some Further Reflections' in JV Roberts and A von Hirsch (eds), *Previous Convictions at Sentencing: Theoretical and Applied Perspectives* (Oxford, Hart Publishing).

Wermink, H, Nieuwbeerta, P, Ramakers, A, de Keijser, JW and Dirkzwager, A (2017) 'Short-Term Effects of Imprisonment Length on Recidivism in the Netherlands' 63 *Crime and Delinquency* 1.

Zara, G and Farrington, D (2016) *Criminal Recidivism: Explanation, Prediction and Prevention* (Abingdon, Routledge).

10

Unpacking Sentencing Algorithms

Risk, Racial Accountability and Data Harms

KELLY HANNAH-MOFFAT AND KELLY STRUTHERS MONTFORD

I. Introduction

Over the past decade, risk scholars and policy makers have noted a 'remarkable resurgence of risk assessment as an essential component of criminal sanctioning' (Hannah-Moffat 2013; Hyatt and Chanenson 2016; Kehl et al 2017; Monahan and Skeem 2014: 158). Many support a utilitarian logic that includes the use of risk-based actuarial instruments to inform sentencing decisions and promote a rational, aggregate and calculative approach to sentencing (see, for example, Bonta 2007; Hyatt and Chanenson 2016; Monahan and Skeem 2016; Oleson 2011; Stoobs, Hunter and Begaric 2017). Assessment technologies are used to inform bail decisions and pre-sentence reports, and are being built into sentencing guidelines (Hannah-Moffat 2013; Hannah-Moffat and Maurutto 2010; *Harvard Law Review* 2017; Hyatt and Chanenson 2016; Kehl et al 2017; van Eijk 2017). Some US states, including Arizona, Oklahoma, Kentucky, Ohio and Pennsylvania, currently *require* the use of risk assessments for criminal sentencing. In other US states and in Canada, sentencing practices permit the use of risk assessments, which can be included as part of a pre-sentence investigation or pre-sentence report (Hannah-Moffat, 2013; Hannah-Moffat and Maurutto, 2010; Kehl et al 2017).[1] Harcourt (2007: 16) noted that 'prediction of criminality has become *de rigueur* in our highly administrative law enforcement and prison sectors – seen as necessary, no longer a mere convenience'. With the emergence of Big Data analytics, this industry is being expanded and reconfigured (Chan and Bennett Moses 2016;

[1] Although in the province of Ontario, pre-sentence report writers have been instructed to not mention their reliance on risk assessment instruments in order to avoid being cross-examined on this matter (Hannah-Moffat and Maurutto 2010).

Hannah-Moffat 2018). The term 'Big Data' then generally refers to a wide array of digitally stored information about individuals, organisations, companies and events. The term can also be used to describe the techniques used to efficiently assemble and disassemble this information for a variety of commercial and non-commercial purposes. In this chapter we consider how various actuarial approaches to sentencing are structured by and reproduce racial inequalities (as well as other biases), despite claims of racial neutrality.

Research has shown that racialised and gendered socio-economic structures and contexts are relevant to the production and composition of the offender population, and that risk-based practices can exacerbate inequalities and generate systemic discrimination (Fass et al 2008; Gavazzi et al 2008; Hudson and Bramhall 2005; Vose et al 2008). Until recently, debates about the use of various types of risk assessment in sentencing have actively resisted scholarship that advocates for a comprehensive, empirical and conceptual analysis of how bias, systemic discrimination and other forms of marginalisation are embedded into and perpetuated by risk technologies. Instead, there is a rather narrow empirical re-affirmation of the value of risk instruments as more accurate than individual decision making. Actuarial instruments are typically defended as appropriate for use on racialised people after having been narrowly tested for predictive validity and reliability, with seeming 'racially neutral' results. Although debates about gender and risk have been influential enough to result in modified tools or security metrics for women (Hannah-Moffat 2016a; Salisbury, Boppre and Bridget 2016; Salisbury, van Voorhis and Spiropoulos 2009; van Voorhis 2012; van Voorhis et al 2010), few scholars have focused on the impact of race, how race intersects with gender, or how systemic aspects of social inequalities are reproduced through social, political and cultural institutions and practices that produce the data collected to develop, score and validate rick instruments.

We argue that the support for actuarially based risk assessment tools – specifically that these are 'fair', ethical solutions to biased decision making in various sectors of the criminal justice system – remain constrained and limited by an outright dismissal of evidence of racism. Next, we will show that because the inputs contained in risk assessment are assumed to be neutral correlates of recidivism rather than correlates of recidivism within a largely White male prison population, these tools may not be valid, predictive or appropriate to use for non-White persons. We will examine how actuarial risk technologies based either on psychological approaches or Big Data technologies are shaped by evidence bases (data) that are always socially mediated and constituted through the discriminatory operation of the criminal justice system and intersecting forms of social disadvantage. It is important to attend to the advent of Big Data technologies as this represents a methodological and epistemological divergence from other forms of algorithmic justice (Hannah-Moffat 2018). It shifts discretion from psychologists or probation officers who make and administer risk assessments to third-party companies, which use Big Data techniques to develop algorithms based on using multiple data sources that are constantly changing and not necessarily designed for use in criminal justice settings. Further, we will show that a focus on predictive validity and reliability allows race-based critiques to be ignored. Finally, we argue for a penology of racial accountability based on the fundamental reality that racialisation cannot be avoided, and thus that social practices, data and actuarial risk assessment tools cannot be constructed or operate in a racially neutral vacuum. Risk assessment research and testing that seriously engages literature on race, gender and social inequality is needed to best understand how risk assessments are predicated on racialised constructs. Such an approach would allow for an analysis of risk of purportedly 'fair' and bias-free instruments that have the potential to operate in discriminatory manners and contribute to the overrepresentation of racialised persons in custody.

II. Biased Judges, Actuarial Solutions

Arguments supporting 'evidence-based' sentencing or risk-based sentencing include the following: (1) judicial discretion and bias leads to unfair and unequal sentencing; (2) risk assessment can remedy the effects of mandatory minimums and mass incarceration in the US, which are both racially discriminatory and expensive; (3) sentencing low-risk offenders to imprisonment creates rather than prevents recidivism; and (4) judicial discretion does not allow for accountability, transparency and consistency in sentencing within and across jurisdictions. Thus, actuarial sentencing, involving the use of risk assessments to guide judicial decisions, is positioned as a way to identify low-risk offenders, who can be diverted to community supervision, and high-risk offenders (Hyatt and Chanenson 2016; James 2015; Monahan and Skeem 2016; Stoobs, Hunter and Begaric 2017). For example, Stoobs, Hunter and Begaric (2017) have argued that the benefits of wide-ranging discretion in sentencing are exaggerated. Instead, they recommend the introduction and 'develop[ment of] an algorithm which accommodates nearly all variables' (2017: 4). They felt that this kind of tool would allow for consistency in sentencing, arguing that judicial bias leads to conventionally attractive persons receiving lighter sentences or to persons belonging to minority groups receiving harsher sentences. According to these authors, it thus follows that sentencing algorithms can standardise sentencing across jurisdictions and courts. They also argued that this kind of tool could alleviate court backlogs and save taxpayer money. This kind of argument represents a shift from the discretion of individual judges to 'the organizations and individuals producing risk templates and providing courts with risk scores' (Hannah-Moffat 2013: 21). It frames actuarial risk technologies, which are often proprietary, as logical and practical remedies to the seemingly biased and imprecise behaviour of individual decision makers (in this case, judges).

However, this line of reasoning – that problems with individual discretion and discrimination can be remedied with algorithmic assessments – overlooks the way in which risk assessment technologies are premised on the norms of Whiteness. Norms often positioned as devoid of race and therefore universally applicable and racially neutral. Recent socio-legal and punishment research on race and crime has revealed the importance of giving serious consideration to the norms of Whiteness that inform criminal justice practices, as well as how race shapes, informs and intersects with penal policy and institutional practices (Hannah-Moffat 2016a; Murakawa and Beckett 2010; van Cleve and Mayes 2015; Ward 2015). Despite variance in context, experience and socio-economic status that shapes the life course of individuals, the classifications used in research about risk impart moral certainty, neutrality and legitimacy, 'allowing people to accept them as normative obligations and therefore scripts for action' (Ericson and Haggerty 1997: 7). Because actuarial forms of risk assessment have been presented as an impartial and objective alternative to judicial bias, criticism of these tools has largely been directed at rates of predictive accuracy rather than how the tools are built and how the inputs tested for reliability and validity are always already premised on norms of Whiteness. We situate these claims as articulable within a 'penology of racial innocence', in which social practices and institutions are taken to be racially neutral until proven otherwise (Murakawa and Beckett 2010).

A penology of racial innocence refers to social scientific research on race and discrimination that takes legal institutions to be racially neutral rather than structured by White cultural norms (Murakawa and Beckett 2010). This taken-for-granted neutrality shapes legal arguments in cases of racial discrimination, the result of which means that discrimination is limited to proving whether an individual or institution intended to discriminate against another because of their race. Murakawa and Beckett (2010) have challenged this hegemonic penological framework. For example, some legal precedents in the US require litigants to prove that their discrimination was the result of another individual acting deliberately (see Kehl et al 2017; Murakawa and Beckett 2010). In reality, this is inconsistent with how racial discrimination functions and is perpetuated in various penal contexts. Murakawa and Beckett argued that most Western criminal justice systems have 'expanded to affect historically unprecedented numbers of people of colour, with penal policies broadening in ways that render the identification of racial intent and causation especially difficult' (2010: 695). Van Cleve and Mayes argued that the presumption of racial neutrality in the criminal justice system, along with a wider racial ideology of being 'post-racial' (ie, the idea that racism is a problem located in the past that has since been overcome) allows 'criminal justice apparatuses [to] produce an illusion of racial neutrality while exacerbating racial disproportionality' (2015: 406). Ward (2015) for example, argues that the impact of racialised discrimination occurs not only in events of 'spectacular violence', but also in the cumulative, recurring, normalised and ongoing nature of structural inequality. Such discrimination often produces data that is not neutral, but is instead a decontextualised marker of inequality that is unwittingly characterised as indicators of *natural* proclivities to crime and violence. This data is then typically uncritically used to inform the identification and codification of risk factors that underpin assessment tools. Consequently, risk indicators become proxies for race (Harcourt 2007) or systemic discrimination (Hannah-Moffat 2016), with assessment tools simply reproducing insidious forms of systemic discrimination. Overall, the idea that actuarial risk assessments function as a solution to otherwise biased judges neglects the reality that bias is already built into risk assessment and that the use of these tools can have racially discriminatory effects.

III. Racial Neutrality and the Evidence Base

Few have explored how shifts towards more actuarial forms of justice and criminal sentencing are informed by race and therefore have individual and structural racialised effects. Those who have explored these issues have mainly focused on methodologies of assessment, predictive accuracy, individual recidivism and enhanced decision making. Some authors have argued that risk assessment tools are gender-neutral or race-neutral because they have been validated for women and racialised people (see, for example, Bonta 1989, 2007; Bonta et al 1997; Coulson et al 1996; Skeem and Lowenkamp 2016). Bonta (2007) argued that risk factors are unrelated to gender or race, while for others, including Skeem and Lowenkamp (2016), the question is not whether the constructs (such as criminal history, education and substance use) are biased, but whether the tools accurately predict who will re-offend across racial groups.

These researchers have tested tools that were designed on largely White, adult, male prison populations to see whether they predict recidivism among minority populations to the same level of accuracy. For example, Skeem and Lowenkamp (2016) tested the Post-Conviction Risk Assessment (PCRA) on a population of 34,794 federal offenders in the US, paying specific attention to the relationship between the tool, race and recidivism. Overall, they concluded that the PCRA 'strongly predicts' re-arrest (the authors' measure for recidivism) for both White and Black offenders at equal levels of accuracy. They also noted that Black offenders are more likely to receive a higher risk score than White offenders (approximately 13.5 per cent higher), so the application of the tool can have a disparate impact for Black persons. However, they stressed that these differences in risk scores are related to criminal history and that the tool itself is not racially biased, writing that 'criminal history is not a proxy for race, but instead mediates the relationship between race and future arrest. Data are more helpful than rhetoric, if the goal is to improve practice at this opportune moment in history' (Skeem and Lowenkamp 2016: 2). Notably, they measured recidivism in terms of re-arrests, not convictions, which ignores the relationship between race and criminal history and factors such as how race and class influence the likelihood of arrests, denial of bail or strict bail conditions that result in a breach and inaccessibility of adequate legal defence. Showing that a tool accurately measures risk of re-arrest does not insulate it from racial bias. In this case, bias could only be proven if the tool did not predict arrest for Black persons at the same rate as it did for White persons. To presume that bias only exists if the tool predicts at a different rate than for White persons ignores the social, political and economic contexts shaping the discriminatory operation of criminal justice systems, and how these influence how seemingly neutral risk factors are scored. Such an approach is tautological and might better measure the relationship between race, surveillance, suspicion, socio-economic status and the factors shaping the likelihood of police to arrest certain individuals. Instead, questions of bias must focus on context and effect to adequately explore how systemic inequality is perpetuated via the application of purportedly neutral risk assessment techniques.

When compared to White Americans and Canadians, Black persons and Indigenous persons experience lower levels of education and employment, as well as increased rates of poverty, child welfare placements, victimisation, police contact, arrest, charges being placed, denial of bail, inadequate legal representation and incarceration (Berdejó 2018; Epp et al 2014; Hudson and Bramhall 2005; Kellough and Wortley 2002; Myers 2009, 2017; Omori 2014; Rudin 2016). For example, in Ontario, Canada, Black and Indigenous children make up the majority of child welfare placements, despite these groups only comprising a minority of the general population (Ontario Association of Children's Aid Societies 2016; Ontario Human Rights Commission 2018). Some have argued that this overrepresentation is a culmination of the heightened surveillance of Black and Indigenous families combined with entrenched notions that families whose structures deviate from White middle-class norms are pathological and inadequate (King et al 2017; Maynard 2017). Placements of children into state care are linked to an increased likelihood of involvement with the criminal justice system. Black and Indigenous students are more likely to be streamed into non-academic education programmes, to be suspended and to drop out of high school (James and Turner 2017). Black and Indigenous high school students are stopped by police at rates almost three times those of their White counterparts – contact that irrespective of an arrest is correlated with lower educational outcomes. The above-mentioned evidence is not a consequence of these persons committing disproportionate amounts of crime, but of the racialisation of suspicion and crime (Fitzgerald and Carrington 2012; Hayle, Wortley and Tanner 2016). These factors restrict employment and earning ability – factors that will later be coded as risk factors.

In adulthood, Black and Indigenous individuals continue to face disproportionate and *routine* police surveillance and contact, are more likely than White persons to be detained prior to trial and are overrepresented in rates of incarceration, as well as in security ratings upon incarceration (Black Lives Matter Edmonton, Institute for the Advancement of Aboriginal Women 2017; Government of Canada 2017; Kellough and Wortley 2002; Mehler Paperny 2017; Owusu-Bempah and Wortley 2014; Rankin et al 2014; Wortley and Owusu-Bempah 2011; Wortley and Tanner 2003). Those denied bail and/or held in pre-trial detention often cannot afford adequate legal counsel and tend to plead guilty to avoid a lenghtly remands (even though some or all of the charges could have been dismissed at trial).

Those denied bail are also more likely to receive longer sentences than those granted bail (Sacks and Ackerman 2014). Upon incarceration, Indigenous and Black persons are more likely to be placed in maximum security and segregation, and to be the recipients of use of force measures, *despite* Black prisoners being assessed as having lower-risk/needs scores overall (Office of the Correctional Investigator Canada 2013). Increased restrictions on confinement result in being unable to access meaningful vocational training, educational programmes and other services when inside – the result of which will be coded as risk factors in probation and parole decision making (Office of the Correctional Investigator Canada 2013, 2017).

Racialised prison populations exacerbate the social stratification already experienced by minority populations outside the justice system (Pager 2003; Wakefield and Uggen 2010; Western 2002). Although race has been specifically excluded as an item on many risk-assessment tools (see Harcourt 2007), items such as education and prior criminal record are racially loaded. As such, the evidence base – ie, the dataset used to correlate individual traits with recidivism – used to construct risk instruments is an amalgam of various forms of cumulative discrimination that permeates the operation of the CJS and the myriad points in time where decision making is informed by assessments about risk. Understandings of risk must then be situated in a broader context that recognises how social context, the racialisation of crime and institutional decisions can contribute to and mediate risk (Hannah-Moffat 2016). It is impossible to treat individuals fairly if they are treated as abstractions, unaffected by the contexts of social life. In addition to being unable to contextualise economic, familial and geographical disadvantage, risk assessments cannot account for racial discrimination and marginalisation that compound as a result of contact with the criminal justice system. These experiences can serve to artifically elevate criminal histories (Crow 2008). These seemingly neutral factors function to increase purportedly neutral risk scores and may generate a 'ratchet effect', wherein profiled populations become an even larger portion of the carceral population, with highly determined consequences for their employment, educational, family and social outcomes (Harcourt 2007).

A risk score tells us the degree to which the individual being measured shares common features with the population on which the tool was normed; this score is related to correlation, not causation, and is always related to the specific evidence base on which the tool was designed. The score then relates to the likelihood that an individual with those characteristics will re-offend. In practice, those interpreting and making decisions based on scores often attribute a degree of certainty to the scores, with the result that the scores can function not as probability, but as 'administrative certainty' (Hannah-Moffat 2013: 278). Research has shown that few criminal justice practitioners are familiar with the nuances of probability statistics and as a result are unable to appropriately interpret risk scores (see Hannah-Moffat 2013; Hannah-Moffat and Maurutto 2010; *Harvard Law Review* 2017). When used to guide sentencing decisions, 'the "abstract" risk score is thus converted into a correctional artefact that structures the management of prison populations, correctional programming, and the experience of incarceration' (Hannah-Moffat 2013: 278). Actuarial tests might be repeated over the course of an individual's trajectory through the criminal justice system and these scores have wide-ranging consequences. Some scholars have noted that in correctional settings, risk scores function as a form of 'branding', mediating how guards assess character, correctional programming, institutional liberty and parole decisions (Berk 2012; Hannah-Moffat 2018).

Silver and Miller (2002) and Reichman (1986) referred to the idea of statistical justice, wherein dispositions are determined based on how closely an offender matches an actuarial profile, with less significance being given to other relevant legal criteria (*cf* Harcourt 2007). In this way, actuarial risk (as it relates to rehabilitation and incapacitation) de-individualises the assessment of risk by categorising offenders based on unalterable group characteristics. This means that decisions about community or custodial punishments, the conditions of probation and levels of supervision are not determined based on what offenders have done, but rather how closely they approximate subgroups of an offender population. In effect, risk assessments often tell us more about the operation of the criminal justice system than about individuals. The science behind risk tools is consistent with a racially neutral approach, in that it is insufficiently advanced and does not exclude the possibility that tools replicate or produce forms of systemic discrimination. Providing evidence that these tools do not have discriminatory effects on racialised persons would require that questions of cultural bias and the appropriateness of tools designed and normed on primarily White male populations for non-white persons, be taken seriously. Despite many criticisms and cautions, proponents of risk-based approaches to sentencing conceive of this issue narrowly. Namely, that bias only exists if the tools can be shown to have a statistically significant predictive effect, ie, if the tools incorrectly predict for members of certain populations (*cf* Fazel, Chapter 11 in this volume). In effect, tools are assumed to be racially neutral until proven otherwise (*Queen v Ewert*;[2] Skeem and Lowenkamp 2016).

IV. New Risk Technologies

Forms of algorithmic risk are constantly in flux. Current approaches are typically designed by psychologists or informed by Big Data technologies and differ in their methodological, epistemological and normative approaches. Psychologically informed risk assessments use a sample population to infer statistical probability, whereas risk algorithms designed using Big Data are based on massive, potentially infinite population data. Big Data analytics are seen as a game changer for risk

[2] *Queen v Ewert* 2016 FCA 203.

assessment in criminal justice because of its phenomenal speed, breadth and depth capacities for calculating data, and due to its ability to amalgamate many types of data from a range of sources, including but not limited to smartphones, digital cameras, Global Positioning System (GPS) tracking devices, internet searches, consumer databases, social media, open data sources and smart software (Hannah-Moffat 2018; Lupton 2015; Smith and O'Malley 2016). In terms of methodological rigour, psychologically informed risk tools must adhere to discipline-specific standards and are subject to peer review. In contrast, Big Data and its attendant risk algorithms are designed using multiple sources of data that are assembled without the constraints of academic standards of rigour. Moreover, the algorithms are often developed by data scientists who are not trained in the social sciences or criminology (see Berk 2012; Hannah-Moffat 2018). Finally, these forms of algorithmic risk differ in terms of application and fixity. Psychologically informed assessment tools remain static unless revised versions are released by the developers. Big data-risk technologies rely on machine learning. In other words, new data is constantly being inputted and processed by the existing algorithms, with the result that the parameters around risk remain in flux. Therefore, the promises of risk assessment must be interpreted in relation not only to the form of algorithmic risk in question, but also to the methodological and epistemological conditions under which the risk tool was developed (*cf* Fazel, Chapter 11 in this volume). Knowing the variables, data and method of calculation used by various risk tools is essential for their legitimacy. Nonetheless, these aspects of risk assessment as often blackboxed and subject to propriety protections, and thus difficult to assess.

Recent research has examined how Big Data technologies are influencing the prediction of risk and are being used to manage the 'crime problem' and to address the discriminatory operation of the criminal justice system that is perpetuated through psychologically informed approaches to crime and risk (Brayne 2017; Eubanks 2018; Ferguson 2017; Smith and O'Malley 2016). Some have noted a trend towards 'computational criminology' that relies on the promise of future technological developments. This shift to the use of Big Data re-frames notions of security and social control as 'pre-crime' and trades on a fantasy of the post-human, where algorithms are constantly digesting, processing, analysing and responding to an ongoing influx of data that allows them to identify patterns and predict social threats at a scale and speed at which humans are unable to do so. Edwards wrote that the proponents of Big Data for predictive security stress that it allows for 'hitherto unrecognisable patterns of social relations can be registered, indeed *anticipated*, through reference to digital databases arising out of the translation into digital format of historical administrative data held in paper-based archives, the shift to near/real-time recording of administrative data in digital datasets that can be accessed rapidly and remotely, and access to the explosion of data generated by users of social media services' (2017: 3). The technology is so appealing because it has the potential to translate linked data into intelligence about crime and the apparatus of control (Edwards 2017: 3). In terms of sentencing, 'words yield to numbers' (Hamilton 2015: 13), with risk assessments based on Big Data potentially superseding traditional forms of sentencing.

For Stoobs, Hunter and Begaric (2017), sentencing is a governmental decision, similar to taxation or the calculation of social benefits. They wrote that 'the process for coding a sentencing algorithm is no different to other decision-making areas which have multiple variables' and argued that appropriate weights could be attributed to mitigating and aggravating factors through research 'involving reading a large number of sentencing decisions in each relevant jurisdiction' (2017: 31). This passage is notable because the data processed by the algorithms are racialised artefacts inasmuch as the data is based on the operation of the criminal justice system. In other words, the sentencing decisions from which the machine learns are not unaffected by, or outside of, the discriminatory manner in which criminal justice systems operate. Stoobs, Hunter and Begaric focused on judges who as individuals have the potential to be biased, and did not focus on the compounding or 'ratcheting' effects of systemic discrimination over time. They argued that because 'computers have no instinctive or subconscious bias, bias can infiltrate computerised sentencing only if an algorithm incorporates existing variables that result in disproportionately harsh sentences being imposed on offenders from minority groups' (2017: 38). To these authors, bias is the result of individual behaviour, such as judges who rule in a discriminatory manner. This focus on individual actors in the perpetuation of discrimination neglects context. Stoobs, Hunter and Begaric were adamant that once the algorithm is properly calibrated, 'there would be no scope for extraneous, racial considerations to have an impact on computerised sentencing decisions' (2017: 39). It is unclear whether they considered prospective sentencing algorithms to be static or responsive to the input of ongoing data.

Edwards correctly noted that Big Data and algorithmic risk cannot be post-human, nor should it be considered 'post-criminological' (2017: 470). We add that it cannot be post-social, in that data is always already socially assembled and constrained by epistemological approaches. For example, those sceptical of the potential of Big Data argue that it 'will always require human input to refresh the algorithms driving predictive machine-learning' (2017: 459). Furthermore, the ability for machines to appreciate context has been central to criticisms regarding their potential as a solution to many social problems. For example, while machines can be taught to replicate, they are 'colossal failures at polymorphic actions, such as writing love letters or the subversion of factory work routines, because they lack the core human qualities of empathy and improvisation' (2017: 458). Initial trials of algorithmic data mining of social media communication have failed to detect racist comments directed at various high-profile individuals. In addition, Microsoft's experimental AI chatbot, named Tay, began to express and repeat 'amplified racist sentiments, Nazi sympathies and expressions of support for genocide, having learnt these through interactions with unscrupulous users of Twitter' (2017: 458). These examples show that data are not neutral, and algorithms, like psychologically informed risk assessments, rely on how correlations and relationships between factors are parsed and detected.

Some scholars have pointed out that because machine learning uses 'training data', bias can be directly incorporated into the algorithm without the human programmer knowing (Barrett 2017; Kehl et al 2017; Kun 2015). In the case of using artificial intelligence to predict crime, Barrett notes that:

> [A]n algorithm that relies on data produced by biased institutions and attitudes does nothing to inherently remove that institutional bias. Machine-learning algorithms, for example, analyse a set of training data and design rules to apply to prospective data based on the relationship between various attributes in that initial set. That means that any correlations between attributes like race and arrest rates can be recognized and replicated by the algorithm. This integrates discrimination into the software in a way that is subtle, unintentional, and difficult to correct, because it is often not the result of an active choice by the programmer. (2017: 340)

It is difficult for both Big Data and psychologically informed risk assessments to meet the requirement of intent for legal challenges based on equal protection violations. Under US law, the current standard for assessing whether a 'facially neutral law, or … a facially neutral factor' results in racially disparate impact comes from the 1976 decision in *Washington v Davis*.[3] This precedent holds that 'strict scrutiny is only triggered if the individuals challenging the law can show that it was also adopted with a racially discriminatory intent' (Kehl et al 2017: 24). In the case of risk assessments, if a person being sentenced wanted to challenge their score or the use of the tool overall on the basis of bias, Kehl et al argued that they 'would have to be able to prove that the variable that correlated heavily to race was included *for the purpose* of racial discrimination, which is an extraordinarily difficult burden to meet' (2017: 24). Given that this is not a realistic legal threshold for defendants to meet, in addition to the fact that software developers can be unaware of the bias in the dataset, and the fact that algorithms are often proprietary and therefore not available for scrutiny, the threshold for disparate impact is unobtainable and unsuitable to questions surrounding algorithmic race and risk. Instead, notions of neutrality and the attendant legal principles shield risk assessment tools from critique and challenge.

Overall, while the promises of algorithmic sentencing – transparency, accountability, the diversion of low-risk offenders from prison, length of incapacitation and the distribution of rehabilitative resources for high-risk offenders – appear progressive and oriented to problems of equity, in practice this is not the case (Hannah-Moffat 2016; Hannah-Moffat and Maurutto 2010; Harcourt 2007; Hudson and Bramhall 2005; Starr 2014; van Cleve and Mayes 2015). By relying on risk assessments during sentencing, issues of race, gender, religion, nationality,

[3] *Washington v Davis* 426 US 229 (1976).

socio-economic status, histories of abuse, mental and physical health, education, employment, substance use, marital status and various other factors are introduced and become relevant to judicial decision making in ways not previously considered. Not only are these factors introduced, but inasmuch as judges are usually given the scores and not the first-hand information upon which the risk score was assessed, issues of social, political and economic inequality are further decontextualised, abstracted and individualised (Hannah-Moffat 2013). In her analysis of the relevant case law and empirical findings, Starr argued that evidence-based sentencing represents 'an explicit embrace of otherwise-condemned discrimination, sanitized by scientific language' (2014: 803). With regard to issues of race and actuarial risk, van Cleve and Meyes argued that 'risk prediction tools are not free of bias or created in a vacuum – but are mere reflections of the very society that has produced virulent racial inequalities in the first place' (2015: 411). However, the relationship between bias in risk assessment and the embedding of systemic inequality for racialised persons is obscured by appeals to scientific objectivity and statistical prediction on which the tools and technologies trade (van Cleve and Meyes 2015).

The shift to algorithmic-informed sentencing has generated new questions about transparency and accountability. For example, in *State v Loomis*,[4] the defendant, Eric Loomis, filed a motion following his conviction against the use of the Correctional Offender Management Profiling for Alternative Sanctions (COMPAS). Loomis, who had pleaded guilty to lesser charges, specifically argued that the use of a COMPAS risk score in the determination of his sentence violated his right to due process and his right to an individualised sentence, as well as his right to be sentenced based on accurate information. His argument centred on how a COMPAS score is calculated as well as what information can be inferred about an individual based on their score. Because the COMPAS relies only on publicly available data and information provided by the defendant, a COMPAS score 'provides only aggregate data on recidivism risk for *groups* similar to the offender' (*Harvard Law Review* 2017: 1532). However, the trial court, the Wisconsin Court of Appeals and the Wisconsin Supreme Court rejected Loomis' claim on the grounds that he could have provided an explanation or refuted aspects of his personal data used for the COMPAS assessment, and therefore his right to be sentenced according to accurate information had not been infringed. The Supreme Court also stated that while a COMPAS score can only predict the behaviour of someone belonging to a group similar to themselves, the COMPAS score was not the sole basis upon which a sentence was determined, and that the court exercised discretion in interpreting risk scores and would disagree with scores if needed. However, the Wisconsin Supreme Court stipulated how risk assessments are to be introduced to trial courts and the degree to which the assessments can influence an offender's sentence. Notably, it ruled that risk scores cannot be used

[4] *State v Loomis* 881 NW2d 749 (Wis 2016).

to determine whether the individual is sentenced to incarceration or the harshness of the sentence. Judges must also provide an explanation of factors other than the risk assessment that justify the sentence.

Furthermore, the Supreme Court stipulated that any pre-sentence investigation including a COMPAS score should include five written warnings addressed to the judge:

> First, the 'proprietary nature of COMPAS' prevents the disclosure of how risk scores are calculated; second, COMPAS scores are unable to identify specific high-risk individuals because the scores rely on group data; third, although COMPAS relies on a national data sample, there has been 'no cross-validation study for a Wisconsin population'; fourth, studies 'have raised questions about whether [COMPAS scores] disproportionately classify minority offenders as having a higher risk of recidivism'; and fifth, COMPAS was developed specifically to assist the Department of Corrections in making *post*-sentencing determinations. (*Harvard Law Review* 2017: 1533, emphasis in original)

This mandatory written advisement demonstrates that using the COMPAS does not contribute to transparency because the algorithm is not available for scrutiny, is likely unsuitable for use at sentencing and possibly operates in a racially discriminatory manner that will have compounding effects for individuals during their sentence and upon release. Therefore, despite the promissory narratives of risk proponents, Big Data approaches to algorithmic sentencing can further shield the criminal justice system from criticism. Judicial bias and discretion are also not alleviated, but judges are now asked to exercise their discretion in the interpretation of risk scores produced using Big Data technologies.

Conversely, Big Data analytics can be used to expose the discriminatory effects of these tools – referred to as 'data harms'. Scholars at the New York Data and Society Research Institute, for example, obtained and analysed the COMPAS risk scores of more than 7,000 people who had been arrested between 2013 and 2014 in Broward County, Florida, as well as the rate at which they had been charged with new crimes over the following two years (the benchmark used by the designers of the algorithm). The findings show that the COMPAS is limited in the prediction of violent crime. In terms of *all* types of crime, such as the misdemeanours of driving with an expired licence, the algorithm was marginally more predictive than a coin toss. However, the analysis, did find significant racial disparities. While the algorithm had a rate of prediction error that was similar for Black and White defendants, the *form* of error varied with significant consequences. COMPAS[5] scores erroneously flagged Black defendants as future criminals (ie, false positives)

[5] Recent research (Dressel and Farid 2018) has shown the COMPAS to be no more accurate in predicting recidivism than humans with no criminal justice expertise who had been presented with a defendant's criminal history and age. Furthermore, both the human assessors and the COMPAS had almost similar rates of false positives (37–40 per cent for Black defendants and 25–27 per cent for White defendants) and false negatives (29–30 per cent for Black defendants and 40–47 per cent for White defendants).

at nearly twice the rate it did for White defendants. Yet, White accused persons were more likely to be incorrectly scored as low risk (ie, false negatives) than Black defendants were (Angwin et al 2016). Despite controlling for the effect of criminal history, these disparities remained (Angwin et al 2016). In other words, the risk factors processed by the COMPAS algorithm reveal the racialisation of crime and risk. COMPAS developers refuted the above findings. In a letter to ProPublica, Northpointe stated that it 'does not agree that the results of your analysis, or the claims being made based upon that analysis, are correct or that they accurately reflect the outcomes from the application of the model' (as cited in Angwin et al 2016: np). Regardless, this example demonstrates the promise of Big Data by rendering tangible the tautological and inner workings of risk assessment. In so doing, Big Data analytics can serve to invalidate claims that risk assessments produce unbiased risk scores.

Big Data analytics are also allowing lawyers and data scientists to conduct research with new levels of efficiency (Markoff 2011). Various individuals are compiling and producing datasets of judicial rulings, precedents and legislative interpretations, as well as various witness and victim statements and court logs that are publicly available. These websites often include a presentation of snapshot analyses, as well as a synthesis of broader systemic patterns and issues of public concern, including discrimination in the criminal justice system. For example, former lawyer and now legal hacker and software engineer David Colarusso has made public a detailed account of how he used the VirginiaCourtData.org website to show the relationship between race and sentencing: 'For a black man in Virginia to get the same treatment as his Caucasian peer, he must earn an additional $90,000 a year' (Colarusso 2016: np). Although his analysis showed that race could only explain six per cent of the variance, he concluded:

> What we see here is the aggregate effect of many interlocking parts. Reality is complex. Good people can find themselves unwitting cogs in the machinery of institutional racism, and a system doesn't have to have racist intentions to behave in a racist way. (Colarusso 2016: np)

Not only does such a statement highlight that individuals ought not *act* in a racist manner for racism to occur, but these findings are also consistent with risk scholars who have shown that many routine risk assessments do not adequately capture the complexities of gender, race and ethnicity. Rather than attending to these complexities, the risk factors contained in tools are often and better characterised as 'needs', but nonetheless become re-framed as 'risks' (Hannah-Moffat 2005, 2009, 2016b).

V. Conclusion

The literature on race and systemic discrimination and on psychologically based risk assessment (see van Ginneken, Chapter 2 in this volume) each emerged separately in the 1980s and developed in parallel with few intersections. Although criminological and socio-legal scholars have offered a sophisticated conceptualisation and analysis of how risk is interpreted using factors such as gender, race, socio-economic status and regional variations, these critiques are largely misunderstood, often narrowly interpreted as a methodological problem or irreconcilable theoretical differences. Much more research and theory on risk (recidivism/classification) has focused on creating abstract, universal, official 'gender-neutral' and 'race-neutral' tools involving offender risk categories. These tools ignore how gendered, stratified and racialised social structures mediate the types of needs of subgroups of individuals, and how differential social histories, pathways and opportunities affect our understanding of criminal involvement (Hannah-Moffat 2016b), as well as how various correlates of 'crime' are used to characterise and define the risk of recidivism. Nonetheless, the empirical literature on race and crime is largely ignored and dismissed by risk scholars. This ontological and epistemological impasse reinforces a continued dismissal of each position by the other. While the courts value human rights and are invested in the erasure of both overt and systemic discrimination *and* can benefit from the information provided by risk instruments, we argue that risk and race scholars need not be polar opposites. Instead, both risk and race scholars ought to understand the others' 'evidence' and re-think methods and effects of risk assessment, particularly as we enter an era of Big Data informed risk assessment.

Debates about whether or not risk tools employ proxies for race will persist until risk research moves beyond its fixation on predictive validity and reliability of risk predictors, and judiciously considers the ample evidence documenting how these variables are themselves racialised. At the crux of this debate are quite different notions of fairness – one that is rooted in human rights law that accounts for forms of systemic discrimination and the other in statistical method, which often considers variables in isolation (see also Ashworth and Zedner, Chapter 8 in this volume). Until these two debates merge to develop a deeper appreciation of how race and risk intersect, it is imprudent to rely heavily on existing methods of assessing risk to determine sentences, as these assessments have yet to demonstrate that the scores they generate are fair and free from systemic bias.

The advent of Big Data will likely catalyse actuarial justice approaches, as the potential of these technologies to process infinite amounts of data imparts further scientific and computational credibility to risk-based sentencing. However, promises of accountability, objectivity and fairness are in conflict with the fact that algorithms are proprietary and are constantly adjusting to the data being processed. As machine learning entails the constant and ongoing processing of data to improve its predictive capacities, it is possible that otherwise equivalent individuals will be sentenced based on risk scores that vary according to what the algorithm considered significant at that time and place. Put another way, machine learning suggests that the decision-making matrix is constantly in flux. As such, the variables that an algorithm considers relevant for sentencing, as well as their relative weights, at time one can change by time two. Furthermore, we suggest that given the capacity of Big Data technologies to process data in real time and from multiple sources – such as social media, GPS trackers, shopping rewards programmes and financial transactions – the risk of slippage between causation and correlation increases as seemingly 'anything and everything' can be linked to offending via the sheer volume of data processed by the algorithm in question.

As Eubanks notes, 'the cheerleaders of the new data regime rarely acknowledge the impacts of digital decision-making on poor and working-class people. This myopia is not shared by those lower on the economic hierarchy, who often see themselves as targets rather than beneficiaries of these systems' (2018: 9). Analyses of race and risk-based sentencing algorithms requires a comprehensive understanding of race and racial harms – one that is not limited to identifying racial discrimination as an intentional act carried out by an individual. We take critical race theorists seriously in their assertion that there is no 'outside' of racial power, and that claims of racial neutrality and universalism are instead claims about the universality of Whiteness and its attendant norms. This conceptualisation offers a more nuanced understanding of how race and risk of recidivism is co-constitutive. Thus, in both psychologically informed risk assessment and Big Data approaches to risk and sentencing, race is constitutive of the inputs that supposedly race-neutral risk assessments employ. For these reasons, we suggest a penology of racial accountability. Such a framework begins from a point of recognition and critique of systemic inequality rather than the prevailing legal and social scientific approaches that assume neutrality until other parties can prove otherwise.

References

Angwin, J, Larson, J, Mattu, S and Kirchner, L (2016) 'Machine Bias: There's Software Used across the Country to Predict Future Criminals. And it's Biased against Blacks', *ProPublica*, available at www.propublica.org/article/machine-bias-risk-assessments-in-criminal-sentencing.

Barrett, L (2017) 'Reasonably Suspicious Algorithms: Predictive Policing at the United States Border' 41 *New York University Review of Law & Social Change* 327.

Berdejó, C (2018) 'Criminalizing Race: Racial Disparities in Plea Bargaining' 59 *Boston College Law Review* 1189.

Berk, R (2012) *Criminal Justice Forecasts of Risk: A Machine Learning Approach* (New York, Springer).

Black Lives Matter Edmonton, Institute for the Advancement of Aboriginal Women (2017) 'Summary and Analysis of Edmonton Carding Data', https://d3n8a8pro7vhmx.cloudfront.net/progressalberta/pages/352/attachments/original/1498688525/Summary_and_Analysis_of_Edmonton_Carding_Data.pdf.

Bonta, J (1989) 'Native Inmates: Institutional Response, Risk and Needs' 31 *Canadian Journal of Criminology and Criminal Justice* 49.
——. (2007) 'Offender Risk Assessment and Sentencing' 49 *Canadian Journal of Criminology and Criminal Justice* 519.
Bonta, J, LaPrairie, C and Wallace-Capretta, S (1997) 'Risk Prediction and Re-offending: Aboriginal and Non-Aboriginal Offenders' 39 *Canadian Journal of Criminology and Criminal Justice* 127.
Brayne, S (2017) 'Big Data Surveillance: The Case of Policing' 82 *American Sociological Review* 977.
Chan, J and Bennett Moses, L (2016) 'Is Big Data Challenging Criminology?' 20 *Theoretical Criminology* 21.
Colarusso, D (2016) 'Uncovering Big Bias with Big Data', https://lawyerist.com/big-bias-big-data.
Coulson, G, Ilacqua, G, Nutbrown, V, Giulekas, D and Cudjoe, F (1996) 'Predictive Utility of the LSI for Incarcerated Female Offenders' 23 *Criminal Justice & Behaviour* 427.
Crow, MS (2008) 'The Complexities of Prior Record, Race, Ethnicity, and Policy: Interactive Effects in Sentencing' 33 *Criminal Justice Review* 502.
Dressel, J and Farid, H (2018) 'The Accuracy, Fairness, and Limits of Predicting Recidivism' 4 *Science Advances* 1.
Edwards, A (2017) 'Big Data, Predictive Machines and Security: The Minority Report' in MR McGuire and TJ Holt (eds), *The Routledge Handbook of Technology, Crime and Justice* (London, Routledge).
Epp, CR, Maynard-Moody, S and Haider-Markel, DP (2014) *Pulled over: How Police Stops Define Race and Citizenship* (Chicago, University of Chicago Press).
Ericson, RV and Haggerty, K (1997) *Policing the Risk Society* (Oxford, Clarendon Press).
Eubanks, V (2018) *Automating Inequality: How High-Tech Tools Profile, Police, and Punish the Poor* (London, Macmillan).
Fass, TL, Heilbrun, K, DeMatteo, D and Fretz, R (2008) 'The LSI-R and the COMPAS: Validation Data on Two Risk-Needs Tools' 35 *Criminal Justice & Behaviour* 1095.
Ferguson, AG (2017) *The Rise of Big Data Policing: Surveillance, Race, and the Future of Law Enforcement* (New York, New York University Press).
Fitzgerald, RT and Carrington, PJ (2012) 'Disproportionate Minority Contact in Canada: Police and Visible Minority Youth' 53 *Canadian Journal of Criminology and Criminal Justice* 449.
Gavazzi, SM, Bostic, JM, Lim, J-Y and Yarcheck, CM (2008) 'Examining the Impact of Gender, Race/Ethnicity, and Family Factors on Mental Health Issues in a Sample of Court-Involved Youth' 34 *Journal of Family & Marital Therapy* 353.
Government of Canada, Statistics Canada (2017) 'Trends in the Use of Remand in Canada, 2004/2005 to 2014/2015', www.statcan.gc.ca/pub/85-002-x/2017001/article/14691-eng.htm.

Hamilton, M (2015) 'Adventures in Risk: Predicting Violent and Sexual Recidivism in Sentencing Law' 47 *Arizona State Law Journal* 1.
Hannah-Moffat, K (2005) 'Criminogenic Needs and the Transformative Risk Subject: Hybridizations of Risk/Need in Penality' 7 *Punishment & Society* 29.
——. (2009) 'Gridlock or Mutability: Reconsidering "Gender" and Risk Assessment' 8 *Criminology & Public Policy* 209.
——. (2013) 'Actuarial Sentencing: An "Unsettled" Proposition' 30 *Justice Quarterly* 270.
——. (2016a) 'Risk Knowledge(s), Crime and Law' in *Routledge Handbook of Risk Studies* (Routledge Handbooks Online).
——. (2016b) 'A Conceptual Kaleidoscope: Contemplating "Dynamic Structural Risk" and an Uncoupling of Risk from Need' 22 *Psychology, Crime & Law* 33.
——. (2018) 'Algorithmic Risk Governance: Big Data Analytics, Race and Information Activism in Criminal Justice Debates' *Theoretical Criminology* 1.
Hannah-Moffat, K and Maurutto, P (2010) 'Re-contextualizing Pre-sentence Reports: Risk and Race' 12 *Punishment & Society* 262.
Harcourt, BE (2007) *Against Prediction* (Chicago, University of Chicago Press).
Harvard Law Review (2017) '*State v. Loomis*: Wisconsin Supreme Court Requires Warning Before Use of Algorithmic Risk Assessments in Sentencing' 130 *Harvard Law Review* 1530.
Hayle, S, Wortley, S and Tanner, J (2016) 'Race, Street Life, and Policing: Implications for Racial Profiling' 58 *Canadian Journal of Criminology & Criminal Justice* 322.
Hudson, B and Bramhall, G (2005) 'Assessing the "Other" Constructions of "Asianness" in Risk Assessments by Probation Officers' 45 *British Journal of Criminology* 721.
Hyatt, JM and Chanenson, SL (2016) 'The Use of Risk Assessment at Sentencing: Implications for Research and Policy', Villanova Law/Public Policy Research Paper No 2017-1040, https://papers.ssrn.com/sol3/papers.cfm?abstract_id=2961288.
James, C and Turner, T (2017) *Towards Race Equity in Education: The Schooling of Black Students in Greater Toronto Area* (Toronto, York University Press).
James, N (2015) *Risk and Needs Assessment in the Criminal Justice System* (Washington DC, Congressional Research Service).
Kehl, D, Guo, P and Kessler, S (2017) 'Algorithms in the Criminal Justice System: Assessing the Use of Risk Assessments in Sentencing', Responsive Communities Initiative, Berkman Klein Center for Internet & Society, Harvard Law School, https://dash.harvard.edu/handle/1/33746041.
Kellough, G and Wortley, S (2002) 'Remand for Plea: Bail Decisions and Plea Bargaining as Commensurate Decisions' 42 *British Journal of Criminology* 186.
King, B, Fallon, B, Boyd, R, Black, T, Antwi-Boasiako, K and O'Connor, C (2017) 'Factors Associated with Racial Differences in Child Welfare Investigative Decision-Making in Ontario, Canada' 73 *Child Abuse & Neglect* 89.
Kun, J (2015) 'One Definition of Algorithmic Fairness: Statistical Parity', https://jeremykun.com/2015/10/19/one-definition-of-algorithmic-fairness-statistical-parity.

Lupton, D (2015) *Digital Sociology* (Abingdon, Routledge).

Markoff, J (2011) 'Armies of Expensive Lawyers, Replaced by Cheaper Software', *New York Times*, 4 March, https://www.nytimes.com/2011/03/05/science/05legal.html.

Maynard, R (2017) *Policing Black Lives: State Violence in Canada from Slavery to the Present* (Halifax, Fernwood Publishing).

Mehler Paperny, A (2017) 'Exclusive: New Data Shows Race Disparities in Canada's Bail System', *Reuters*, 19 October, https://www.reuters.com/article/us-canada-jails-race-exclusive/exclusive-new-data-shows-race-disparities-in-canadas-bail-system-idUSKBN1CO2RD.

Monahan, J and Skeem, JL (2014) 'Risk Redux: The Resurgence of Risk Assessment in Criminal Sanctioning' 26 *Federal Sentencing Reporter* 158.

——. (2016) 'Risk Assessment in Criminal Sentencing' 12 *Annual Review of Clinical Psychology* 489.

Murakawa, N and Beckett, K (2010) 'The Penology of Racial Innocence: The Erasure of Racism in the Study and Practice of Punishment' 44 *Law & Society Review* 695.

Myers, NM (2009) 'Shifting Risk: Bail and the Use of Sureties' 21 *Current Issues in Criminal Justice* 127.

——. (2017) 'Eroding the Presumption of Innocence: Pre-trial Detention and the Use of Conditional Release on Bail' 57 *British Journal of Criminology* 664.

Office of the Correctional Investigator Canada (2013) *Annual Report of the Office of the Correctional Investigator of Canada 2012–2013* (Ottawa, Office of the Correctional Investigator Canada).

——. (2017) *Annual Report of the Office of the Correctional Investigator 2016–2017* (Ottawa, Office of the Correctional Investigator Canada).

Oleson, JC (2011) 'Risk in Sentencing: Constitutionally Suspect Variables and Evidence-Based Sentencing' 64 *Southern Methodist University Law Review* 1329.

Omori, M (2014) 'Cumulative Racial Inequality of Drug Defendants', PhD thesis, University of California, Irvine.

Ontario Association of Children's Aid Societies (2016) 'One Vision One Voice: Changing the Ontario Child Welfare System to Better Serve African Canadians', http://www.oacas.org/wp-content/uploads/2016/09/One-Vision-One-Voice-Part-1_digital_english.pdf.

Ontario Human Rights Commission (2018) 'Report Interrupted Childhoods: Over-representation of Indigenous and Black Children in Ontario Child Welfare', Ontario Human Rights Commission (2018) Report Interrupted Childhoods: Over-representation of Indigenous and Black children in Ontario Child Welfare.

Owusu-Bempah, A and Wortley, S (2014) 'Race, Crime, and Criminal Justice in Canada' in S Bucerius and M Tonry (eds), *The Oxford Handbook of Ethnicity, Crime, and Immigration* (New York, Oxford University Press).

Pager, D (2003) 'The Mark of a Criminal Record' 108 *American Journal of Sociology* 937.

Rankin, J, Winsa, P, Bailey, A and Ng, H (2014) 'Carding Drops But Proportion of Blacks Stopped by Toronto Police Rises', *Toronto Star*, 26 July, https://www.thestar.com/news/insight/2014/07/26/carding_drops_but_proportion_of_blacks_stopped_by_toronto_police_rises.html.

Reichman, N (1986) 'Managing Crime Risks: Towards an Insurance Based Model of Social Control' 8 *Research in Law, Deviance & Social Control* 151.

Rudin, J (2016) 'Aboriginal Peoples and the Criminal Justice System', research paper delivered to the Attorney General of Canada, https://www.attorneygeneral.jus.gov.on.ca/inquiries/ipperwash/policy_part/research/pdf/Rudin.pdf.

Sacks, M and Ackerman, AR (2014) 'Bail and Sentencing: Does Pretrial Detention Lead to Harsher Punishment?' 25 *Criminal Justice Policy Review* 59.

Salisbury, EJ, Boppre, B and Bridget, K (2016) 'Gender-Responsive Risk and Need Assessment: Implications for the Treatment of Justice-Involved Women' in FS Taxman (ed), *Handbook on Risk and Need Assessment: Theory and Practice* (New York, Taylor & Francis).

Salisbury, EJ, van Voorhis, P and Spiropoulos, GV (2009) 'The Predictive Validity of a Gender-Responsive Needs Assessment: An Exploratory Study' 55 *Crime & Delinquency* 550.

Silver, E and Miller, LL (2002) 'A Cautionary Note on the Use of Actuarial Risk Assessment Tools for Social Control' 48 *Crime & Delinquency* 138.

Skeem, JL and Lowenkamp, CT (2016) 'Risk, Race, and Recidivism: Predictive Bias and Disparate Impact' 54 *Criminology* 680.

Smith, GJD and O'Malley, P (2016) 'Driving Politics: Data-Driven Governance and Resistance' 57 *British Journal of Criminology* 275.

Starr, SB (2014) Evidence-Based Sentencing and the Scientific Rationalization of Discrimination 66 *Stanford Law Review* 803.

Stoobs, N, Hunter, D and Begaric, M (2017) 'Can Sentencing Be Enhanced by the Use of Artificial Intelligence?' 41 *Criminal Law Journal* 261.

Van Cleve, NG and Mayes, L (2015) 'Criminal Justice through "Colorblind" Lenses: A Call to Examine the Mutual Constitution of Race and Criminal Justice' 40 *Law & Social Inquiry* 406.

Van Eijk, G (2017) 'Socioeconomic Marginality in Sentencing: The Built-in Bias in Risk Assessment Tools and the Reproduction of Social Inequality' 19 *Punishment & Society* 463.

Van Voorhis, P (2012) 'On Behalf of Women Offenders' 11 *Criminology & Public Policy* 111.

Van Voorhis, P, Wright, EM, Salisbury, E and Bauman, A (2010) 'Women's Risk Factors and Their Contributions to Existing Risk/Needs Assessment: The Current Status of a Gender-Responsive Supplement' 37 *Criminal Justice & Behaviour* 261.

Vose, B, Cullen, FT and Smith, P (2008) 'The Empirical Status of the Level of Service Inventory' 72 *Federal Probation* 22.

Wakefield, S and Uggen, C (2010) 'Incarceration and Stratification' 36 *Annual Review of Sociology* 387.

Ward, G (2015) 'The Slow Violence of State Organized Race Crime' 19 *Theoretical Criminology* 299.

Western, B (2002) 'The Impact of Incarceration on Wage Mobility and Inequality' 67 *American Sociological Review* 526.

Wortley, S and Owusu-Bempah, A (2011) 'The Usual Suspects: Police Stop and Search Practices in Canada' 21 *Policing & Society* 395.

Wortley, S and Tanner, J (2003) 'Data, Denials, and Confusion: The Racial Profiling Debate in Toronto' 33 *Canadian Journal of Criminology & Criminal Justice* 367.

11

The Scientific Validity of Current Approaches to Violence and Criminal Risk Assessment

SEENA FAZEL

I. Introduction

Criminal justice systems in many high-income countries use some form of structured risk assessment tool or instrument to inform decisions about sentencing, parole, release and probation (see van Ginneken, Chapter 2 in this volume). These tools typically consider two aspects: the future risk of an individual for re-offending and also the criminogenic needs to mitigate this future risk. One estimate is that there are more than 300 such risk assessment tools (Singh et al 2014), many of which are heavily marketed and sold commercially. In the US alone, one report based on a review from 1970 to 2012 documented that 39 states have their own risk assessment tools (Desmarais, Johnson and Singh 2016). In contrast, in England and Wales, there is one risk tool in place for prisons and probation, called OASys (Offender Assessment System), which has been revised, as its first edition was found to have poor predictive performance (Howard and Dixon 2012). Typically, such tools include a set of risk factors, which may or may not be weighted, to provide a classification of risk (such as high, medium or low), a probabilistic score (ie, a percentage probability of re-offending within a certain timeframe) or both. At its most basic, a small number of static (or unchangeable) risk factors, such as sex, age and previous offending, are used to determine high, medium or low risk, but without any information as to what these categories actually mean in terms of probabilities, data on accuracy, or how these risk factors translate into one of these categories. The increasing use of these tools has been driven by the need to provide more consistent and defensible estimates of future risk and, in tools that are more focused on needs, better matching of treatment and interventions in criminal justice with their limited resources. The needs-based approaches attempt to assess individual factors that are thought to be related to offending, such as certain attitudes, stable accommodation, relationship problems and family support. The uptake of these tools can also be explained by research findings, which suggest in general terms that they are better at prediction than human beings (Ægisdóttir et al 2006) and that unstructured clinical judgement (or the subjective judgement of individuals without any explicit framework of assessment) may be biased for many different reasons, including recent experience, prejudice against minority groups and attitudes towards certain offences.

This chapter will present a brief overview of performance measures for risk assessment instruments and will then summarise a number of recent systematic reviews examining the accuracy of commonly used instruments. I will then identify some gaps in the field and discuss whether the current tools are fit for purpose.

II. Measuring the Statistical Performance of Risk Assessment Tools

There are two approaches to test to the performance of such instruments: discrimination and calibration. Discrimination measures a particular tool's ability to distinguish between those who have offended and those who have not by assigning a higher risk score or category to those who offend. Discrimination is tested by reporting sensitivity, specificity, positive predictive value and negative predictive value (see the definitions below), which can only be calculated at specific risk cut-offs. In addition, an overall measure of discrimination across all possible cut-offs is the area under the curve (AUC, reported as a *c* statistic or c-index in some studies), which tests the probability that a randomly selected offender has a higher score on a tool than a randomly selected non-offender. The curve is the Receiver Operating Characteristic Curve (or ROC curve), which plots true positives against true negatives. To take one example, an AUC of 0.70 is the equivalent of saying that a tool will correctly assign a higher score 70 per cent of the time to a randomly selected offender than a randomly selected non-offender. Many studies rely on simply presenting discrimination statistics, and even then, only the AUC, which on its own is uninformative. For example, a tool can correctly classify individuals into higher and lower risk groups at all possible cut-offs, but is only used at a specific cut-off, where its discrimination is much poorer. This can be exemplified in the case of a risk assessment tool that has 30 items and is scored from 0 to 30. If the tool is tested in a research study and it correctly assigns all the offenders with a score of 2 compared to all non-offenders who score 0 and 1, then it will have a perfect AUC of 1. However, the guidelines for the use of the tool state that a score of 5 and above should be used to determine high risk of offending, and therefore the AUC statistic masks its poor intended performance. If used as intended with a cut-off of 5, this would mean that everyone in the sample is assigned a low risk score, even though some of these individuals are offenders. Depending on the number of offenders and non-offenders, this would mean that the AUC is closer to 0.5 or chance. AUCs below 0.5 are worse than chance – in other words, such models are systematically wrong. This is one of the reasons why presenting a range of performance measures is important, particularly true and false positives and negatives. Indicative values of good discrimination measures have been discussed, but there is no clear consensus (Singh 2013).

Further, an instrument may be accurate in identifying risk groups, but may do so in a way that is very different from their real offending rates. In such a case, a tool may estimate rates of offending of 10 per cent to higher-risk offenders compared to 9 per cent to lower-risk offenders, and hence perfectly discriminates between these two groups. But if the higher-risk offenders are more likely to offend at rates of around 40 per cent and the lower-risk offenders at 1 per cent, then it is very poorly calibrated and has little if any practical utility as a prediction model (Lindhiem et al 2018). Calibration refers to the agreement between observed outcomes (ie, offending) and predictions from a particular tool. For example, if there is a prediction of a 30 per cent re-offending risk following release from prison in one year, the observed frequency for re-offending should be around 30 out of 100 released prisoners with such a prediction.

Sensitivity (the proportion of people who have offended that an instrument correctly classified as high risk) needs to be high if the aim is to screen individuals for a disease (eg, for further costly or more invasive investigations) and is important from a public policy perspective, as the consequences of 'missing' an individual who offends needs to be considered. The corollary of sensitivity is the false negative rate (which is calculated as 1-sensitivity) – the proportion of individuals who commit crimes that the tool misses. A false negative rate of, say, five per cent is equivalent to the tool not correctly identifying five out of every 100 individuals who have offended. Specificity (the proportion of individuals who have not offended that are correctly identified) should be high if the implications of being labelled high risk are harmful (eg, longer sentences or preventative detention). The false positive rate is the inverse of specificity (1-specificity) – the proportion of people that the tool incorrectly estimates will commit crimes. The relative proportion of true and false positive and negative rates will be determined by a range of legal, ethical and political concerns. Low false negative and positive rates will clearly be preferred, but a high false positive rate could be acceptable if the consequences of being labelled higher risk are not harmful. To exemplify this, if a tool does not miss individuals who re-offend on release (a low false negative rate), but also identifies many people as high risk who do not re-offend (a high false positive rate), this is less concerning if the consequences for those incorrectly identified as high risk are not harmful, such as additional support on release. Where it will be problematic is if the high-risk group have their prison sentences extended.

These decisions will need some alternatives to consider, such as the relative balance without using such tools or when two approaches can be compared. Some tools have tried to maximise the combination of sensitivity and specificity by adjusting cut-off points (eg, looking at the inflection point of a ROC curve – the point at which there is a change in concavity of the curve). Here, researchers would look at the best possible cut-off by examining the inflection point. By finding the inflection point, this will translate into a cut-off to the nearest whole number for a tool that has the best discrimination for that particular sample being studied. The problem with this approach is that it is unlikely to be applicable to other samples, and pre-specifying a cut-off is preferable methodologically. In other words, taking this approach to identifying the best cut-off statistically will likely only apply to the specific sample being studied rather than new populations.

Some commentators have suggested that positive predictive value (PPV – the proportion of people that a tool identifies as high risk that actually offend) and negative predictive value (NPV – the proportion that are identified as low risk that do not offend) are more relevant to criminal justice as it is how these tools are used in practice (Buchanan and Leese 2001; Coid, Ullrich and Kallis 2013). The main limitation with this approach is that these two measures, alongside sensitivity and specificity, are also sensitive to the base rate, so the PPV will be low if the rate of offending in the population of interest is low, and the NPV will be high. Nevertheless, the NPV is increasingly important in some countries where decarceration is a public policy priority, which provides information on the proportion of prisoners that can be safely released (ie, not re-offend within a specified time period). It is also important for some populations such as juveniles and women, where prison should be avoided if possible, due to secondary effects on education, work, family and social networks, and mental health (Abram et al 2015). Sensitivity, specificity, PPV and NPV will change if a tool's cut-off changes – if the threshold for high risk increases, then sensitivity and NPV will decrease, and correspondently specificity and PPV will increase. This is one reason why the AUC is often presented as a summary statistic as it presents measures of discrimination (sensitivity and 1-specificity) at all possible cut-offs. At the same time, using AUCs to compare risk tools is problematic as very different numbers of false negative and false positive predictions resulting from different shapes of receiver operating curve may have the same overall AUC (Mallett et al 2012).

The other key measure of a tool's performance is calibration. This asks how closely the tool's predicted risk matches the observed risk. For example, a tool that predicts a 20 per cent chance of offending in a particular sample, but only 10 per cent actually offended, is poorly calibrated. Calibration can be examined graphically by plotting predicted risk versus observed offending behaviour or through statistical tests to measure the typical level of miscalibration, such as the Brier test or HL statistic (Lindhiem et al 2018). Calibration is the key performance measure if only probability scores are used – as the discrimination measures are only possible if there are a limited number of cut-offs. One important area of contention relevant to calibration is the group to individual problem, and proponents of this view have argued that it is not possible to apply group information to individuals due to a lack of precision, also known as the G2I ('group to individual') problem. The argument is put forward that when an actuarial tool provides a probability score of 30 per cent, applying this to an individual is subject to the potentially large variation underlying the probability score. Hence, this view proposes that 30 per cent actually means 10–50 per cent for an individual and so is not informative. However, this position is based on a misunderstanding of statistics – all individual predictions are based on group data, and their precision will be a consequence of sample size (Imrey and Dawid 2015). The probability score of 30 per cent for a risk assessment tool can be interpreted by stating that it refers to an individual with the same risk factor profile who will on average re-offend at a rate of 30 per cent.

III. The Overall Performance of Currently Used Risk Assessment Tools

So what do we know about the performance of currently used tools in criminal justice? There have been a number of systematic reviews that have outlined their performance. Interestingly, none of them has reported calibration statistics, as it seems that this is very rarely reported in the research literature. In fact, one 2013 review of how AUCs were presented in 50 studies did not report one calibration metric (Singh et al 2013). The review by Yang and colleagues in 2010 looked at head-to-head comparisons of nine violence risk assessment tools and identified 28 studies in no more than 7,221 individuals, which reported AUCs and a measure of effect size (Cohen's d). It concluded that there was little difference in the included risk assessment measures, which varied in AUCs between 0.65 and 0.71 (Yang, Wong and Coid 2010). A later and more comprehensive review of an overlapping but different set of nine instruments identified 73 studies including 24,827 people (Fazel et al 2012). This review presented a broader range of discrimination statistics, and also separately by violent offending and any criminal offending. The findings were different by type of predicted outcome – for violent crime, sensitivity was high (0.92) and specificity was low (0.36), with moderate PPV (41 per cent) and high NPV (91 per cent). For any offending, sensitivity was low (0.41) and specificity was high (0.80), with moderate PPV (52 per cent) and NPV (76 per cent). In terms of AUCs, for violent offending it was 0.72 and for criminal offending it was 0.66. Overall, these are mixed discrimination metrics – moderate AUCs and NPVs – which suggests that their use in practice needs to reflect these differing performance metrics. One possibility is to screen out low-risk offenders. Another is to only use these tools as adjuncts in the decision-making process due to positive predictive values of around 40–50 per cent. Finally, due to the low specificity of violence risk assessment, they should only be used when the consequences of high-risk categories are non-harmful interventions, such as additional management or treatment. Another way of looking at these findings is to focus on false negative and false positive rates – for tools predicting violent outcomes, it was 8 per cent and 64 per cent, respectively, while for tools predicting any criminal outcomes (such as the Level of Service Inventory (LSI-R)), it was 59 per cent false negative and 20 per cent false positive. If the implications of false positive rates are not harmful, this would suggest that instruments predicting violent outcomes should be prioritised over those focusing on any crime. In other words, this review found that the balance between false negatives (low for tools focusing on violent crime, but more than 50 per cent for tools with any crime outcomes) and false positives (high for tools focusing on violent crime, but lower for those predicting any crime) favours the violence risk assessment tools if the consequences of false positive (ie, being labelled high risk and not re-offending) are not harmful. The 59 per cent false negative rate for tools predicting any crime is arguably too high for their widespread use in criminal justice.

A third notable review summarised research on the predictive validity of 19 instruments used in US corrections from 1970 to 2012 (Desmarais, Johnson and Singh 2016). This review underscores the problems with the reporting of this literature. It found that only summary statistics were presented and solely for general recidivism (as distinct from violent recidivism). The median AUC of these tools typically ranged from 0.64 to 0.71 for new offences, and in real-life settings, the LSI-R, which is a commonly used tool, had an AUC of 0.63 and the RMS an AUC of 0.66. As with the other reviews, no information on calibration was reported, which is problematic as all the 19 included tools provide probabilistic scores of re-offending (and, in some cases, parole violations).

Overall, based on these recent systematic reviews of current risk assessment tools, there are major shortcomings in how these instruments are reported, with insufficient information on their performance. In addition, there are other problems with transparency (see also van Ginneken, Chapter 2 in this volume). The statistical contribution of individual risk factors to the final model, and the process by which they were chosen and categorised should be outlined. This transparency is important as it allows for the models to be critically appraised by experts, such as the nature of the sample that it was derived in, the choice of predictors and how they were categorised, the statistical power of the study, and the precision of the performance measures. This is particularly important if harm follows from a tool's use, such as longer sentences, certain interventions, and more restrictions in the community (cf Hannah-Moffat, this volume; Hester, this volume). Another problem are the potential financial and non-financial conflicts of interests among researchers in this field, and many of the tools being studied are conducted by individuals who developed or translated them (Singh, Grann et al 2013). Such potential conflicts need to be disclosed, which currently rarely occurs.

Scalability and cost need to be considered – some of the tools have commercial licences (such as the COMPAS or Correctional Offender Management Profile for Alternative Sanctions), which takes up to 60 minutes to complete. Many of these tools also assess individual needs and treatment (and linked to responsivity, which is the extent to which an intervention is responsive to the individual needs identified), and their predictive validity is one element in their potential value. However, conflating risk and needs can lead to loss of performance on risk, and empirically robust risk calculators are required before more careful assessment of needs and treatment. Further, there have been some recent attempts to focus on causal risk factors as these will lead to reductions in recidivism once treated (Howard and Dixon 2013). However, one problem with this approach is that the most predictive factors (eg age, previous crime) are not causal, and excluding such factors will lead to poorer performance in terms of prediction. If the next stage of any risk management process is needs assessment, then identifying causal risk factors will be informative but will require different approaches (such as quasi-experimental designs and treatment trials rather than correlational studies of risk factors). Another issue is that the performance of current tools shrinks when used in real-world settings as distinct from research studies. A recent example was reported for the commonly used Psychopathy Checklist, revised edition (PCL-R). In a field trial in Belgium, its predictive validity was poor with an overall AUC of 0.63 for general recidivism and 0.57 for violent recidivism (Jeandarme, Edens et al 2017), which compares unfavourably to mostly research studies that have reported higher AUCs of 0.66-0.67 (Singh, Grann et al 2011; Yang, Wong et al 2010). The LSI-R, when used prospectively in over 22,000 prisoners in Washington State in the US, was associated with an AUC of 0.64 for violent recidivism (Barnoski and Aos 2003), which is lower than its performance in psychiatric samples and research studies. This shrinkage is a consequence of a number of methodological weaknesses in the design of these tools (see below for more on the LSI-R).

IV. A Practical Guide to Evaluate Risk Assessment Tools

So what can we make of this in practice? How can individuals in criminal justice and public policy determine whether a tool is fit for purposes? We have proposed a 10-point guide (Fazel and Wolf 2018), which I will summarise. I will start with criteria relevant to the derivation (or discovery or development) study and will then move on to criteria relating to the validation of risk assessment tools. The relevant criteria are as follows.

A. Did the Study Deriving the Tool Follow a Protocol?

This is a key component if a study is to provide an accurate representation of a tool's performance. Without a protocol, the likelihood of creating a tool that reports strong statistical performance but performs poorly in practice is high as it possible that the original methods were changed to optimise performance. The sample, candidate variables, outcome(s), follow-up periods, statistical analyses and output should all be pre-specified before any data analysis is performed. This protocol should be published, and any deviations from it in any particular study should be clearly explained and justified (such as a predictor being dropped because of large proportions of missing data).

B. How were Candidate Variables Selected for the Tool?

The more variables that have been tested in a derivation study, particularly if the sample was not sufficiently large, the more likely the chance that associations are found, and the reported model performance will not perform well in external validation. One rule of thumb is that for each variable tested, the derivation sample should have at least 10 outcomes (Royston and Sauerbrei 2008). Further, the choice of which variables to test and how they are categorised should have followed a protocol, and multivariable regression should have been conducted to determine their independent association with the outcome (typically criminal reoffending) before inclusion in a model. Otherwise, tools will include variables that do not add incremental predictive accuracy and will lead to overcomplicated and time-consuming instruments.

C. How were Variables Weighted?

Many tools in criminal justice give equal weighting to all included items. This makes two assumptions: first, that all included predictors have the same association with the outcome; and, second, that the variables are all independently related to the outcome. In terms of weighting, previous violent crime and living in a poor neighbourhood are both associated with higher risk of crime, but they are not equally important. Tools that have not weighted individual items will perform worse (Hamilton et al 2015).

D. How were Other Parameters Selected?

Other key aspects of any research study should be determined beforehand and outlined in a protocol, such as the time for follow-up for the tool. If this has not been done, to take an example, a particular tool may perform better at three years rather than one or two years, and the researchers might decide that three years is the primary outcome. The problem with this approach is that it is a form of multiple testing and the consequence will be that the tool performs considerably worse in real-world settings.

E. Has Internal Validation Been Done?

This is typically done using a method called bootstrapping, which takes a number of random samples from the dataset to provide an estimate of accuracy of performance measures.

F. Has the Tool Been Externally Validated?

This question examines whether the tool's performance has been investigated in a new sample. In many ways, this is the most important question as tools tend to perform considerably better in the sample in which they were derived (Khoury, Gwinn and Ioannidis 2010, Monahan and Skeem 2016) and an external validation is necessary to test how accurate it is. Splitting the original derivation sample into two random groups is a form of internal validation, but is not external validation due to the equal distribution of predictor variables. Such a split will lead to comparable performance because the predictors will have a very similar distribution in the derivation and the randomly split samples. To achieve this, the sample should be split on other variables, which are not related to the outcome (Fazel et al 2016).

G. Has This Validation Been Done in the Population of Interest?

Here the key issue is whether the new population for which the tool will be used has similar characteristics, risk factors, baseline risk and outcome(s) to the sample where the tool was created. This may explain why some tools, such as the PCL-R, which was not developed to predict violence risk, but to identify a form of personality disturbance, performs among the worst of commonly used tools (Singh et al 2011). In addition, this is problematic for some tools developed in selected samples of high-risk offenders (which appears to have been the case for the LSI-R) that are then used in general criminal justice samples, such as all individuals in prison or on probation. Particularly important is using the same or very similar outcome as intended because differences in outcome prevalence will inevitably lead to reductions in performance.

H. Has the Validation Been Conducted Using Robust Methods?

Validation studies should stay true to the original model and be based on a protocol, and anticipated changes should be discussed beforehand in a protocol (eg, recalibration will be considered if the underlying base rate of offending is different, and how this recalibration of the model will be tested). Otherwise, what appears to be a validation is no longer an external validation, but the derivation of a new model. The sample size is also important and should aim for at least 100 events (or outcomes) for statistical power (Collins, Ogundimu and Altman 2016). Results should be published in peer-reviewed journals, but, on its own, this is not a marker of methodological quality. Studies should provide sufficient methodological detail in order to be replicable.

I. Has the Validation Study Reported Essential Information?

As described above, tools should report both measures of discrimination (especially rates of true and false positives and negatives) and calibration (ideally with a graphical plot that compares observed with predicted risks).

J. Is the Risk Assessment Tool Useful, Feasible and Acceptable?

The tool should provide useful information, including a relevant outcome (eg, prediction of re-offending), and clearly defined risk categories. The tools and their constituent predictors should also be easy to complete, reliable and clearly defined. For example, rating scales (eg, 1–5 Likert scales) may vary between raters. The tool should have face validity by including essential items (for example, age and sex) and should justify the inclusion of other items. There are advantages in having interview-independent tools to reduce the possibility of observer bias.

If a particular tool has not been externally validated, we argue that it should not be used in practice apart from rare circumstances when alternatives are not appropriate or available, and external validation is ongoing (Fazel and Wolf 2018). And even if it has been externally validated, instruments should undergo prospective validation after implementation to monitor their ongoing accuracy.

V. Applying Quality Criteria to Individual Risk Assessment Tools

The extent to which risk assessment tools currently used in criminal justice meet these 10 criteria needs to be systematically evaluated, but few of them meet more than one or two. To take some examples of commonly used tools, on these five criteria for derivation discussed above, two such instruments, the Historical Clinical Risk Management-20 (HCR-20) and the Violence Risk Appraisal Guide (VRAG), meet few criteria. The HCR-20 chose its 20 predictors based on expert opinion in 1997 rather than a systematic review of the evidence or testing them in multivariable models (an approach the authors reported in the following way: 'What variables might clinicians and administrators consider as they attempt evaluations of risk of violence in cases where psychiatric disorders are thought to be involved?'; Webster et al 1997: 251). The derivation did not include any statistical performance measures. Each item is scored as '0' (item not present), '1' (item possibly present) or '2' (item definitely present) rather than assigning any weighting to them (Douglas and Reeves 2010). Age and sex, two of the strongest predictors of violence that are considered important for face validity, were not included. In developing the VRAG, 42 candidate variables were collected from a single sample of 618 mentally disordered Canadian offenders (of whom 191 re-offended). Of those, 332 individuals had been admitted to a maximum-security prison, while the remaining 286 had been admitted to a secure hospital for a brief pre-trial psychiatric assessment – not a sample that will be generalisable to most prisoners. With regard to the outcome, 191 re-offenders does not provide sufficient statistical power for 42 candidate variables (Harris, Rice and Quinsey 1993), and good practice would suggest that at least double the number of re-offenders would be required for derivation. The VRAG's derivation study reports performance measures at five different cut-offs (which were not pre-specified) and does not provide an overall performance measure. As with the HCR-20, the offender's sex was not one of the variables considered and hence was not included in the final model, which consists of 12 items (that are weighted).

Two other widely used tools are difficult to evaluate due to a lack of published information about certain aspects of their derivation and original validation. The LSI-R is based on 54 dynamic items, and the OASys Violent Predictor (OVP) in England and Wales, which is given to all individuals who receive sentences of 12 months or more, is derived from the 100-item OASys (Howard and Dixon 2012). However, the LSI-R does not include some of the most powerful predictors such age or gender, and has items that appear to be unreliable psychometrically (such as 'could make better use of time', has 'very few prosocial friends' and four items on current attitudes). Importantly, the original derivation study has not been published to my knowledge. The OASys is better reported and has some selected publications explaining aspects of its derivation, but lacks detail on some key areas (Howard and Dixon 2011, 2013). At the same time, both the LSI-R and the OASys have weighting for individual predictors that were tested using logistic regression in developing the model, along with relatively simple scoring methods, and have been subject to external validation.

Putting this altogether, I would argue that the most commonly used tools in criminal justice are not fit for purpose for prediction purposes. None of them meet all the 10 tests outlined above to my knowledge, and few meet more than one or two of the criteria outlined. At the same time, some of these instruments may provide a useful framework for organising information, may act as a reminder for those working in criminal justice to assess certain risk factors and domains, and may match individuals for treatment based on needs. The first two of these justifications are arguably too high a price to pay for those instruments that are resource-intensive.

VI. The OxRec Model

After reviewing this literature, I have been part of a team that has developed the Oxford Risk of Recidivism tool (OxRec), using Swedish national data, which provides a probabilistic score for violence and any re-offending in one and two years post-release from prison, and also low/medium and high categories based on pre-specified levels. It can be completed in 5–10 minutes using 14 routinely collected predictors and using a freely available online calculator (Fazel et al 2016). The weighting of the individual predictors and how they are combined to create a probability score has been published (with the original protocol), with a full range of discrimination and calibration statistics, making it a fully transparent risk prediction model. It has been externally validated in Sweden in more than 10,000 individuals leaving prison (Fazel et al 2016), with another recent external validation in the Netherlands (Fazel et al 2019) and some ongoing in other countries, and provides a methodological rigorous approach with which to develop risk assessment instruments. The probability score is relatively precise as it was derived based on a study of 37,100 released prisoners.

VII. Summary

In summary, I have outlined some key ways of evaluating the performance of risk assessment instruments in criminal justice and have highlighted the importance of both investigating measures of discrimination and calibration. I have outlined some systematic reviews of the field, which suggest that many current tools, such as the LSI-R and the PCL-R, have at best moderate performance in discrimination with no information on calibration. Most tools currently used in criminal justice have not been included in these reviews because research on their external validation has not been published. Further, the development of risk assessment tools in criminal justice has lagged behind methodological improvements in prognostic models in science, and particularly in medicine.

Finally, I have provided a 10-point checklist that can be used to evaluate any risk tool. On this basis, I have argued that current widely used tools should probably not be used for prediction. At the very least, their use should be reviewed in the light of the 10 tests outlined, and information that is lacking should be requested from these tool's developers and commercial entities marketing them. In terms of its implications for predictive sentencing, risk predictions from commonly-used tools – either as categories such as high, medium or low, or as probability scores – do not have a sufficient evidence-base in support that they can currently be used in court. As I have shown, the current risk assessment tools have not met some basic criteria in terms of how they were derived or in subsequent validations of their performance. Furthermore, when empirically tested on a range of performance measures and mostly in research studies, they typically lead to unacceptably high false positives and false negative rates, particularly in tools aimed at any recidivism. I have also discussed the development and validation of a new scalable prediction tool, OxRec, which represents a methodological advance and provides a model for transparent reporting of such tools.

References

Abram, KM, Zwecker, NA, Welty, LJ, Hershfield, JA, Dulcan, MK and Teplin, LA (2015) 'Comorbidity and Continuity of Psychiatric Disorders in Youth after Detention: A Prospective Longitudinal Study' 72 *JAMA Psychiatry* 84.

Ægisdóttir, S, White, MJ, Spengler, PM, Maugherman, AS, Anderson, LA, Cook, RS, Nichols, CN, Lampropoulos, GK, Walker, BS and Cohen, G (2006) 'The Meta-analysis of Clinical Judgment Project: Fifty-Six Years of Accumulated Research on Clinical Versus Statistical Prediction' 34 *Counseling Psychologist* 341.

Barnoski, R and Aos, S (2003) 'Washington's Offender Accountability Act: An Analysis of the Department of Corrections' Risk Assessment' (Olympia, Washington State Institute for Public Policy).

Buchanan, A and Leese, M (2001) 'Detention of People with Dangerous Severe Personality Disorders: A Systematic Review' 358 *Lancet* 1955.

Coid, JW, Ullrich, S and Kallis, C (2013) 'Predicting Future Violence among Individuals with Psychopathy' 203 *British Journal of Psychiatry* 387.

Collins, GS, Ogundimu, EO and Altman, DG (2016) 'Sample Size Considerations for the External Validation of a Multivariable Prognostic Model: A Resampling Study' 35 *Statistics in Medicine* 214.

Desmarais, SL, Johnson, KL and Singh, JP (2016) 'Performance of Recidivism Risk Assessment Instruments in US Correctional Settings' 13 *Psychological Services* 206.

Douglas, KS and Reeves, KA (2010) *Historical-Clinical-Risk Management-20 (HCR-20) Violence Risk Assessment Scheme: Rationale, Application, and Empirical Overview* (Abingdon, Routledge).

Fazel, S, Chang, Z, Fanshawe, T, Långström, N, Lichtenstein, P, Larsson, H and Mallett, S (2016) 'Prediction of Violent Reoffending on Release from Prison: Derivation and External Validation of a Scalable Tool' 3 *Lancet Psychiatry* 535.

Fazel, S, Singh, JP, Doll, H and Grann, M (2012) 'Use of Risk Assessment Instruments to Predict Violence and Antisocial Behaviour in 73 Samples Involving 24,827 People: Systematic Review and Meta-analysis' 345 *British Medical Journal* e4692.

Fazel, S and Wolf, A (2018) 'Selecting a Risk Assessment Tool to Use in Practice: A 10-Point Guide' 21 *Evidence-Based Mental Health* 41.

Fazel, S, Wolf, S, Vasquez Martez, M and Fanshawe, T (2019) 'Prediction of violent reoffending in prisoners and individuals on probation: a Dutch validation study (OxRec)' *Scientific Reports* doi: 10.1038/s41598-018-37539-x.

Hamilton, Z, Neuilly, M-A, Lee, S and Barnoski, R (2015) 'Isolating Modeling Effects in Offender Risk Assessment' 11 *Journal of Experimental Criminology* 299.

Harris, GT, Rice, ME and Quinsey, VL (1993) 'Violent Recidivism of Mentally Disordered Offenders: The Development of a Statistical Prediction Instrument' 20 *Criminal Justice and Behavior* 315.

Howard, PD and Dixon, L (2011) 'Developing an Empirical Classification of Violent Offences for Use in the Prediction of Recidivism in England and Wales' 3 *Journal of Aggression, Conflict and Peace Research* 141.

——. (2012) 'The Construction and Validation of the OASys Violence Predictor: Advancing Violence Risk Assessment in the English and Welsh Correctional Services' 39 *Criminal Justice and Behavior* 287.

——. (2013) 'Identifying Change in the Likelihood of Violent Recidivism: Causal Dynamic Risk Factors in the OASys Violence Predictor' 37 *Law and Human Behavior* 163.

Imrey, PB and Dawid, AP (2015) 'A Commentary on Statistical Assessment of Violence Recidivism Risk' 2 *Statistics and Public Policy* 1.

Jeandarme, I, Edens, JF, Habets, P, Bruckers, L, Oei, K and Bogaerts, S (2017) 'PCL-R Field Validity in Prison and Hospital Settings' 41 *Law and Human Behavior* 29.

Khoury, MJ, Gwinn, M and Ioannidis, JP (2010) 'The Emergence of Translational Epidemiology: From Scientific Discovery to Population Health Impact' 172 *American Journal of Epidemiology* 517.

Lindhiem, O, Petersen, IT, Mentch, LK and Youngstrom, EA (2018) 'The Importance of Calibration in Clinical Psychology' *Assessment*, doi.org/10.1177/1073191117752055.

Mallett, S, Halligan, S, Thompson, M, Collins, GS and Altman, DG (2012) 'Interpreting Diagnostic Accuracy Studies for Patient Care' 345 *British Medical Journal* e3999.

Monahan, J and Skeem, JL (2016) 'Risk Assessment in Criminal Sentencing' 12 *Annual Review of Clinical Psychology* 489.

Royston, P and Sauerbrei, W (2008) *Multivariable Model-Building: A Pragmatic Approach to Regression Anaylsis Based on Fractional Polynomials for Modelling Continuous Variables* (Chichester, John Wiley & Sons).

Singh, JP (2013) 'Predictive Validity Performance Indicators in Violence Risk Assessment: A Methodological Primer' 31 *Behavioral Sciences & the Law* 8.

Singh, JP, Desmarais, SL, Hurducas, C, Arbach-Lucioni, K, Condemarin, C, Dean, K, Doyle, M, Folino, JO, Godoy-Cervera, V, Grann, M, Ho, RMY, Large, MM, Nielsen, LH, Pham, TH, Rebocho, MF, Reeves, KA, Rettenberger, M, de Ruiter, C, Seewald, K and Otto, RK (2014) 'International Perspectives on the Practical Application of Violence Risk Assessment: A Global Survey of 44 Countries' 13 *International Journal of Forensic Mental Health* 193.

Singh, JP, Desmarais, SL and Van Dorn, RA (2013) 'Measurement of Predictive Validity in Violence Risk Assessment Studies: A Second-Order Systematic Review' 31 *Behavioral Sciences & the Law* 55.

Singh, JP, Grann, M and Fazel, S (2011) 'A Comparative Study of Violence Risk Assessment Tools: A Systematic Review and Metaregression Analysis of 68 Studies Involving 25,980 Participants' 31 *Clinical Psychology Review* 499.

——. (2013) 'Authorship Bias in Violence Risk Assessment? A Systematic Review and Meta-analysis' 8 *PloS One* e72484.
Webster, CD, Douglas, KS, Eaves, D and Hart, SD (1997) 'Assessing Risk of Violence to Others' in C Webster and M Jackson (eds), *Impulsivity: Theory, Assessment, and Treatment* (New York, Guilford Press).
Yang, M, Wong, SC and Coid, J (2010) 'The Efficacy of Violence Prediction: A Meta-analytic Comparison of Nine Risk Assessment Tools' 136 *Psychological Bulletin* 740.

12

Risk Assessment at Sentencing

The Pennsylvania Experience

RHYS HESTER

> If you can look into the seeds of time,
> and say which grain will grow and which will not,
> speak, then, to me[.]
>
> Banquo (to the Three Witches), *Macbeth*

I. Introduction

Risk prediction has been introduced at virtually every stage of criminal justice – from policing, prevention and pre-trial to probation, parole and re-entry – and, increasingly, at sentencing. 'Evidence-based sentencing' seems to deeply divide academics and practitioners. There are many thoughtful, even impassioned arguments praising the possibilities of fairer and more accurate judgments on the one hand, and decrying actuarial approaches as biased, non-transparent and unjustifiable on the other (Hannah-Moffat and Struthers Montford, Chapter 10 in this volume).

I am a risk agnostic. I resonate with arguments that actuarial assessment could exacerbate racial disparities and that – *taken to the extreme* – punishment solely on an algorithm could result in some eerie, dystopian justice system. Yet I am persuaded that a judicial equivalent of unstructured clinical risk assessment is a defining feature of utilitarian-based theories of punishment and that using actuarial instruments can be consistent with hybrid punishment theories like limiting retributivism (Frase 2013; Morris 1974; see also Husak, Chapter 3 in this volume). Rehabilitation, specific deterrence and incapacitation are all aimed at reducing the causes or consequences of future criminal conduct (Hester et al 2018). For decades, perhaps centuries, judges in the Western tradition have assessed risk (see, eg, Hogarth 1971). In a favourable light, actuarial (rather than clinical) risk assessment is simply a different tool to assist court personnel in assessing risk. Of course, like most tools, risk instruments have the potential for both utility and misuse, and the questions (for me anyway) are whether risk instruments can be integrated into sentencing practices in a way that sufficiently avoids the potential misuse – and whether or not they are an improvement on practitioners' clinical judgements.

While a risk agnostic, I spent some time preparing the sacraments in the employ of an American sentencing commission as that agency worked its way through the development of a risk assessment instrument to be used at sentencing.[1] In what follows in this chapter, I attempt to use the Pennsylvania experience to put some flesh on the bones of the arguments and concerns about predictive sentencing raised in this volume and elsewhere. American states have been likened to policy laboratories – jurisdictions sufficiently autonomous that they can experiment with novel approaches to vexing social issues (see Reitz (2010), quoting *New State Ice Co v Liebman*).[2] Some experiments will fail, and others succeed, but without experimentation, there is little opportunity for progress. The concerns raised about the use of actuarial risk tools have some analogues in the status quo, where practitioners assess risk based on judgement, experience and intuition. Judges currently make informal assessments about a defendant's likelihood of re-offending, and these informal assessments can also result in punishment for the prospective. Judges may also fail to understand the context of subgroups, their decisions may generate race and gender disparities, and their sentencing practices can suffer from a lack of transparency. Thus, most of the leading concerns over the use of actuarial risk instruments are also salient concerns of the status quo of judicial clinical assessment. More research is needed to determine whether clinical or actuarial assessments are better or worse for these areas of concern; in particular, more work establishing the consequences of the baseline clinical approach is needed. Consequently, I take the position that since there is the potential for improvement with actuarial risk assessment, inclined jurisdictions should mindfully proceed with experimentation.

Pennsylvania's experience has been a protracted exercise with substantial debate over many of the issues raised in the literature. The state's experience is instructive as additional jurisdictions experiment with predictive instruments at sentencing and as scholars refine the issues that demand attention. This chapter proceeds with a brief contextual overview of Pennsylvania's approach.

[1] I served as Deputy Director of the Pennsylvania Commission on Sentencing during part of the time the Commission worked to develop a risk assessment instrument for use at sentencing. The views expressed do not necessarily represent the views of the Commission or its staff. Throughout this chapter, I try to present my understanding of the Commission's decisions and, where possible, I cite the Commission's reports on the risk assessment process. However, why a decision was made is not always clearly documented and there may be multiple, even competing, reasons why members support a particular decision. This chapter offers my interpretation of key parts of the Pennsylvania experience with an eye towards contributing to the larger conversation about risk at sentencing.

[2] *New State Ice Co v Liebman* 285 US 262 (1932), Justice Brandeis, dissenting.

I then address several specific issues that appear as central themes of concern in the risk literature through the lens of the Pennsylvania process. These include: (1) transparency in how risk instruments were constructed and operate; (2) decisions over how risk information would be used (eg, to divert low-risk offenders, increase punishment for high-risk individuals, identify cases for additional information etc); (3) concerns over accuracy and false positives; and (4) issues related to demographic characteristics like race, gender and age. I draw directly on the process of the Pennsylvania Commission on Sentencing for several points and illustrate other issues by constructing a demonstrative risk assessment instrument using Pennsylvania data. Through survival analysis and receiver operating characteristic analysis, I demonstrate why concerns over false positives continue to be a live issue in the risk assessment arena and I explore the impact of including and excluding age and gender. But first, I begin with a brief contextualisation of Pennsylvania's experience with developing and implementing a risk instrument for use at sentencing.

II. The Pennsylvania Risk Assessment Approach

This section provides an overview of the Pennsylvania's development of risk instruments. I describe the approach and focus on two overarching issues: first, transparency in the development of the instruments and in their operation in a given case; and, second, implementation of the instruments to mitigate concerns over blind reliance on labels or straddling decision makers with a strict adherence to punishment based on probability.

A. Overview

Although not the first US state to integrate risk assessment at sentencing, Pennsylvania is among the first jurisdictions to attempt to do so on a state-wide level. In 2010, the Pennsylvania Commission on Sentencing received a legislative mandate to develop and adopt a risk assessment instrument to be used at sentencing (Pennsylvania Commission on Sentencing 2015a). Over the next eight years, the Commission would traverse along the winding path of the risk assessment project. The initiative went through a number of significant changes in direction, some of which are addressed below. As of late 2018, the ultimate fate of the Pennsylvania risk assessment approach was unclear. Following public hearings on a proposed version of the approach in 2018, the Commission voted to postpone adoption of the instrument and provide the public the opportunity to submit alternative proposals that would fulfil the legislative mandate (Pennsylvania Commission on Sentencing 2018b). This decision was made in response to pushback from those who opposed the Commission's approach and risk assessment instruments in general, largely over concerns of potential differential racial impact.[3] Regardless of the ultimate fate of the Pennsylvania approach, the Commission's eight years of experience has amassed a considerable body of analysis and reporting which should provide valuable lessons for those interested in risk assessment at sentencing.

In what follows, I describe the approach as developed over the first eight years of the project. As currently conceived, there are several defining features of the Pennsylvania risk assessment approach:

(1) multiple instruments based on the guideline severity level;
(2) assessment based only on static factors;
(3) use of a standard deviation convention for establishing low-risk and high risk cut-points; and
(4) the implementation of risk designation to generate additional information for the court rather than recommend type or dosage of punishment.

Each of these is expounded in turn.

First, separate scales were constructed for each guideline severity level, so there are actually multiple instruments. All were constructed in the same manner (the Burgess method based on logistic regression analysis) with the same potential static risk factors, but tailored specifically to the guideline offence severity level (Bruce, Burgess and Harno 1928). The hope here was to treat like offenders alike and to increase the accuracy of the individual instruments. (There are 14 'offense gravity score' levels on the Pennsylvania matrix; the staff research team collapsed the six most serious categories into a single OGS 9–14 category, resulting in a total of nine scales.)

Second, the instruments are 'second-generation' risk assessments, meaning they use only static information about the individual and his or her prior criminal justice record (see van Ginneken, Chapter 2 in this volume). The decision was

[3] The opposition voiced at the June 2018 public hearings took on an emotional and strongly racialised tone, fuelled by slogans and social media. For example, one testifier diagnosed law makers with 'Obsessive Racial Hatred Disorder' for pursuing the risk assessment and likened the use of risk assessment to the whipping of Black slaves (written copies of the testimony included a graphic historical photograph of a slave with extensive scarring on his back) (http://pcs.la.psu.edu/guidelines/proposed-risk-assessment-instrument/testimony/ceatrice-beard-private-citizen.-philadelphia-june-6-2018/view). Other testimony received announced 'This tool on its own won't be racist. However, the humans programming the tool definitely are, and so without proper oversight the recommendations of the tool will be, too' and 'No racist "risk assessment" tool for PA judges! Don't be a cracker state, PA!' (http://pcs.la.psu.edu/guidelines/proposed-risk-assessment-instrument/testimony/color-of-change.-submitted-petition-june-13-2018/view). Over 30 individuals and organisations testified, and the strong turnout appeared to be spurred by opposition voiced on social media by two of the Commission's most recent appointments, who tweeted artwork with the words 'NO RACIST RISK ASSESSMENT AT SENTENCING' and hashtags of '#minorityreport' (see, eg, Representative Joanna McClinton's retweet of https://twitter.com/powerinterfaith/status/1003704424907333632). Notably, racial impact analysis showed the Commission's risk instrument actually had a moderate intercept bias in favour of minority offenders (ie, the instrument underestimated minority risk compared to Whites) (Pennsylvania Commission on Sentencing 2018c). Nevertheless, in this highly racially charged climate, the Commission voted to table the risk assessment approach and take public testimony later in 2018 on alternative ways to fulfil its statutory mandate for a risk assessment tool.

made not to pursue a third- or fourth-generation assessment that would contain criminogenic needs and dynamic factors related to relationships, employment, attitudes, substance abuse etc due to the desire that the assessments be automated from the information currently available to the court. The factors include:

- the offender's gender;
- the offender's age;
- the number of prior convictions;
- the types of prior convictions;
- the current offence type;
- whether there are multiple current offences; and
- whether the offender has a prior juvenile adjudication.

The scales were constructed using the Burgess method to allocate points based on whether a given factor was statistically significant in the respective offence severity-specific logistic regression predicting three-year recidivism for any re-offence (Pennsylvania Commission on Sentencing 2011, 2016).

Third, low-risk, typical-risk and high-risk designations were based on the offender's score being within or outside one standard deviation of the mean risk score for each severity level. This approach provided a less arbitrary standard for selecting cut-points for high- and low-risk designations (see further below).

Fourth, and finally, for offenders designated as low or high risk, the recommendation is that the court should order a more comprehensive risk-needs or risk-needs-responsivity assessment for that offender. The proposed risk instrument provisions state:

> For those offenders who are identified as high or low risk by the sentence risk assessment, the Commission recommends, but does not require, that the court seek additional information in the form of a pre-sentence investigation (PSI) report or a fuller risk-needs assessment. Thus, the risk assessment does not make any recommendation regarding the sentence to be imposed. Instead, the assessment is incorporated as an informational tool that targets individuals with risk profiles that are higher or lower than average. Since these individuals are not typical offenders with respect to their risk of reoffending, the court will likely benefit from seeking additional information prior to imposing the sentence. (Pennsylvania Commission on Sentencing 2018a)

B. Atypical Risk, More Information

Given the realities of an overburdened criminal justice system, and the necessities of making significant decisions on the basis of little information and in a short window of time (eg, Albonetti 1991), the Commission's approach is to identify a subset of cases that would most likely benefit from the investment of additional time and more information. The system currently cannot support the completion of more expansive risk-needs-responsivity assessments for all offenders. Thus, this static assessment is a way to meet the legislature's mandate to provide an actuarial risk assessment on all offenders, while encouraging consideration of criminogenic needs and appropriate intervention for those identified as high or low risk. One hopeful benefit of not directly tying risk category to punishment recommendation is that implementation could avoid the concerns over mandating strict adherence to a risk designation (Hannah-Moffat 2013) and fears related to 'Hollywood's images of regimes in which prisoners are selected according to genetic makeup or brain chemistry' (Slobogin 2012: 205).

Despite the Commission's direction that the sentencing risk assessment should only be used to trigger additional information, the approach is not a panacea for the concerns articulated by Hannah-Moffat (2013: 277) that: 'Risk scores impart a sense of moral certainty and legitimacy into the classification they produce, allowing people to accept them as normative obligations and therefore scripts for action.' This concern is particularly salient since, in the abstract, 'high risk' does not indicate the risk of *what* (Vigorita 2003). Less than seven per cent of Pennsylvania offenders in the risk development sample ($n > 130{,}000$) recidivated for a felony-level offence against the person – the closest available approximation for identifying serious violent recidivism. The majority of offenders commit lower-level property, drug and public order offences. Thus, most 'high-risk' offenders are also low-stakes offenders who do not pose a serious threat to public safety. Clemons and McBeth discuss the tendency for humans in complex policy arenas to:

> [N]arrow, simplify, analogize, and separate problems into specialized, solvable chunks – losing valuable information and ignoring interrelatedness. We utilize models, metaphors, analogies, taxonomies, hierarchies, and categories to impose structure on the world, to provide a frame of reference, and to reduce the number of considerations and alternatives we face. (2009: 53)

We often forget, they argue, that 'just because we have given something a name or placed it in a certain group does not make the abstract real' (2009: 53).

Therefore, it is critical to educate practitioners as users of risk instruments and risk information on the limited meaning of probability scores and risk designations. There remains a strong intuitive, human appeal to seeing the label 'high risk' and jumping to thoughts of violent predatory offending. Continued efforts must be undertaken to educate practitioners on the proper meaning and use of risk tools, even when they are not intended to directly impact punishment levels.

Further, Pennsylvania's method of implementation may be of no comfort to opponents of risk since the encouragement to courts to generate and consider more advanced risk assessments simply brings the questions full circle to concerns over those third- or fourth-generation assessments and how information derived from them will be used by the court. The Commission's intent, as expressed in the proposed risk instrument provisions, is that this information will be useful for individualising a sentence. The additional information could help to divert low-risk offenders from custodial sentences and could help identify recidivism-reducing programming. But even tools that are only used to divert low-risk individuals can result in unfairness as certain groups may benefit from diversion over others (Laskorunsky 2017). Further, information from more advanced assessments could be used to enhance punishment for some offenders, and the instruments could suffer from issues related to fairness and bias discussed throughout the literature. Therefore, the ultimate impact remains to be seen, and additional research will be needed.

C. Transparency

Another defining feature of the process in Pennsylvania has been the Commission's efforts at transparency in terms of how the risk instruments were constructed and how any given offender's risk score is derived. Two varieties of objections over transparency have been raised in the literature: first, some risk instruments are proprietary and defendants may not have access to the factors or the algorithm that gives rise to their risk score; and, second, even if the factors are known, risk instruments may obfuscate the underlying details that give rise to a risk score as those factors become buried in a worksheet (see Hannah-Moffat 2013; and Hannah-Moffat and Struthers Montford, Chapter 10 in this volume).

The Commission chose to construct its own instrument rather than relying on a proprietary one and made a concerted effort to carefully document the instrument construction process. By 2017, the Commission had published 14 reports detailing its journey with risk assessment, with several more published since.[4] These reports outline the initial approaches, document the statistical and methodological processes used to generate various versions of the instruments, and articulate the changes in direction undertaken along the way. At the individual offender level, for everyone on whom an assessment is generated, the Commission's sentencing software creates a risk summary sheet that provides the eligible factors and point allocations for the given scale, how that offender was scored, the average recidivism rates by score and the unique prior conviction tracking numbers used to calculate the offender's score. As a result, defendants have full access to the information used to generate both the general scheme and their particular score, perhaps alleviating some of the 'black-box' concerns.

With the context of the Pennsylvania approach in mind, the next sections address how Pennsylvania's experience with some more contentious issues might be instructive for other jurisdictions and for refining the larger debate over risk at sentencing. I begin with concerns over accuracy levels and false positives, and then take up the inclusion of demographic characteristics.

[4] See http://pasentencing.us.

III. False Positives, Cut-Points and Punishment Concerns

Whatever progress has been made in terms of instrument sophistication and accuracy, concerns over false positives remain as salient and palpable as ever. Most risk instruments have comparable accuracy levels, as measured by the area under the curve statistic.[5] But issues of false positives and predictive values are affected by risk designation cut-points, which are inherently policy decisions. The final cut-points selected can drastically alter conclusions about how accurate an instrument is in practice. I illustrate this, first, by constructing a demonstrative risk assessment instrument using a subset of the Pennsylvania risk project data and, second, by discussing the Pennsylvania Commission's struggles with constructing a violent or person offence risk instrument.

A. False Positives and Cut Points

Risk assessment accuracy is often measured with Receiver Operatorship Characteristic (ROC) analysis, which generates an Area under the Receiver Operatorship Curve (AUC) statistic. The AUC provides a metric for comparing true positive rates and false positive rates in the instrument (see Fazel, Chapter 11 in this volume). We know from a given sample which offenders go on to recidivate and which do not. If we randomly chose one recidivist and one non-recidivist and compared their prediction scores, we would expect the recidivist to have a higher score than the non-recidivist. How well an instrument predicts can be measured by the percentage of instances the randomly drawn recidivist would have a higher score than the randomly drawn non-recidivist. A perfect predictor would achieve 100 per cent accuracy: the recidivist would always have a higher score than the non-recidivist. The baseline for an inutile predictor is one that does no better than chance, correctly classifying only 50 per cent of the time (which one could achieve with a coin toss). Risk instruments frequently have AUCs in the 60–80 per cent range, so the AUC can be a helpful tool to the extent that it can identify an instrument with a 75 per cent accuracy level versus one with a 65 per cent accuracy level, or for gauging the loss in accuracy experienced when removing a factor from a risk scale. In practice, however, risk assessment approaches are not always based on a

[5] Risk instruments generally have an AUC accuracy of around 65–72 per cent (Monahan and Skeem 2016) and 'there is not compelling evidence that one validated tool forecasts recidivism better than another' (Monahan and Skeem 2014: 162). For example, Monahan and Skeem (2014) discuss a meta-analysis which found that nine risk instruments were essentially interchangeable. They also discuss a study by Kroner, Mills and Reddon (2005), in which the researchers placed 101 factors taken from four well-established risk instruments into an empty coffee can, mixed them together and randomly selected 13 of the factors. They repeated the exercise a total of four times, compared their four coffee can instruments with the originals, and found the coffee can instruments predicted as well as the originals.

full score; instead, the approach is sometimes to designate low-risk and high-risk cut-points along that score, and those choices have direct implications for accuracy and error rates.

To illustrate this, I created a risk instrument based on a sample of around 55,000 felony offenders from the Pennsylvania risk assessment project data[6] (see Pennsylvania Commission on Sentencing 2011, 2016). This instrument uses the following set of static factors (the factors are similar to those used for the Commission's instruments, but contain a few differences):

- Prior Conviction Count Category (0; 1; 2–3; 4–5; 6–7; 8+).
- Multiple Current Charges (yes, no).
- Juvenile Adjudication on Record (yes, no).
- Type of Prior Offence:
  - Prior Personal Offence (yes, no).
  - Prior Property Offence (yes, no).
  - Prior Drug Offence (yes, no).
  - Prior Other Offence (yes, no).
- Current Offence Type (person, property, drug or other).
- Offence Severity Level ≤11 (yes, no).
- Age (<21; 21–24; 25–29; 30–34; 35–39; 40–44; 45–49; 50+).
- Male (yes, no).

Using these predictors, I estimated a Cox proportional hazards regression model (the results are given in Table A1 of the Appendix) and generated a risk score using the Burgess approach of assigning points based on statistical significance in the model.

The resulting instrument ranged from 0 to 18 points. Due to small numbers in the 0 and 18 categories, I collapsed categories to create the 1–17 point scale. Figure 12.1 provides a bar graph of recidivism rates by instrument score. The recidivism rate ranges from 9 per cent for those with a score of 1, to 84 per cent for those with those with a score of 17.

The AUC statistic for this instrument is a respectable 0.70 (Standard Error = 0.002), meaning that a randomly drawn recidivist in this sample would have a higher score than a randomly drawn non-recidivist on this 17-point scale 70 per cent of the time, a 20 per cent improvement over a coin toss. This AUC of

[6] The sample consists of 55,656 non-DUI offenders initially sentenced in Pennsylvania in 2004–06 and subjected to a three-year recidivism follow-up upon release to community supervision or from incarceration. In addition, the models control for race (White, Black or Hispanic; 'other' was dropped); to adjust for potential heteroscedasticity, county fixed effects are included (not reported) (see Steffensmeier, Painter-Davis and Ulmer 2017). For additional information on sample selection, see Hester (2018).

Figure 12.1 Recidivism rates by risk instrument score

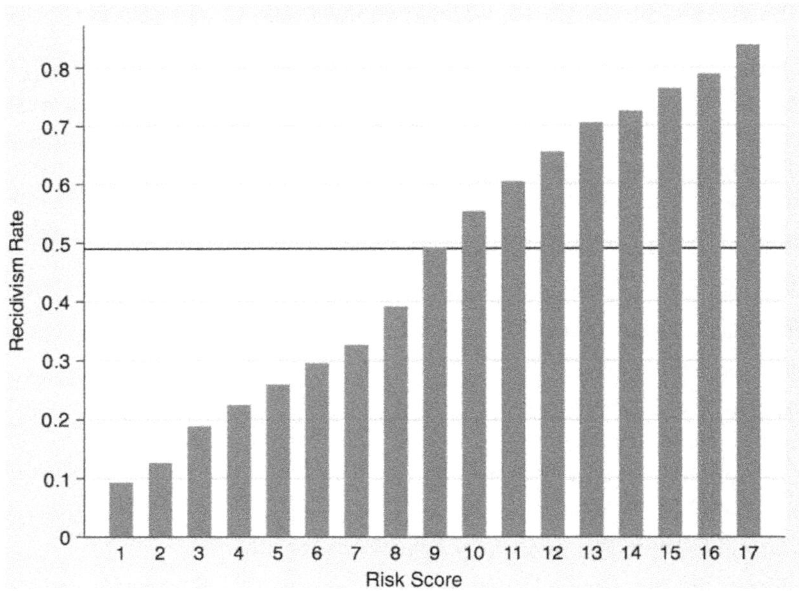

Note: bars represent the recidivism rates for the designated risk instrument point score. The horizontal line indicates the overall mean recidivism rate. The figure illustrates a recidivism rate of less than 10 per cent of individuals scored as a 1, ranging up to well over 80 per cent for those scored as 17, with a fairly linear distribution between.

0.70 is consistent with the Pennsylvania scales and falls within the range of AUCs which Monahan and Skeem (2016) note are generally in the range of 0.65–0.72.[7]

Yet, as noted, implementing most risk assessments involves the additional step of identifying cut-points along the score to designate low-risk and high-risk offenders. Once this is done, the AUC provides little insight.

To illustrate, suppose a policy maker must choose a cut-point on the 17-point scale presented in Figure 12.1 to distinguish some offenders as 'high risk' – where should he or she draw the line? Suppose the policy maker wanted to be as accurate as possible and impose as few false positives as possible, so he or she designates only the scores of 17 as high risk. This would maximise accuracy, but for this sample would cover just 123 offenders out of 55,656, a rate of 0.2 per cent. Suppose instead she wanted to make a prediction on the top 25 per cent. (The score bins do not allow for a perfect partition at 25 per cent, but we can get close: 26 per cent of offenders have a score of 11 or higher.) This more expansive cut-point would direct a decision for one in four defendants, but it would do so at a cost of more false positives. As shown in Figure 12.1, scores of 11 approach the mean recidivism rate, and with every stair-step down from a score of 17, the recidivism rate gets 'diluted',

[7] See n 5 above.

with more and more false positives. The policy maker is forced to choose between lesser coverage and greater accuracy, or greater coverage and lesser accuracy.

Table 12.1 presents this trade-off in the form of confusion matrices, essential evaluation tools in the field of predictive analytics.[8] The data reduces to a two-by-two confusion matrix for each of the two high-risk policies mentioned above: each offender is predicted to be either at high risk of recidivism or not, and each offender actually recidivates or does not. These four possibilities are represented by familiar labels: false positives, false negatives, true positives and true negatives.[9] All four carry independent significance, but of chief concern are false positives: labelling a person high risk and being wrong. Predictive analysts typically refer to two statistics related to false positives. The *positive predictive value* (PPV) calculated as *TP / (FP + TP)* and the *false positive rate* (FPR) calculated as *FP / (TN + FP)*. The PPV refers to the likelihood of an accurate prediction of recidivism, while the FPR refers to the rate at which individuals who will actually succeed are wrongly flagged as likely recidivists.

Table 12.1 Confusion matrices for high-risk examples

PANEL A **High-risk = Score of 17**			*PANEL B* **High-risk = Score of 11+**		
	Risk Predictions			*Risk Predictions*	
Observed	p(Success)	p(Re-offend)	*Observed*	p(Success)	p(Re-offend)
Success	TN: 28,224	FP: 20	Success	TN: 23,917	FP: 4,327
Re-offend	FN: 27,309	TP: 103	Re-offend	FN: 17,319	TP: 10,093
Positive Predictive Value:		84%	Positive Predictive Value:		70%
False Positive Rate:		0%[10]	False Positive Rate:		15%

Notes: FP = false positive; FN = false negative; TP = true positive; TN = true negative. Positive Predictive Value = *TP / (FP + TP)*. False Positive Rate = *FP / (TN + FP)*. The comparison of the positive predictive values and false positive rates in the bottom portion of the table shows that the choice of who is classified as high risk on the 17-point risk scale has measurable consequences for accepted errors: moving from the more a restrictive to an inclusive definition in the example discussed in the text results in a 14 per cent decline in predictive accuracy and a 15 per cent increase in the rate at which individuals are erroneously designated as high risk.

As the positive predictive values and false positive rates reported for each decision in Table 12.1 show, the same risk score can generate markedly different error

[8] See Berk et al (2018) and Chouldechova (2018) for excellent treatments of confusion tables, and discussions of fairness and accuracy measures derived from them, tailored to risk assessment in the criminal justice context.

[9] False positives are predictions of recidivism that turn out to be wrong, and true positives are recidivism predictions that turn out to be correct. True negatives are success predictions that turn out to be correct, while false negatives are success predictions that turn out to be wrong.

[10] More precisely, the FPR = 0.0007.

consequences depending on how risk is operationalised (ie, whether it falls below or above a chosen cut-point). With the highly selective cut-point (score of 17) in Panel A, the risk instrument is quite accurate – 84 per cent of those identified as high risk do in fact go on to recidivate. (Reciprocally, the error rate among high risk predictions is 16 per cent.) However, this application is so narrow as to render the risk instrument almost irrelevant. We would only be making a positive prediction for about one in every 500 offenders. The more expansive application in Panel B may have greater utility as it attempts to identify the riskiest quartile of offenders. But the error rate almost doubles from 16 per cent to 30 per cent for predictive value. Further, in terms of false positive rates, the more restrictive designation almost never classified a person as likely to recidivate when they would go on to remain successful. With the more expansive designation, this happens 15 per cent of the time.

Therefore, the choice in cut-point is a crucial policy decision and is independent of overall evaluations of accuracy as measured by the AUC. In the example given above, the scale's AUC remained constant at 0.70, but the choice in cut-point rendered substantial differences in the prediction error rates and false positive rates. As such, when implementing risk, policy makers are inevitably presented with the challenge of balancing broader utility with increased error.

As noted in the initial overview, Pennsylvania's approach was to determine the cut-points with reference to a standard deviation convention. This approach had the appeal of removing some arbitrariness from the decision by adhering to conventional statistical definitions for higher and lower than average. This was all the more desirable since the Commission chose to pursue multiple severity level-specific scales which ranged in points: selecting a cut-point of 11 has different implications if the scale has a maximum of 17 compared to a scale with a maximum of 14. Another approach would be to identify predictive values and error rates that are acceptable from a policy standpoint, and to select cut-points that adhered to those policy decisions. The error rates in the Commission's scales are more along the lines of the instrument in Panel B above, though they vary by instrument.[11]

[11] If the Commission's standard deviation approach were applied to the example above, the mean score of 9.29 (SD = 3.15) would result in the following cut-points: 1–5 points = low risk; 6–12 points = typical risk; 13–17 points = high risk. What might be viewed as a downside to this approach is that the score bins do not consistently allow for drawing the line at near the 16 per cent mark one would expect for a standard deviation approach because one cannot split a point bin (eg, there is a forced choice between a cut-point of 5 or 6, since you cannot split the 6 bin to account for the actual value of 6.14). In this example, 16.4 per cent in the sample had a score of 13 or higher, getting quite close to what one would expect, but only 12.5 per cent are designated as low risk. Thus, the final percentage depends on how offenders are binned within the score points, and sometimes a small change in the standard deviation could capture the next bin, resulting in a much larger percentage of affected individuals. For instance, if a score of 12 were added to high risk, this would be more than 5,000 additional cases and would raise the percentage of high-risk designations to 26 per cent (with implications for accuracy and errors). Indeed, this happenstance variance can be seen in the high-risk and low-risk designations among the Commission's scales.

B. The Pennsylvania Efforts for a Violent Risk Predictor

Overreliance on the AUC as a measure of accuracy can prove problematic in a narrower context where the prevalence of the recidivism outcome is low. In the Pennsylvania account, this problem was encountered in the effort to generate a violent or offence-against-the-person recidivism instrument.

As noted above, for a general recidivism event, the 'high risk' designation may be less than fully satisfying to some, since it refers to high risk of all offences, and most offences are of low severity and non-violent. Pursuing the laudable desire to identify significant public safety threats, at some point well into the process (but prior to my joining the Commission), nine 'person' offence outcome scales were constructed. These mirrored the severity level-specific approach of the primary 'any recidivism' scales, but provided separate information on an individual's relative risk to commit a 'person' offence.

Fortunately for the Commonwealth, but problematically for researchers, violent recidivism outcomes are exceedingly rare. Less than seven per cent of offenders recidivated for a felony-level person offence (and even this may be overly inclusive as some felony-level person offences are not classified as violent). Consequently, the outcome was expanded to include non-felony-level person offences such as simple assaults. This boosted the prevalence of the new person offence outcome up to around 11 per cent. The scales constructed for this outcome performed respectably as measured by the area under the curve, and the two sets of scales (18 in all) were submitted for public hearings in 2017.

Late on in the process, new concerns were raised over the person offence scales. Chief among these was that while the AUCs were consistent with other risk assessments, the AUC as a measure of accuracy masked two very different predictive processes with the person scales: the scales were remarkably predictive for their low-risk indications (the negative predictive value (NPV)), but quite poor for high-risk indications (the PPV). Staff presented the Commission with the comparisons, provided below in Figure 12.2, which showed an NPV of around 95 per cent, but a PPV of around 20 per cent for the person scale.[12] This meant that when the instrument designated someone as low risk of person offence recidivism, the prediction was correct 95 per cent of the time, but when the instrument designated someone as high risk, the prediction was correct only 20 per cent of the time. The AUC of around 65 per cent masked this differential effect, which is an artefact of attempting to predict a low prevalence event. Since only 11 per cent re-offended on this outcome, one could guess that every offender would be low risk and be correct almost nine times out of 10.

[12] These statistics are based on a single all-severity level scale rather than showing 18 different scales.

Figure 12.2 Accuracy measures for general and person offence recidivism instruments

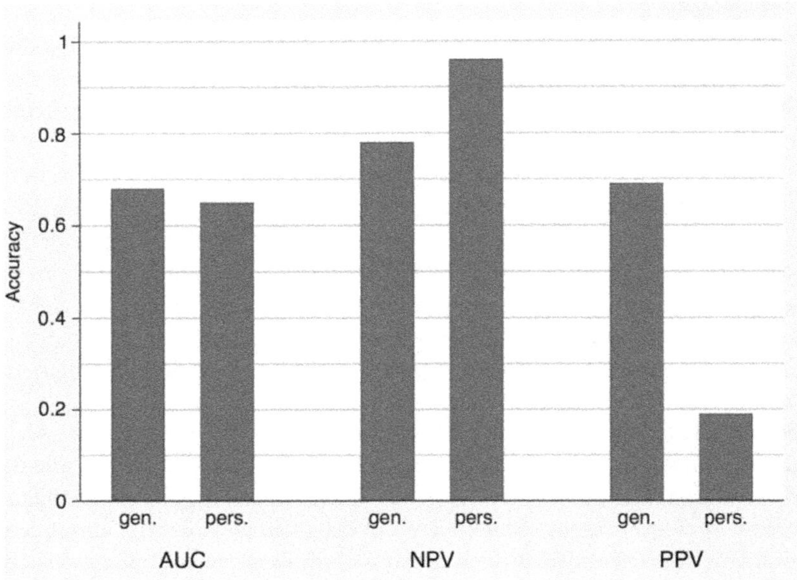

Note: AUC = area under the curve statistic; NPV = negative predictive value; PPV = positive predictive value; gen. = general recidivism scale; pers. = person offence recidivism scale. Comparing the general and person recidivism measures, note that while the AUCs are quite similar, there are substantial underlying differences in the accuracy of the predictions: for individuals labelled low risk, the person offence instrument is accurate more than 95 per cent of the time, but for those labelled high risk, the instrument is correct less than 20 per cent of the time. Thus, over four in every five individuals labelled as high risk of person level re-offending would have been erroneously labelled as such.

Upon reconsideration of this information, a divided Commission voted to only use information related to low risk of a person offence in the very rare occurrence where an individual scores high on the general risk scale, but low on the person risk scale. (The likelihood of this combination is about 0.0006, affecting about six in every 10,000 cases.)[13]

The lesson for this purpose is that, given a low-prevalence outcome, prediction error rates can be substantial, but can be masked by the AUC. While there are suggestions that some violence predictors can be quite accurate (eg, Monahan 2006), it is doubtful whether these instruments are appropriate for a general population of offenders, since many violence indicators appear to have been developed on very specific populations such as persons institutionalised for psychiatric treatment.

[13] Consequently, the overview of the process provided above is overly simplified. There is actually a tenth scale – the offence against a person scale – but its effect is so rare and anomalous I omitted discussion of that scale from the overview to streamline the presentation.

IV. Demographic Factors

Another set of issues that have played a prominent role in the larger debate on risk at sentencing and in the Pennsylvania experience are those related to demographic characteristics (eg, Starr 2014; Tonry 2014). Concerns over risk and demographics are expressed in at least three different forms. First, to the extent that risk instruments are created from samples that are predominantly white and male, and are based on theories that fail to adequately account for the contextualisation of a given subgroup, using these instruments presents validity and fairness problems. Second, using factors that directly measure demographic features (like age and gender) or which are correlated with personal characteristics (eg, in the way in which race may be correlated with residential location, employment status, prior record etc) can perpetuate minority disadvantage. Third, equal protection objections are raised over the inclusion of factors like age, gender and race (Hannah-Moffat 2016; Hannah-Moffat and Struthers Montford, Chapter 10 in this volume; Harcourt 2008; Laskorunsky 2017; Starr 2014; see also Ashworth and Zedner, Chapter 8 in this volume). In this final part of the chapter, I address some of the ways in which the Pennsylvania approach has dealt with these issues and some areas that should be subject to continued consideration.

A. Race, and County as Proxy for Race

Race was never contemplated for inclusion as a point factor (ie, the Commission never contemplated having the risk instrument allocate a point for the defendant's race, even if race was statistically significant in the regression models);[14] instead, the Commission's approach was to include race in the logistic regression models that generated the scales, but to never assign points on the basis of race, regardless of statistical significance. Stated differently, staff included race as a control variable to provide more race-neutral estimates of the other covariates that were correlated with race.[15]

The Commission did initially include county as a possible factor, but it was eventually removed over racial concerns. There was a race-neutral justification for the inclusion of county. Case processing practices and norms can vary tremendously by county (see, eg, Eisenstein, Flemming and Nardulli 1988; Hester 2017; Ulmer 1997). There may also be true differences in offence and offender profiles across counties – for instance, among offenders in Pittsburgh and Philadelphia

[14] Although one practitioner once emphatically expressed concern to the author that White offenders would be disadvantaged since race was not factored in.

[15] While this approach might have a substantial effect under a weighted Burgess or similar scheme, it is unclear how much difference it made given the non-weighted Burgess approach. The differences would have to come from factors that were statistically significant in the race-controlled model, which would have fallen short of statistical significance in the race-omitted model.

compared to the more rural parts of the Commonwealth. However, the racial composition of the state's population – and its criminal justice population – is also correlated with county. Further, Commission members and external stakeholders expressed particular concern over the possibility of the overpolicing of minorities in parts of Philadelphia. Prior to my service, the Commission staff had determined that removing county from the models would result in statistically significant reduction in prediction in only two of the nine scales, and for those two the difference was less than one per cent (Pennsylvania Commission on Sentencing 2015b). Nevertheless, it was recommended that county be retained as a risk factor. Yet, from a policy standpoint, the race proxy objections were persistent and compelling. Ultimately, the Commission chose to remove county as an eligible point factor, retaining it in the models for control purposes.

A second set of issues related to race involves the question of whether an instrument predicts similarly or differently for racial subgroups. A substantial literature has developed on how to evaluate issues of fairness and bias for race (see Berk et al 2018; Chouldechova 2018; Flores, Bechtel and Lowenkamp 2016; Skeem and Lowenkamp 2017; Skeem, Monahan and Lowenkamp 2016). The general approach is currently to compare AUCs between groups and to perform a block regression approach where risk score or designation predicts recidivism and where race is then entered into the model, first as a direct effect and then as an interaction with risk score, to determine whether information related to offender race alters the ability of the score to predict recidivism at a statistically significant level. This analysis was the primary reason why the Commission proceeded with scales that used prior convictions as a risk factor rather than prior arrests.

Others, including Berk et al (2018) and Chouldechova (2018), discuss additional metrics to consider related to evaluating race (and gender) bias. Their discussions highlight that when base rates of recidivism differ (which would appear to be the case across both race and gender), it is statistically impossible to achieve fairness among the several leading definitions of fairness (related to the predictive values and error rates presented above). A full elaboration of these issues is beyond the scope of this chapter, but how instruments perform on these examinations of fairness and predictive bias will likely play a prominent role in the evaluation of risk assessment in sentencing in the future. Unlike offender race, the Commission has from the outset included gender and age as potential risk factors.

B. Age and Gender

Fairness and equity issues related to demographic factors may manifest in several different ways. For example, there is a preliminary question as to whether instruments developed on primarily male populations should be used on female offenders at all, since they may be predominately based on theories and research about white male offenders, divorced from the context and processes that define female offender involvement in the criminal justice system (Hannah-Moffat 2013; *cf* Hannah-Moffat 2009; Smith, Cullen and Latessa 2009). As Hannah-Moffat (2009: 211–12) explains:

> [B]ecause the criminogenic factors included in generic risk tools are derived from statistical analyses of aggregate male correctional population data and are based on male-derived theories of crime, a gender problem is built into them. The gender problem results from a failure to acknowledge and reply to the vast feminist literature that theoretically and empirically critiques mainstream criminology and other disciplines for their treatment of female correctional populations as 'afterthoughts' and for their uncritical use of male norms in the management and treatment of female offenders.

It is unclear whether Pennsylvania's implementation of static risk assessment provides a satisfactory avenue for addressing these concerns or not. The leading criticisms over the failure to account for gendered context seem to focus on problems related to the needs aspects of third- and fourth-generation instruments. For example, Hannah-Moffat (2016: 436) notes the extensive body of research that has 'criticized the use of universal criminogenic need categories without comprehensive analysis of how needs differ among various subgroups, and how these categories affect how offender populations are defined, assessed, targeted, and managed'. Likewise, Salisbury, Boppre and Kelly (2016: 222) argue that male-based risk assessments are insufficient when they 'do not measure women's gender-specific criminogenic needs and strengths'. Since the Pennsylvania instruments capture only second-generation risk factors, the question of whether female offender needs are adequately addressed is answered at the subsequent stage where more information in the form of RNA (risk and needs assessment) or RNR (risk-need-responsivity assessment) is sought (see van Ginneken, Chapter 2 in this volume). Here, these objections about failure to use a gender-responsive assessment may come full circle. However, it is also possible that a gender-responsive assessment (see, eg, van Voorhis et al 2008) is ordered at this stage.

Another issue relates to whether a risk instrument should include gender as a risk factor. Starr (2014), among others, objects to this on equal protection grounds. In contrast, Monahan argues that judged against the US constitutional standards applying intermediate scrutiny, gender-based risk policies 'should have little difficulty surviving an equal protection challenge due to the importance of governmental police powers and because gender differences in violent offending are 'genuine and not hypothesized' (2006: 431).

While these gender-based concerns over validity persist, critics also raise a separate question as to whether consideration of gender violates equal protection. On this question, it is actually male offenders who are positioned to object, since analysis consistently finds males at higher risk of recidivism and therefore would add score points on the basis of being male. The counter-argument in favour of including gender as a risk factor is that to fail to do so would unjustifiably disadvantage females and decrease accuracy (resulting in more false positives). The Commission staff's analysis of previous versions of the scales found that overall accuracy was lower in four of the nine scales when gender was removed and remained unchanged in four of the other scales (for the ninth scale – OGS 1, the lowest severity level – gender was not a statistically significant factor and thus was not included in the scale to begin with) (Pennsylvania Commission on Sentencing 2015b). However, in each of the four scales, the reduction in accuracy was less than one per cent (Pennsylvania Commission on Sentencing 2015b).

Similar arguments involve the use of age as a predictor. While in the US, age-based policies would be treated under lower constitutional scrutiny than gender, some commentators still object to the unfairness of including age as a predictor (Tonry 2014). Again, the counter is that failing to account for age would actually be the unfair policy because offending rates vary substantially by these characteristics and attempting to ignore them simply imputes the mean characteristic to the entire population.

To illustrate these issues, I return to the sample recidivism model and risk assessment instrument constructed above. Using the results of the Cox regression model (see Table A1 in the Appendix), I estimated recidivism survival functions for a hypothetical case. I assumed a profile of an offender with: two prior convictions; no prior person or drug offences; one prior property and other offence; and a current property offence. Figure 12.3 shows the survival functions separately by age category and then by gender.

The survival rates (the reciprocal of recidivism rates) are provided on the y-axis, while the line plots show the different success/failure rates over time for the subgroups of age and gender. In each plot, the subgroup average is indicated with the bold black line. The plots simply illustrate that failing to distinguish between age and gender in a risk model means choosing to assign the average values for the entire population. Beginning with the age plot, to disregard age would be to impose the risk level of the average age category, in this case effectively treating all individuals as if they had the approximate risk profile of a 25–29 year old. All other things being equal, the baseline failure rate would be about 55 per cent (reciprocally, the baseline survival rate would be about 45 per cent). We would thus be imposing a failure rate of 55 per cent on individuals over the age of 50 even though their actual failure rate is less than 35 per cent. At the other extreme, we would be imputing to offenders under 21 an average success rate of 45 per cent when their actual success rate is less than 25 per cent. Any criminal justice intervention that offered a span of 45 per cent variation in recidivism would be viewed as miraculous. If normative objections are to prevail over the use of age, they must at least do so in the face of the empirical reality that the age of the offender is among the most pertinent pieces of information related to the likelihood of further criminal involvement. The age-crime curve is one of the few things criminologists can agree on and it is firmly supported by recidivism analysis.

Figure 12.3 Demonstration case: survival curves by age and gender

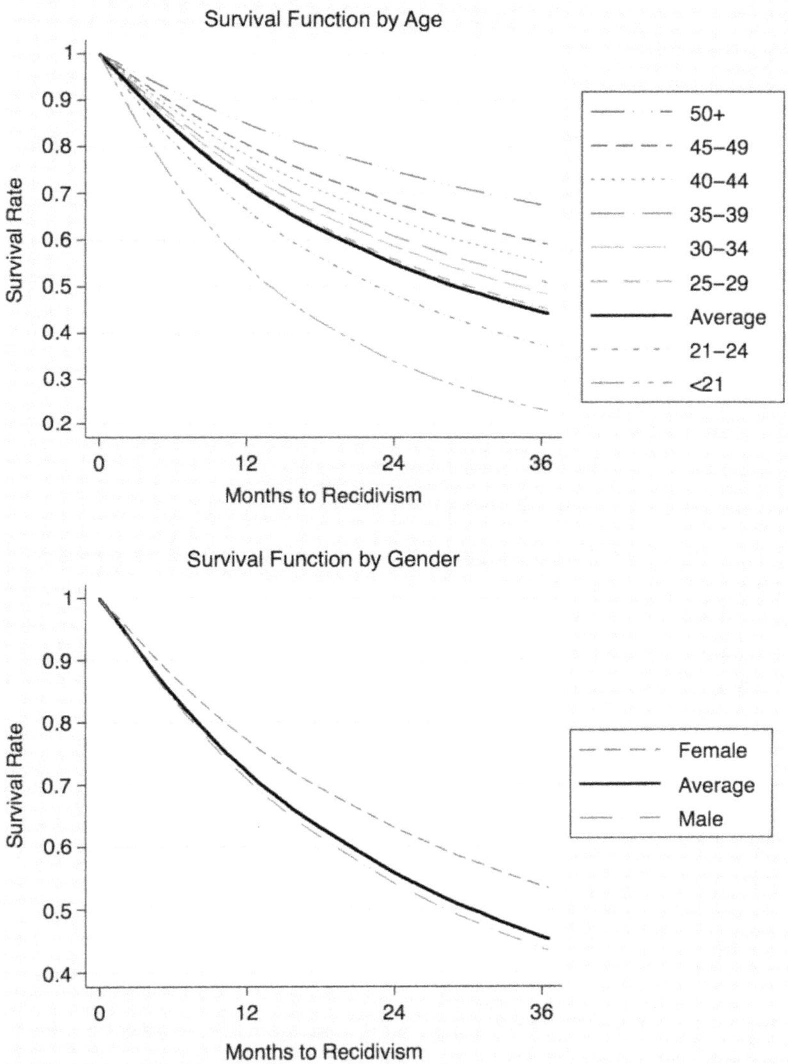

Note: these plots show the survival functions for the stated subcategories over the three-year recidivism period. The survival rate (y-axis) provides the percentage of cases that remain crime-free (thus: 1 – survival rate = recidivism rate). All other factors from the Cox regression are controlled for as stated in the text. Survival rates vary by about 45% depending on age category, and 10 per cent depending on gender. The models assume an offender with two prior convictions, no prior person or drug offences, one prior property and other offence, and a current property offence.

The bottom half of the figure repeats the exercise for gender. Attempting to ignore the offender's sex effectively equates to treating women as if they have the same risk level as men. For this example profile, women succeed more often than they fail, but by ignoring gender and effectively treating women as men (since men, at around 82 per cent of the sentenced population, drive the average results), we would treat them as if they fail more often than they succeed.

But these survival analysis results do not get to the question of how instruments that do or do not incorporate age and gender as predictors vary in terms of predictive accuracy. To address this question, I return to the example risk assessment instrument constructed above. That instrument, which ranged from 1 to 17, included both age and gender as predictive factors. Taking that 'Instrument 1' as a point of departure, I then created three additional risk instruments by removing the combinations of age and gender (see Pennsylvania Commission on Sentencing (2015b) for a similar analysis). Thus, the four instruments are as follows:

Instrument 1	Full Instrument
Instrument 2	Full Instrument minus age
Instrument 3	Full Instrument minus gender
Instrument 4	Full Instrument minus age and gender

Using Receiver Operatorship Curve (ROC) or AUC analysis, I compared the predictive accuracy of these four instruments. For ease of demonstration, Table 12.2 reports the comparison of Instrument 1 (which contains all factors including age and gender) and Instrument 4 (which excludes both age and gender, but contains the other factors).

Table 12.2 AUC comparison for instruments with and without age and gender

	AUC	**SE**
Full instrument	0.70	0.00
Full instrument minus age and gender	0.65	0.00
$chi^2(1) = 751.41$ $p = 0.000$		

Note: AUC = Area under the Curve; SE = Standard Error.

As Table 12.2 confirms, the instrument which includes age and gender performs substantially better than the instrument without them. Instrument 1 has an accuracy of 70 per cent compared to Instrument 4's 65 per cent, and the difference between the instruments is statistically significant. However, most of this difference is attributable exclusively to the inclusion of age. Instrument 2 (not shown), which omitted only age, had an AUC of 0.66, while Instrument 3 (not shown), which omitted gender but which retained age, had an AUC of 0.69 (almost the same as the instrument which differed only terms of in the inclusion of gender).

The argument for retaining age appears more compelling from an accuracy standpoint – almost a quarter of the improvement of the instrument over chance is attributable to age. Given that gender differences in offending and recidivism are quite pronounced, it may seem surprising that the impact of including gender is so negligible. It is possible that under a weighted point assignment method, the impact of gender would be greater. As it is, using the Burgess method here, gender can only account for one point on the scale, while factors like age and prior record, which have multiple categories, account for a much larger share of the scale. A separate question worthy of further investigation is how the distributions of individuals under the different low-risk and high-risk designations might shift when gender is removed. For example, it is possible that while the overall gender effect appears to wash out in the AUC comparison, a substantial number of female offenders would be shifted out of a low-risk category.

In conclusion, from a descriptive standpoint, the survival plots suggest a potential unfairness in omitting gender since doing so would impute a male risk level to females, despite the fact that, all other things being equal, women appear to be about 10 per cent less likely to re-offend than men. In application, however, the inclusion of gender in the model results in only a minor change in the accuracy of the instrument. Nevertheless, with age, the change becomes more appreciable. Further, as suggested above, the generality of the AUC masks underlying differences. While inclusion of gender affects overall accuracy by only one per cent, the distribution of score points would be affected and, depending on the cut-points and how the re-distribution grouped for males and females, the application could vary more substantially by gender. In addition, a reduction in accuracy of 1–2 per cent may appear inconsequential for any one factor, but as two, three or four factors are objected to partly on the basis of their modest 1–2 per cent contribution in accuracy, an instrument could quickly depreciate from moderate to poor predictive efficacy.

Finally, it is worth noting that the questions as to whether an instrument is racially biased may also be raised for gender (see Berk et al 2018; Chouldechova 2018). In the end, whether the inclusion of age, gender and other factors is justifiable should be subjected to further scrutiny and both empirical and normative analysis. Here again, while there are useful methods of examining these issues, at some point the questions are not just how actuarial approaches do on fairness and bias examinations, but how the actuarial approaches compare to the counterfactual status quo of clinical approaches (Laskorunsky 2017).

V. Conclusion

This chapter has offered a mixed approach to highlighting some of the issues that feature in the debate over risk assessment at sentencing by drawing on both the risk development reports and on some original research. Pennsylvania's approach does not offer a panacea for all risk-at-sentencing problems. Legitimate bases for debate remain. The Pennsylvania experience does demonstrate some decisions worthy of consideration. While the shortcomings of a static instrument are acknowledged, the approach of identifying atypical cases for which more information and attention should be given (rather than directing punishment on the basis of score) could avoid some of the greatest fears of deterministic punishment for the prospective. Still, some may criticise the approach for simply passing many of these 'hot potato' issues to later stages. This chapter has also emphasised the significance of policy decisions related to cut-points and the need for continued diligence in examining the details of the consequences of those policy decisions.

Among the most troubling questions remaining are those related to race and gender fairness. These fall into conceptual questions over whether risk assessments are properly contextualised for subgroups and over whether an instrument predicts similarly across subgroups or is biased. What would be particularly helpful is more research on the counterfactual to actuarial risk assessments – ie, the risk-related judgments made by court personnel in the absence of an actuarial risk assessment. Questions include: how much of a sentence is assigned on the basis of a non-actuarial evaluation of risk versus retribution, how much does the weight afforded clinical evaluation of risk vary by judge or courtroom workgroup, how much does this vary by offence type and other context, what kinds of error rates can be approximated for clinical determinations, and are clinical judgements free from predictive bias on factors like race and gender? Whatever progress can be made in terms of fairness and accuracy, it would be helpful to have a better sense of the alternative.

With the proliferation of forecasting algorithms and predictive analytics, the application of risk assessment to the weighty issues of crime and justice was inevitable, and absent a currently unforeseeable paradigm shift away from the new penology (Feeley and Simon 1994), the use of analytic instruments will only increase. But the debate should be welcomed in the ongoing effort to direct risk tools in ways that will be useful while avoiding misuse.

References

Albonetti, CA (1991) 'An Integration of Theories to Explain Judicial Discretion' 38 *Social Problems* 247.

Berk, R, Heidari, H, Jabbari, S, Kearns, M and Roth, A (2017) 'Fairness in Criminal Justice Risk Assessments: The State of the Art' *arXiv preprint* arXiv:1703.09207.

Bruce, A, Burgess, EW and Harno, AM (1928) 'A Study of the Indeterminate Sentence and Parole in the State of Illinois' 19 *Journal of Criminal Law & Criminology* 259.

Chouldechova, A (2017) 'Fair Prediction with Disparate Impact: A Study of Bias in Recidivism Prediction Instruments' 5 *Big Data* 153.

Clemons RS and McBeth MK (2009) *Public Policy Praxis: A Case Approach for Understanding Policy and Analysis*, 2nd edn (New York, Routledge).

Eisenstein, J, Flemming, RB and Nardulli, PF (1988) *The Contours of Justice: Communities and Their Courts* (Boston, Little, Brown).
Feeley MM and Simon J (1994) 'The New Penology: Notes on the Emerging Strategy of Corrections and its Implications' 30 *Criminology* 449.
Flores, AW, Bechtel, K and Lowenkamp, CT (2016) 'False Positives, False Negatives, and False Analyses: A Rejoinder to "Machine Bias: There's Software Used Across the Country to Predict Future Criminals. And it's Biased against Blacks"' 80 *Federal Probation* 38.
Frase, RS (2013) *Just Sentencing: Principles and Procedures for a Workable System* (New York, Oxford University Press).
Hannah-Moffat, K (2009) 'Gridlock or Mutability: Reconsidering "Gender" and Risk Assessment' 8 *Criminology & Public Policy* 209.
——. (2013) 'Actuarial Sentencing: An "Unsettled" Proposition' 30 *Justice Quarterly* 270.
——. (2016) 'Purpose and Context Matters: Creating a Space for Meaningful Dialogues about Risk and Need' in FS Taxman (ed), *Handbook on Risk and Need Assessment: Theory and Practice* (New York, Routledge).
Harcourt, BE (2008) *Against Prediction: Profiling, Policing, and Punishing in an Actuarial Age* (Chicago, University of Chicago Press).
Hester, R (2017) 'Judicial Rotation as Centripetal Force: Sentencing in the Court Communities of South Carolina' 55 *Criminology* 205.
——. (2018). 'Prior Record and Recidivism Risk' *American Journal of Criminal Justice*, https://doi.org/10.1007/s12103-018-9460-8.
Hester, R, Frase, RS, Roberts, JV and Mitchell, KL (2018) 'Prior Record Enhancements at Sentencing: Unsettled Justifications and Unsettling Consequences' 47 *Crime and Justice: A Review of Research* 209.
Hogarth, J (1971) *Sentencing as a Human Process* (Toronto, University of Toronto Press).
Kroner, DG, Mills, JF and Reddon, JR (2005) 'A Coffee Can, Factor Analysis, and Prediction of Antisocial Behavior: The Structure of Criminal Risk' 28 *International Journal of Law and Psychiatry* 360.
Laskorunsky, J (2017) 'Assessment of Offender Risk at Sentencing: A Potential for Disparity?' in JT Ulmer and MS Bradley (eds), *Handbook on Punishment Decisions: Locations of Disparity* (New York, Routledge).
Monahan, J (2006) 'A Jurisprudence of Risk Assessment: Forecasting Harm among Prisoners, Predators, and Patients' 92 *Virginia Law Review* 391.
Monahan, J and Skeem, JL (2014) 'Risk Redux: The Resurgence of Risk Assessment in Criminal Sanctioning' 26 *Federal Sentencing Reporter* 158.
——. (2016) 'Risk Assessment in Criminal Sentencing' 12 *Annual Review of Clinical Psychology* 489.
Morris, N (1974) *The Future of Imprisonment* (Chicago, University of Chicago Press).
Pennsylvania Commission on Sentencing (2011) 'Interim Report 1: Review of Factors Used in Risk Assessment Instruments', http://pcs.la.psu.edu/

publications-and-research/research-and-evaluation-reports/risk-assessment/phase-i-reports/interim-report-1-review-of-factors-used-in-risk-assessment-instruments/view.

——. (2013) 'Interim Report 7: Validation of Risk Scale', http://pcs.la.psu.edu/publications-and-research/research-and-evaluation-reports/risk-assessment/phase-i-reports/interim-report-7-validation-of-risk-scale/view.

——. (2015a) 'Risk Assessment Project, Phase 2. Interim Report 1: Development of a Risk Assessment Scale by Offense Gravity Score for All Offenders', http://pcs.la.psu.edu/publications-and-research/research-and-evaluation-reports/risk-assessment/phase-ii-reports/Interim-Rpt-1-Phase-2/view.

——. (2015b) 'Special Report: Impact of Removing Demographic Factors', http://pcs.la.psu.edu/publications-and-research/research-and-evaluation-reports/risk-assessment/phase-ii-reports/special-report-impact-of-removing-demographic-factors/view.

——. (2016) 'Risk Assessment Project, Phase 2. Interim Report 2: Validation of a Risk Assessment Instrument by Offense Gravity Score for All Offenders', http://pcs.la.psu.edu/publications-and-research/research-and-evaluation-reports/risk-assessment/phase-ii-reports/interim-report-2-validation-of-risk-assessment-instrument-by-ogs-for-all-offenses-february-2016/view.

——. (2018a) 'Proposed Risk Assessment Instrument', http://pcs.la.psu.edu/guidelines/proposed-risk-assessment-instrument/proposed-sentence-risk-assessment-instrument-approved-for-publication-for-public-comment.

——. (2018b) 'Responses to Public Comments; Request for Proposals', http://pcs.la.psu.edu/guidelines/proposed-risk-assessment-instrument/sentence-risk-assessment.-public-hearings-comments-and-responses-and-call-for-proposals.

——. (2018c) 'Racial Impact Analysis of the Proposed Risk Assessment Scales', http://pcs.la.psu.edu/guidelines/proposed-risk-assessment-instrument/additional-information-about-the-proposed-sentence-risk-assessment-instrument/racial-impact-analysis-of-the-proposed-risk-assessment-scales/view.

Reitz, KR (2010) 'Brandeis's Laboratories of Sentencing and Corrections: Making Better Use of Knowledge from the States' 12 *Justice Research and Policy* 169.

Salisbury, EJ, Boppre, B and Kelly, B (2016) 'Gender-Responsive Risk and Need Assessment: Implications for the Treatment of Justice-Involved Women' in FS Taxman (ed), *Handbook on Risk and Need Assessment: Theory and Practice* (New York, Routledge).

Skeem, JL and Lowenkamp, CT (2016) 'Risk, Race, and Recidivism: Predictive Bias and Disparate Impact' 54 *Criminology* 680.

Skeem, J, Monahan, J and Lowenkamp, CT (2016) 'Gender, Risk Assessment, and Sanctioning: The Cost of Treating Women Like Men' 40 *Law and Human Behavior* 580.

Slobogin, C (2012) 'Risk Assessment' in J Petersilia and KR Reitz (eds), *The Oxford Handbook of Sentencing and Corrections* (New York, Oxford University Press).

Smith, P, Cullen, FT and Latessa, EJ (2009) 'Can 14,737 Women Be Wrong? A Meta-analysis of the LSI-R and Recidivism for Female Offenders' 8 *Criminology & Public Policy* 183.

Starr, SB (2014) 'Evidence-Based Sentencing and the Scientific Rationalization of Discrimination' 66 *Stanford Law Review* 803.

Steffensmeier D, Painter-Davis N and Ulmer J (2017) 'Intersectionality of Race, Ethnicity, Gender, and Age on Criminal Punishment' 60 *Sociological Perspectives* 810.

Tonry, M (2014) 'Legal and Ethical Issues in the Prediction of Recidivism' 26 *Federal Sentencing Reporter* 167.

Ulmer, JT (1997) *Social Worlds of Sentencing: Court Communities under Sentencing Guidelines* (Albany, NY, SUNY Press).

Van Voorhis, P, Salisbury, E, Wright, E, and Bauman, A (2008) 'Achieving Accurate Pictures of Risk and Identifying Gender Responsive Needs: Two New Assessments for Women Offenders', University of Cincinnati Center for Criminal Justice Research, National Institute of Corrections, Washington DC.

Vigorita, MS (2003) 'Judicial Risk Assessment: The Impact of Risk, Stakes, and Jurisdiction' 14 *Criminal Justice Policy Review* 361.

Appendix

Table A1 Cox proportional hazards model of recidivism

	HR	SE	
Prior Convictions (0 base)			
Priors: 1	1.13	0.02	***
Priors: 2–3	1.29	0.03	***
Priors: 4–5	1.47	0.04	***
Priors: 6–7	1.70	0.06	***
Priors: 8+	2.03	0.07	***
Juvenile Adjudication	1.30	0.03	***
Prior Personal Offence	1.14	0.02	***
Prior Property Offence	1.29	0.02	***
Prior Drug Offence	1.21	0.02	***
Prior Other Offence	1.11	0.02	***
Offence Type (Property base)			
Person Offtype	0.88	0.02	***
Drug Offtype	0.85	0.02	***
Other Offtype	0.87	0.02	***
Age (50+ base)			
<21	3.71	0.14	***
21–24	2.50	0.09	***
25–29	2.00	0.07	***
30–34	1.83	0.07	***
35–39	1.71	0.07	***
40–44	1.51	0.06	***
45–59	1.33	0.06	***
Male	1.33	0.03	***
Race (White base)			
Black	1.29	0.02	***
Hispanic	1.15	0.03	***
n = 54,798			

Note: HR = hazard ratio; SE = standard error; *** $p < 0.001$.

13

Predictive Sentencing

An Analysis of Public Views

JAN W DE KEIJSER AND SIGRID GC VAN WINGERDEN

I. Introduction

To date, in most Western jurisdictions, offenders' risk of re-offending is pivotal in the criminal justice system. Scarce resources are used to control high-risk offenders and to divert low-risk offenders from prison (Kopkin, Brodsky and DeMatteo 2017; Skeem, Monahan and Lowenkamp 2016). Risk assessment is used to address a myriad of criminal justice applications at different stages in the criminal justice process. To identify high-risk offenders, social scientific evidence about factors associated with re-offending is used, usually integrated into structured risk assessment tools. Such instruments attempt to predict future dangerousness using static and dynamic criminogenic factors (see Mills, Kroner and Morgan 2011; Otto and Douglas 2010). Risk assessment at sentencing (the main focus of this chapter) is called smart, evidence-based, risk-based or predictive sentencing (Hannah-Moffat 2013; see also Van Ginneken, Chapter 2 in this volume, for an overview of the development and use of risk assessment instruments).

The widespread use of risk assessment instruments at sentencing seems to imply a high degree of consensus amongst criminal justice practitioners on an instrumental sentencing approach. However, as many contributions to this volume show, it is quite difficult to reconcile predictive sentencing with normative principles of punishment. The legitimacy of predictive sentencing is still subject to debate. Critics point out, for instance, the discriminatory effects of predictive sentencing (Starr 2014) and the cultural bias of the instruments (Hannah-Moffat and Struthers Montford, Chapter 10 in this volume; Shepherd and Esqueda 2018).

The legitimacy of predictive sentencing may be approached from two directions. The first considers normative legitimacy, ie, the extent to which a sentencing practice reflects and implements sound moral legal principles (Roberts and Plesničar 2015). From a retributivist point of view, predictive sentencing conflicts with principles of desert and proportionality. From a utilitarian perspective, predictive sentencing may be questioned because of false positive risk predictions or for collateral societal damages (such as the adverse effects of punishment on employment opportunities; see, eg, Husak, Chapter 3 in this volume). Such issues of normative legitimacy are extensively addressed in other contributions to this volume (eg, van Ginneken, Chapter 2; Husak, Chapter 3; Ryberg, Chapter 4; and Hoskins, Chapter 6 in this volume).

However, legitimacy is not only about normative principles of justification and application. Another dimension of legitimacy is 'empirical legitimacy'. This concerns community views of and support for sentencing practices. Responsiveness to public attitudes, and the extent to which sentencing practice reflects community views are associated with legitimacy by scholars, politicians and practitioners alike (eg, Hinsch 2008; Nonet and Selznick 1978; Roberts and Plesničar 2015; Robinson 2007; Robinson and Darley 1997; Tyler 2007). In recent years, there has been a push in the literature arguing that criminal justice practice has become so disconnected from public views that the legitimacy of the entire system is at stake. Consequently, criminal justice practice needs to become democratised or, in other words, to be directly and much more closely connected to public views (eg, Barker 2009; Bibas 2012; Dzur 2012; Robinson 2013). There are, however, good reasons to question both the justification and the supposed effectiveness of such a direct link between community views and legitimacy of the criminal justice system (*cf* de Keijser 2014; de Keijser and Elffers 2009; Roberts and de Keijser 2014). Despite these discussions and debate, the fact remains that many criminal justice policy makers and practitioners have a strong inclination to value and incorporate some form of public opinion into their decision making (Casey and Mohr 2005; de Keijser, Elffers and van de Bunt 2008; Tonry 1999). Such desires may be deontological, instrumental or straightforwardly populist in nature.

It is well documented that general public opinion is uninformed and undeliberated, resulting in attitudes towards crime and punishment that are unnuanced and punitive (*cf* Casey and Mohr 2005; de Keijser, van Koppen and Elffers 2007; Green 2006; Mirrlees-Black 2002; Roberts and Hough 2005). Moreover, it has been demonstrated that in order to get more guilty suspects of dangerous crimes behind bars, the public is willing to accept more wrongful convictions for serious crimes than for less serious crimes (de Keijser, de Lange and van Wilsem 2014). Apparently, in the eyes of the general public, concerns for future safety are strong enough to override some of the core values in criminal justice. As such, we should expect strong support amongst the general public for the use of risk assessments at sentencing.

The importance of risk predictions in contemporary sentencing processes raises the question of how closely that practice actually reflects community sentiments: is there strong public support for predictive sentencing? Moreover, are community attitudes to the role of risk assessment known to begin with? However, to date, public support for predictive sentencing seems to be a blind spot in the literature. In what follows, we will first briefly describe the sparse empirical research that has been conducted on public views of predictive sentencing. We then explain our own research approach and present findings of our public opinion survey as well as three experiments with members of the public. This chapter ends with a discussion of the findings and the limitations. We will draw a tentative conclusion on the empirical legitimacy of predictive sentencing. We will also indicate a way forward for further research in this underexplored area of popular opinion.

II. What Do We Know?

A vast amount of research has explored community attitudes to punishment. Such studies focus, for example, on the punitiveness gap between courts and public (Hough and Roberts 2012; Roberts and de Keijser 2014). They consistently show that outcomes depend on the research method used, as well as the amount of information provided to the respondent. People are less punitive when sentencing concrete cases than in their general attitudes towards punishment. Punitiveness decreases when the public is better informed about the case at hand and about sentencing practices in general.

Public support for predictive sentencing has rarely been addressed in prior research, and if so, then mostly indirectly. One such study focused on public support for the use of certain risk factors at sentencing. In response to legal scholars criticising predictive sentencing for being covertly discriminating with respect to sex, age and race (eg, Starr 2014), Scurich and Monahan (2016) investigated whether such concerns are shared by the public. To study public reaction to using these risk factors at sentencing, they surveyed 600 MTurk participants, exploring whether they would support offender age, gender and race being taken into account at sentencing. Half of the respondents opposed predictive sentencing, but this percentage depended strongly on the risk factor: 18 per cent said that offender's age should definitely not affect sentencing outcomes, 55 per cent said that offender's gender should not matter at sentencing and 79 per cent said that offender's race should not play a role at sentencing. The public thus seems to be divided on the issue of predictive sentencing. Scurich and Monahan (2016) further found that demographic characteristics of the participants did not explain the public division on the matter.

Singh and Sprott (2017) investigated the role of the offender's ethnicity in sentencing preferences of the public. They presented vignettes to 500 respondents and found that harsher sentences were imposed for the Black offender, and also when the respondents perceived the offender to be more dangerous, more culpable or to have a higher risk of re-offending. Participants rated the Black offender as being more dangerous than the White offender, but offender race had no effect on estimates of the risk of re-offending. After controlling for perceptions of dangerousness, culpability and risk of re-offending, there was still a small effect of the race of the offender, but the strongest predictor of the preferred sentence was how dangerous respondents viewed the offender. This study thus presents evidence that risk does play a role in public attitudes towards sentencing.

Hester et al (2017) investigated public attitudes towards the recidivist premium at sentencing. Since offenders with prior convictions are punished more severely because of their assumed higher risk of re-offending, prior record enhancements can be seen as an example of predictive sentencing (see Roberts and Frase, Chapter 9 in this volume). The study showed that the public supports harsher punishment when the offender has prior convictions, but also that there is less support for taking older priors and juvenile priors into account. Public support for prior record enhancements – and thus for predictive sentencing – turned out to be less robust than expected.

In an older study, Monahan and Ruggiero (1980) studied the relationship between culpability and prior offences by providing psychology students with a robbery case. The offender had either prior offences or no prior offences, and was either at high or at low risk of re-offending. Respondents were asked: (1) how much punishment the offender morally deserved?; (2) how much punishment should be imposed to protect society (ie, incapacitation)?; and (3) how much punishment should the judge impose? Sentences aiming to incapacitate the offender to protect society were more severe than sentences aiming for desert. Punishments for all three questions were harsher when the offender had prior offences and when he had a high risk of re-offending. Thus, contrary to expectations, a high risk of re-offending not only increased the punishment imposed to protect society, but also the punishment that was deemed to be morally deserved. Public support for predictive sentencing can consequently be linked to both utilitarian and retributive perspectives.

Starr (2014) performed a small experimental study using vignettes among 83 criminal law students to investigate whether a scientific risk assessment score affected sentences. The effect of the risk information on sentencing outcomes was strong. When deciding on punishment for two variants of a grand larceny case, low risk led to shorter prison terms as compared to no risk information. Conversely, when provided with high risk information, prison terms were significantly longer compared to no risk information.

III. Current Study: Research Approach

Our study contributes to the existing literature by investigating the empirical legitimacy of predictive sentencing. The research questions are: to what extent does the public support predictive sentencing? Does the public prefer harsher punishment for high-risk offenders than for low-risk offenders? Does the public support specific risk factors like age, ethnicity and sex to affect sentencing? Does the public support the use of risk information at sentencing and does this depend on the type and severity of the crimes committed? To answer these questions, both a survey and a series of experiments with members of the public have been carried out.[1]

In the survey, we measured awareness and general knowledge of, and support for the use of risk predictions at sentencing. We asked questions about the impact that high or low risk predictions should have on sentencing outcomes for different categories of crime. We related these attitudes to preferred goals of punishment. Furthermore, we asked people how supportive they were of specific risk factors that are commonly incorporated into contemporary risk prediction instruments. The survey questions were general and abstract on the one hand, and more tailored to the context of types of cases on the other hand.

The experiments were designed to isolate the extent to which risk assessments influence sentencing outcomes as preferred by the public, specifically sentence severity. Concise descriptions of crime cases were provided together with information about predicted risk and validity of the risk prediction instrument. We carried out two experiments with criminal law students, who may be considered relatively informed, and compared the outcomes using a sample of the general public. Within the three experiments, the type and severity of the crime cases was varied in conjuncture with levels of assessed risk. Through the experiments, we are able to show the public's use and impact of risk information at sentencing, whether or not this use depends on the severity and nature of the crimes under consideration and whether this is affected by awareness of the error margins that risk predictions have.

IV. Survey: Public Attitudes to Predictive Sentencing

A. Procedure for Collecting Our Survey Data

Participants for both the survey and the third experiment were recruited online by distributing a Qualtrics weblink[2] on social media and by email. Asking people to further share the link on their Facebook or Linked In pages, or to forward the email to others, led to a snowballing effect. Participants were randomly assigned to either the survey or the experiment. After 382 participants had participated in the experiment, all participants from that moment on were directed to the survey.

Data was collected between December 2017 and March 2018. Respondents aged 17 or older were eligible. Since the use of prizes is known to increase online participation (Kypri and Gallagher 2003; Laguilles, Williams and Saunders 2011),

[1] We are grateful to Noëlle Vos, Micha van Egteren and to our colleagues from the Criminal Law Department at Leiden University for their assistance with data collection for these studies.

[2] Qualtrics is a web-based software tool to create and distribute online surveys.

a reward of €250 was raffled among the respondents. Participants filled out the online survey in their own time. The tendency to respond in socially desirable ways is expected to not distort the findings, since the social desirability bias mostly emerges when there is an interviewer present and the questions involve sensitive issues (Baker et al 2010); none of these triggers were at play in our study.

B. Participants in the Survey

There were 645 participants in the survey. The mean age of the participants is 39 (median 34), ranging from 17 to 85. Females and highly educated people are over-represented in the study: 65 per cent were female and 44 per cent had obtained a university degree. To make the sample more representative of the Dutch population, post-stratification weights were applied to the sample to match the demographics of the Statistics Netherlands 2017. Weights were applied to participant's sex and educational level, and were calculated by dividing the percentage in the population by the percentage in the sample.[3] These weights were used for all survey analyses.

C. Findings from the Survey

i. Knowledge of Predictive Sentencing

Risk assessment is common in criminal justice practices, but to what extent does the public know that judges use risk assessments? Three out of four participants said they were aware of judges' use of risk assessments.[4] These participants were subsequently presented with specific types of judicial decisions and asked whether they think risk assessments are used. Where nine out of 10 participants correctly identified the decisions to impose or extend the TBS-measure (for dangerous mentally ill offenders), fewer people knew that judges use risk assessments for the decision on punishment type and severity (75 per cent and 64 per cent respectively). Participants thus underestimate the use of risk assessment at sentencing. On the other hand, one in five participants wrongly thought that judges use risk assessments to decide upon the offender's guilt.

ii. Attitudes towards Predictive Sentencing

Participants were further asked the extent to which they agree with statements regarding the role that the offender's risk of re-offending *should* play at

[3] Weights used are 2.777 for lower-educated males, 5.309 for medium-educated males, 0.587 for higher-educated males, 1.820 for lower-educated females, 1.966 for medium-educated females and 0.302 for higher-educated females.

[4] Figure 13.1 provides a literal translation of the survey items.

sentencing. Although the participants were presented with five-point scales (completely disagree – disagree – neutral – agree – completely agree), these are condensed to three-point scales (disagree – neutral – agree) for presentation purposes.

Figure 13.1 shows that 75 per cent of the participants support risk of re-offending playing a role at sentencing. Nearly one out of every five participants (18 per cent) feels that risk should not be taken into account at sentencing. However, as questions become more specific, public support for predictive sentencing diminishes. Whereas 75 per cent of the participants believe that offender's risk of re-offending can be taken into account at sentencing, only 54 per cent think that an offender with a high risk of re-offending *deserves* a more severe punishment. Public support for low-risk offenders deserving lesser punishment is even lower: 24 per cent think they deserve less punishment. So there are twice as many people in favour of high-risk offenders deserving more severe punishment than of low-risk offenders deserving less severe punishment. Thus, from the perspective of deservedness, there is more support for high risk as an aggravating factor than for low risk as a mitigating factor. Further, if it were certain that the offender would not commit new crimes, 85 per cent of the participants think there is still a role for punishment. With a consequentialist eye on the protection of society, 59 per cent thinks that high-risk offenders should be punished more severely.

To find out whether public support is affected by the severity of the crime, more specific statements were presented. A majority (58 per cent) of the participants agree that offenders' risk of re-offending should play a greater role at sentencing for serious crimes. However, when asked more specifically whether they agree that a high-risk offender who stole a bicycle should be punished more severely than he deserves considering the minor severity of the crime, only 23 per cent agree. And with the converse statement, whether a low-risk murderer should be punished less severely than he deserves considering the severity of the crime, only 5 per cent agree. Thus, although 75 per cent of respondents agree that in general, offenders' risk of re-offending should affect sentencing, when put in a more concrete perspective, there is much less support for predictive sentencing.

iii. Attitudes in Relation to Preferred Goals of Punishment

Since predictive sentencing is intrinsically utilitarian in origin, we expect that public support for predictive sentencing is related to generally preferred punishment goals: the more incapacitation is endorsed as a sentencing goal, the more support for predictive sentencing we would expect. We asked participants to rate how important in general they find the sentencing goals of desert, incapacitation, rehabilitation, deterrence and reparation (very unimportant – unimportant – neutral – important – very important). We use correlation coefficients to determine the relation between these generally preferred punishment goals and support for predictive sentencing.

Table A1 (in Appendix 2) shows that the goals are related to support for predictive sentencing in the expected directions. However, it also becomes clear that these correlations are only weak to moderate.[5] As expected, the findings show that the more importance participants ascribe to incapacitation, the more supportive they are of predictive sentencing. For rehabilitation, we found the opposite: more support for rehabilitation is associated with less support for predictive sentencing.

Further, the more participants are in favour of desert, incapacitation and deterrence, the more they agree that high-risk offenders *deserve* more severe punishment. For rehabilitation, the direction of this relation is again opposite. Similar correlations are found for the utilitarian version of this statement, with the highest association with the goal of incapacitation: the more importance participants adhere to incapacitation, the more they agree that high-risk offenders should be punished more severely in order to protect society.

Except for rehabilitation, preferences for all other punishment goals are positively related to the statement that risk of re-offending should play a greater role at sentencing for major than for minor crimes. Participants who value the goal of incapacitation and deterrence particularly agree with this idea. Further, the more importance ascribed to rehabilitation, the more one agrees that low-risk murderers should be punished less severely. For all other punishment aims, this relation is inverted: the more importance for retribution, incapacitation or deterrence, the less participants agree that low-risk murderers should be punished less severely. But again, the correlations between preferred punishment aims and public support for predictive sentencing are only weak to moderate.

iv. Accuracy of the Prediction

For the participants who agreed that the risk of re-offending can be taken into account at sentencing, we further examined their view on the issue of false positives: to what extent is the quality of the prediction important for its use at sentencing? Figure 13.1 further shows that 75 per cent of the participants agree that the extent to which the risk of re-offending affects sentencing should depend on the accuracy of the risk assessment. Moreover, 72 per cent think that risk assessment can only play a role at sentencing when it is almost certain that the risk assessment is correct. The public thus requires high-quality predictions about future offending. Further, they require risk assessments of high quality, regardless of the severity of the crime: 59 per cent disagreed with the statement that for major crimes, the accuracy of the risk assessment is less important than for minor crimes.

[5] Correlations smaller than 0.3 are generally considered weak to modest.

Figure 13.1 Public opinion on aspects of predictive sentencing

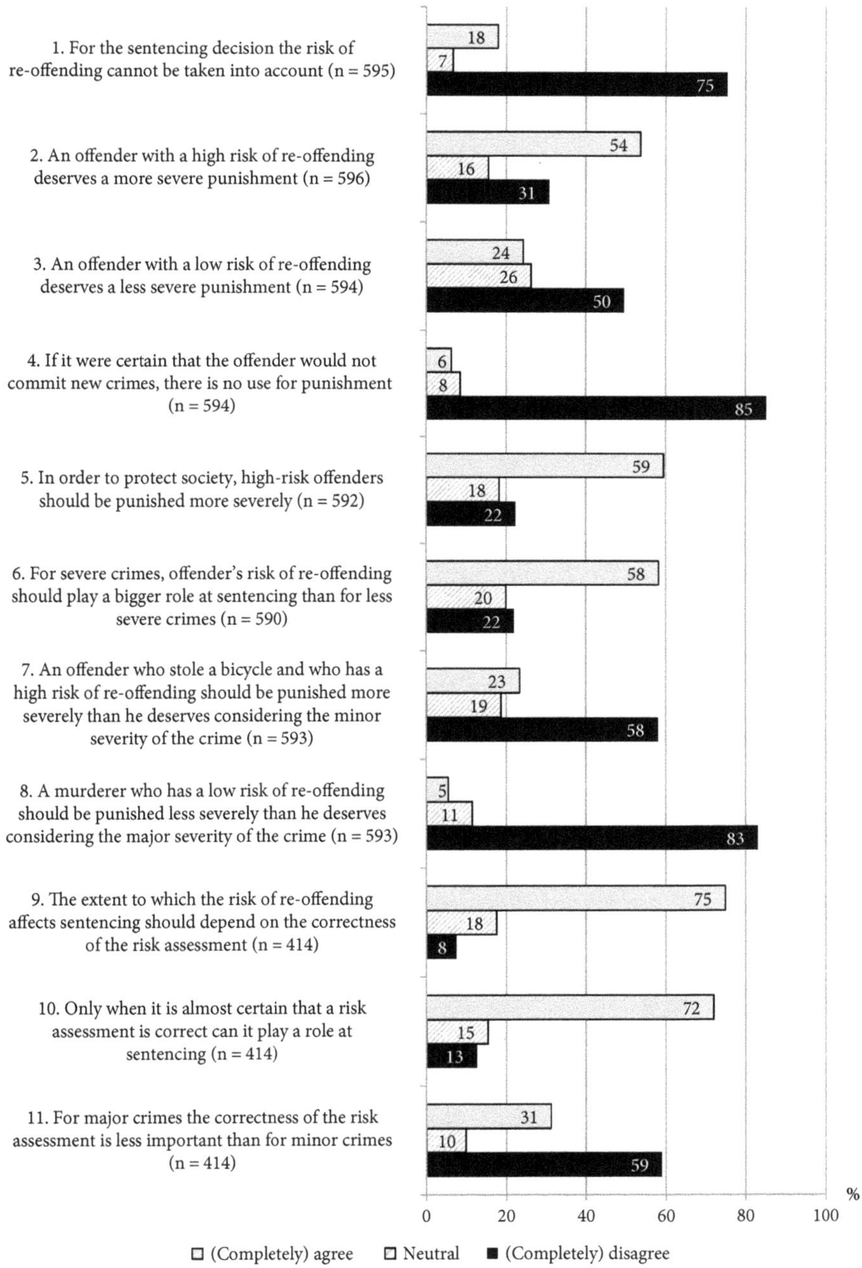

v. Support for Specific Risk Factors in Risk Assessment and Sentencing

Predictive sentencing is often criticised by legal scholars for being discriminatory with respect to sex, age and race (eg, Starr 2014). In a similar fashion to Scurich and Monahan (2016), we investigated whether these concerns expressed by legal scholars are shared by the public. Participants were first asked to what extent they think it is good that offender sex, age, ethnicity, employment and relations with delinquent friends are taken into account to assess the risk of re-offending. Thereafter, they were asked to what extent they think these characteristics should be taken into account at sentencing.

Figure 13.2 shows that more people support these offender characteristics being taken into account for assessing the risk of re-offending than for actual use at sentencing. For example, while 77 per cent of the participants think that having delinquent friends should be taken into account for assessing the risk of re-offending, only 48 per cent think that having delinquent friends should play a role at sentencing. Moreover, the figure also shows that public support for risk-related offender characteristics depends heavily on the characteristic. There is less support for sex and ethnicity being taken into account at risk assessment and sentencing than for employment, age and relations with delinquent friends. For example, 12 per cent of the participants agree that offender ethnicity and sex can be taken into account at sentencing, while over half of the participants agree that offender age can be taken into account at sentencing. These differences show that the public is divided on the admissibility of risk-related offender characteristics at sentencing.

Figure 13.2 Public support for specific risk-related offender characteristics to be taken into account for *risk assessment* and for *sentencing*

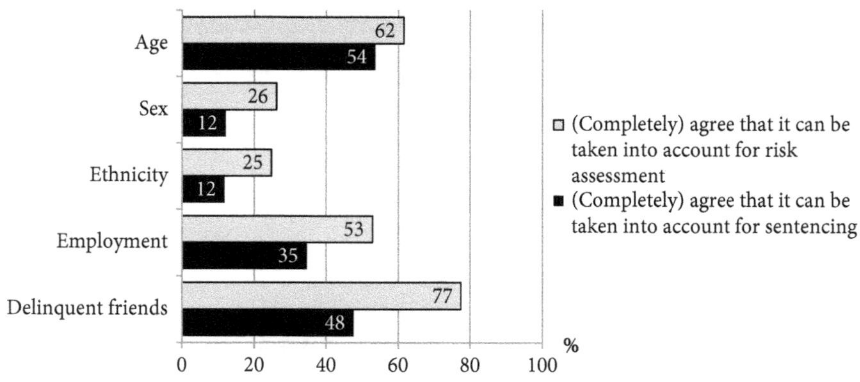

D. Conclusions Based on the Survey

The public is well aware that judges use risk assessments for their decision making. When asked generally, 75 per cent of the participants agreed that an offender's risk of re-offending should be taken into account at sentencing, but in response to more specific questions, public support declines: low-risk murderers should not receive less punishment and high-risk bicycle thieves should not be punished more severely. Although we found that the more importance participants ascribe to incapacitation, the more supportive they are of predictive sentencing, we found similar patterns for retribution and deterrence, and the opposite for rehabilitation. However, preferences for punishment goals in general are only weakly to moderately related to support for predictive sentencing. Further, when asked to what extent participants agree with specific risk-related offender characteristics being taken into account, participants are less supportive with respect to sentencing than assessing risk. Moreover, public support for risk-related offender characteristics depends strongly on the specific characteristic. This is in line with the findings from Scurich and Monahan (2016). As in other public opinion research on issues related to punishment (*cf* de Keijser and Elffers 2009), our survey shows that public support for harsher sentencing policies diminishes as the questions on the role of risk assessment become more specific.

V. The Effects of Risk, Crime Seriousness and Predictive Validity: Three Experiments

A. First Experiment: Risk and Crime Seriousness in an Informed Sample

i. Design of the Experiment and Expectations

The experiment was designed to examine the effect of different levels of risk on sentence severity within the context of concrete crime scenarios. The second aim of this experiment was to test whether the magnitude of an effect of risk depends on the type and seriousness of the crime under consideration.

It was (obviously) expected that a more serious crime would yield harsher sentencing outcomes than a less serious crime. It was further expected that a *higher level* of predicted risk would produce harsher sentences than a benchmark of *no information* about predicted risk and that a *low level* of predicted risk would result in the most lenient sentences. Finally, an interaction effect was expected between the seriousness of the crime and the level of predicted risk. In line with the above-mentioned instrumental public attitudes on wrongful convictions, we expected that the effect of risk levels on sentence severity would be *stronger* for the more serious crime scenario than for a less serious crime scenario.

Two crime scenarios (vignettes) were devised with a clear contrast in severity between them: a residential burglary and an aggravated assault (see Appendix 1 for translations). Each vignette had three risk variants: (i) high level of predicted risk; (ii) no information about predicted risk; and (iii) low level of predicted risk.

Each participant received both vignettes, but within participants, both vignettes mentioned one and the same risk level.[6]

The outcome measure was sentence severity. We asked participants for their sentencing preference, restricting their choice to imprisonment (in years, months or days).[7] To limit extreme variation in sentencing choices, we provided participants with an anchor – or starting point – for their choice of punishment. This was done by noting the (actual) average sentence that Dutch courts impose for the particular type of crime.[8] For residential burglary, this was three months' imprisonment, while for the aggravated assault, this was six months' imprisonment. After determining the length of the prison sentence, participants were asked to indicate which punishment goal(s) they wanted to achieve with the sentence. They could choose one or more from concise descriptions of *desert*, *individual deterrence*, *incapacitation*, *rehabilitation* and *general deterrence*.

ii. Procedure for Collecting the Data

Participants were third-year bachelor students of criminal law at Leiden University. During working group sessions, the professors distributed the questionnaires and asked students to participate individually during the session. In total, 150 questionnaires were distributed in December 2016.

There were six distinct variants of the questionnaire: three risk-level variants by two order variants. Half of the questionnaires started with the residential burglary, while the other half started with the aggravated assault.[9] The questionnaires were randomly assigned to the participants.

iii. Findings of the First Experiment

Of the 150 questionnaires distributed, 142 were completed. Respondents' prison sentences were transformed into numbers of days. For determining effect sizes and statistical significance of differences, repeated measures analysis of variance was employed.[10]

Figure 13.3 shows the average prison sentences for the burglary and for the assault per risk level. Table A2 in Appendix 2 provides the statistical details.

[6] In technical terms, this is a 3 (risk) by 2 (crime) factorial design, where risk level is a between subjects factor and crime seriousness a within subjects factor.

[7] Participants were asked: 'What length of prison term would you impose?'

[8] The literal (translated) instruction was: 'Because determining a punishment is rather difficult, we inform you that in practice for residential burglary, on average three months of imprisonment is meted out.'

[9] While both vignettes could be read at the respondents' own leisure, varying the presentation sequence of vignettes counter-balances systematic order effects.

[10] Preceding the analysis, extreme values (outliers) on the prison sentence variable were identified. This resulted in the identification and removal of eight extreme values for the residential burglary and nine extreme values for the aggravated assault.

Despite the fact that this concerns a relatively well-informed sample, all average sentence lengths, with the exception of the low risk variant of the burglary, are well above the court average that was provided to respondents. The figure further shows a clear and strong main effect of crime seriousness; all sentencing levels for the assault are well above those for the burglary.

Moreover, Figure 13.3 shows that for both cases, sentences increase from low level of risk, through no information to high level of risk. The effect, although statistically significant, is of a moderate magnitude.[11] The differences between the risk levels further seem to indicate that low level of risk has more of a mitigating effect on sentence severity, as compared to 'no risk information', than the aggravating effect of a high risk level. Two explanations may be offered for this finding. First, in our materials, 'low level of risk' has been formulated as a high probability that the offender will *not* commit further crimes. In daily practice, however, risk levels are commonly stated in positive probabilities of re-offending – eg, low, medium or high risk. Second, this finding may be illustrative of an earlier documented tendency for members of the public to have the worst-case scenario in mind when responding to questions about crime (Casey and Mohr 2005; Roberts 1992) or to favour harsh treatment because they see no hope of rehabilitation (*cf* Slobogin and Brinkley-Rubinstein 2013). If that is the case here, it may be expected that participants who received no risk information had a high-risk offender in mind when sentencing.

Figure 13.3 Experiment 1: Average prison sentence (in days) by crime vignette and risk levels (n=127)

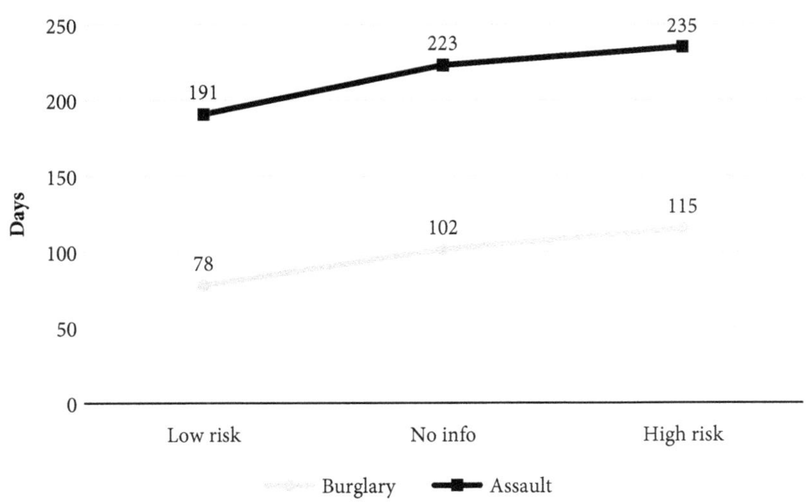

[11] The 'partial eta squared' for the effect size of seriousness is 0.69, which is very strong indeed. The effect size of risk is much lower at 0.09 – a moderate effect (*cf* Table A2).

We further expected that the effect of risk level on sentencing would be stronger for the aggravated assault (the more serious crime) than for the domestic burglary. Figure 13.3 shows no such combined (interaction) effect of risk and seriousness; the lines run parallel to one another (see also Table A2).

Figures 13.4 and 13.5 show the preferred goals of punishment per risk level for the burglary and the assault respectively.[12] The ordering of goal preferences is similar across the crime vignettes, with *desert* and *individual deterrence* being the most-preferred objective and *incapacitation* the least-preferred objective. Preferences for the goals of sentencing are significantly affected by risk levels in two instances. For the burglary (Figure 13.4), more risk means a stronger desire for *incapacitation*. For the aggravated assault (Figure 13.5), there is a significant effect of risk on preference for *rehabilitation*: a high risk level clearly invites a stronger preference for rehabilitation than a low risk level.

Figure 13.4 Experiment 1: burglary – public support for sentence goals by offender risk level (**χ^2 test p<.01)

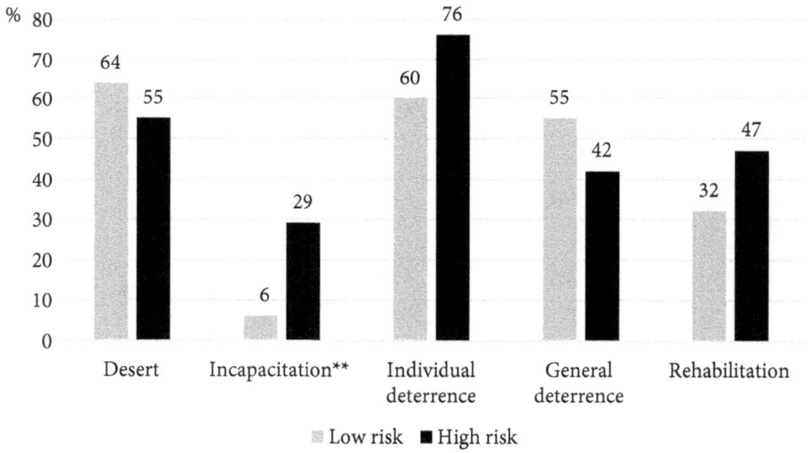

iv. Conclusions from First Experiment and Implications for Subsequent Experiments

While the preferences for the goals of sentencing, given different levels of risk, are generally consistent with common sense and theoretical rationales, these findings reveal differential support for our expectations. There was an effect of risk information, and that was in the expected direction. However, the effect of risk was weaker than we had anticipated. Moreover, there was no support for the expected interaction between risk and seriousness. This implies, at least within the context

[12] The percentages for the individual goals of punishment add up to over 100 per cent because respondents were free to choose more than one goal.

Figure 13.5 Experiment 1: aggravated assault – public support for sentence goals by offender risk level (*χ^2 test p<.05)

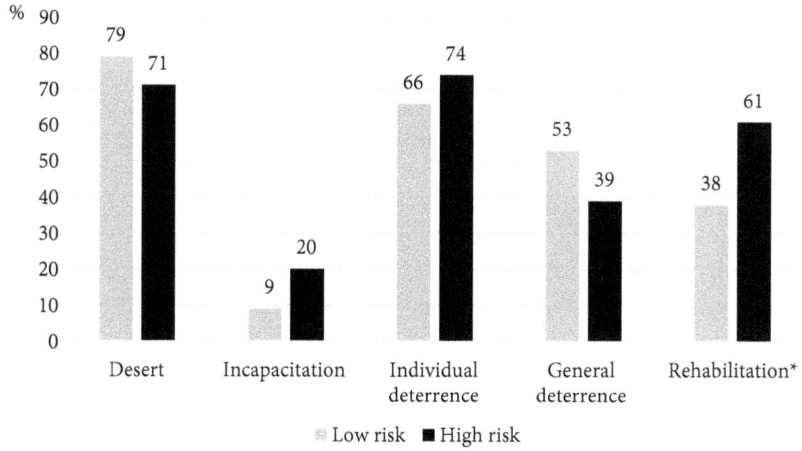

of this sample and materials used, that there is only moderate public support for the use of risk predictions at sentencing.

The moderate effect of risk and the absence of interaction with seriousness may be attributed to the characteristics of our sample. After all, this was a relatively informed group of criminal law students. As a result, these participants may have been inclined to consider risk information an irrelevant or even illegal sentencing factor. This calls for a replication of the experiment with a sample of the general public, to which we will turn in the third experiment below. But there is another possible explanation. It may be expected that the anticipated effects of risk and the subsequent interaction between risk and seriousness would be much stronger with a more extreme *seriousness contrast* between the crimes in the experiment. Perhaps the aggravated assault simply did not trigger enough concern for the consequences of future dangerousness. This calls for a replication of the study with similar participants, but with a larger crime contrast. The latter is the focus of our second experiment.

B. Second Experiment: Replication with Greater Seriousness Contrast

i. Design of the Experiment and Expectations

The purpose, design and measures were identical to the first experiment. We replaced the aggravated assault with a case of vehicular manslaughter. It is a case of drunk driving that resulted in the death of a young female pedestrian (see Appendix 1). This is typically the type of case that causes very strong public sentiment. We expect the effect of risk information to be strong for this type of case.

The residential burglary was identical to the one used in the first experiment. The drunk driver described in this new vignette had been warned by his friends in the bar not to drive home. Driving at high speed on his way home, he hits and kills an 18-year-old woman at a pedestrian crossing and flees the scene of the accident. As in the first experiment, the average sentence that Dutch courts impose for this type of case was provided: three months' imprisonment for the burglary and two years' imprisonment for the drunk driving and subsequent death of the pedestrian.

In the first experiment, we speculated that participants who were not given risk information in the vignette may have had worst-case scenarios in mind concerning the future dangerousness of the offender. In this subsequent experiment, in a final question, we asked participants to estimate recidivism rates for eight types of crime, including residential burglary and vehicular manslaughter. Our hypothesis would be confirmed if estimated recidivism rates for participants who did not receive risk information in the vignettes are closer to those who received high-risk vignettes than to those who received low-risk vignettes.[13]

ii. Procedure for Collecting the Data

This experiment was conducted with a new sample of third-year bachelor students of criminal law at Leiden University, during the same course as in experiment one. Questionnaires were randomly distributed and completed during working group sessions. In total, 336 questionnaires were distributed in such sessions from 8 to 14 November 2017.

iii. Findings

Of the 336 distributed questionnaires, 300 were completed. Prison sentences were transformed into number of days and the data was analysed using repeated measures analysis of variance.[14]

Figure 13.6 shows the average prison sentences for the burglary and for the vehicular manslaughter per risk level. Table A2 provides the statistical details. As with the previous sample, the average preferred sentences were well above the actual court averages. The figure further shows that we were successful in creating a much greater seriousness contrast between the vignettes as compared to the first experiment. As a result, there is an even stronger seriousness effect on the sentences.[15] Moreover, while the burglary vignette was identical to the one used

[13] This is based on a supposed priming effect of risk information on the general question about recidivism rates.

[14] Preceding the analysis, outliers were identified and removed. This resulted in the identification and removal of 25 extreme values for the residential burglary and 13 extreme values for the DUI manslaughter.

[15] Partial eta squared is now 0.79. It was 0.69 in Experiment 1. See Table A2.

in the first experiment, sentences for that case are now higher than in the first experiment across the risk levels. Since the type of sample is exactly the same, we interpret this as a framing effect (*cf* Kahneman, Slovic and Tversky 1982) resulting from the seriousness of the DUI manslaughter case.[16]

Analyses (*cf* Table A2) further reveal that, in contrast to the first experiment, there is no statistically significant effect of risk on sentencing and there is no combined (interaction) effect of risk and seriousness. While, as a result of introducing a much more serious case in the experiment, we had expected a strong(er) effect of risk, no such effect emerged.

Figure 13.6 Experiment 2: average prison sentence (in days) by crime vignette and risk levels (n=264)

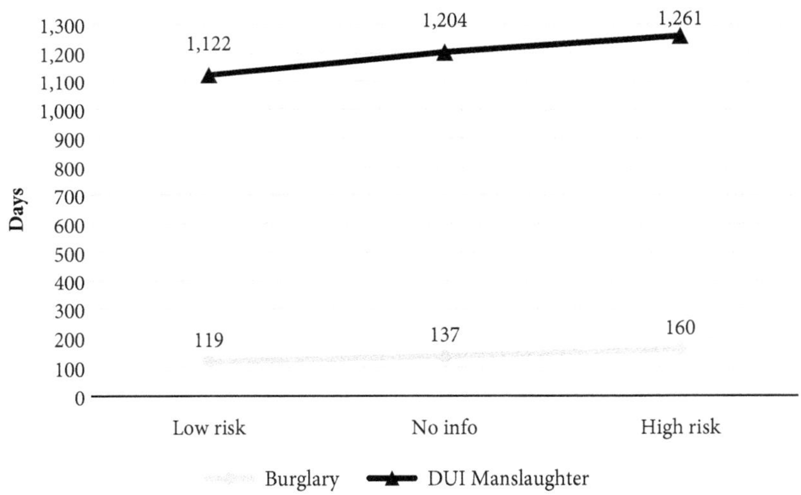

Analysis of the general estimates of recidivism risk for different types of crime reveals no support for the hypothesis that participants who received no information about risk in the vignette had worst-case scenarios in mind when considering the future dangerousness of the offender. In fact, this analysis provides support for the opposite: participants with no risk information in the vignette provided similar estimates of general recidivism rates for burglary and for manslaughter in traffic as participants who were given low risk levels in these vignettes.[17]

[16] In an earlier Dutch experiment, it was demonstrated that when judging a series of crimes, the most serious crimes have an effect on people's attitudes towards the less serious crimes, in the sense that these become more punitive (de Keijser and Elffers 2008).

[17] Estimated recidivism rates for burglary: low risk 45.5 per cent; no info 46.2 per cent; high risk 54.4 per cent ($F(2,291)=4.74$, $p<0.01$). Estimated recidivism rates for vehicular manslaughter: low risk 12.7 per cent; no info 10.4 per cent; high risk 17.2 per cent ($F(2,290)=5.96$, $p<0.01$).

C. Intermezzo: What Have We Learned from the First Two Experiments?

The two experiments examined the effect of risk information on sentence severity. We expected strong effects of risk on sentencing and we expected that such an effect of risk would be considerably stronger for more serious crimes. In the first experiment, we found a moderate effect of risk in the predicted direction. A stronger seriousness contrast between the crimes as adopted in the second experiment did not strengthen the effect; rather, it disappeared. Moreover, in both experiments we found no evidence for the expectation that risk information would have a stronger effect in more serious crime cases than in less serious cases.

Across crime cases (in the first experiment), preference for two goals associated with individual prevention (ie, incapacitation and rehabilitation) increased with higher risk levels. A final finding is that the absence of risk information in a specific case does not seem to result in participants having high-risk offenders in mind when sentencing. Rather, the findings of the first experiment seem to indicate that, in comparison with crime scenarios without risk prediction, low risk has more of a mitigating effect than high risk has an aggravating effect.

A preliminary conclusion would be that in the minds of the public, risk should play only a limited role at sentencing. The effect of risk appears to be more nuanced than we expected. The public, who are generally uninformed and punitive, are not as overtly instrumental concerning the use of risk information as might be expected.

However, our samples in the first two experiments were relatively informed samples. In the third and final experiment, we focus on an uninformed, more general sample of the public.

D. Third Experiment: Effects of Risk, Crime Seriousness and Predictive Validity in a Less Informed Sample

i. *Design of the Experiment and Expectations*

The third experiment was designed with two purposes in mind. The first was a replication of the previous experiments. In a more general sample of the Dutch public, does risk information affect sentencing preferences and does it elicit more or less preference for certain goals at sentencing? Is an effect of risk information stronger for a more serious crime than for a less serious crime?

Apart from replicating the first two experiments, we added a third experimental factor: information about the predictive accuracy of risk assessments. It was expected that any effect of risk assessment on sentencing for a given crime scenario would be affected by the prediction error margins provided. We further expected that the public would attach less weight to prediction errors when accounting for risk levels in the more serious (and violent) case than in the less serious (property) case. This expectation was informed by the findings of earlier research (discussed in section II), where in order to get more guilty suspects of dangerous crimes behind bars, the public is willing to accept more wrongful convictions for serious crimes than for less serious crimes (de Keijser, de Lange and van Wilsem 2014).

Since the more extreme seriousness contrast between the vignettes in the second experiment yielded neither a stronger effect of risk on sentencing nor the expected interaction effect between risk and crime seriousness, we use the burglary and the aggravated assault of the first experiment. Risk information was again varied between low risk, no information on risk and high risk. Information on the accuracy of risk assessment was varied between three categories: no information on error margins; 10 per cent of the predictions are incorrect; and 40 per cent of the predictions are incorrect (see Appendix 1). The measures for sentencing and goal preferences were identical to those in the first experiment.

ii. Procedure for Collecting the Data

Data for this experiment was collected from December 2017 to January 2018 using the self-administered online Qualtrics procedure described above. In total, 382 respondents were randomly assigned to one of the versions in the experimental design.

iii. Findings

Of the 382 self-administered questionnaires, 379 were completed. The prison sentences that were imposed by our participants were transformed into number of days and the data was analysed using repeated measures analysis of variance.[18]

The mean age of the participants in this experiment was 38 (median 33), ranging from 17 to 88 years old. Females were overrepresented (64 per cent). Half of the respondents had university-level education. However, this does not make our sample inappropriate for the current purposes. After all, we are looking for the particular effects of differential risk information on sentencing preferences rather than aiming to draw general conclusions about the attitudes of the Dutch population. We refrained from weighing the experiment data.

Figure 13.7 shows the average prison sentences for the burglary and for the assault per risk level. Table A2 provides the statistical details. Similar to the other two experiments, the preferred sentences are much higher than the court average.

[18] Preceding the analysis, extreme values were identified. This resulted in the identification and removal of 22 extreme values for the residential burglary and 30 extreme values for the aggravated assault. After the removal of outliers, 340 cases remain for analyses.

Moreover, just like in the other experiments, the figure shows a clear and strong effect of crime seriousness; sentences for the assault are well above those for the burglary. Further, risk level has an effect on sentence outcomes, but although statistically significant, the effect size is small. Moreover, there is no combined (interaction) effect of risk and seriousness. Thus, similar to the other two experiments, the effect of risk on sentence severity is *not* stronger for the more serious crime than for the less serious crime.

We also hypothesised that information on the predictive validity of the risk information would affect the role of risk at sentencing. This interaction between risk and error information was tested overall as well as separately for the burglary case and for the assault case. The findings, reported in Table A2, show that there is no significant interaction between risk and error margin information for either crime scenario.

Thus, this third experiment shows that the use of risk at sentencing is a very modest one and does not interact with crime seriousness or with information about predictive accuracy.

Figure 13.7 Experiment 3: average prison sentence (in days) by crime vignette and risk levels (n=340)

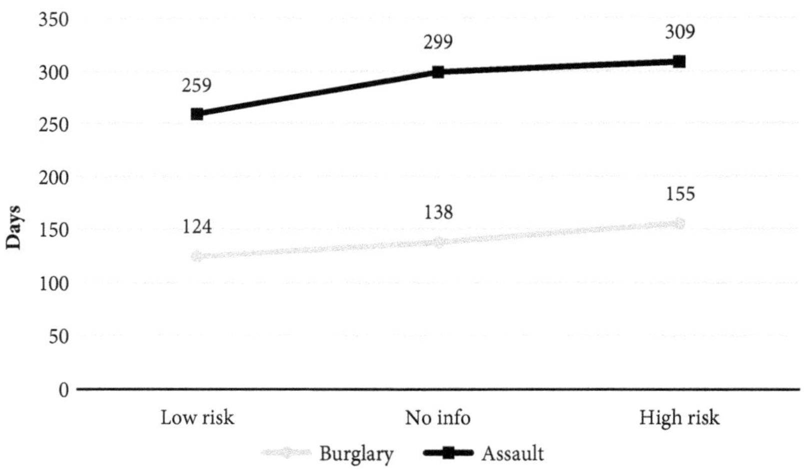

Regarding the goals of punishment, Figures 13.8 and 13.9 show that *individual deterrence* and *rehabilitation* are the most preferred goals and that *incapacitation* is least preferred. In contrast to the law students, the general public is less inclined to have *desert* in mind when sentencing these two crimes.

Preferences for the goals of sentencing are significantly affected by risk levels in three instances. For the burglary, *rehabilitation* is favoured more for high-risk than for low-risk offenders. For the assault, we find support for increased preferences for both *incapacitation* and *rehabilitation* with higher risk levels. The preference for *rehabilitation* is 20 percentage points (assault case) and 19 percentage points (burglary case) higher for high-risk compared to low-risk offenders. As such, the effects of risk on punishment support an increase in consequentialist thoughts, not only in a punitive but also in a rehabilitative sense.

Figure 13.8 Experiment 3: burglary – public support for sentence goals by offender risk level (**χ^2 test p<.01)

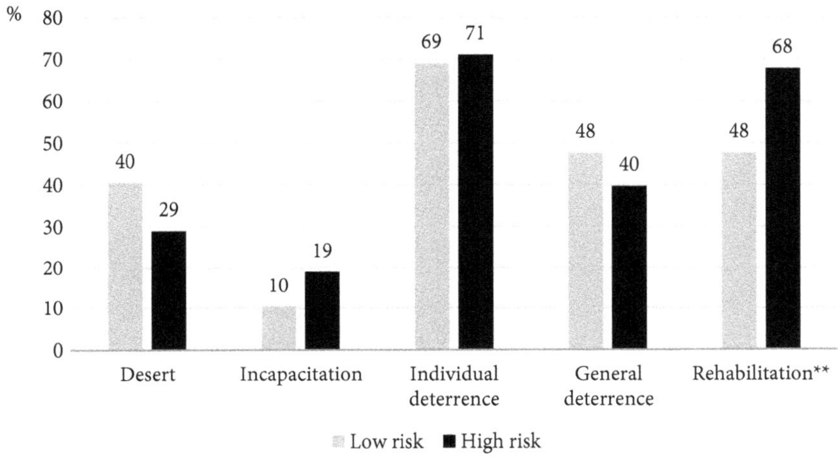

Figure 13.9 Experiment 3: aggravated assault – public support for sentence goals by offender risk level (**χ^2 test p<.01)

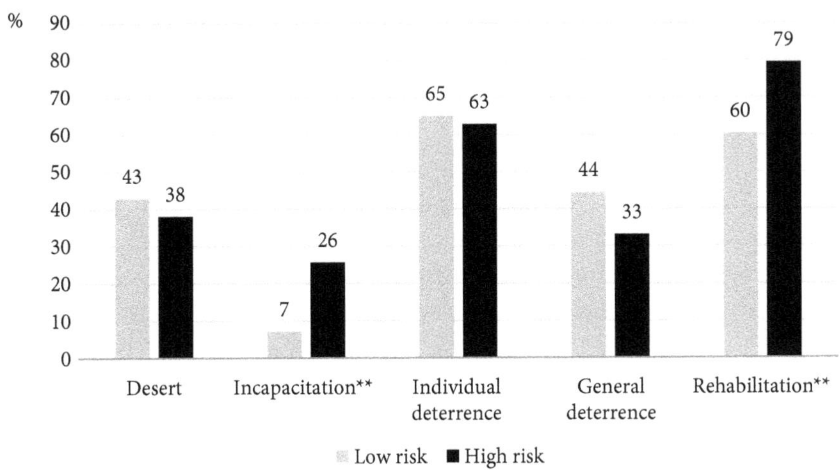

E. Conclusion Based on the Three Experimental Studies

In one of the three experiments, no statistically significant effect of risk on sentencing outcomes was found, while the other two experiments demonstrated only a moderate effect (first experiment) and a small effect (third experiment). Thus, in our studies with informed samples and with a sample from the general public, we found only modest support at most for the role of risk assessment in forming people's punitive preferences.

Given our three independent experiments and sample variation, we consider this a robust finding. Not only is the role for risk assessment a modest one in the minds of the public, it is also independent of the type (property or violent) and seriousness of the crime, as well as of information about the predictive accuracy of risk assessments. Even when risk assessments are said to be quite reliable, this does not increase the effect of risk on sentencing above the modest levels demonstrated here.

While the sample in the third experiment was relatively highly educated, it can still, overall, be considered less educated and less informed in matters of sentencing than the criminal law students. Indeed, in line with what has been documented before, the sentence severity preferred by the general public exceeded that of the more informed samples. Nevertheless, even in the more general sample, there was only modest support for a direct effect of risk on sentencing and no support for risk having a stronger effect in the more serious cases.

VI. Conclusions

We had expected a strong public preference for predictive sentencing. Moreover, we expected that such support would be stronger for serious crimes. Both the survey and the experiments show modest public support for predictive sentencing. When asked globally in the survey, three-quarters of the participants favoured predictive sentencing. This would imply quite a strong public support base for the practice. Although still indicative of public support, the percentage of participants who favour harsher sentences for high-risk offenders because they *deserve* it is 54 per cent and for the *protection of society* 59 per cent. And, placed in even more concrete perspectives, public support for the use of risk information at sentencing diminished substantively. Such differences between answers on general and on more specific questions mirror findings of studies on public punitiveness (de Keijser, van Koppen and Elffers 2007; Green 2006; Roberts and Hough 2005; Stalans 2002). However, our survey questions focused on increases or decreases in sentencing severity as a result of more or less risk. Yet, there may also be public support for using risk assessment in order to tailor an intervention to the rehabilitative (criminogenic) needs of the offender. As a result of our focus on the meaning of risk for sentence severity, we cannot speculate on levels of public support for a rehabilitative variant of predictive sentencing.

Across the three experiments, we also found at best only modest public support for predictive sentencing. The moderate support is independent from crime type and severity. Furthermore, information about the predictive accuracy of risk assessments did not affect the public's use of risk information at sentencing. This latter finding contrasts with the survey findings, where seven out of 10 participants agreed that the permitted use of risk predictions should depend on their accuracy. Again, this appears to highlight differences between responses to general survey questions and responses to questions within the context of concrete cases.

While there is a positive relationship between risk and harsher sentencing, our experiments were not constructed to explore the rehabilitative dimension of predictive sentencing. When an offender has a high risk of re-offending, he may be considered to be in need of rehabilitation: more severe punishment is not of help in such a case. This reasoning was found among judges in previous research (van Wingerden 2014). Indeed, the experiments showed that in some instances, a high risk of re-offending led to a (much) stronger preference for rehabilitation as a sentencing goal than a low risk of re-offending. However, the participants in our experiments were not able to express any rehabilitative concerns in the outcome measure, as the question was restricted to a prison term.

To our knowledge, our studies are the first to specifically examine public support for predictive sentencing. They show a more nuanced picture of the Dutch public's views on the use of risk assessment than we expected. While the main conclusions of both the survey and the experiments seem clear and robust, these studies were confined to examining the relationship between risk and sentence severity. As a result, there is certainly much more research to be done into public attitudes towards predictive sentencing. Such future work could focus on public preferences for rehabilitative interventions in conjunction with risk assessments. Apart from a wider focus on differential sentencing outcomes, replication of these first study findings is called for in this early pioneering phase. While our findings did not appear to be particularly sensitive to sample characteristics within the Netherlands (eg, law students versus the general population), it would be valuable to have replications of our studies with other Dutch samples over time. Moreover, we do not know whether our findings are restricted to the Dutch context. From cross-jurisdictional comparisons of survey questions concerning punitiveness (*cf* de Keijser and Elffers 2009), we do know that in using the same questions across jurisdictions, there are large similarities between the Dutch and the British, but also some notable differences. Cross-jurisdictional replications of our studies would shed light on this question. Also, as far as public attitudes within the context of specific crimes were addressed in our survey and experiments, we should be aware that other crime scenarios may generate different responses. Although the patterns and effects were broadly similar across the first two experiments, where we had changed the more severe crime from aggravated assault into DUI manslaughter, there are so many other types of crime that we do not know about in terms of public preferences for predictive sentencing. Future research should vary the types of crime.

To conclude, with the above reservations squarely in mind, while the normative aspects of predictive sentencing remain clearly contested, there is also reason to question the empirical legitimacy of the use of risk assessments at sentencing.

References

Baker, R, Blumberg, S, Brick, JM, Couper MP et al (2010). 'American Association for Public Opinion Research Report on Online Panels' 74 *Public Opinion Quarterly* 711.

Barker, V (2009) *The Politics of Imprisonment: How the Democratic Process Shapes the Way America Punishes Offenders* (Oxford, Oxford University Press).

Bibas, S (2012) *The Machinery of Criminal Justice* (Oxford, Oxford University Press).

Casey, S and Mohr, P (2005) 'Law-and-Order Politics, Public-Opinion Polls and the Media' 12 *Psychiatry, Psychology and Law* 141.

De Keijser, JW (2014) 'Penal Theory and Popular Opinion: The Deficiencies of Direct Engagement' in J Ryberg and JV Roberts (eds), *Popular Punishment: On the Normative Significance of Public Opinion* (New York, Oxford University Press).

De Keijser, JW, de Lange, EGM and van Wilsem, JA (2014) 'Wrongful Convictions and the Blackstone Ratio: An Empirical Analysis of Public Attitudes' 16 *Punishment & Society* 32.

De Keijser, JW and Elffers, H (2009) 'Public Punitive Attitudes: A Threat to the Legitimacy of the Criminal Justice System?' in ME Oswald, S Bieneck and J Hupfeld (eds), *Social Psychology of Punishment of Crime* (Chichester, John Wiley & Sons).

De Keijser, JW and Elffers H. (2008) 'Straffen in Context: Het Effect van Referentiekaders op de Publieke Opinie over Straf' 50 *Tijdschrift voor Criminologie* 233.

——. (2009) 'Cross-jurisdictional Differences in Punitive Public Attitudes?' 6 *European Journal on Criminal Policy and Research* 47.

De Keijser, JW, Elffers, H and van de Bunt, H G (2008) 'Responsive But Misunderstood: Dutch Judges on Their Relation to Society' in H Kury (ed), *Fear of Crime – Punitivity: New Developments in Theory and Research* (Bochum, Universitätsverlag Dr N Brockmeyer).

De Keijser, JW and van Koppen, PJ (2007) 'Paradoxes of Proof and Punishment: Psychological Pitfalls in Judicial Decision Making' 12 *Legal and Criminological Psychology* 189.

De Keijser, JW, van Koppen, PJ and Elffers, H (2007) 'Bridging the Gap between Judges and the Public? A Multi-method Study' 3 *Journal of Experimental Criminology* 131.

Dzur, A (2012) *Punishment, Participatory Democracy, and the Jury* (New York, Oxford University Press).

Green, DA (2006) 'Public Opinion versus Public Judgment about Crime: Correcting the "Comedy of Errors"' 46 *British Journal of Criminology* 131.

Hannah-Moffat, K (2013) 'Actuarial Sentencing: An "Unsettled" Proposition' 30 *Justice Quarterly* 270.

Hester, R, Roberts, JV, Frase, RS and Mitchell, K (2017) 'A Measure of Tolerance: Public Attitudes on Sentencing Enhancements for Old and Juvenile Prior Records' 3 *Corrections* 137.

Hinsch, W (2008) 'Legitimacy and Justice' in J Kuhnelt (ed), *Political Legitimation without Morality* (London, Springer).

Hough, M and Roberts, JV (2012) 'Public Opinion, Crime and Criminal Justice' in M Maguire, R Morgan and R Reiner (eds), *The Oxford Handbook of Criminology* (Oxford, Oxford University Press).

Kahneman, D, Slovic, P and Tversky, A (1982) *Judgment under Uncertainty: Heuristics and Biases* (Cambridge, Cambridge University Press).

Kopkin, MR, Brodsky, SL and DeMatteo, D (2017) 'Risk Assessment in Sentencing Decisions: A Remedy to Mass Incarceration?' 9 *Journal of Aggression Conflict and Peace Research* 155.

Kypri, K and Gallagher, SJ (2003) 'Incentives to Increase Participation in an Internet Survey of Alcohol Use: A Controlled Experiment' 38 *Alcohol and Alcoholism* 437.

Laguilles, JS, Williams, EA and Saunders, DB (2011) 'Can Lottery Incentives Boost Web Survey Response Rates? Findings from Four Experiments' 52 *Research in Higher Education* 537.

Lippke, RL (2008) 'No Easy Way out: Dangerous Offenders and Preventive Detention' 27 *Law and Philosophy* 383.

Mills, JF, Kroner, DG and Morgan, RD (2011) *Clinician's Guide to Violence Risk Assessment* (New York, Guilford Press).

Mirrlees-Black, C (2002) 'Improving Public Knowledge about Crime and Punishment' in JV Roberts and M Hough (eds), *Changing Attitudes to Punishment: Public Opinion, Crime and Justice* (Cullompton, Willan).

Monahan, J and Ruggiero, M (1980) 'Psychological and Psychiatric Aspects of Determinate Criminal Sentencing' 3 *International Journal of Law and Psychiatry* 143.

Nonet, P and Selznick, P (1978) *Law and Society in Transition* (New York, Harper & Row).

Otto, RK and Douglas, KS (eds) (2010) *Handbook of Violence Risk Assessment* (New York, Routledge).

Richardson, JTE (2011) 'Eta Squared and Partial Eta Squared as Measurements of Effect Size in Educational Research' 6 *Educational Research Review* 135.

Roberts, JV (1992) 'Public Opinion, Crime, and Criminal Justice' 16 *Crime and Justice: A Review of Research* 99.

Roberts, JV and de Keijser, JW (2014) 'Democratising Punishment: Sentencing, Community Views and Values' 16 *Punishment & Society* 474.

Roberts, JV and Hough, M (2005) *Understanding Public Attitudes to Criminal Justice* (Maidenhead, Open University Press).

Roberts, JV and Plesničar, MM (2015) 'Sentencing, Legitimacy, and Public Opinion' in G Meško and J Tankebe (eds), *Trust and Legitimacy in Criminal Justice: European Perspectives* (New York, Springer).

Robinson, P (2013) *Intuitions of Justice and the Utility of Desert* (New York, Oxford University Press).
Robinson, PH and Darley, JM (1997) 'The Utility of Desert' 91 *Northwestern University Law Review* 453.
Scurich, N and Monahan, J (2016) 'Evidence-Based Sentencing: Public Openness and Opposition to Using Gender, Age, and Race as Risk Factors for Recidivism' 40 *Law and Human Behavior* 36.
Slobogin, C and Brinkley-Rubinstein, L (2013) 'Putting Desert in its Place' 65 *Stanford Law Review* 77.
Shepherd, SM and Willis-Esqueda, C (2018) 'Indigenous Perspectives on Violence Risk Assessment: A Thematic Analysis' *Punishment & Society*, doi.org/10.1177%2F1462474517721485.
Singh, AM and Sprott, JB (2017) 'Race Matters: Public Views on Sentencing' 59 *Canadian Journal of Criminology and Criminal Justice* 285.
Skeem, J, Monahan, J and Lowenkamp, C (2016) 'Gender, Risk Assessment, and Sanctioning: The Cost of Treating Women Like Men' 40 *Law and Human Behavior* 580.
Stalans, LJ (2002) 'Measuring Attitudes to Sentencing' in JV Roberts and M Hough (eds), *Changing Attitudes to Punishment* (Cullompton, Willan).
Starr, SB (2014) 'Evidence-Based Sentencing and the Scientific Rationalization of Discrimination' 66 *Stanford Law Review* 803.
Tonry, M (1999) 'Rethinking Unthinking Punishments Policies in America' 46 *UCLA Law Review* 1751.
Tyler, TR (1990) *Why People Obey the Law* (New Haven, Yale University Press).
Van Wingerden, SGC (2014) *Sentencing in the Netherlands: Taking Risk-Related Offender Characteristics into Account* (The Hague, Eleven International).

Appendix 1 Vignettes Used in the Experiments (Translated from Dutch)

Aggravated assault in gym (Experiments 1 and 3)
On 2 May, Eric has just finished working out in the gym where he has a weekly session. He is tired from working out and has just packed his things to go home. He picks up his sports bag and wants to walk out when Pieter passes by. Eric has not noticed Pieter and accidentally bumps into him. As a result, Pieter spills the sporting drink that he was holding on his white sports trousers, which become soaked and dirty. Pieter yells at Erik that he is 'an asshole who is blind'. Then Eric loses his self-control and pushes Pieter hard. Pieter trips over one of the pieces of fitness apparatus and falls backwards on the ground. Eric, who is still furious, starts kicking Pieter very hard while he is lying defenceless on the ground. Eric keeps on kicking until Pieter finally loses consciousness. In the meantime, the manager of the gym has arrived. He immediately calls 911 while Eric runs away. Pieter is taken to the hospital by an ambulance, where his injuries are treated. Somewhat later, Eric is arrested by the police in his house. Eric is being prosecuted for aggravated assault.

Residential burglary during a holiday (Experiments 1, 2 and 3)
On 18 July, Harry and Liesbeth van Dam arrive at home from their holiday in Spain. At the door, they immediately notice that it has been opened by force. The house has been burgled during their absence. Several items, including a laptop and a DVD player, are missing. Harry and Liesbeth immediately call the police to report the burglary.
The police investigate and soon find Mark, the perpetrator. On the night of 15 July, Mark had forced open the door and took off with the items. He had noticed a large quantity of mail in the mailbox and concluded that the residents had been absent for a while, so the house would be an easy target. Nevertheless, the police quickly found Mark and took him to the station for questioning. Mark is being prosecuted for residential burglary.

DUI with fatal consequences (Experiment 2)
Mariska (18) is on her way home after a night out. She is walking to the nearest tram stop. When the traffic light at a pedestrian crossing turns green, she walks across and does not notice a car approaching at high speed. The car does not reduce its speed, ignores a red traffic light and runs into Mariska. Mariska dies on the spot. The driver of the car, Peter, drives on. Bystanders saw it happening and make a note of the car's number plate. Peter is arrested that same night at his home. It turns out that Peter has twice the legal maximum of alcohol in his blood. At the police station, he states that his friends at the bar had warned him not to drive, but that he felt good and it only was a short ride home. Peter claims he had not noticed the red traffic sign, nor had he seen Mariska on the pedestrian crossing. When he realised that he had hit someone, he drove on in shock. Peter is being prosecuted for manslaughter.

The probation service has examined [Eric's/Mark's/Peter's] living situation and criminal history. This examination shows that it is very unlikely that [Eric/Mark/Peter] will commit any more crimes.

The probation service has examined [Eric's/Mark's/Peter's] living situation and criminal history. This examination shows that it is very likely that [Eric/Mark/Peter] will commit new crimes.

Only in Experiment 3:

However, risk assessments do not provide certainty that someone will or will not re-offend. In 10 per cent of cases, the risk assessment proves to be wrong.

However, risk assessments do not provide certainty that someone will or will not re-offend. In 40 per cent of cases, the risk assessment proves to be wrong.

What is the length of the prison term you would impose?

Appendix 2 Tables and Statistics

Table A1 Survey: Spearman's correlation coefficients between agreement on predictive sentencing statements and importance of sentencing goals in general

	Retribution	Incapacitation	Rehabilitation	Deterrence	Reparation
1. Risk of re-offending cannot be taken into account at sentencing	−0.07	−0.17**	0.15**	−0.07	−0.03
2. An offender with a high risk of re-offending deserves a more severe punishment	0.25**	0.27**	−0.26**	0.27**	0.12**
3. An offender with a low risk of re-offending deserves a less severe punishment	−0.07	0.06	−0.05	0.03	0.05
4. If it were certain that the offender would not commit new crimes, there is no use for punishment	−0.15**	−0.24**	0.08	−0.09*	−0.14**
5. In order to protect society, high-risk offenders should be punished more severely	0.24**	0.34**	−0.23**	0.31**	0.21**
6. For severe crimes, offender's risk of re-offending should play a greater role at sentencing than for less severe crimes	0.14**	0.27**	−0.05	0.26**	0.15**
7. An offender who stole a bicycle and who has a high risk of re-offending should be punished more severely than he deserves considering the low seriousness level of the crime	0.11*	0.03	−0.11**	0.17**	0.03
8. A murderer who has a low risk of re-offending should be punished less severely than he deserves considering the high seriousness level of the crime	−0.23**	−0.13**	0.13**	−0.12**	−0.08*

* $p<.05$, ** $p<.01$.

Table A2 Repeated measures and univariate ANOVAs, and effect sizes[A]

Effects	**F**		**Partial η^2**
Experiment 1			
Main effects			
Crime seriousness	F(1, 124)=	278.96**	0.69
Risk	F(2, 124)=	5.80**	0.09
Interaction effect			
Crime seriousness × Risk	F(2, 124)=	0.14	0.00
Experiment 2			
Main effects			
Crime seriousness	F(1, 261)=	977.12**	0.79
Risk	F(2, 261)=	2.09	0.02
Interaction effect			
Crime seriousness × Risk	F(2, 261)=	0.73	0.01
Experiment 3[B]			
Main effects			
Crime seriousness	F(1, 337)=	294.50**	0.47
Risk	F(2, 337)=	3.82*	0.02
Interaction effects			
Crime seriousness × Risk	F(2, 337)=	0.88	0.01
Risk × Error info	F(2, 216)=	1.04	0.01
Crime seriousness × Risk × Error info	F(2, 216)=	0.49	0.01
Per crime scenario (univariate): *Interaction risk × Error info*			
– Burglary	F(2, 224)=	0.68	0.01
– Assault	F(2, 224)=	1.04	0.01

* p<.05. ** p<.01

[A] Suggested norms for effect size as represented by *Partial* η^2: small = 0.01; medium = 0.06; large = 0.14 (*cf* Richardson 2011).

[B] Analyses including the factor 'Error info' only carried out for those respondents who received (high or low) risk information.

14

Sentencing and Prediction

*Old Wine in Old Bottles**

MICHAEL TONRY

People's views about the use of predictions of future violence in sentencing sometimes appear to be irreconcilable, as two high-profile exchanges demonstrate. Hart, Michie and Cooke (2007) evaluated the use of several well-known instruments and concluded that the 'group and individual risk estimates' they produce are too wide to be useful. The predictions are too often wrong, they said; using them does serious unjustifiable harm to individuals who would not have been violent. Imrey and Dawid (2015) responded, insisting that the best-known instruments, their results and their applications are based on sound statistical practice.

Imrey and Dawid did not understand, or pretended not to understand, the critics' objection. Individuals are not treated unjustly, they wrote: decisions are 'individualized'. A judge saying that would mean that he or she took into account all available information concerning a particular individual and thought carefully about what to do. What Imrey and Dawid meant was that 'individualized risk [is] derived from an external group and projected onto the subject' (2015: 39); that is, the riskiness attributed to an individual is not his or her own, but the average of a group of which he or she is a member. They distinguished this from 'latent individual risk intrinsic to the subject herself', which though obscurely phrased is what individualised usually means.

The second exchange began when Angwin et al (2016) analysed Broward County, Florida data on use of COMPAS, a proprietary prediction instrument. Their title tells their conclusion: 'There's Software Used across the Country to Predict Future Criminals. And it's Biased against Blacks.' Their three key findings: Blacks had higher average risk scores than Whites, relatively more Blacks than Whites were wrongly predicted to be violent (exposing them to harsher treatment),

* I am grateful to John Monahan, Jan de Keijser and Douglas Husak for insightful comments on drafts, and to Richard Berk and John Monahan for guiding me to the pertinent specialist literature. A somewhat different, extended version of this chapter appears in M Tonry (ed), *Crime and Justice: A Review of Research*, vol 48 (Chicago, University of Chicago Press, 2019).

and relatively fewer Blacks than Whites were wrongly predicted to be non-violent (making them less eligible for milder treatment). These foreseeable racial disparities are what the critics meant by 'bias'.

Flores, Bechtel and Lowenkamp (2016) did not refute the racial-disparity findings, but insisted that the critics had not shown *statistical* bias. Blacks have higher crime rates than Whites, they explained, and more often have socio-economic and other characteristics correlated with offending: no bias, just sound statistical practice. They sidestepped the critics' objections.

Talented, passionate people were on both sides of those exchanges, but could not find common ground. The prediction defenders viewed the issues as primarily technical let the chips fall where they may. The critics viewed the issues as primarily substantive: knowingly treating Black people more harshly than Whites is wrong.

Many faultlines permeate prediction debates. Some consider it irresponsible not to use state-of-the-art prediction methods. Others believe that punishments should be closely proportioned to offenders' blameworthiness and that it is unjust to punish some more severely than others because of predictions. Still others believe that reducing the use of imprisonment depends on identifying offenders likeliest to re-offend and locking them up, so that others need not be. Some people believe that racial, ethnic and class disparities caused and exacerbated by prediction instruments are morally wrong and want them to end.

In writing the preceding paragraphs, I tried to avoid polemic. The facts, ma'am, just the facts, as Sergeant Joe Friday used to say. I did not mention assertions that political and ideological agendas, and racial, ethnic and class biases, both conscious and implicit, underlay adoption in the US of incapacitative crime control policies, including the increased use of prediction. Those allegations may be true, but here I set them aside. My interest is in the intellectual challenge posed by widely different, good-faith views about prediction and whether and how they can be reconciled.

The difficulty, as Isaiah Berlin (2002) explained long ago, is that the implications of equally valid first principles often conflict. Few would disagree that the maintenance of public order and security is a good thing. Were that the only relevant consideration, it would be self-evident that efforts to diminish crime's effects on victims should be maximised.

However, other no less important values are at stake. If assuring that offenders be punished precisely as much as they deserve was all that mattered, predictions about future offending would be irrelevant. If only equal treatment mattered, people convicted of equally serious crimes should be punished equally severely; predictions would again be irrelevant. If avoidance of policies that cause or aggravate racial and ethnic disparities, or that rely on factors tinged with invidious bias, was overridingly important, all existing prediction systems would have to be abandoned.

The values underlying all of those things matter and they conflict. People resolve the conflicts in different ways. Some allow one goal to trump others (eg, reducing mass incarceration: Flores, Bechtel and Lowenkamp 2016; reducing social and racial injustice: Harcourt 2008; preventing crime: Slobogin, Chapter 7 in this volume). Peter Imrey and Philip Dawid (2015: 40), in an article sometimes described as the leading statistical work on actuarial risk assessment instruments, observe: 'If groups of individuals with high and low propensities for violence recidivism can be distinguished, and courts act upon such distinctions, recidivism will decline to the extent that groups most prone to violence are incapacitated … And both society and offenders will be better served even if we cannot be sure … from precisely which individual offenders this betterment derives.' Offenders who are imprisoned, or held longer, because they were mistakenly predicted to be violent are seldom likely to agree that they have been 'better served'.

Some writers acknowledge the problem but take no position. When writing about punishment theory generally, Douglas Husak (forthcoming) observes: 'Sentencing according to the principle of proportionality is crucial if the state is to treat offenders as they deserve.' However, concerning risk prediction, he adopts a 'pluralist' stance and writes: 'Retributivists should preserve the role of desert while weakening its strength … We can preserve proportionality, but allow exceptions when we have a good rationale for them … If we have good reason to inflict different amounts of punishment on two offenders who have committed equally serious crimes, we should not be worried that our decision does not preserve proportionality … Admittedly, the results produced [may be] messy; sentencing, like morality more generally, is not governed by an algorithm' (Husak, Chapter 3 in this volume).[1]

Not everyone sidesteps. Monahan and Skeem (2016; see also Monahan 2017) survey the literature, work through all the major problems and propose ways to limit unwanted effects of prediction (notably by allowing them to be used to reduce, but not to increase sentence severity).[2] Berk et al (2018: 1), in the latest of a series of increasingly subtle analyses of trade-offs between ethical issues and predictive accuracy, observe: 'Except in trivial cases, it is impossible to maximize accuracy and fairness at the same time, and impossible simultaneously to satisfy all kinds of fairness.' However, they too throw up their hands: 'In the end, it will fall to stakeholders – not criminologists, not statisticians and not computer scientists – to determine the tradeoffs … These are matters of values and law, and ultimately, the political process' (Berk et al 2018: 33). This is not terribly helpful or reassuring to anyone concerned about the just treatment of individuals. The political process produced mass incarceration and three-strikes, life without parole and similar laws.

[1] The newest and purportedly most accurate prediction devices employing Big Data and machine learning *are* algorithms (Berk et al 2018; Kleinberg et al 2018).

[2] However, this does not reduce racial and class disparities. Minority and lower social class offenders systematically score worse on risk prediction instruments and are thus less likely to benefit from mitigated sentences predicated on 'good' risk scores.

In this chapter, I examine fundamental issues raised by the use of prediction instruments in sentencing.[3] Mostly I discuss predictions of violence. Re-offending is so common among chronic minor property, drug, prostitution and public disorder offenders that the use of predictive incapacitation strategies would generate palpably unjust punishments for minor crimes. Blumstein, Farrington and Moitra (1985) long ago showed that the probability of a subsequent arrest exceeds 90 per cent for anyone who had been arrested eight or more times. Section I canvasses familiar objections, including the instruments' inaccuracy; their reliance on ascribed characteristics such as age and gender;[4] their use of status characteristics such as education, marital status and employment; and their reliance on criminal history indicators that are based in large part on discriminatory police practices. All of the practices discussed systematically disadvantage poor and minority offenders relative to White and more privileged offenders.

Section II addresses justifications offered for predictive sentencing. One is that normative considerations related to punishment theories are too contested, unrealistic or indeterminate to guide real-world decisions. Another is that racial, ethnic, age and gender disparities caused by predictions are not troubling because they reflect real differences between groups. A third is that predictive sentencing raises issues that are indistinguishable from public health quarantines and the use of actuarial predictions in medicine, public health, credit scoring and insurance. A fourth is that predictive sentencing is an essential tool for the minimisation of crime.

In the final section, I show diverse ways competing claims and aspirations can be reconciled. I also discuss the realpolitik claims that predictions will be used one way or another, that crime is too emotional a topic for rational argument and analyses to be relevant, and accordingly that there is no point in explaining why predictive sentencing is unjust. I disagree with all those propositions. Better that officials treating other human beings unjustly be reminded again and again that that is what they are doing. Someday they may want and decide to do better.

This is not an unworldly aspiration. Conventional beliefs change. Some American southerners before the Civil War and during the Jim Crow period consistently opposed racial discrimination on moral grounds. Theirs eventually became the prevailing view. Early feminists and sympathisers, notably including John Stuart Mill (1997 [1869]), argued, again against the odds, that subordination of women is wrong. This became the prevailing view. Other countries' criminal law systems are committed to ideas of proportionality and equal treatment that leave

[3] I discuss some of these issues in fuller detail elsewhere (Tonry 1987, 2014a).

[4] Changes in gender self-identification are more common or more often declared in our time than in earlier times. However, it remains relatively rare and in the text, I use 'gender' in its traditional bimodal sense. Inevitably, though, the issue will be raised in individual cases, in which gender attributions matter, whether individuals may or must be categorised according to birth-identified or self-identified gender (including none).

little room for predictive sentencing (eg, in Scandinavia; Lappi-Seppälä 2016). This may someday happen in the US.

I. The Indictment

Three sets of problems bedevil the use of predictions in sentencing. The first is that they are seldom very accurate. When the aim is to predict serious sexual or other violence, more predictions are wrong ('false positives') than are right ('true positives'). If used to determine prison sentence lengths, many people who would not have committed serious violence will be held longer. The second set of problems concerns the variables used in nearly all prediction instruments: some over which individuals have no control, such as age and gender, are fundamentally unjust; some concern inherently personal matters such as marriage, work and education; and some relate to aspects of criminal records that are contaminated by conscious and implicit bias and discriminatory practices. The third set of problems concerns racial and ethnic disparities; almost all variables used in prediction instruments correlate with race and ethnicity and inexorably make punishments of members of minority groups harsher than those of Whites.

A. Accuracy

Violence is rare, even among known offenders. Predicting rare events accurately is inherently difficult. As a result, the technology of violence prediction is not very good. The predictions are more often inaccurate than accurate. I was astonished to learn, when reviewing the contemporary literature as background for writing this chapter, that accuracy is little better now than it was four decades ago.

Norval Morris (1974), in an influential early synthesis, concluded that predictions of future violence were wrong two-thirds of the time. The most exhaustive contemporaneous analysis by psychologist John Monahan (1981) reached the same conclusion. Predictions that people will not be violent were overwhelmingly correct, but that is trivial: if only 10 per cent are violent, a prediction that no one will commit a violent crime will be correct 90 per cent of the time. Morris argued that the then current knowledge did not justify imposing longer prison terms on people predicted to be violent: '"Dangerousness" must be rejected for this purpose, since it presupposes a capacity to predict future criminal behaviour quite beyond our present technical ability' (1974: 62). Locking up three people predicted to be violent when only one will be is, he said, deeply unjust. Two would be wrongfully deprived of extended periods of freedom.

Analyses of prediction studies conventionally distinguish, as Morris did, between true and false positives. True positives are predicted to re-offend and do. False positives are predicted to re-offend, but do not. True and false negatives are defined similarly. In Morris' time, the state of the predictive art, as Table 14.1 shows using Morris' example, was that two-thirds of individuals predicted to be violent were false positives.

Table 14.1 Violence prediction, true and false positives and negatives: an illustration

Crime Type	Prediction	Result – no violence	Result – violence
No violence	70	65 (true negatives)	5 (false negatives)
Violence	30	20 (false positives)	10 (true positives)
Total	100	85	15

Source: adapted from Morris (1974: Table 1).

The technology of violence prediction is vastly more sophisticated than it was four decades ago. The early studies were based on clinical predictions by doctors, mental health specialists, judges and correctional personnel. The contemporary literature is actuarial and based on mathematical models, sophisticated statistical analyses, machine learning and 'Big Data'. One might expect that violence predictions today would be vastly more accurate than in the 1970s. They aren't.

One leading meta-analysis concludes that further improvements in accuracy are unlikely: 'After almost five decades of developing risk prediction tools, the evidence increasingly suggests that the ceiling of predictive efficacy may have been reached with the available technology' (Yang, Wong and Coid 2010: 759). Consistently with this caution, two major meta-analyses conclude that the most commonly used violence prediction instruments are indistinguishable in terms of their accuracy.[5]

The most influential meta-analysis, analysing research on the nine most commonly used instruments, concluded that positive violence predictions are on average correct 42 per cent of the time (Fazel et al 2012; Fazel, Chapter 11 in this volume). Morris, let us recall, was troubled that only one-third of positive predictions (two of six) were correct. Fazel et al's 42 per cent, put differently, is that two out of five positive predictions are correct. As in Morris' time, substantially more than half of people predicted to be violent will not be.

Two of the leading meta-analyses conclude that positive predictions of future violence are too inaccurate to be used in sentencing:

> Because of their moderate level of predictive efficacy, they should not be used as the sole or primary means for clinical or criminal justice decision making that is contingent

[5] Yang, Wong and Coid (2010: 259): 'If prediction of violence is the only criterion for the selection of a risk assessment tool, then the tools included in the present study are essentially interchangeable.' Campbell, French and Gendreau (2009: 253): 'This analysis found little difference among the predictive validities of actuarial and structured instruments for violent reoffending.' Meta-analyses of research on instruments used to predict any, as opposed to only violent, re-offending reach the same conclusion: 'Overall, no one instrument stood out as producing more accurate assessments than the others, with validity varying with the indicator reported' (Desmarais, Johnson and Singh 2016: 213).

> on a high level of predictive accuracy, such as preventive detention. (Yang, Wong and Coid 2010: 761)
>
> These tools are not sufficient on their own for the purposes of risk assessment … The current level of evidence is not sufficiently strong for definitive decisions on sentencing, parole, and release or discharge to be made solely using these tools. (Fazel et al 2012: 5, 6)

Even outspoken defenders of risk prediction agree. Flores, Bechtel and Lowenkamp (2016: 39), whom I discussed above concerning disagreements about racial bias, emphasised that 'we want to make it clear that we are not supporting or endorsing the idea of using risk assessment at sentencing'.

There is thus no credible scientific case to be made in favour of the use of predictions of future violence in sentencing.

B. Unjust Variables

Except for race and, though they are seldom explicitly discussed, presumably also ethnicity, nationality and religion, developers of prediction instruments include as variables any offence and offender characteristics on which they can obtain data. In other public policy settings – for example, education, public health and medical research – equivalent strategies including the use even of racial and other usually verboten data makes sense. The aims are to improve public services generally, to understand and address problems affecting subpopulations or to diagnose and treat individual health problems.

Violence prediction in courts is different.[6] The aim is usually to identify high-risk individuals for pre-trial or post-conviction preventive detention (though as Monahan (2017) argues, it could in theory be used to identify low-risk individuals for more humane treatment; I will discuss this below). Public health and educational research and related policies seldom target individuals. Medical decision making does, but the aim is to attempt to prevent or minimise human suffering. Sentencing decisions are intended to cause human suffering. That is why Jeremy Bentham called all punishment, even when warranted, 'evil'.

Suspect variables fall into three categories. Race, gender and age ought to be off-limits because they are basic human characteristics for which individuals bear no causal, personal or moral responsibility. Increased punishments for any of these reasons are per se unjust. A host of socio-economic characteristics,

[6] Different considerations may be pertinent concerning some uses of prediction instruments in correctional settings. Some 'culturally appropriate' treatment programmes, for example, target the special needs of women or members of specific minority groups. Other treatment programmes target 'higher-risk' offenders on the efficiency rationale that low-risk offenders will usually not re-offend, whether or not they participate. Prediction instruments are used to match offenders to treatment programmes generally, to set or vary treatment or supervision intensity and to measure changes relative to programme goals. They are also used in institutional custody-level decisions, which may raise issues similar to those concerning sentencing.

including employment, education, marital status, living arrangements and parental responsibilities, are correlated with offending, but are not the criminal law's business. These are matters of individual choice in a free society. Punishing people for making the 'wrong' choices is also per se unjust. Socio-economic status (SES) and other personal characteristics, including many related to criminal history, are highly correlated with race and ethnicity; many are shaped by invidious discrimination. Their use causes and exacerbates adverse racial and ethnic disparities.

C. Immutable Characteristics

No one would think that people should be punished more severely because of their eye or hair colour or adult height, characteristics over which they have no control. Gender, race and ethnicity, and age raise the same issue – so, despite their greater mutability, would religion and nationality most of the time.

i. Age

Individuals have no more control of their age than of their eye colour. Mentally responsible individuals do have control over their behaviour. All other things being equal, the age of an offender should not matter, with one major exception.[7] Traditionally in all Western countries, including the US, young offenders have been punished less severely than adults and usually in specialised courts using specialised procedures.[8]

The reasons for this are self-evident. Most young offenders are less experienced and mature than most adults, are at a developmental stage during which risk taking, thrill seeking and experimentation are common and are more malleable.[9] Research on 'age/crime curves' and desistance has long shown that

[7] The other exception is advanced age. Many European countries have created strong legal presumptions against imprisonment of the elderly (typically 70 or older). That is why former Italian Prime Minister Silvio Berlusconi was sentenced to community service as a hospital orderly rather than to the multi-year prison sentence he would otherwise have received following conviction for public corruption offences. As the Madoff Ponzi scheme and Bill Cosby cases and the reluctance of most American prisons to release terminally ill and elderly prisoners demonstrate, the US, as in many penal policy matters, is an outlier.

[8] In Western European countries, for example, the age of criminal responsibility is typically 14 or 15 (in Belgium 18 for most offences). In most, waiver of young offenders to adult courts is not legally possible, nor is direct prosecution in adult courts. In German courts, the vast majority of 18 and 19-year-olds convicted of serious crimes are sentenced as if they were juveniles (Tonry and Chambers 2012).

[9] Douglas Husak (personal communication) notes that not all young offenders have the characteristics that I describe and that some adults do. This is no doubt true, but not insoluble. In American juvenile courts, prosecutors and judges almost always have authority to refer especially difficult cases to adult courts (in most European legal systems, this is not possible; even especially difficult cases must be handled within the juvenile system). Conversely, judges and prosecutors have authority, and decent ones exercise it, to take account of the emotional immaturity and cognitive impairment of adults.

many adolescents commit crimes as teenagers, but most soon desist (the classic sources are Farrington (1986) and Laub and Sampson (2001)). Recent neurological and developmental research has documented details of adolescent brain development and behavioural controls that strengthen the rationale for more forgiving handling of young offenders (Monahan, Steinberg and Piquero 2015). Even the conservative US Supreme Court is convinced. Banning mandatory life sentences without parole for juveniles, it emphasised that 'children are constitutionally different from adults for purposes of sentencing' and that 'mandatory penalties, by their nature, preclude a sentence from taking account of an offender's age and the wealth of characteristics and circumstances attendant to it'.[10]

Nonetheless, youth is widely used as a variable in prediction instruments and as an aggravating factor in sentencing. I discuss Virginia's notorious sentencing guidelines, which have been in use for more than 25 years, because they are premised on prediction-based incapacitation. They call, all other things being equal, for harsher punishments for younger than for older offenders. This is wrong in principle and, in light of a growing body of research showing that imprisonment is criminogenic, perverse (eg, Nagin, Cullen and Lero Jonson 2009).

The Virginia guidelines set out criteria that identify non-violent offenders for whom prison sentences are specified, but whom judges are encouraged to divert to community-based punishments. In fraud guidelines,[11] 22 'points' are given for being aged 20 or younger (Virginia Sentencing Commission 2014). Being male adds 10 more points, for a total of 32. Only offenders who receive 31 or fewer points qualify for diversion; thus, no matter how minor the offence or the criminal record, no male under 21 meets the diversion criteria.

Virginia's remarkable treatment of young people becomes starker when compared with provisions for offenders aged 30 and over; they receive seven 'age points'. Five points are given for having one or two prior felony convictions and four points for having been incarcerated as an adult one to nine times. Put it together: a 30-year-old (7 points) male (10) with two prior felony convictions (5) and two prior adult incarcerations (4) totals 26 points and satisfies the diversion criteria. An 18-year-old with no criminal record does not.

There are three explanations for this strange policy. First, Virginia's guidelines were developed at the height of the 'tough on crime' period under the administration of Republican Governor George Allen, who ran for office on a 'parole abolition' platform (Tonry 2016). They were developed under the leadership of former US Attorney General William Barr, author while in office of the 1992 tract *The Case for More Incarceration* (1992). Second, selective incapacitation had long before been repudiated as a crime control strategy by the National Academy of Sciences (Blumstein et al 1986), but Barr nonetheless made incapacitation the

[10] *Miller v Alabama* 132 S Ct 2455, 2467 (2012).

[11] The details are slightly different for larceny. Being male adds nine, not 10 points. The system is otherwise similar.

premise for the Virginia guidelines. Third, because of the age/crime curve, age is a powerful predictor of future offending (though most offences involve property or drugs and most young offenders soon desist).

The more general question is whether age should be included in any prediction instrument meant to be used, or that might be used, in deciding whom to imprison or for how long. The trade-off is between predictive accuracy and punishing people because they are young. If the trade-off concerned eye colour, race or religion, few people would consider it. Even if any of them predicted re-offending, basic requirements of justice forbid their use. Age is equally inappropriate.

ii. Gender

Gender cuts in different directions in different contexts. Assiduous efforts are made in education, employment and public health to prevent or minimise differential treatment of women. This is so even when actuarial justifications exist. Because they typically live longer than men, women traditionally paid lower life insurance premiums, but also received lower monthly pension benefits. Those practices have been attacked as unjust, increasingly successfully, despite their actuarial justifications. So have higher automobile insurance premiums paid by men.

The early American sentencing commissions commissioned research on past sentencing patterns and invariably found that women typically received less severe punishments than men. However, no commission chose to promulgate separate, less severe guidelines for women or to make gender a mitigating factor. Gender-blind guidelines were expected to increase sentence severity for women, but everyone involved agreed that was required by respect for gender equality (eg, Knapp 1984; Tonry 1996).

Gender blindness is a powerful idea. Treating people differently because they are male or female is wrong in the same way that treating people differently because they are of a particular race or religion is wrong. Gender blindness is sometimes set aside for sympathetic policy reasons. Examples targeting women include healthcare, maternity leaves, flexible work schedules and childcare. Even with such policies, movements are afoot as a matter of fairness to make comparable policies available to men. What distinguishes these gender-conscious policies is that they aim to do something for women, not to them. They do not aim to treat men worse, but to meet the gender-specific needs of women.

This has not stopped developers of prediction instruments from incorporating maleness as a factor. Nor has it stopped policy makers from using maleness, all other things being equal, to increase punishment severity. The 10 points given under the Virginia fraud guidelines for being male (compared with one point for being female) is an example. Theft and drug sale guidelines vary in detail, but all treat men and women differently.

The rationale is actuarial. Across crime, time and country, men's offending rates are higher than women's. Locking up more otherwise comparable men than women will predictably prevent more future offences. However, just as with eye colour, race, ethnicity and age, that cannot justify punishing some equally culpable offenders more severely than others.

iii. Race and Ethnicity

No American jurisdiction explicitly incorporates race or ethnicity into criteria for sentencing or parole release. Many do so indirectly through the use of socio-economic and criminal history variables that are correlated with race and ethnicity. On average, Black and Hispanic Americans have lower incomes, weaker employment records, less extensive educations and less residential stability compared to Whites. All are correlated with higher offending risks. This is one major reason why prediction instruments produce higher false positive rates for Blacks than for Whites and higher false negative rates for Whites than for Blacks. Table 14.2, showing the false positive and false negative rates calculated by Flores, Bechtel and Lowenkamp (2016) in their re-analysis of COMPAS data illustrates this. Half of new arrests of Whites were people predicted not to re-offend, compared with only 28 per cent of Black arrestees. Conversely, only 22 per cent of Whites who were not arrested were predicted to be re-arrested, compared with 42 per cent of Blacks. The false positive rate for Blacks was twice that for Whites.

Table 14.2 Prediction errors, any arrest within two years, by race: an illustration

	False positive rates	False negative rates
Whites	22%	50%
Blacks	42%	28%

Source: Flores, Bechtel and Lowenkamp (2016: Table 3).

Anyone who believes in equal justice should oppose reliance on the use of race-skewing variables in sentencing generally, including in prediction instruments. That is why, more than 30 years ago, the US Parole Commission removed socio-economic variables from its prediction instrument, even though that weakened its accuracy (Hoffman 1983).[12]

Bernard Harcourt (2008) has shown that predictive sentencing has a ratchet effect that worsens racial and socio-economic disparities. When risk predictions are used, minority and disadvantaged defendants are treated more severely than others the first time they are convicted. Each subsequent conviction has compounding effects and further increases increments of additional severity that they suffer. Racial differences in criminal history are a primary cause of racial disparities in imprisonment (Hester et al 2018).

[12] The US Parole Commission was concerned for decades about racial skewing in the use of its Salient Factor Score (Hoffman 1976, 1983, 1995).

Correlations between offending and race and ethnicity are not random. Crime rates for many offences are higher for Blacks than for Whites. The social and economic disadvantages that disproportionately afflict Black and Hispanic people in America, and are correlated with offending, are partly the results of historical and ongoing discrimination and of diminished life chances at birth. Mentally responsible minority offenders, like other offenders, should be punished as they deserve for the offences they commit; few people disagree.[13] However, it should be at least discomforting that the use of SES factors in prediction instruments exacerbates the effects of disadvantage and causes minority offenders to be punished more harshly than they deserve.

D. Socio-economic Characteristics

All of the early sentencing commissions rejected the use of socio-economic variables in their sentencing guidelines systems. Section 994(d) of the Sentencing Reform Act of 1984, for example, explicitly directed the federal sentencing commission: 'The Commission shall assure that the guidelines and policy statements are entirely neutral as to the race, sex, national origin, creed, and socioeconomic status of offenders.' Section 994(e) elaborates: 'The Commission shall assure that the guidelines and policy statements, in recommending a term of imprisonment or length of a term of imprisonment, reflect the general inappropriateness of considering the education, vocational skills, employment record, family ties and responsibilities, and community ties of the defendant.'

The US Congress and other early sentencing commissions forbade the use of socio-economic factors because using them is unjust. Even the Virginia Sentencing Commission, not renowned for its sensitivity to moral issues, removed the SES factors – employment and marital status – initially included in its diversion guidelines (Ostrom and Kauder 2012). The correlation of many SES characteristics with race makes their use doubly unjust. Whether an offender is rich or poor, well or inadequately educated, married or single has nothing to do with blameworthiness.

There is another fundamental reason to object to the use of socio-economic and similar characteristics as reasons for harsher punishment. Many result from legitimate lifestyle choices, including whether to marry, obtain higher education or hold a steady job, that in a free society are not the state's business. Maintenance of public order and security is given high priority in a free society so that citizens can live their lives in peace and as they wish.

Committing offences, selling illicit drugs and actively participating in criminal gangs also reflect personal choices, but they are choices of a different kind. So are

[13] Minority and other deeply disadvantaged offenders may often deserve less severe punishments than do others (Tonry 2014).

choices by sentenced offenders to violate lawful conditions imposed on community punishments, such as abstention from drugs, desisting from crime and not associating with former criminal associates. These behaviours are unlawful; people who engage in them assume risks of arrest, prosecution, conviction and punishment. They choose to risk criminal consequences.

Lawful lifestyle choices are different. Free citizens are entitled to live hand-to-mouth. Many artists, musicians and writers do so by choice or necessity. Free citizens are entitled to choose to work, or not, or only intermittently, and to live on income from casual work or from trust funds or indulgent parents.

However, many offenders do not – in a fundamental sense – choose to be poorly housed, poorly employed or unemployed, poorly educated or unmarried. Even if poor people's choices are more constrained than those of more privileged people, they are lawful choices all the same. Punishing people because of their lawful lifestyle choices raises the same ethical issues for a disadvantaged inner-city man as it would for a privileged trust fund beneficiary.

E. Criminal History

Criminal history raises more complex issues than is usually recognised, despite widely held intuitions that prior convictions justify harsher punishments for subsequent offences (Roberts 2008). Retributivists believe that any punishment more severe than an offender deserves is per se unjust. Immanuel Kant, the archetypal retributivist, averred that punishment should be precisely calibrated to the seriousness of the offence:

> But what kind and what amount of punishment is it that public justice makes its principle and measure? None other than the principle of equality (in the position of the needle on the scale of justice), to incline no more to one side than to the other. Accordingly, whatever undeserved evil you inflict on another among the people, that you [deserve] … Only the law of retribution (*jus talionis*) … can specify definitely the quality and the quantity of punishment. (2017 [1797]: 115)

This requires strict proportionality so that equally serious crimes are punished equally severely and more and less serious crimes are punished appropriately differently. Almost all retributive philosophers and criminal law theorists who have considered the matter conclude that there is no convincing moral justification for treating people with prior convictions more severely than first-timers (eg, Fletcher 1978; Lippke 2016).[14]

Utilitarians in principle could permit harsher punishments for recidivists, but only if the reductions in suffering attributable to reduced crime are greater than

[14] A 'progressive loss of mitigation' argument is sometimes offered to justify punishing first-time offenders *less* than they deserve based on the rationale that their crimes may have been 'out of character' and may demonstrate less than typical blameworthiness.

the additional suffering imposed on offenders. For Jeremy Bentham, any punishments that are more severe than concerns for utilitarian proportionality otherwise permit are per se wrong: 'All punishment is mischief: all punishment in itself is evil … If it ought at all to be admitted, it ought *only* to be admitted in as far as it promises to exclude some greater evil' (1970 [1789]: 158, emphasis added).

The problem in our time for utilitarian supporters of predictive sentencing is that contemporary knowledge of deterrence, incapacitation (the rationale for prediction) and rehabilitation cannot 'promise to exclude some greater evil'. I have several times recently surveyed the relevant literature (Tonry 2016, 2018a), as have many others, including most notably the National Academy of Sciences Committee on the Causes and Consequences of High Rates of Incarceration (Travis, Western and Redburn 2014: Chapter 5). This august body concluded that deterrent and incapacitative effects of punishment are modest at best and that imprisonment is on balance criminogenic, making ex-prisoners more rather than less likely to re-offend. The evidence on rehabilitation is stronger. Well-designed, well-targeted, well-managed and well-funded programmes can reduce re-offending (MacKenzie 2006). However, assignment to diagnostically appropriate treatment programmes does not require that individuals receive longer prison sentences.

Even if punishment theories are set aside, difficult ethical issues relating to race and ethnicity remain. The use of criminal history factors systematically disadvantages members of minority groups. Richard Frase (2009), in the most comprehensive study ever published on racial disparities in a state sentencing system, found that two-thirds of racial disparities in the Minnesota imprisonment rate result from the use of criminal history factors in sentencing.

Group differences in some criminal history factors – including age at first arrest, custody status, and numbers of prior arrests, convictions and punishments – result in substantial part from explicit and implicit racial bias and from conscious police targeting of poor and minority neighbourhoods and individuals. Young Black and Hispanic people are arrested at younger ages and more often than Whites partly because of racially differentiated practices.[15] Police sometimes arrest more young Black people for invidious reasons, but often would prefer to avoid arrests if they can. However, White and middle-class young people can more frequently than minority offenders be returned to stable homes or referred to private treatment and mental health facilities. Schools refer more minority than White students to the police for conduct problems. Racial profiling by the police targets minority neighbourhoods and individuals. Drug enforcement policies disproportionately target substances sold by minority drug dealers and the places where they sell them (Fellner 2013). All of these practices exaggerate the criminal records of poor and minority individuals compared with other people.

[15] The classic Philadelphia birth cohort studies, for example, found that 48.7 per cent of non-White offenders in the 1945 cohort had their first police contact before the age of 14, compared with 30.8 per cent for Whites. The corresponding figures for the 1958 cohort were 41 and 27 per cent (Tracey, Wolfgang and Figlio 1990: ch 10).

II. The Defences

The indictment is pretty formidable. Predictions of future violence are more often wrong than right (Fazel et al 2012): Of five positive predictions, three will be mistakes (false positives). The false positives are disproportionately Black and other minority offenders (Angwin et al 2016; Flores, Bechtel and Lowenkamp 2016). Many prediction instruments incorporate variables such as youth and gender that are per se unjust: in most other settings, gender is simply not an acceptable basis for distinguishing between people; common practice in all Western countries and recent neurological and developmental research call for treating young offenders more sympathetically and less severely than adults. All prediction instruments incorporate SES variables that produce systematically harsher dispositions of Black, other minority and disadvantaged offenders. All prediction instruments incorporate criminal history variables that are inflated for Black and other minority offenders by racially biased and disparate practices, racial profiling and street-level drug enforcement that targets minority individuals and neighbourhoods.

The defences are less weighty. One is that normative punishment theories provide no meaningful bar to reliance on predictions (Husak, Chapter 3 in this volume). A second is that the prevention of predicted harms to victims is so overwhelmingly important that it trumps concerns about proportionality and equal treatment (see Ryberg, Chapter 4 in this volume, as devil's advocate). A third is that there is nothing special about subordinating individuals to collective or organisational interests on the basis of predictions. This happens all the time: actuarial statistics are used in credit scoring and setting insurance premiums; statistical analyses underlie public health policies and medical practices; quarantines confine individuals (see Douglas, Chapter 5 in this volume, as to quarantines). A fourth is that concerns about racial and other disparities in punishment are misplaced: people who score badly on predictive variables commit disproportionate numbers of crimes and should bear disproportionate preventive burdens (Slobogin, Chapter 7 in this volume).

A. Punishment Theory

If everyone agreed that punishment policies and practices should be assessed only in relation to their crime-reductive effects, the elements of the indictment would be immaterial. So far as I can tell, no one believes this concerning themselves and people they care about.[16] The Christian New Testament and Kant's

[16] As a matter of political self-interest, American politicians often support policies such as life without parole for minors, three-strikes sentences of 25 years to life imprisonment for minor property offenders and decades-long prison sentences for street-level drug sellers that cannot be justified by any principled theory of punishment. However, throughout a long life of observing the criminal law, my experience has been that politicians and other powerful people charged with crimes believe in relation

categorical imperative agree that we should want and do for others what we want done for ourselves. Everyone believes that crime seriousness matters. Probably no one disagrees that lengthy imprisonment for routine traffic or parking offences would be unjustly severe, even if it acted as an effective deterrent, and that probation for stranger rapes would be unduly lenient, even if harsher punishments had no preventive effects.

The likeliest theoretical justifications for predictive sentencing are utilitarian, trading justice to individual offenders for greater crime prevention. Jeremy Bentham, however, did not believe that the prevention of crime justifies injustice to individuals. He endorsed strong criminal law defences – including insanity, intoxication and ignorance of law – so that only blameworthy people are convicted. He argued that punishment is evil and should be imposed only when the offender's suffering would be outweighed by greater suffering averted for others. He insisted that punishments be proportioned to the seriousness of offences – for deterrent and not retributive reasons – and that sentencing decisions take sympathetic account of myriad personal characteristics of offenders (Bentham 1970 [1789]: 52, 158, 169). The only contemporary mainstream consequentialist theory, Braithwaite and Pettit's 'Republican Theory of Justice' (1990, 2001), recognises proportionate retributive upper limits on punishment. It otherwise rejects retributive values and calls in every case for the least punitive disposition on which the victim, the offender and others close to them agree.

Retributive theories vary. Kant's foundational account insists that offenders receive 'definitely the quality and quantity of punishment' they deserve, no more, no less (2017 [1797]: 115). This leaves no role for predictions, although it may permit them to be taken into account in choosing between punishments of equal severity (eg, Ryberg, Chapter 4 in this volume).[17] This was Andreas von Hirsch's view three decades ago (von Hirsch, Wasik and Green 1989). In practice, however, it could apply to only a small minority of crimes. Few minor crimes would warrant imprisonment in place of a community punishment. For serious crimes, no sanction other than capital punishment has the same or greater incapacitative effect as imprisonment.

Two retributivist possibilities are left. One is to develop a broad negative retributivist analysis (blameworthiness only sets upper limits on severity). This

to themselves, their families and close colleagues that justice requires the full panoply of procedural protections, compassionate consideration of personal circumstances and observance of general principles of justice in punishment, including the imposition of the least severe possible sentence.

[17] Kant (2017 [1797]: 115) wrote explicitly of substitution of punishments so that they would be subjectively comparably burdensome. One example is that 'someone of high standing given to violence could be condemned not only to apologize for striking an innocent citizen inferior to himself but also to undergo a solitary confinement involving hardship; in addition to the discomfort he undergoes, the offender's vanity would be painfully affected, so that through his shame like would be fittingly repaid with like' for an offence for which a 'social inferior' would only be called on to apologise.

may be what Husak (Chapter 3 in this volume) has in mind when he says: 'If we have good reason to inflict different amounts of punishment on two offenders who have committed equally serious crimes, we should not be worried that our decision does not preserve proportionality.' However, the consensus view noted above among authors of leading meta-analyses that violence predictions should not be used in sentencing casts serious doubt as to whether current knowledge provides 'good reason' to allow the pursuit of predictive goals to trump proportionality.

Husak's position rejects Kantian retributive and Benthamite utilitarian insistence on comparable treatment of people who committed comparable crimes.[18] It also abandons the almost ubiquitous belief among retributivists that proportionality between offence seriousness and punishment severity is a fundamental requirement of justice. This is regrettable, since retributive proportionality provides a framework for punishment systems that aspire to equal treatment of comparably blameworthy offenders.

Although it can never be self-evident in a given case precisely what punishment respect for retributive proportionality requires, that problem was solved as a practical matter long ago. Wide agreement exists on the relative seriousness of different crimes. Uncontroversial scales of relative offence seriousness can be devised for particular places and times. So can parallel scales of punishment severity (Duus-Otterström, forthcoming). The two can then be linked. Comparably severe punishments can be specified for comparably serious crimes and proportionately different ones for diversely serious crimes. There is no room for prediction; the overarching goals are to ensure equal treatment by linking blameworthiness to punishment.

The alternative to Kant's and others' (eg, von Hirsch 2017) thoroughgoing retributivism is a negative retributivist account. John Monahan (2017), for example, has argued that predictions can properly be used so long as upper limits based on offence seriousness are respected and predictions are used to mitigate sentences for low-risk offenders, but not to increase them for high-risk offenders. He refers to Virginia's policy that incorporates predictions into guidelines for diversion to alternative punishments of offenders otherwise bound for imprisonment.[19]

Norval Morris' (1974) version of negative retributivism, 'limiting retributivism', provided a more fully developed proposal. For every crime, there is a maximum punishment that may justly be imposed. This varies with offence seriousness and

[18] But with major differences. Both want sanctions – for Kant, calculated on the gravity of wrongdoing and for Bentham, calculated on deterrence calculations – to be adjusted to take account of subjective differences (which Bentham called sensibilities) between offenders.

[19] This doesn't really work, at least in Virginia, because the main guidelines are only advisory and judges may depart both downwards and upwards. Negative retributivist theories envision an unbreachable upper limit. The 'normal' Virginia guideline recommendation is only that, not an upper limit. I will discuss other problems below.

thus provides proportionate limits. For some crimes – I used stranger rape earlier as an example – there may be minimums that must ordinarily be observed. The default is always the minimum; like Bentham, Morris urged recognition of a principle of parsimony that forbade the imposition of unnecessary suffering. However, the minimum can be exceeded for good reason.

From a predictive sentencing perspective, so far so good. Morris insisted that there be good evidence-based reasons to justify harsher-than-minimum punishment. Concerning predictions of dangerousness, he was emphatic: four false positives for every two true positives is not good enough. That would cause too much undeserved suffering. It is unlikely that improvements in accuracy over four decades – three false positives for every two true positives – would have changed his view. The general case to be made is weaker now than in 1974. Morris wrote before much evidence had accumulated on the racial disparities inexorably produced by predictive sentencing and without considering the implications of use of youth, gender, race-correlated SES, and bias-contaminated criminal history variables. Morris' limiting retributivism does not provide the licence that prediction proponents might wish for.

Predictive sentencing is thus incompatible with mainstream retributive punishment theories. This is confirmed by the theoretical literature on the role of prior criminal history in sentencing new crimes. It is a cliché but true that past crimes are the best predictor of future crimes, which is why criminal history variables are the most predictively powerful (Hoffman 1983; Monahan 2017). Empirical evidence and common experience document that there is a 'recidivist premium' that results in harsher punishments for repeat offenders (Reitz 2010). There is solid evidence that most people think there should be (eg, Roberts 2008, 2011).

Nonetheless, nearly every retributivist philosopher who has considered the matter has concluded that it cannot be justified (eg, among many more, Bagaric 2010; Fletcher 1978; Lippke 2016; Ryberg 2001): 'Did the crime, did the time'; 'Paid his or her debt to society'. More punishment now for this crime for predictive reasons, because there was an earlier crime, is double counting, in effect attaching an increment of additional punishment to this crime more fully to punish the earlier one.

Several efforts have been made to argue that committing an earlier crime somehow increases an offender's culpability in respect to the new one. One argument is that recidivists deserve additional punishment because their behaviour demonstrates defiance of the judge or the state or is evidence of bad character (eg, Lee 2010). These claims have no place in a free society: citizens are entitled to be defiant, eccentric and difficult. 'Bad character' is in the eyes of the beholder and in any case is not a criminal offence anywhere. The other argument is that recidivists have a greater obligation than others to be law-abiding (Bennett 2010). However, the law makes the same demands of all citizens. No one except possibly the arguments' proponents has been persuaded by either of these analyses.

If punishments may not justly be increased to take account of earlier convictions, it is difficult to imagine principled arguments for why punishments may be increased on the basis of predictions of future offending that are in turn substantially based on criminal history variables. Jesper Ryberg (Chapter 4 in this volume) intensively mines retributive theories looking for an overlooked nugget that can justify predictive sentencing. No such luck. He concluded thusly: 'Though there is some appeal in pursuing justice and in preventing future crimes, you cannot to a full extent get both.'

B. Public Safety

Everyone is in favour of public safety, but that is not the only fundamental value involved. Sentencing also implicates fairness, proportionality, equal treatment and parsimony (Tonry 2018a). Any rational person would want these additional values to be honoured if he or she or a loved one was charged with a crime. It is difficult to develop a morally persuasive explanation for why we as individuals deserve those things, but other people whom we do not personally know or care about do not. Unless someone can develop a fully elaborated consequentialist theory of punishment that does not incorporate these values and justifies predictive sentencing, a principled case for predictive sentencing cannot be made.

This does not mean that the pursuit of crime prevention and public safety need be abandoned. Systems such as those in Scandinavian countries, Germany and the Netherlands, in which punishment is based primarily on blameworthiness and which allow only minor increases for criminal history, do not have higher crimes rates than the US. Insofar as the operation of the criminal justice system deters wrongful behaviour, systems of proportionate punishment will continue to do so. They will contribute to moral education by reinforcing the basic social norms of right and wrong. Deserved terms of imprisonment will continue to incapacitate inmates from committing new offences in the community. Other demonstratively effective strategies of community, developmental and situational crime prevention will, if pursued, continue to do their work.

Expecting more than that from predictive sentencing is in any event unrealistic. The best available evidence cautions against believing that changes in sanctions policies have significant crime reduction effects (Tonry 2016; Travis, Western and Redburn 2014: Chapter 5).

C. Actuarial Analogies

Two arguments are made. The first is that, ho hum, there is nothing special about predictive sentencing: actuarial risk calculations affect private lives throughout modern society. There has been a 'proliferation of statistical and other algorithmic prediction tools in banking, insurance, marketing, medicine, and other fields … Prediction need not be highly accurate at the individual level for major collective benefit to accrue' (Imrey and Dawid 2015: 25, 30).

So what is the problem? There are several. The most important is that the application of predictions in sentencing causes undeserved suffering to individuals whose punishments are increased, usually through the lengthening of prison terms. Most other uses of actuarial prediction affect people's private lives as private citizens. It may be disappointing to be denied a loan, insurance policy or an apartment lease, or be asked to pay higher rates, or not be offered a marketing opportunity. However, these burdens are not comparable to being imprisoned when otherwise a community punishment would be imposed, or receiving a longer prison term. Actuarial predictions in medicine are used to benefit individuals by means of improved diagnostic capacities, not to cause suffering.

A criminal conviction is an authoritative declaration by the state that an individual engaged in morally blameworthy behaviour. Punishment is meant to cause suffering – some philosophers approvingly refer to 'hard treatment' – and is inherently stigmatising in the eyes of the general public. Other uses of actuarial prediction are private and are neither intended to cause suffering nor handled in ways that expose individuals to public stigma. People who are denied loans or insurance policies may feel regretful, humiliated, even stigmatised, but only in private. No one else need know.

Arguments have been offered that predictive sentencing can be justified by analogy to public health quarantines. People carrying or exposed to contagious diseases are sometimes confined to eliminate or minimise the spread of contagion. However, except for rare circumstances such as the early periods of awareness of HIV when drug users and homosexuals were 'blamed' for their afflictions, having a contagious disease (eg, measles, typhoid, malaria or Ebola) is seldom personally stigmatising. In rare circumstances when stigma attaches, decent people regard it as unjust and morally wrong. In any case, quarantines are not for lengthy fixed terms; they end when the risk passes or reaches acceptable levels. People subject to quarantines are not held in prisons and in a decent society receive sympathy and compassion. They are afforded the greatest material comfort that conditions allow, with as few limitations as possible on the freedoms enjoyed by other citizens. Preventive confinement on the basis of risk predictions is not like that.

The arguments that preventive detention is morally equivalent to quarantine are unconvincing. Douglas (Chapter 5 in this volume) tries mightily to demonstrate that quarantine is, or under some circumstances could be, indistinguishable. He assumes that both sets of restrictions are morally undeserved. He sets aside the question of 'Soft Moral Difference', whether preventive detention is typically more morally suspect than quarantine, and considers only the narrower question of 'Hard Moral Difference', whether preventive detention is always in at least one respect more morally suspect.

Douglas concludes that preventive detention is not always in at least one respect worse. He may or not be right, but in the real world, as he acknowledges, that is not important:

> Whether preventive detention is *typically* more problematic than quarantine will depend heavily on the facts about how these two practices are typically imposed and what effects they normally have on those subject to them, on those whom they are intended to protect and on those required to fund them. (Emphasis in original)

Other arguments that quarantine offers a valid analogy to preventive detention are no more convincing. Gregg Caruso (2016) and Derek Pereboom (2014) argue that quarantine and preventive detention are indistinguishable to adherents of free will scepticism: 'What we do, and the way we are, is ultimately the result of factors beyond our control and because of this we are never morally responsible for our actions in the basic desert sense – the sense that would make us truly deserving of blame or praise' (Caruso 2016: 26).

Caruso and Pereboom agree that neither 'dangerous' offenders nor carriers of serious contagious diseases are morally responsible for the risks they pose and may be subjected to state controls to minimise risk. They posit reciprocal state obligations to offer minimal intrusions, humane conditions and serious treatment efforts. Given their premise of free will scepticism, these are plausible and necessary ethical propositions.

Arguments about free will, hard determinism and compatibilism are intellectually interesting and conceptually important. However, accepting the validity of Caruso's and Pereboom's analyses requires first accepting the validity of free will scepticism. This is unlikely to occur on a widespread basis anytime soon.

D. Group Differences in Offending

The argument is that the aim of prediction instruments is to predict crimes, that some instruments (eg, COMPAS) predict future offending by Black and White people with comparable accuracy, and accordingly that the instruments are not statistically biased (Flores, Bechtel and Lowenkamp 2016). It may be regrettable, but Black, other minority and disadvantaged offenders generally disproportionately have characteristics that predict future offending. So be it:

> COMPAS is based on an actuary designed to inform the probability of recidivism across its three stated risk categories. To expect the COMPAS to do otherwise would be analogous to expecting an insurance agent to make absolute determinations of who will be involved in an accident and who won't. Actuaries just don't work that way. This error discredits their [Angwin et al 2016] main finding that Black defendants were more likely to be incorrectly identified as recidivists (false positives) while white defendants were more likely to be misclassified as non-recidivists (false negatives). (Flores, Bechtel and Lowenkamp 2016: 45)

Two things about this quotation warrant comment. First, the quotation acknowledges no reason for concern about suspect variables: COMPAS uses every variable discussed in this chapter except race.[20] Second, the claim that Flores, Bechtel and Lowenkamp's analysis 'discredits' Angwin et al's conclusions about racial distributions of false positives and false negatives is contradicted by their own findings (see Table 14.2 above presenting their findings concerning general recidivism). What they presumably meant is that racial disparities do exist, but are not important because they are simply byproducts of an algorithm that is not statistically biased.

Flores, Bechtel and Lowenkamp (2016) are interested only in predictive accuracy. This is made explicit when they offer two prediction models with very different false positive and negative rates, but reject out of hand the model that makes fewer mistakes, as if any reasonable person would agree:

> The [second model's effects] – a decrease in false positive rates and an increase in false negative rates – might be preferred by some, as it limits the number of individuals that are identified as 'high-risk'. For others with a low tolerance for recidivism and victimization, the [first model] would be preferred. (Flores, Bechtel and Lowenkamp 2016: 42)

Use of SES and criminal history variables that differentially affect Blacks and Whites does not to them, as Lady Catherine de Bourgh would put it, signify. To people concerned about racial and punitive justice, it does.

III. The Summation

Predictive sentencing can thus be justified neither empirically nor morally. However, to many people, predictive sentencing, especially concerning violence, is intuitively plausible. It provides supporters with the opportunity to express sympathy towards hypothetical future victims and to express disdain for people who are believed likely to be violent. Probably in realpolitik terms, predictive sentencing will continue to command support from elected politicians and many criminal justice officials. What to do? A number of options are available.

A. Abandon Predictive Sentencing

This would be the most morally justifiable approach. Prevention of crime is an important public policy goal, but so are justice, fairness, equal treatment and

[20] They note that when they added an interaction term between race and COMPAS into their analyses, it did not improve predictive accuracy (Flores, Bechtel and Lowenkamp 2016: 43). This is irrelevant, as modellers have recognised for four decades (Berk et al 2018; Fisher and Kadane 1983). Because race and other variables covary, most or all of any race effect is carried by the other variables. They most likely found no separate race effect because it was already present.

parsimony. Importantly, they differ from crime prevention. Each derives from fundamental ideas about human dignity and limits state power over individual lives (Dan-Cohen 2002; Luban 2007; Waldron 2014). By contrast, predictive sentencing focuses only on hypothetical victims.

The way forward concerning punishment becomes clear when we recognise that punishment implicates multiple, competing values, including not only deserved punishment and crime prevention, but also fairness and equal treatment. A comprehensive jurisprudence of just punishment would incorporate four propositions:

- *Justice as proportionality*: offenders should never be punished more severely than can be justified by their blameworthiness in relation to the severity of punishments justly imposed on others for the same and different offences (Morris 1974).
- *Justice as fairness*: processes for responding to crimes should be publicly known, implemented in good faith and applied even-handedly (Rawls 1958).
- *Justice as equal treatment*: defendants and offenders should be treated as equals; their interests should be accorded concern and respect when decisions affecting them are made (Dworkin 1977).
- *Justice as parsimony*: offenders should never be punished more severely than can be justified by appropriate, valid, normative purposes (Tonry 1994).

No country's legal system perfectly observes these values, but many in Western and Northern Europe try. In the US, the case against predictive sentencing is likely to fall on deaf ears. Less bold options that would do less injustice are available.

B. Constrained Predictive Sentencing

Prevention concerns and prevailing emotionalism may make the elimination of preventive sentencing unachievable. An unprincipled but more saleable option might be to establish limits on the increments of additional punishment that can be imposed. Roberts and Frase (Chapter 9 in this volume) propose maximum sentence increases of no more than 100 per cent of the deserved sentence as a limit. I have proposed 50 per cent (Tonry 2016: 244).

A more discriminant proposal needs to be worked out. Under Roberts and Frase's proposal, for example, predictions could justify a two-month sentence if the starting point was one month, or a 40-year sentence if the starting point was 20 years, as it often could be in the US. A more constrained approach might allow increments ranging from the greater of 100 per cent or one year for less serious offences to the lesser of 100 per cent or three years for more serious ones.

However, these proposals make heroic assumptions about the willingness of American policy makers to constrain judges' authority and limit sentencing severity.

C. Predictive Mitigation

This is what John Monahan (2017) proposes. It has the great defect that it will usually worsen racial and class disparities, all other things being equal, because predictions of lower risk usually result from the absence of SES, criminal history and other characteristics disproportionately associated with minority and disadvantaged offenders. The end result will be the diversion of more White and advantaged offenders.[21] Norval Morris and I (1990) long ago argued that there is something perverse about the argument that if some offenders will be treated unduly severely, concern for equal treatment requires that others also suffer unduly. Monahan's proposal might thus reduce severity for some offenders. Some people no doubt believe that this is desirable, even if it exacerbates racial disparities (so Morris believed; I was doubtful). *But* – a big but – Monahan's proposal can work only if there are strong 'normal' limits on sentencing severity, from which the mitigated sentence offers a reduction. Otherwise there will be nothing to stop judges and prosecutors from providing mitigated sentences to low-risk offenders and continuing to impose aggravated sentences on high-risk offenders. This is what happens under Virginia's 'advisory' guidelines.

D. Limiting Retributivism

A stronger version of Monahan's proposal is to allow mitigation for low-risk offenders, but establish strong upper limits for all offenders based on offence seriousness. Only a handful of presumptive (Minnesota, Washington and Kansas) and mandatory (North Carolina) American guidelines systems establish meaningful upper limits. In such places, Norval Morris' proposals might work. The presumptive normal sentence in every case would be set at the bottom of the guideline range. Low-risk offenders could receive sentences below the normal minimum, most offenders the normal minimum and highest-risk offenders up to the maximum. This, however, could only work if guidelines systems were radically reformulated. Current approaches provide ranges for particular offenders that take account of both offence seriousness and criminal history. The limiting retributivism approach could work only if ranges were based solely on offence seriousness. Otherwise the use of criminal history variables in prediction instruments would be double counted.

[21] Kleinberg et al (2018: 41), on the basis of a machine learning exercise using data from bail hearing decisions in New York City from 2008 and 2013, conclude that 'a properly built algorithm can reduce crime and jail populations while simultaneously reducing racial disparities. In this case, the algorithm can be a force for racial equity'. The conclusion was based on a comparison of predicted releases if only the algorithm was used and judges' actual decisions. In real courts, judges take into account numerous factors that were not included in the algorithm.

E. Sanctions and Measures

Debates raged a century ago in the US and Europe over the wisdom and justice of indeterminate sentencing (Pifferi 2012, 2016). Supporters argued that criminal behaviour results primarily from environmental and psychological influences on individuals, and that a rational sentencing system would reject retributive ideas and focus on rehabilitation of the vast majority of corrigible offenders and incapacitation of the rest. Opponents argued that moral blameworthiness should not be abandoned as an animating idea, but should instead set limits on the state's punishment powers.

American jurisdictions – every one of them by the 1930s – adopted indeterminate sentencing. European countries, including those in the UK, rejected it as unjust. However, to deal with the problem of seemingly incorrigible dangerous offenders, European countries established a distinction between sanctions, deserved punishments which are based on blameworthiness, and measures, which are crime prevention actions based on assessments of risk. In theory, measures are not punishments, but extraordinary actions designed to deal with special problems. This is hypocritical, of course, since extended confinement will feel like additional punishment to any affected offender, but it has worked much as was intended (*cf* de Keijser 2011). Measures targeting violence prevention are rarely used in any country (eg, in Scandinavia; Lappi-Seppälä 2016), but they are available for special cases. Anders Brejvik, the Norwegian mass murderer, was sentenced to 21 years' imprisonment, the longest term possible, but was also made subject to a measure. If when his 'sanction' expires he continues to be considered dangerous, the measure provides authority to continue to hold him.

The sanctions and measures distinction could in theory provide a mechanism for taming predictive sentencing in the US. All offenders would receive proportionate sanctions based on the seriousness of their crimes and respecting concerns for fairness, equal treatment and parsimony. A tiny number, a small fraction of one per cent if the European pattern were followed, might also be the objects of measures predicated on their dangerousness and permitting continued confinement after the expiration of their prison sentences. Predictions could be used to identify cases in which a measure might be appropriate. However, for such a system to be a realistic option, there would need to be radical transformations in American popular, political and legal cultures. That is unlikely in any foreseeable future.

References

Angwin, J, Larson, J, Mattu, S and Kirchner, L (2016) 'Machine Bias: There's Software Used across the Country to Predict Future Criminals. And it's Biased against Blacks', https://www.propublica.org/article/machine-bias-risk-assessments-in-criminal-sentencing.

Bagaric, M (2010) 'Double Punishment and Punishing Character: The Unfairness of Prior Convictions' 19 *Criminal Justice Ethics* 10.

Barr, W (1992) *The Case for More Incarceration* (Washington DC, US Department of Justice, Office of Policy Development).

Bennett, C (2010) '"More to Apologise for": Can We Find a Basis for the Recidivist Premium in a Communicative Theory of Punishment?' in JV Roberts and A von Hirsch (eds), *Previous Convictions at Sentencing: Theoretical and Applied Perspectives* (Oxford, Hart Publishing).

Bentham, J (1970 [1789]) *An Introduction to the Principles of Morals and Legislation*, JH Burns and HLA Hart (eds) (Oxford, Clarendon).

Berk, R, Heidari, H, Jabbari, S, Kearns, M and Roth, A (2018) 'Fairness in Criminal Justice Risk Assessments: The State of the Art', *Sociological Methods and Research*, https://doi.org/10.1177/0049124118782533.

Berlin, I (2002) *Liberty*, H Hardy (ed) (Oxford, Oxford University Press).

Blumstein, A, Cohen, J, Roth, JA and Visher, CA (eds) (1986) *Criminal Careers and 'Career Criminals'* (Washington DC, National Academies Press).

Blumstein, A, Farrington, DP and Moitra, S (1985) 'Delinquency Careers: Innocents, Desisters, and Persisters' in N Morris and M Tonry (eds), *Crime and Justice: An Annual Review of Research*, vol 6 (Chicago, University of Chicago Press).

Braithwaite, J and Pettit, P (1990) *Not Just Deserts: A Republican Theory of Criminal Justice* (New York, Oxford University Press).

——. (2001) 'Republicanism and Restorative Justice: An Explanatory and Normative Connection' in J Braithwaite and H Strang (eds), *Restorative Justice: Philosophy to Practice* (Burlington, VT, Ashgate).

Campbell, MA, French, S and Gendreau, P (2009) 'The Prediction of Violence in Adult Offenders: A Meta-analytic Comparison of Instruments' 36 *Criminal Justice and Behavior* 567.

Caruso, GD (2016) 'Free Will Skepticism and Criminal Behavior: A Public Health-Quarantine Model' 32 *Southwest Philosophy Review* 25.

Dan-Cohen, M (2002) *Harmful Thoughts: Essays on Law, Self, and Morality* (Princeton, Princeton University Press).

De Keijser, JW (2011) 'Never Mind the Pain, it's a Measure! Justifying Measures as Part of the Dutch Bifurcated System of Sanctions' in M Tonry (ed), *Retributivism Has a Past: Has it a Future?* (New York, Oxford University Press).

Desmarais, SL, Johnson, KL and Singh, JP (2016) 'Performance of Risk Assessment Instruments in US Correctional Settings' 13 *Psychological Services* 206.

Duus-Otterström, G (forthcoming) 'Weighing Relative and Absolute Proportionality in Punishment' in M Tonry (ed), *Fitting Punishments to Crimes: Is Proportionality Possible?* (New York, Oxford University Press).

Dworkin, R (1977) *Taking Rights Seriously* (Cambridge, MA, Harvard University Press).

Farrington, DP (1986) 'Age and Crime' in M Tonry and N Morris (eds), *Crime and Justice: An Annual Review of Research*, vol 7 (Chicago, University of Chicago Press).

Fazel, S, Singh, JP, Doll, H and Grann, M (2012) 'Use of Risk Assessment Instruments to Predict Violence and Antisocial Behavior in 73 Samples Involving 24,827 People: Systematic Review and Meta-analysis' 345 *British Medical Journal* e4692.

Fellner, J (2013) 'Race and Drugs' in S Bucerius and M Tonry (eds), *The Oxford Handbook of Ethnicity, Crime, and Immigration* (New York, Oxford University Press).

Fisher FM and Kadane JB (1983) 'Empirically Based Sentencing Guidelines and Ethical Considersations' in A Blumstein (ed), *Research on Sentencing: The Search for Reform* (Washington DC, National Academies Press).

Fletcher, G (1978) *Rethinking Criminal Law* (Boston, Little Brown).

Flores, AW, Bechtel, K and Lowenkamp, CT (2016) 'False Positives, False Negatives, and False Analyses: A Rejoinder to "Machine Bias: There's Software Used across the Country to Predict Future Criminals. And it's Biased against Blacks"' 80 *Federal Probation* 38.

Frase, R (2009) 'Racial Disproportionality in Minnesota's Prisons and Jails' in M Tonry (ed), *Crime and Justice: An Annual Review of Research*, vol 38 (Chicago, University of Chicago Press).

Harcourt, BE (2008) *Against Prediction* (Chicago, University of Chicago Press).

Hart, SD, Michie, C and Cooke, DJ (2007) 'Precision of Actuarial Risk Assessment Instruments. Evaluating the "Margins of Error" of Group v Individual Predictions of Violence' 190 *British Journal of Psychiatry* s60.

Hester, R, Frase, RS, Roberts, JV and Mitchell, K (2018) 'Prior Record Enhancements at Sentencing: Unsettled Justifications and Unsettling Consequences' in M Tonry (ed), *Crime and Justice: A Review of Research*, vol 47 (Chicago, University of Chicago Press).

Hoffman, PB (1976) 'Salient Factor Score Validation: A 1972 Release Cohort' 6 *Journal of Criminal Justice* 69.

——. (1983) 'Screening for Risk: A Revised Salient Factor Score (SFS 81)' 11 *Journal of Criminal Justice* 539.

——. (1995) 'Twenty Years of Operational Use of a Risk Prediction Instrument: The United States Parole Commission's Salient Factor Score' 22 *Journal of Criminal Justice* 477.

Husak, D (forthcoming) 'The Metric of Punishment Severity: A Puzzle about the Principle of Proportionality' in M Tonry (ed), *Fitting Punishments to Crimes: Is Proportionality Possible?* (New York, Oxford University Press).

Imrey, PB and Dawid AP (2015) 'A Commentary on Statistical Assessment of Violence Recidivism Risk' 2 *Statistics and Public Policy* 25.

Kant, I (2017 [1797]) *The Metaphysics of Morals*, revised edn, M Gregor (trans) (Cambridge, Cambridge University Press).

Kleinberg, J, Lakkaraju, H, Leskovec, J, Ludwig, J and Mullainathan, S (2018) 'Human Decisions and Machine Predictions' 2018 *Quarterly Journal of Economics* 237.

Knapp, K (1984) *The Impact of the Minnesota Sentencing Guidelines: Three-Year Evaluation* (St Paul, Minnesota Sentencing Guidelines Commission).

Lappi-Seppälä, T (2016) 'Nordic Sentencing' in M Tonry (ed), *Sentencing Policies and Practices in Western Countries: Comparative and Cross-national Perspectives* (Chicago, University of Chicago Press).

Larson, J, Mattu, S, Kirchner, L and Angwin, J (2016) 'How We Analyzed the COMPAS Recidivism Algorithm', *ProPublica*, https://www.propublica.org/article/how-we-analyzed-the-compas-recidivism-algorithm.

Laub, JH and Sampson, RJ (2001) 'Understanding Desistance from Crime' in M Tonry (ed), *Crime and Justice: A Review of Research*, vol 28 (Chicago, Chicago University Press).

Lee, Y (2010) 'Repeat Offenders and the Question of Desert' in JV Roberts and A von Hirsch (eds), *Previous Convictions at Sentencing: Theoretical and Applied Perspectives* (Oxford, Hart Publishing).

Lippke, RL (2016) 'The Ethics of Recidivist Premiums' in J Jacobs and J Jackson (eds), *The Routledge Handbook of Criminal Justice Ethics* (Abingdon, Routledge).

Luban, D (2007) *Legal Ethics and Human Dignity* (Cambridge, Cambridge University Press).

MacKenzie, DL (2006) *What Works in Corrections: Reducing the Criminal Activities of Offenders and Delinquents* (Cambridge, Cambridge University Press).

Mill, JS (1997 [1869]) *The Subjection of Women* (New York, Dover).

Monahan J (1981) *The Clinical Prediction of Violent Behavior* (Washington DC, National Institute of Mental Health).

——. (2017) 'Risk Assessment in Sentencing' in E Luna (ed), *Reforming Criminal Justice: Punishment, Incarceration, and Release* (Phoenix, Academy for Justice, Arizona State University Press).

Monahan, J and Skeem, JL (2016) 'Risk Assessment in Criminal Sentencing' 12 *Annual Review of Clinical Psychology* 489.

Monahan, K, Steinberg, L and Piquero AR (2015) 'Juvenile Justice Policy and Practice: A Developmental Perspective' in M Tonry (ed), *Crime and Justice: A Review of Research*, vol 44 (Chicago, University of Chicago Press).

Morris, N (1974) *The Future of Imprisonment* (Chicago, University of Chicago Press).

Morris, N and Tonry, M (1990) *Between Prison and Probation: Intermediate Punishments in a Rational Sentencing System* (New York, Oxford University Press).

Nagin, DS, Cullen, FT and Lero Jonson, C (2009) 'Imprisonment and Reoffending' in M Tonry (ed), *Crime and Justice: A Review of Research*, vol 38 (Chicago, University of Chicago Press).

Ostrom, BJ and Kauder, NB (2012) 'The Evolution of Offender Risk Assessment in Virginia' 25 *Federal Sentencing Reporter* 161.

Pereboom, D (2014) *Free Will, Agency, and Meaning in Life* (Oxford, Oxford University Press).
Pifferi, M (2012) 'Individualization of Punishment and the Rule of Law: Reshaping Legality in the United States and Europe between the 19th and the 20th Century' 52 *American Journal of Legal History* 325.
——. (2016) *Reinventing Punishment: A Comparative History of Criminology and Penology in the 19th and 20th Century* (Oxford, Oxford University Press).
Rawls, J (1958) 'Justice as Fairness' 67 *Philosophical Review* 164.
Reitz, K (2010) 'The Illusion of Proportionality: Desert and Repeat Offenders' in JV Roberts and A von Hirsch (eds), *Previous Convictions at Sentencing: Theoretical and Applied Perspectives* (Oxford, Hart Publishing).
Roberts, JV (2008) *Punishing Persistent Offenders: Exploring Community and Offender Perspectives* (Oxford, Oxford University Press).
——. (2011) 'The Future of State Punishment. The Role of Public Opinion in Sentencing' in M Tonry (ed), *Retributivism Has a Past: Has it a Future?* (New York, Oxford University Press).
Roberts, JV and von Hirsch, A (2010) *Previous Convictions at Sentencing: Theoretical and Applied Perspectives* (Oxford, Hart Publishing).
Ryberg, J (2001) 'Recidivism, Multiple Offending, and Legal Justice' 36 *Danish Yearbook of Philosophy* 69.
Tonry, M (1987) 'Prediction and Classification: Legal and Ethical Issues' in DM Gottfredson and M Tonry (eds), *Prediction and Classification* (Chicago, University of Chicago Press).
——. (1994) 'Proportionality, Parsimony and Interchangeability of Punishments' in RA Duff, SE Marshall, RE Dobash and RP Dobash (eds), *Penal Theory and Penal Practice* (Manchester, Manchester University Press).
——. (1996) *Sentencing Matters* (New York, Oxford University Press).
——. (2014) 'Can Deserts Be Just in an Unjust World?' in AP Simester, U Neumann and A du Bois-Pedain (eds), *Liberal Criminal Theory: Essays for Andreas von Hirsch* (Oxford, Hart Publishing).
——. (2016) *Sentencing Fragments* (New York, Oxford University Press).
——. (2018a) 'An Honest Politician's Guide to Deterrence: Certainty, Severity, Celerity, and Parsimony' in DS Nagin, FT Cullen and C Lero Jonson (eds), *Deterrence, Choice, and Crime: Contemporary Perspectives* (New York, Routledge).
——. (2018b) 'Making American Sentencing Just, Humane, and Effective' in M Tonry (ed), *Reinventing American Criminal Justice* (Chicago, University of Chicago Press).
Tonry, M and Chambers, C (2012) 'Juvenile Justice Cross-nationally Considered' in BC Feld and DM Bishop (eds), *The Oxford Handbook of Juvenile Crime and Juvenile Justice* (New York, Oxford University Press.).
Tracey, PE, Wolfgang, ME and Figlio, RM (1990) *Delinquency Careers in Two Birth Cohorts* (New York, Plenum).

Travis, J, Western, B and Redburn, S (eds) (2014) *The Growth of Incarceration in the United States: Exploring Causes and Consequences* (Washington DC, National Academies Press).

Virginia Criminal Sentencing Commission (2014) *Manual*, 17th edn (Richmond, Virginia Criminal Sentencing Commission).

Von Hirsch, A (2017) *Deserved Criminal Sentences: An Overview* (Oxford, Hart Publishing).

Von Hirsch, A, Wasik, M and Greene, J (1989) 'Punishments in the Community and the Principles of Desert' 20 *Rutgers Law Review* 595.

Waldron, J (2014) *What Do the Philosophers Have against Dignity?* Public Law and Legal Theory Research Series, Working Paper 14-59 (New York, NYU Law School).

Yang, M, Wong, SC and Coid, J (2010) 'The Efficacy of Violence Prediction: A Meta-analytic Comparison of Nine Risk Assessment Tools' 136 *Psychology Bulletin* 740.

INDEX

www.ingramcontent.com/pod-product-compliance
Ingram Content Group UK Ltd.
Pitfield, Milton Keynes, MK11 3LW, UK
UKHW021910150926
475560UK00003B/282